BANTU, BOER, AND BRITON:
THE MAKING OF
THE SOUTH AFRICAN
NATIVE PROBLEM

BANTU, BOER, AND BRITON:

THE MAKING OF THE
SOUTH AFRICAN NATIVE PROBLEM

BY

WILLIAM MILLER MACMILLAN

SOMETIME ASSOCIATE MEMBER OF
ALL SOULS COLLEGE, OXFORD

"Ω πόποι, οἷον δή νυ θεοὺς βροτοὶ αἰτιόωνται.
'Εξ ἡμέων γάρ φασι κάκ' ἔμμεναι· οἱ δὲ καὶ αὐτοὶ
Σφῆσιν ἀτασθαλίῃσιν ὑπὲρ μόρον ἄλγε' ἔχουσιν.
HOMER, *Od.*, I., 32

[*How idle it is for men to blame the gods for cruel
fate when foolish pride still rules their hearts.*]

LONDON
FABER & GWYER LIMITED
24 RUSSELL SQUARE

FIRST PUBLISHED IN MCMXXIX
BY FABER & GWYER LIMITED
24 RUSSELL SQUARE LONDON W.C.I
PRINTED IN GREAT BRITAIN
BY BUTLER & TANNER LIMITED
FROME AND LONDON

TO

J. M.

SECRETARY, EDITOR, CRITIC

PREFACE

THIS book, like *The Cape Colour Question*, evolved from the study of the private papers of Dr. John Philip, now acquired by the Witwatersrand Council of Education for the University of the Witwatersrand. These papers throw new light especially on Dr. Philip's personal share in the politics of his day. But chiefly they point to the necessity for a radically new interpretation of known and generally undisputed facts, suggesting in particular that the predicament of the natives, involved perforce in a struggle with encroaching European colonists, has never been taken into account.

To say this is in no way to make light of the hardships stoutly endured by European pioneers, or to minimize their sufferings at the hand of the natives whom in the end they subjugated and conquered. Even now the condition of the victorious white farming community of South Africa is matter for grave concern. For years past, in articles, papers and pamphlets, I have done what I could to call attention to the facts and causes of the sordid poverty, white no less than black, that rests like a blight on the common weal of Golden South Africa; and I hope shortly to re-embody the results of first-hand study of modern conditions in a single book by way of commentary on the pages of history here dealt with.

The social problems of mixing and of intermarriage, which are a modern nightmare, happily do not arise so far as the South African Natives are concerned. The Native Problem is economic and political, and, so long as economic stress is not allowed to undermine and destroy the moral fibre of the race, the Bantu are a pure stock, with a fair share of the white man's antipathy to race-mixture. In truth, the diseases of the body politic of the Union to-day are the sins of the fathers visited upon the children of the third and fourth generation, who are as far as ever from an understanding of the true significance of the happenings of seventy years ago. The Native Problem as it is now is what the

vii

disintegration of the Amaxosa by the Kafir wars, and the wide-spread dispossession of tribes by the Great Trek, made it in the eighteen-fifties, when Government and Trekkers alike failed to take just account of the economic needs and human interests of the native population. And now, in the full bloom of ' young nationhood ', the Union bids fair to repeat this fundamental mistake. It is a sign of ill-omen that South African opinion is absorbed in the political aspect of a problem that is one of administration, and, above all, of economics. For good or ill the country is made up of black as well as white, and to satisfy the complex needs of her varied population is the essential Native Problem. Civilization, being of the East as well as of the West, knows no Colour Bar.

Nowhere is there such danger of political disaster as in a country, constitutionally democratic, which denies political rights to a section of its own people. In South Africa, though Parliament is more than usually sensitive to electoral opinion, that opinion is not only incompletely representative, but, through fear, definitely antagonistic to the interests of a large part of the community. Instead of seeking the best possible representation of Native opinion, South Africans deny the first principles of their own cherished Parliamentary system, leaning heavily to a ' solution ' of the Native Problem by measures expressly calculated to make their Parliament more one-sided than ever—proposals for ' reform ' being inspired, chiefly, by a desire to restrict the Native vote in the interests of ' White ' Civilization. The plan, much favoured, of a fixed maximum of separate or *communal* Native representation must place the effective control of the country's future in the hands of a Parliament whose members (all but the communal ' five ' or ' seven ') will be expressly freed from the compelling electoral necessity of remembering that natives exist. The Natives ready to qualify for the jealously guarded privilege of the franchise are a mere handful, and their number increases all too slowly. Wisdom demands that White South Africa bind this handful to itself, and secure their co-operation in devising a policy for leading up to civilization the great backward masses who must, for many years, remain incapable of independent political thought and action. To doubt its ability to do this is to despair of the soundness of the political system and the civilization of which it boasts. For the Union —in blindness born of fear—to baulk or retard their progress will be to sow dragons' teeth that must soon spring to dreadful life in the not infertile seed-plot of South Africa. If knowing is understanding, it may be that new light upon the pages of history will serve to prepare the ground for a happier issue.

Obligations acknowledged in the Preface to the *Cape Colour Question* hold for this which was originally designed to form part of that book. I must now add that the later chapters owe a very great deal to the researches of Miss L. S. Sutherland and of Dr. C. W. de Kiewiet in the Public Records of London and Cape Town. Dr. de Kiewiet has put me under an additional obligation by compiling the index. In very early days Miss G. E. Edwards, of Wynberg, read the draft of certain chapters which her invaluable suggestions helped to transform past her own powers of recognition.

The map, unearthed for me by Mr. D. Chamberlin of the London Missionary Society, is of interest as showing certain limitations and imperfections in the knowledge of South African geography in the eighteen-thirties.

W. M. MACMILLAN.

University of the Witwatersrand,
Johannesburg,
December, 1928.

CONTENTS

xi

CONTENTS

ABBREVIATIONS, ETC.

CORY—*The Rise of S. Africa.* 4 vols. Sir G. E. Cory. Longmans.

THEAL—*History of S. Africa.* 5 vols. G. McC. Theal. Sonnenschein. 1908.

C. C. RECORDS—*Records of the Cape Colony.* 35 vols. ed. by G. M. Theal.

WALKER—*A History of S. Africa.* Prof. E. A. Walker. Longmans. 1927.

BROOKES—*History of Native Policy.* Prof. E. H. Brookes.

BIRD—*Bird's Annals of Natal.* 2 vols. Pietermaritzburg.

EYBERS—*Select Documents Illustrative of S. A. Constitutional History.* G. W. Eybers. Routledge.

GIE—*Geskiedenis vir S. Afrika.* 2 vols. Dr. S. F. N. Gie.

AGAR HAMILTON—*Native Policy of the Voortrekkers.* J. Agar-Hamilton. C. Town. 1928.

DURBAN MSS.—Typewritten volumes, copied by Dr. Theal, in S. A. Library, Cape Town.

GUBBINS—Private Library of J. G. Gubbins, Esq., of Ottoshoop, Western Transvaal.

CAPE COL. QN.—*The Cape Colour Question.* W. M. Macmillan. Faber & Gwyer. 1927.

LETTERS AND DOCUMENTS cited by name or date only are usually among the Philip MSS., University of Witwatersrand, Johannesburg.

BANTU, BOER, AND BRITON:

THE MAKING OF
THE SOUTH AFRICAN
NATIVE PROBLEM

CHAPTER 1

INTRODUCTORY

THE development of a small colony into a self-governing community, and ultimately into an independent nation, is not without parallel, and does not in itself account for the peculiar interest of South African history. The sister Dominions, indeed, Canada and Australia, two other ' virile young nations ', are stronger, wealthier, and more prosperous than the South African Union. In South Africa, from very early days, colonial pioneers had to adapt themselves to the presence of a growing, rather than a vanishing, indigenous coloured population, and very special problems have continually arisen from the juxtaposition of advanced and backward races in one state. Ineluctable fate has decreed that South Africa must make provision in its national system not only for the needs and aspirations of a homogeneous community of Europeans, but also for the potential and progressive development of its far more numerous backward Natives.

In a former book I have described how the problems arising from the contact of advanced and backward peoples were dealt with inside the bounds of the old Cape Colony, where European colonists met with hardly any opposition from the aboriginal Hottentots—nomadic tribes, with little or no organization, no skill in agriculture, and no power of military resistance—and gradually ousted them from their grazing lands, reducing them before the eighteenth century was out to abject dependence, economic, legal and political. In the first generation after the British occupation of the Cape in 1806 the legal status of these people was thrashed out, and the year 1828 marked the freeing of the Hottentots by the efforts of Emancipationists whose ideals led them to fight for the overthrow of slavery ' in all its roots and branches '. The ' Philip ' Party of South African tradition was, in truth, the local manifestation of a world movement in whose current the Cape, tiny and remote as it was at that time, became engulfed. After 1833 the emancipated slaves,

an exotic element of the population, reinforced the ranks of the
' free ' people of colour ; and by 1853—when the Cape attained
to ' Representative ' Government with a franchise open to all—
Hottentots and ex-slaves, with a strong admixture of European
blood, were beginning to merge into what have come to be known
as the ' Cape Coloured People ', or, latterly, ' Eurafricans '.
These people differ endlessly amongst themselves in shade and
in physical characteristics, according as they inherit more from
Hottentot, Negro, Malay or European ancestors—the Malays
indeed, by their adherence to the faith of Islam, maintaining a
somewhat separate existence. But socially, *vis-à-vis* the European population, the least trace of colour suffices to throw the
various elements into one class. Politically, only their own
Cape Colony allows coloured people potentially equal rights
with Europeans, so that the great majority of them are still
inhabitants of the old Colony.

To-day the ' Coloured ' people number only about half a
million, and memories are so short that it is often asserted that
it is precisely because their numbers are so small that they have
been allowed political rights which the dominant Europeans
' dare ' not allow to the more numerous Bantu. The truth is,
on the contrary, that at the time when the coloured people's
rights were won they outnumbered the Europeans in the Colony
by two to one, a disproportion not much less than that between
White and Bantu in the present Union, and that the freeing of
the Hottentots led directly to the disruption of South African
unity by the Great Trek. The grand climacteric of South
African history came in the early 'fifties, when the British Government, dismayed by the effects of disruption, and turning back
on the principles of freedom, abandoned the control of the larger
part of the Bantu population to those who expressly repudiated the
ideals which had inspired the Emancipationists twenty years earlier.

Even while the first, largely internal, Colour Question was
being worked out, this second and far more formidable problem,
South African more than Cape, was coming into being on the
colonial frontiers and beyond. The very feebleness of Hottentot
opposition to the expansion of the Colony hastened the day when
isolated families of Trek-Boers (the typical South African colonists) were to meet with really formidable opposition from the
better organized and warlike Bantu of the more distant interior.
In the east indeed, on the natural geographical line of advance,

colonial expansion was stayed after 1779 for half a century and more, the boundary remaining fixed at or about the Great Fish River. At first the effect of this check was not very serious ; for in the north, where at this time the Bantu hardly counted, the old advance continued almost unnoticed, so that by 1826 the boundary had been pushed forward from the Stormberg to the Orange River. At this point, however, though pioneers still pushed on, further annexation was stopped even in the north, where the London Society's missionaries stood firm for the land rights of their protégés, the ' Bastards ' or Griquas, who were themselves for the most part emigrants from the Cape Colony. So it was that by 1836 the natural advance and the land hunger of the colonists were sharply checked on two fronts, in the north by Griqua interests, in the east by the Kafirs, or Bantu, and by the British Government's hesitation about provoking more ' Kafir Wars '.

In setting its face, as far as it could, against expansion, the British Government was but following in the steps of its Dutch predecessors. But it had gone further and given mortal offence to many colonists by the recognition of Hottentot or ' Coloured ' rights within the Cape Colony. The discontents of the 'thirties, therefore, had two main sources ; some colonists were thwarted in their desire to satisfy their land hunger ; and almost all resented what they felt to be vexatious legal restraints upon the treatment of their coloured and native servants. The result was the great explosion of South African history, the Great Trek, by which some thousands of Boers sought a way of escape from these restraints by abandoning the Colony altogether. Up to this point the impact of European colonists upon the Bantu, and the resulting wars, had been confined to a short front extending only from the Winterberg or Katberg to the sea. There could be but few settled farms, if any, in Bantu country, and except for stray refugees like the ' Fingos ' and some Bechuanas, the Cape Colony had no Bantu subjects to complicate its problems of government. All within two or three years the issue was forced. By the Great Trek the colonial front was enormously extended. Dangers attended the old slow penetration of the interior by isolated families, but strongly organized parties of Trekkers now began to spread themselves over the whole of the interior from the Winterberg to the Orange River, thence over the High Veld plains of what are now the Orange Free State and Transvaal, as well as across the Drakensberg

into Natal. In military language, the Bantu flank was turned.
At a time of internal confusion continuing after the Chaka
Wars, Bantu tribes, which never had been effectively united,
were taken in detail and conquered, and their land in large
slices cut up into Boer farms—the people themselves, like the
Hottentots before them, being gradually reduced to economic
dependence and political subjection.

This book is the story of how European colonization in South
Africa, driven forward by its own inner momentum, at first
almost unchallenged, came thus into collision with the far more
numerous Bantu of the interior. After a long military phase
of wars and of ultimate conquest, the problem became social,
political, and above all economic, complicating at every turn
the domestic policy of the country to the present day. By
about 1854 the main issues were settled. Downing Street,
while it still occasionally intervened, abandoned the attempt to
control South African policy as a whole. Tribes like the Zulus
kept alive in the minds of scattered and out-numbered Europeans
a sense of possible Native ' danger ' or ' menace '. But there
was no more question of what was feared in 1835—a rising
that would sweep from the Fish River even to Cape Town.
Essentially the Bantu were now a broken people. Yet without
real justification the old fear of the Bantu has lived on, blended
now with a widespread feeling of contempt, shown in the use
of the colloquial Afrikaans ' Kaffer '. In muddled fashion,
perhaps, the ' menace ' is now thought of as economic. The
competition of the Native is felt to threaten the poorer whites,
and his rise to civilization that of children yet unborn. Fear,
therefore, clamours to keep the Native down, with incredible
waste of productive man-power ; and White South Africa,
as a whole, refuses to see how its own economic ills are the
direct result of the backwardness and poverty of the Native
majority. ' Policy ' has never faced the changed conditions.

In this book finally the influence of ' Exeter Hall ', represented
in South Africa most conspicuously by Dr. John Philip, must
now come under review, in substantiation of the claim formerly
made, that in so far as the missionary or ' Exeter Hall ' policy
has been applied, as to the Cape Coloured People, there is to-
day little difficulty ; whereas the Bantu, with whom for the
most part ' colonial ' views have had their way, now present a
most baffling problem. Contrary to the tradition that the

troubles of South Africa have been largely due to outside ' inter-ference ' with the instinctive wisdom of its own colonists, it would appear that even in their hey-day of 1836–8 the warnings of Humanitarians went almost unheeded. The Cape Colony, it is true, thanks to its distinctive, missionary-born, tradition of freedom, has made a notable success of the Transkeian Territories, though in the Ciskei, the old scene of the ' Kafir Wars ', it has less reason for self-satisfaction. In Natal again, comparatively adequate ' Reserves ' were secured to the Natives by direct inter-vention of the British Government ; but the Native administra-tion of this Colony has not been conspicuously successful in promoting progress or, latterly, even contentment. In the two Republics the pre-1828 colonial policy has, on the whole, been faithfully adhered to, with severe restrictions on the right to acquire property in land (or its total denial), and the complete exclusion of people of colour from any share in political privileges. The Orange Free State, almost destitute as it is of Native ' Reserves ', was saved from the worst penalties of a Native land problem by the very intervention it so hotly resented in 1868 when Basutoland was taken under British protection ; and in the Transvaal it was only in terms of Conventions with Britain in 1881 and 1884, that definite, though still rather fragmentary, Native Reserves began to be saved from the all-absorbing land-hunger of the burghers.[1] It may be true that the apprehension of Downing Street intervention on Native behalf served to numb the tender growth of the colonial conscience in Native affairs ; but it was none the less the indirect liberal influence of what is loosely and opprobriously denounced as ' Exeter Hall ' which thus often saved South Africa from itself.

Now that the Union is mistress of her own destinies, the Natives are known to contrast the benefits they enjoyed, according to a still lively tradition, from the government of the Great White Queen, Victoria, with the restraints and restrictions that now threaten them. The old Downing Street is no more, and the Native people stand sorely in need of re-assurance. A stable settlement cannot be reached in isolation, without regard to the rights enjoyed by other Bantu people, and to the progress and development of our relatively near neighbours in the Rhodesias, in Tanganyika, even in Kenya and Katanga. The defenders of ' White ' civilization must now plead their case before the Supreme Court—the moral conscience of the world.

[1] Brookes, c. iv.

CHAPTER II

THE BANTU TRIBES—CUSTOMS AND INSTITUTIONS—CHAKA AND OTHERS

THE Bantu are now so much with us that it tends to be forgotten that in the days of the Dutch East India Company, apart from imported slaves, the only people of colour in the Colony were the weak and helpless Hottentots. The Bantu races, first seriously encountered towards the end of the Company's days, were still a frontier and external distraction. The essential colour problem of the Colony, thorny as it proved to be, concerned only Hottentot rights and status. Till the nineteenth century, the Bantu, however serious a complication, remained a military and frontier problem, and except for a handful of refugees, and Sir Benjamin D'Urban's ill-starred experiment in 1835, it was only some years after the Great Trek that the British Colonial Government extended its protection to subjects of Bantu race.

Of the origin of the Bantu [1] it is impossible to speak with certainty, the name itself being a philological (and ethnological) abstraction. The term Bantu suggests common physical features, such as, for example, the black woolly hair and thick lips of the Negroid, similar social customs, and, especially, a group of languages apparently derived from some common ancestor ; but it connotes no single political group. History knows only scattered tribes, loosely connected with one another like those of ancient Germany and Gaul, the very multitude of names indicating that the tribes were constantly breaking up and new combinations forming. The Bantu most prominent in South African history fall into four groups, Ama-Xosa, Ama-Zulu, Bechuana, and Basuto.[2] The Ama-Xosa, or ' Kafirs ', held

---

[1] See Theal, i, cc. 14, 15.

[2] See Theal, *History since 1795*, vol. ii, c. xiii. The Bantu make use of prefixes, *ama*, or *ba*, to denote the whole tribe, as in *Ama*-Xosa; an individual is a *Mo*suto, *Mo*chuana ; the language, *Se*chuana or *Se*suto ; the country *Le*suto.

the old Cape Frontier; the Ama-Zulu, the coastal belt farther
east, in Natal and beyond ; the Bechuana, considerably mixed,
it may be, with Korannas or Hottentots, inhabited the country
bordering on the Kalahari and much of what is now the Western
Transvaal ; there remained on the eastern edge of the High
Veld, on the upper waters of the Orange River and the Caledon,
the Basuto—scattered remnants gathered together and organized
after the Chaka wars (below, p. 14) by the great chief Moshesh
in the South African Switzerland still known as Basutoland.
The term ' Kafir ', derived from the Islamic *giaour*, meaning
Gentile or unbeliever, which is often loosely used for individuals
of any of these tribes and rather disliked by some of them,
stands as a reminder of an East Coast origin and of early contact
with Islam ; by long association the name serves to distinguish
those of the eastern frontier of the Cape Colony who were long
the only ' Kafirs ' known to the Europeans.

It was, in fact, in South East Africa that the Bantu first
figured in history. Like some famous prehistoric migrations,
whether merely from the internal pressure of population or, as
perhaps in the days of Chaka, from a combination of causes,
they had in the centuries preceding European settlement at the
Cape of Good Hope gradually penetrated from Central Africa
to the south. For the most part they followed the lower coastal
terraces, similar to those still farther south favoured first by
Hottentots and later by Europeans, settling in the coastal and
warmer levels of Natal and the eastern Cape, on the well-watered
slopes of the Drakensberg, and in the Low or Bush Veld of the
Transvaal, on a line running east and north of Lydenburg-
Pretoria-Rustenburg. Rather avoiding the High Veld with its
cold winter—where the wide open plains gave little cover
from enemies—they settled also farther west, not only in Bechuanaland, but in part of what is now the Transvaal, this dry belt
being well suited to cattle-rearing, since even near the Kalahari
Desert there are good springs,[1] and bushes and trees which
afford the herds both shade and sustenance.

By the eighteenth century the Bantu were firmly established
as the only effective occupants of territory stretching from far
away in the north down at least to the Kei. In the course of
their expansion they displaced, and doubtless slew, the Bushmen,
and either expelled or absorbed the Hottentots. The Bantu,

[1] The spring at Kuruman, for example, is estimated to yield four
or five million gallons of water daily.

therefore, it is often held, are no more South African ' aboriginals ' than their own European conquerors. But if mere conquest gives valid title this assertion is hardly warranted ; it probably owes its vogue to the fact that the Bantu became a serious factor comparatively late in the history of the old Colony, as if they were really only new-comers. Kafir conquest had, in fact, absorbed more of southern Africa than is usually admitted, including especially the tract from the Fish River to the Kei, which the Bantu, like the Boers, coveted for the sake of the attractive districts from Bedford to Kingwilliamstown,[1] not because the arid Fish River bush might sometimes afford cover for thieving.

The earliest recorded conflict between white colonists and Kafirs was in 1702, when a cattle ' bartering ' expedition in the time of the younger Van der Stel (Governor 1699–1707) had a serious skirmish with Kafirs ' three or four days ' west of the Gamtoos.[2] The first time the Government was obliged to take cognizance of this new racial factor was more than seventy years later, in the so-called ' First Kafir War ', when the Fish River was made a dividing line between advancing colonists and the Kafirs. Following petty ' wars ' in 1789 and 1799, the British Government were in 1812 still attempting to ' clear ' the ' Zuurveld ' (the country *west* of the Fish River), and Grahams-town was established as an outlying frontier post to hold the Fish River line. Undoubtedly the Kafirs were in effective occupation [3] down to the Fish River long before the Europeans, and even the outposts still farther west in the Zuurveld must have been fairly strongly held. The Fish River front was, indeed, the scene of the most prolonged and bitter contest of

[1] ' The Kat and Koonap rivers are the finest part of the Colony ', wrote the settler Thos. Pringle to Philip, July 1821, ' and still unoccupied . . . and highly eligible for a missionary settlement.' This belt had been newly cleared to form a ' Neutral Territory '.

[2] The Kafirs were probably also a scouting party, some days from their own ' land ', but as documents make no mention of any river east of the Gamtoos, it seems likely that the Bantu scouts were far to the west of the Kei—some distance west of the Fish, and possibly even of the Sundays River. Annexures M ff. in the *Defence of W. A. van der Stel*, ed. Leibbrandt, Cape Town, 1897.

[3] Williams, of the London Missionary Society, the first missionary to the Kafirs, took up residence at the ' great place ' of the paramount chief, Gaika, in 1816. The ' great place ' of a chief is not an outpost, and Williams' grave remains to show that Gaika was within three miles of the later Fort Beaufort, which is quite near the Fish River.

white and black in all South African history. So far from being
an affair of outposts, this was, in the language of the Great War,
the ' Western Front ' of the long struggle, and European supremacy .was not finally established over this much coveted and
long disputed area for fully eighty years. The territory from
the Kei to the Natal border is still almost wholly Bantu ; and
to this day the fearful congestion of the native population from
the Fish River, indeed from Bathurst, to the Kei, in the area
where the struggle began, bears witness, not to any new or
recent influx, but to the thoroughness, and heedlessness, with
which the older population was not only conquered, but dispossessed. The first phase in the history of Bantu relations
with Europeans is this long struggle, and there is evidence to
show overwhelmingly how it was not a mere lust for colonial
cattle, but the attempt to defend their own earlier acqusition,
which kept chiefs like Maqomo, the most ' turbulent ' of the
Xosa leaders, in chronic unrest till their final disaster in the
eighteen-fifties.

For a primitive people the Bantu were comparatively advanced,
and a formidable obstacle in the way of advancing colonists.
Unlike the Hottentots, they had some skill in metal work, being
armed with assegais. Like Caesar's Germans, whom, in fact,
they closely resembled, they did not specially devote themselves
to agriculture, living rather on milk—that is, the nutritious
curdled milk [1] which they preserve in gourds known as *kalabashes*
—on beef, and to some extent on the game they took. Yet even
their rough and superficial cultivation of maize and Kafir corn
(millet)—the latter used especially to make their native beer—
raised them many stages above the merely nomadic Hottentots.
If their tillage was, and is, wretched, they had in older, roomier
days a shrewd eye for the best patches of soil, and habitually
settled in one spot from five to seven years ; then, even if the
ground was not exhausted, their huts needed to be renewed
for hygienic reasons, and they moved slowly on, ' picking out
the eyes ' of the country in their progress. This, no doubt,
was highly wasteful, but the Bantu were tribally rather than
territorially organized, and since land was plentiful, their ideas
of boundaries were as vague and rudimentary as their notions
of land ownership. Yet they were definitely attached to their

---

[1] Cf. Song of Deborah : ' He asked water and she gave him milk ;
she brought forth *butter* in a lordly dish ' (Judges v. 25).

own ' country ', and the traditional reverence for the graves of
their great chiefs suggests that the Bantu were no mere nomads.
Thanks to their agriculture, and to the fact that in winter, or in
time of drought, their cattle got some sustenance from the stubble
of the fields, their food supply was far more regular than that of
the Hottentots. This may account for the generally magnificent
physique of these Bantu peoples. It also explains how, whatever
their actual numbers, they were relatively closely settled, and
for that reason more formidable. The Hottentot mode of life
under the best circumstances could hardly support as many as
three to the square mile, whereas the Bantu system could probably, without undue pressure, maintain a population of at least
ten, and possibly more, anywhere in the important Cape-Natal
area.[1] Conditions in the north-west or Bechuana area being less
favourable, but the country less important, there the rather
scanty population has been forced into relatively large villages
in the immediate neighbourhood of the stronger springs ; whereas
in the east, except where they clumped together for defensive
reasons, the *kraals* (huts belonging to a family unit) tended to
be scattered broadcast.

This comparatively settled life made in its turn for a quite
highly developed social organization. The possibility of accumu-
lating cattle, for cattle's sake—they sell or slaughter their ' wealth '
but sparingly—raised individuals above the dead level of poverty
which marked the Hottentots ; and though to this day the
communal life and instincts of the Bantu are very strong, they
are by no means equalitarian. Thus their stronger men, being
relieved from the pressure of immediate want, could leave most
of the necessary tillage to the women, and were free to follow
the pleasures of hunting or, in some circumstances perhaps,
the ' predatory instincts ' with which historians have too liberally endowed them. No doubt, as with others similarly placed,
the first rise above the pressure of grinding want stimulated
their fighting and acquisitive instincts ; but the leaders of their
marauding bands were seldom to be classed as mighty warlike
chiefs. There is no reason to believe that a military despot

---

[1] Estimates place the population of the rather more favourable
plains of western Europe at anything up to 30 to the square mile in the
times of the very similar early Celts and Teutons. At the present
day several Transkeian districts have about 100 persons to the square
mile, but these are dependent on supplementary wages, earned on
the mines and elsewhere.

like Chaka was anything but a startling exception to the rude democracy that prevailed among them. The normal Bantu tribe, to this day, has its body of Custom, widely recognized by European administrators as Law. It has also its *Pitso* (folkmoot), and the chief his *Likothla* (Witan), an inner council of wise men and advisers. In practice, no doubt, the ' democracy ' would vary with the strength or weakness of the chief, and the composition of the ' Likothla ' would be as elastic as that of the early English ' Witan '. But there seems little doubt also that as a free people the Bantu had strong political instincts; drastic decisions would not normally be taken by a chief except on the advice of the ' Likothla ', and with something like the general consent of the tribe as a whole. Even on their ' Western Front ', the scene of the long series of ' Kafir Wars ' in the old Cape Colony, there was no effective Paramount chief. Governor Somerset, for example, for official convenience made a paramount of Gaika. But Gaika was neither acknowledged by the Kafirs generally, nor capable of making effective the greatness that was thrust upon him; and many difficulties arose after 1819 from the attempt to enforce recognition of the cession of territory which had been wrung from this chief.

In later times the disciplined military prowess of the Zulus made so great an impression on their neighbours in Natal and the Transvaal, that there is now a tendency to generalize about the military instincts and warrior chiefs of the Bantu ; when called upon to interpret Native Custom, even courts of law tend to ascribe to ordinary Bantu chiefs absolute powers that were in fact enjoyed only by a few outstanding ' kings ' [1]—the *amapakati* (counsellors) of old Kafirland being confused with the *indunas* (military captains) of the Zulus. The almost constitutional chief, with his body of councillors, and not the despot, was more generally true to Bantu type, however the type may have been modified by the revolution forced upon the Bantu in the last hundred and fifty years. So the European tradition of the ' unmitigated savagery ' of these Bantu tribes is hardly just.

[1] E.g. the Zulu Kings, Chaka and Dingaan, their pupil Moselekatze of the Matabele, and possibly some pale imitators in Swaziland. On these points I am indebted to suggestions in a paper lent me by Mr. J. W. Honey, lately Resident Commissioner of Swaziland, whose impressions are confirmed independently by informed Europeans and Natives like Mr. Aston Key, now of Herschel, and Mr. R. W. Selope Thema, a Native of the Transvaal.

The uncertainty and insecurity of their savage existence, even before they came to feel acutely the pressure of the civilized races, must have been unsettling enough. No doubt the Bantu were cattle-reivers, and highly dangerous and troublesome neighbours. Doubtless also they were sufficiently military to make war an inevitable preliminary to reaching any stable equilibrium on frontiers where they and European colonists made contact. But the natural life of the Bantu, and their chief interests, centred not in ' thieving ', but in land. Their primitive methods, and the droughts and difficulties inseparable from South African life, can have left but little economic margin of safety ; and their own population difficulties may easily account for some of their internal dissensions. Since they have no records of their own on which to draw, we are dependent for knowledge of their old conditions either on random travellers, or on colonists to whom they were a cause for alarm, if not a menace. The evidence of missionaries is, therefore, of special value, as for example that of the French missionary Casalis, who, writing from the spot, of disorders on the Basuto border, comments significantly :

' I fear much confusion arises from the very limited and erroneous ideas generally entertained respecting the statistics of the Bantu country. The population is under-rated, the actual and future wants of the tribe are not taken into consideration. It is no childish debate about the useless waste that takes place at this moment. The present lamentable war of the Basutos and the Mantatees, *which originated in nothing else than a land question*, shows sufficiently how keen and deep are the feelings of the natives on the subject.' [1]

The Bantu tribes, it is clear, did not always fall out with each other merely from innate quarrelsomeness and love of fighting. Nor is there any justification for an unfortunate phrase used by Sir Benjamin D'Urban, who in 1835 wrote of them as ' irreclaimable savages '.[2] The Bantu as a people are long-suffering and law-abiding. A mere handful of European police [3]

[1] Casalis to Philip, Feb. 1848.

[2] Even in the war of 1835 there is evidence that while they discriminated against traders—some of whom were not above suspicion —they habitually spared women and children (Cory, iii, pp. 72, 73). Though missionaries were repeatedly cut off by war, and completely in their hands, one of them was unmolested, though all but an eye-witness of the Retief massacre. There is hardly a recorded instance of a martyr missionary to the Bantu.

[3] Apparently about 250 all told, including a ' mobile squadron ' of over 100.

is enough to keep order in the wide area of the Transkei, with
its million inhabitants. In their own territories—though not
necessarily in the artificial European-made conditions of mining
camps and towns—all experience shows that white women, for
example, are as safe as, or safer than, in a European capital. Indeed,
history and administrators agree that the Bantu are singularly
amenable to just government, and are very easily led and controlled. They have never known slavery. Even in defeat, and
in conditions in which they have little voice, their leaders state
their case not only with eloquence and logic, but with amazing
good humour and tact. They are kindly and cheerful and, as
in the famous story of the last days of Dr. Livingstone, faithful
—a people most suitably summed up in one inimitable German
word, *gemütlich*. Dr. Theal—following tradition rather than
interpreting it—sweepingly suggests that in their primitive
condition the Bantu, when they were not stealing colonial cattle,
were ' slaughtering each other '.[1] But the measured judgment
of Bishop Stubbs on Caesar's account of the early Germanic
tribes, is a corrective to exaggerations of this kind :

> ' The features remarked on by Caesar—the perpetual state of war,
> the neglect of agriculture for pastoral pursuits and hunting, the annual
> migrations of tribes—are, it is true, commonly viewed as characteristic
> of the first steps out of barbarism into civilization ; but the first two
> are extremely liable to exaggeration by rumour, and the prominence
> of the whole three in this description is owing to the generally unsettled
> state of all tribes bordering on the Roman conquests.' [2]

The first quarter of the nineteenth century, when the European
onset first became serious, was just such a period of unsettlement
and of ' perpetual war ' among the Bantu tribes behind the
western or European front. Some years after 1783, on the banks
of the Umfolosi in what is still called Zululand, a ' younger
son ' of the then undistinguished Ama-Zulu tribe, by his athletic
and warlike prowess, provoked the jealousy of the chief his
father.[3] This lad, named Chaka, ran away from home and
took refuge and service with a rather greater chief, his own
tribe's overlord, Dingiswayo—himself a man out of the ordinary.

[1] Theal, v, p. 254 and elsewhere.

[2] Select Charters, 8th edition, p. 52.

[3] There are several recent examples of this. In 1925 the heir of
the well-known Khama had had about twenty years in exile, and about
the same time a common labourer, as it seemed, was recalled from the
farm of a European to succeed his father Mpefu as chief of the Zoutpansberg Bavenda.

In his own youth Dingiswayo too had fled from his father. In his wanderings he obtained some knowledge of the European military system and was impressed by the value of discipline. Returning at last to rule his own people, he applied the lessons he had learned from Europeans to the refurbishing of the traditional military methods of his own people, laying the foundations of the military system afterwards developed by Chaka, and long to be associated with his name. The unit was the regiment (*impi*), subject to an iron, and, if reports be true, a bloody discipline. As in some other savage armies, the braves were taught to regard marriage as a reward reserved for those who had worthily ' washed their spears ' and had their baptism of blood. Their characteristic weapon was the assegai, hurled from a distance, or, in the last resort, when it came to ' push of pike ', it might be broken off short and used as a two-edged sword or dagger. The regular formation in attack was the crescent, backed by reserves kept ready to be pushed forward to any point that was specially threatened. At the very outset, Dingiswayo's manifestation of Bantu militarism reflected European example.

Chaka himself first came into prominence while still in the service of Dingiswayo, rising by the patronage of his master to the chieftainship of his own Zulu tribe. Finally, when Dingiswayo himself died without direct heir, he was thrust by the army, of which he was now the most distinguished leader, into the position of supreme power. Then, by all accounts, there began ten years or more of storm and stress for the whole of the Bantu people of southern Africa. Though dates, detailed facts, and estimates of the numbers involved are alike doubtful, it seems fairly certain, by unanimous Bantu tradition, that from a little before 1820 Chaka entered on the career of a Timurlane, attacking, murdering, or putting to flight, over an area wider than modern Natal and Zululand. In September 1828 he met the common fate of tyrants, being murdered in his own kraal in a ' palace conspiracy ' by his two brothers ; one of these, Dingaan by name, succeeded him as King of the Zulus, and crowned his career by the murder of Retief and his fellow-trekkers in the February of 1838.

The effects of the Chaka wars were by no means confined to the Natal and coastal strip in which they originated, but reacted even on tribes far away in the interior. The High Veld itself probably owes some increase of its comparatively small

Bantu population to the dispersal of tribes by the wars of the
eighteen-twenties, though the carrying of war on to the High
Veld was not the work of Chaka himself. One of his early
victims was a certain Matiwana who, as Sir George Cory puts
it, ' unable to oppose the Great King, carried on the process
of extermination on his own account ', and, crossing the Drakensberg, sent wave upon wave of refugees flying or plundering over
the plains beyond. Of these the best known are the bearded
Mantatees who, in the middle of 1823, began to fall upon the
unwarlike Bechuana of the west. These Bechuana were now
under the influence of the London missionaries, and Robert
Moffat at this point stood them in good stead, calling in the
help of the Griquas (or Bastards), mounted and armed with
guns (see Chapter IV), who met and defeated the Mantatee
invaders in the neighbourhood of Kuruman. Thereafter the
Mantatees themselves appear only a broken remnant, as in origin
they always were ; in spite of the picturesque term ' horde '
commonly applied to them, their defeat was effected by only
two or three hundred Griquas. We hear of them again in 1848
on the Caledon River, at loggerheads with the Basuto on the
perennial quest for land for new homes. In the north also,
though they were united against the Mantatees, these Griquas
had their own feuds, which were encouraged by such disturbances among the Bantu. Bands of them rejected the government-
favoured authority of chiefs like Waterboer and took to the
' mountains ',[1] whence their name Bergenaars—whence also
they carried on illicit trade with the Colony, and themselves
kept the North in confusion by their plundering raids upon the
unlucky Bechuana.

The Chaka wars also first forced the Bantu in considerable
numbers across the mountain barrier of the Amatolas and the
Katberg, into country one remove from the influence of the
sea-breezes, hitherto left to clans of Bushmen.[2] Round about
1820, the remnants of a royal tribe, the Tembus, began to occupy
the country near what is now Queenstown, figuring in the frontier
history of that time as the ' Tambookies ', to the further considerable complication of the troubles of the Kafirs (and colonists)
on the eastern frontier. About 1824 numbers of Bechuana
refugees, flying both from Mantatees and from Bergenaars,

[1] Cape Col. Qn., pp. 252 ff.
[2] As late as 1843 the Rev. James Read was exerting himself in these
parts on behalf of a Bushman chief described as ' King ' Madoor. .

made their appearance inside the Cape Colony and were readily
' apprenticed ' or ' *ingeboekt* ' to farm labour. A little later,
about 1828, refugees from Chaka himself began either to disturb
the uneasy peace of the Kafir frontier, or to appear as ' Fingos '
in the Colony itself ; and so for the first time the farmers began
to draw on men of Bantu race for the supply of farm-labourers
of which they were so short.[1]

But not all the victims of the wars were mere refugees,
destined to become detribalized labourers dependent on white
farmers. Above all, the troubles of these days gave his great
opportunity to one of the most sagacious and statesmanlike of
Bantu chiefs, one who was no mere bloodthirsty warrior. The
Basuto chief, Moshesh, soon showed that he knew how to use
his geographical advantages to make an impregnable fortress of
his famous capital, Thaba Bosigo—more than once also, alike
against Bantu, British, and Boer, that he knew something of
the arts of peace, and when to make or keep the peace. He
it was who, in 1832, sent an embassy to ' buy ' a missionary
from Dr. Philip, then on tour at Philippolis [2] ; and though the
price, a thousand head of cattle, was carried off by border robbers
(Korannas) and never reached its destination, Dr. Philip was
directly instrumental very shortly afterwards in diverting the
French Protestant missionaries from their disturbed first station
among the Bechuana to Basutoland, with which they have been
identified ever since. Moshesh's great feat was to bind the broken
tribes of the broad valleys of the Drakensberg into a homogeneous
people, the Basuto. This chief was yet to play a highly important
part in the history of the country (see Chapter XVII), and Basutoland, in origin the promised land to an exodus of the Bantu
under the control and guidance of their own Moshesh,[3] remains,
like the Transkei, a densely crowded but compact island of
Bantu in the mixed and troubled South African scene.

Further, there was an important off-shoot of the Zulu army

---

[1] *Cape Col. Qn.*, pp. 252 ff.

[2] Moshesh was so determined to have a teacher that he seems to
have urged Adam Kok to come himself if no one else was available.

[3] It is significant that in the eastern Transvaal, in parts separated
from ' Basutoland ' by a large stretch of High Veld with only detribalized fragments of a farm-native population, the most widely spoken
Bantu dialect is still *Sesuto*. The Boer Republics, therefore, must
have driven a wedge into these Sesuto-speaking tribes, so that Moshesh's
claim to need more land than the Free State was willing to concede,
was not wholly unjustified.

itself, a division that broke away under Moselekatze (Umziligazi).
This almost equally famous warrior fell out with Chaka and,
being threatened with vengeance, took his army off to the north-
west through parts of the northern Free State and western
Transvaal, following this new route in order, it would seem, to
escape the raids of slave-traders in the north. Moselekatze
seems to have modelled his rule on that of his master, Chaka,
and practised a similar despotism. It is just possible, however,
that tradition in its report of this warrior is none too reliable,
exaggerating, if not his savagery, then at least his power and
its effective organization. Some evidence suggests strongly that
this potentate often went more like a fugitive in terror of enemies,
than like an all-conquering tyrant.[1] In 1829 Moselekatze was
visited by Robert Moffat, and in 1832 by some of the newly
arrived French missionaries ; one of these, as one M. Lemue
reported to Dr. Philip, Moselekatze was anxious to detain, forcibly,
' for himself '—rather a bear's embrace, no doubt, for the mere
proximity of the Matabele soon drove the Frenchmen to abandon
work they had begun in Bechuanaland among the ' Bahurutsi '.

This desire for a missionary was, perhaps, political rather than
spiritual. ' Moselekatze ', Moffat wrote to Philip on 15 August 1832,

' appears ever since Berends' commando to entertain some doubts as to the
real character and motives of missionaries, well knowing that the Banditti who treacherously assailed his territories and murdered his subjects
emanated from the Missionary Station. . . . Notwithstanding his
apparent attachment and confidence in me, he has some fears that I
am a powerful chief, and had some part in the nefarious proceedings
of old Berend '.[2]

---

[1] One Jan Viljoen, a well-known elephant hunter, who in later
years was intimate with the chief, tells how Moselekatze himself claimed
that his wholesale massacres were ' an act of policy ' : ' I was like a
blind man ', he is reported to have said, ' feeling my way with a stick.
We had heard tales of great *impis* that suddenly popped up from under-
ground, or swept down on you from high mountains ' (referring, it
seems, to cave-dwelling tribes with mountain strongholds in the Zoutpansberg) ' and we had a dread of the Korannas, mounted and armed
with rifles. I had to keep open veld around me.' (Quoted in the
Star, 17 October 1925, by Adv. Eugene Marais, who adds a remarkable
story of the privileges allowed to a certain Barolong, who had guided
Moselekatze from before the Boers on the Marico to safety in his later
home in ' Matabeleland '.)

[2] Presumably Barend Barends, who, with one Hendriks, made a
raid on the Matabele in April or May 1832, and seized some cattle.
The raiders seem to have been ambushed, with loss of guns and horses,
on their return journey.

At all events little came of his overtures,[1] and Moselekatze's
'country' (if any such there was) never had the same settled
attractions as that of Moshesh for missionary work. In 1832
he had the far north-west in terror, and Dr. Philip, returning
from one of his tours of inspection in January 1833, warned the
authorities at Graaff-Reinet of possible danger to the colony
itself. As a matter of fact this unrest, which prevented Dr.
Philip from visiting the tyrant's kraal, was perhaps due to the
lawlessness of some of the Griquas who at that very time, by
Moffat's account, suffered chastisement at the hands of Moselekatze himself. As late as August 1835 Moffat appears again to
have paid him a visit. In his Journal of that year he reported
that Moselekatze was still wanting a missionary; he would
have 'only Mosheti' (Moffat), and wished 'to throw away
his spears and live in peace'. For a short time American missionaries settled with him; but about 1837, when the Voortrekkers
came to blows with his *impis* at Vechtkop and Mosega in the
centre and west of the High Veld, they seem to have removed
to Natal.

Fortunately the Matabele, as they came to be called, left
the Colony alone. For some years they engaged in a struggle
with the Boers for ownership of the land, and though not all
their fights were against the Matabele, the Boers of the early
Transvaal were almost annually on 'commando' and the country
knew little peace or settlement. In the more open country of
the north-west there was no natural fortress like Thaba Bosigo
to make the rallying centre of a second Basutoland, even had
Moselekatze learned like Moshesh to make his military power
merely defensive, and the Matabele were soon driven out. The
ruins of their kraals are plentiful in the western Transvaal, and
fragments of the Matabele themselves remain in that province.
But the main body drifted far to the north, and Moselekatze's
son was the Lobengula who was finally conquered in the 'nineties,
near the site of Bulawayo, by the Chartered Company.

How far this great upheaval among the Bantu must be
attributed, in Bishop Stubbs' words, to the 'generally unsettled
state of all tribes bordering' on European conquests can never

---

[1] As late as April 1834 Rolland, one of the French missionaries,
wrote urging upon his colleagues, who had gone from Bechuanaland
to Moshesh in Basutoland, the need for some one to 'propitiate' Moselekatze, even 'for the protection of Moshesh'.

be fully known. While from the nature of the case the effects of the frontier wars on the remoter tribes are not directly evident, the suggestion that there was a connexion is not wholly to be dismissed. It is significant that the rise of Chaka came at the very moment when things were moving towards a climax on the Cape frontier, and that his wars synchronize with those of Gaika and Ndhlambi on the borders of the Colony (see p. 34). It may very well be that the check to their vanguard on the Fish River, in the severe set-back which began in 1812, was not without direct influence on the Bantu in Natal and Zululand. At all events the real source of all this war and tumult has never otherwise been explained.

Further, to meet the demands of European planters, slave-traders had not only raided on their own account for a hundred years past, but set tribe against tribe in such ruthless fashion that if the consequences were often bloody it is not for Europeans to cast a stone. There is no reason to believe that the slave-trade left the southern part of Africa unaffected ; in 1823 Governor Somerset was discussing the desirability of annexing Delagoa Bay, significantly near the scene of Chaka's devastations, as a check on the slave-trade ; and not long afterwards, Dr. Philip writing from Bechuanaland in the end of 1832 [1] quoted hitherto unnoticed evidence that even South African Bantu tribes had direct cause to fear the ravages of the slave trade. The tyrant warrior Moselekatze, it appears, when he fled before Chaka, first went to the north. There, however, he encountered ' brown-skinned men armed with guns ', slave-raiders from Portuguese ports ; which serves to explain, what is in itself surprising, the westward route followed by the Matabele in the devastating raid that carried them at last across mountains and open plains towards Bechuanaland. To his friend, Rev. J. Campbell, Philip wrote at the same time :

[1] Dr. Philip's evidence is important, resting as it does on that of Mr. Moffat and of the French missionaries, who had visited Moselekatze in person in 1829 and 1832 respectively—drawing perhaps also on current native gossip. In 1830 he writes categorically from Kafirland : ' Farewell and others (i.e. pioneers at Port Natal) have stirred up war wherever they have gone. To Farewell's establishment at Port Natal we are to trace the devastations of Chaka.' Moffat's own comment (15 August 1832) suggests how the doings of the earliest Natal settlers appeared to the Natives : ' Moselekatze knows well how many white men live with Dingaan, and how far they have assisted him in his sanguinary expeditions.'

'The people of Moselekatze have for ages past had to maintain an incessant struggle against the Portuguese slave-traders, and war has become their element.'

Finally, whatever their origin, the Chaka wars, contemporaneous with the growing impact of the European colonists upon the Native people, had incalculable consequences for the European population. Sooner or later delicate and difficult problems of frontier and legal relationships were bound to arise from the contact of races. But the devastation caused by the wars made the Boers believe that the land they coveted now lay empty before them, and aggravated the disease of colonial acquisitiveness. The feeble resistance of the Bantu gave the impression that they had been all but wiped out by their own wars, and so much of the land seemed to lie open that the Great Trek presently became in effect a Grand Dispersal. The Colonists were growing in strength, and mere pressure of population and land hunger drove them more and more upon the war-ravaged Bantu. Their own hard life and pioneering achievements have too largely filled the picture. Even at the time they were not without warning of the consequences of their heedless encroachment upon the Natives' land. As early as 1824 Dr. Philip was writing :

'I consider it highly impolitic to drive the Caffres to desperation by depriving them of their cattle, by illicit trade, or by encroachment on their grazing land. . . . Deprive a commercial people of their property, their ingenuity is still left, and may be turned to advantage ; deprive an agricultural people of the produce of their fields and they will continue to sow for themselves in the hope of obtaining some return ; but if you deprive a pastoral people of their herds, you instantly convert them into banditti . . . they have no resources left and they inevitably betake themselves to the thickets and attempt to live by plunder.' [1]

This warning fell on deaf ears. Even now it tends to be forgotten that the Natives were still in large numbers at no great distance from the advancing colonists, a social if not a military problem. [2]

[1] Dr. Philip's *Memo on Settlers*, written in 1824. *Cape Col. Qn.*, p. 114.
[2] According to census of 1921 the population of the Union was made up of 1,519,488 Europeans, 5,409,092 non-Europeans (i.e. Bantu, 'Coloured' and Asiatics). Of the non-Europeans, 4,697,813, or 67·80 *per cent.* of the total population, were Bantu.

CHAPTER III

THE FRONTIER BOERS AND THE FIRST GREAT TREK—FIRST CONTACT WITH THE BANTU

IT was not for a hundred years after 1652 that the Bantu tribes began to affect the course of colonization in the Cape Colony. The very monotony of the first uneventful century of European settlement is important, since it moulded Boer character and habits, and helped to determine at least the general attitude of the colonists to the later Colour Problem. Geographical conditions in the first instance decided the course of South African colonization : the scanty rainfall, the distance from one water-hole or fountain to the next, the difficulties of transport and the almost total want of markets for produce and, most of all, the vast extent of the country itself. The Company Government instead of trying in any way to counteract embarrassing geographical influences merely reinforced them. Officially, indeed, it set its face against any extension of its responsibilities by colonial expansion—it was interested only to make the Cape serviceable as a port of call—but by cutting the prices it offered for produce, and by the restrictions it laid on private trade of any kind, the Company made Cape Town a place to be avoided, and itself drove colonists to that dispersal over the country which it was utterly powerless either to prevent or control.

Very early two classes of Boers began to emerge : a minority, with the French Huguenots, it may be, as a solid nucleus, became real settlers ; the majority developed as 'trekkers' and pioneers. The Western Province alone had considerable agricultural possibilities. In the interior, where only grazing was possible, even the land laws rather encouraged dispersal. The normal tenure was the *leenings-plaats*, or one year lease, for which the uniform charge was 24 Rix Dollars per annum, regardless of the value of the land. On the death of the owner the *opstal*

21

(buildings and permanent improvements) was put up to auction (fees being an important source of revenue) and the proceeds of sale divided equally among the heirs.[1] Even though the purchase of the *opstal* carried with it the right to a renewal of the lease, abandonment was so easy that there was little inducement to close or intensive culture. For if the *leenings-plaats* was given up—and purchases appear to have been brisk amongst neighbours who wished to acquire land for their sons nearby—whole families sold up and moved on.

Outside the agricultural west, the universal dependence on cattle breeding, with the recurrence of drought, made large farms inevitable ; fencing and camping as a means of husbanding the pasture still commonly require costly imported materials, and even yet winter-feeding of stock by the use of hay or ensilage is too little practised. In the conditions of the eighteenth century there was no inducement to work at and develop the family farm. It was almost normal to move ever farther on and take up more farms on the same easy leasehold terms. The old Boers, indeed, can hardly be blamed. In the total absence of markets intensive cultivation was futile, while to sub-divide a mere grazing farm was to reduce what little value it had. Only a formidable enemy could have compelled the mass of the Colonists to dig themselves in round their base at Cape Town, and the Hottentot aborigines, as it happened, were utterly incapable of resistance. So long, therefore, as land was plentiful, families trekked, the trek outspanned, the more favourable outspans became settlements, the Hottentot aboriginals moving on, or else sinking into dependence as servants. Confronted at last with a *fait accompli* the Government could hardly refuse to recognize effective and almost entirely peaceful occupation ; but it was thus, step by step, that the official boundary of the Cape Colony was pushed out far beyond the original Hottentots' Holland to the distant Orange River.[2]

Now at first sight this unresisted colonial expansion, and the habit of mind which it induced, ought to have been sharply checked in the seventeen-seventies when contact with the great

[1] The desire of the settler-farmer to keep a family home intact would explain how in the West the extremes of the Roman-Dutch tradition of equal inheritance were sometimes modified, some of the sons taking their ' share ' out of the estate in education or training instead of in land—thus preventing sub-division going to such disastrous lengths in the West as farther inland.

[2] E. A. Walker, *Historical Atlas*, O.U.P., Maps 7 and 10.

Bantu people about the Fish River put some term to the direct advance. It was no longer safe for mere families to push out into ' Kafirland ' ; and the Fish River, in truth, first indicated as the boundary as early as 1774, and definitively so about 1780, remained the eastern boundary for over fifty years—in fact till 1847. Such a prolonged check was something new, but it was only a partial barrier to Boer penetration. The urgency of eastern frontier affairs has somewhat obscured the significance of the advance that continued uninterruptedly in the north. As early as 1778 the erection of Plettenberg's Beacon (near Coles-berg) to mark the northern boundary of the Colony was a sign that the ' first Great Trek ', as Dr. Gie [1] rightly calls the expansion of the eighteenth century, was being diverted at last away from the coastal belt ; a few years later, in 1786, Graaff-Reinet was established as a ' landdrostdy ' (magistracy) to serve the popula-tion of a large new district. Gradually this new northern area filled up, and by 1826, even while the direct eastward advance was stayed, the Government by simple proclamation acknow-ledged the Orange River as the boundary. Thus, in spite of the Kafirs, and in mere extent if not in its capacity to support a large population, the expansion of the Colony went on just as it had done before. Even Bantu opposition did little to break what was now settled habit, or to mitigate that land-hunger which has remained the great characteristic of South African rural life.

In the north, that is to say, where there were no ' Kafirs ', the old isolation of the days before 1779 was but intensified. The early trek-Boers, by whose efforts and for whose benefit Graaff-Reinet was established in 1786, now found themselves in country with a rainfall ever smaller and less regular ; but there were springs in fair abundance and, for a small population, highly desirable farms in the kloofs and valleys about the great mountain knot of the Sneeuwberg, behind Graaff-Reinet. Even along the base of the Camdeboo Mountains, in the rather arid neighbourhood of the later hamlets of Willowmore and Aberdeen, there are many delectable farms. Mountains being no barrier, before long the Graaff-Reinet district had a ward of field-cornetcy significantly known as *Achter*-Sneeuwberg. Here at last the Boers began to touch the great inland plateau of the High Veld which figures so largely in later history. The dry western, or ' Karoo ', portion of this plateau had on the whole been left unoccupied except in the neighbourhood of Graaff-Reinet itself.

---

[1] *Geskiedenis vir Suid Afrika*, i, by S. F. N. Gie.

Beyond the Sneeuwberg the Boers began to find themselves for the first time on *grass veld*, country with rather more reliable summer rains. Even there, it is true, there were droughts enough, and locusts, but in those days there was little danger of over-stocking, and comparatively little grass-burning. The *vleis*, with their sponge of vegetation, retained their moisture, and the drought-resisting powers of the country were probably greater than now. The superabundance of game also made mere living comparatively easy, incidentally sparing farmers the need to slaughter cattle for food. Yet because of mere distance, the risk of drought, and the chronic scarcity of water, farms were inevitably more and more scattered. The isolation and self-dependence of the Boers were, if anything, intensified in these northern districts from which the bulk of the Trekkers of 1836 were destined to come. Even on the troubled and insecure Kafir frontier, where land-hunger was less easily assuaged,[1] the observations of one constant traveller reveal conditions very similar. Writing from near the Koonap on 11 April 1830, Dr. Philip comments :

'This morning about 5 o'clock some farmers passed us going to Beaufort to meet Mr. Stockenstrom to solicit farms in this country formerly belonging to the Caffres, and now to be divided among the colonists [i.e. land from which chief Maqomo had been expelled in 1829]. This craving for grants of land on the part of the Boers, and the means taken by Governments to gratify (it) call for some strictures in this place.

'The habits of a great proportion of the Boers belonging to this colony are perfectly Scythian in their character. Accustomed to large grants of land when land was abundant and colonists few, they still think that they cannot subsist unless a farm includes the same range of country which it did in the days of their ancestors. Their habits are pastoral, they seldom cultivate more ground than is necessary for their own use, and their wealth is in their cattle. Having extensive herds they not only require much pasture, but are not satisfied if they have not different places to resort to at different seasons of the year. On these occasions, when they change their residences, their families generally accompany them, and they live in their waggons. Besides what they require for their herds, to save them, they must have game also, and each farmer living in this manner, instead of a moderate sized farm, must have a district for himself. Their children are brought up with the ideas of their parents ; (they seldom learn trades) unless it be as much knowledge of smith and carpenter work as may enable them to do something for themselves or their neighbours. Anything

---

[1] In 1796, for example, Graaff-Reinet burghers were petitioning the newly arrived General Craig for land 'unto the Konab, or it may be unto the Kat River'. They were put off with vague promises of 'later' (*C.C. Records*, vol. i).

done by slaves or Hottentots is quite beneath them and it is very seldom
indeed that you meet with the son of a farmer following a trade or
serving another for wages (unless perhaps in rare instances confined
to the neighbourhood of Cape Town). . . . from infancy their first
thoughts, and those of their parents, to provide new places for them.
(Occasionally) you will find a married son and a married daughter as
permanent, nor are they contemplated as desirable longer than till
they can be provided with establishments of their own. The practice
along the whole extended frontier has been for many years to appropriate for the children the spots occupied by the Natives in their immediate neighbourhood. All they can see they consider their own, and
when needed, the Natives are obliged to remove (to make room for)
their cattle or their children. By this means they first take possession
and afterwards get the Government to sanction the deed. (Nor is
this practice) confined to those on the colonial boundary. Like the
breaking out of water, although that nearest the break runs out first,
that behind, even to the extremity of the dam, soon follows. Allured
by the prospects of an estate in the new territory, such as have interest
with those that have it in their gift soon swell the tide of emigration,
and others who are poor sell their estates to their next neighbours who
want them for their sons and daughters, and with the price they receive
stock their new farms.

'Supposing things to proceed in this order, it is obvious, considering
the large families generally found among the Boers, that the colony
must *double its extent* every thirty or thirty-five years. This is not
mere theory, it is what has happened, and must happen, while the
system which has hitherto been acted upon continues . . .' (Dr. Philip
goes on to instance the Northern expansion between 1802 and 1825).

Under these easy-going and yet arduous conditions, Dutch
and Huguenots, with possibly a dash of Germans, were welded
into South Africans—with a predominantly Calvinistic religious
tradition, and, for the rest, a love of sun and open spaces, hardy
self-reliance, consummate skill in handling a gun, and withal
a kindly if robust sense of humour. On the other hand the
Boer's self-reliance and love of independence tended to harden
not only into an impatience of Government control, but into an
incapacity for co-operation even with his own fellows. The
Boers, Dr. Philip commented later, ' are gregarious but not
social '. The habits fostered by the life of the eighteenth century
go far to explain how it was that these sturdy sons of nature
became not a little contemptuous, and at the same time regardless,
of the coloured population.

Though in the early days of contact with the Bantu, a hundred
and fifty years ago, the Europeans were a very small community,
the natural tendency has been to interpret the course of history
almost exclusively as it affected the fortunes of the white colonists.

Just because the Colony was so small and dispersed, it was fifty years before the effects of the check on the Fish River were generally felt. Life was dangerous enough for those Europeans who chose to farm on the frontier, but their troubles and difficulties were not matter of life and death for the Colony as a whole ; as late as the 'twenties, even frontier Grahamstown was almost more concerned about the Cape struggle for political rights than with the Bantu in their near neighbourhood. It was only after 1825 that expansion northward as well as eastward was somewhat hindered, and the population being now rather larger, the issue was no longer to be deferred. At last, in the 'thirties, the stage was fairly set for the inevitable trial of strength between the European colonists and their Bantu rivals for possession of the land, and in the twenty years that followed all other questions seemed to take second place.[1]

The definite clash between Boers and Bantu was only the final stage in a gradual development. The skirmish of 1702 did nothing to discourage further ' cattle-trading ' expeditions —if indeed the discovery of Bantu wealth in cattle did not serve as a positive inducement to the more venturesome of the Colonists to improve their fortunes. The Company, however, having no stomach for new responsibilities, habitually set its face against intercourse between its burghers and the natives, repeatedly issuing *Placaats* against such trade ; [2] but as the *Placaats* had no administrative force behind them, there were continual comings and goings between the Colony and Kafir-land, not without occasional appeals, on either side, to *Faust Recht*, the rule of the strong arm. It was in an attempt to put some limit to the prevailing disorders that in 1778, following ' non-intercourse ' edicts in 1770 and 1774, Governor van Plettenberg undertook something in the nature of a Grand Tour of the frontier districts. On the ' Kafir ' frontier he seems to have concluded a ' treaty ', solemnly ratified by his Council of Policy, fixing ' the Fish River ' as the dividing line between the Colony and the Bantu territories.

Now it seems probable that van Plettenberg's primary object was not to fix carefully defined *territorial* boundaries [3] but

---

[1] *Cape Col. Qn.*, cc. ix and xiv.

[2] About 1700 the restraints on the cattle-trade were temporarily lifted.

[3] Sir Charles Lucas's suggestion, *Historical Geography*, vol. iv, pt. i, p. 82, *note*. ' The Dutch would presumably not have admitted the right of other Europeans to settle beyond them.'

merely to strengthen the colonial jurisdiction in a danger zone which was also the principal scene of the illicit barter that was rife between Colonists and Kafirs ; that is to say, he had an eye for general policy rather than for troublesome local details, or even for topography. In the first place the ' treaty ' seems to have been concluded without reference to any of the greater chiefs west of the Kei—like Rarabe, the reputed Paramount, of blood royal ; and while it is very doubtful if even a paramount had power to cede territory, it is quite certain that lesser chiefs had neither power nor authority to bind any but themselves. Indeed, it is clear that Governor and Bantu thought in different languages, and not much attempt was made to arrive at a real mutual understanding. Europeans are apt to read into such treaties the assumptions of ' civilization ', without being at any pains to understand the ways of Bantu thinking. To European minds the fixing of the colonial boundary at the Fish River carried with it the idea of annexation, with exclusive rights of control up to that point. Bantu custom, on the other hand, like that even of late medieval Europe, knew only *usufructory* rights in land ; Bantu chiefs habitually granted the use of land, in return for cattle, to men who virtually became their vassals ; but the idea of title and private *ownership* in land was as foreign to their ways of thinking as to those of feudal Europe. This fundamental difference in standards would account for much of the friction that ensued. The Bantu treaty-makers of 1778 probably did no more than agree to anything the Governor proposed in order to rid themselves of an embarrassingly formidable visitor ; but neither was the Governor at pains to be very precise in his definitions.

' The Fish River ' may sound definitive, but in all its long history as the boundary of the Colony it was so little precise as to be the endless source of disputes. Except in occasional seasonal floods the ' great ' river is, in fact, no barrier at all, but fordable almost dry shod along the greater part of its course. Even more serious, there was always a certain vagueness about what was meant by the Fish River line ; for a matter of forty miles, from near the later Fort Beaufort to the sea, the line of the river might serve ; but above that point the main stream runs parallel to the coast, almost at right angles to any natural dividing line between Colony and Kafirs ; so that to follow the river where it bends back to the south-west was, in effect, to make a full right turn which cut out of the Kafir territory some of

its most valuable districts—the relatively well-watered inland
country at the base of the Winterberg and Katberg ranges.
The ' Treaty ' of 1778 was unsatisfactory from beginning to
end. If, as is doubtful, there was any chief capable of binding
the whole of the Xosa tribes, he had no hand in the bargain.
There was no attempt to make clear to the Kafir chiefs concerned the European conception of a boundary or of land-
ownership, and, in the last resort, the boundary line itself was
vague and indefinite. Thomas Pringle comments in MSS. of
the eighteen-twenties :

' Nominally, the Governor had the consent of some of the Caffres,
but not of the chiefs. The Ghonaquas (Hottentots) who inhabited
the land between the Gamtoos and the Fish were never even considered. The Boers were left to deal with them as they had dealt
with their brethren already extinct.'

Hence, he concludes, the ' wars ' of 1781 and 1789—and, he might
have added, the unusually active part played by remnants of
the Hottentots in the troubles of 1799–1803.[1]
The result was as might have been expected. It has never
been suggested that the Fish River was a boundary of ' effective
occupation ', or that in 1778 there were no Bantu west of the
Fish River, that is to say—in the new language—within the Colony.
Even if white colonists now for the most part confined their enterprises to the country west of the line, they observed the colonial
limits in a new spirit of assertive ownership. The very next year
one of the Xosa treaty-makers was forcibly driven across the Fish
River ' out of the colony '—[2] and when the Xosa made very
natural reprisals upon colonists' cattle, the farmers, who were
now fairly numerous in the neighbourhood of the later Somerset
East, formed themselves into a ' commando ' and the ' First '
Kafir War followed. The Government itself, however unwillingly,
sanctioned action by the burghers, and by 1781 ' the Kafirs ',
we are told, had been driven across the Fish River, a fair share
of their cattle being divided among the triumphant victors by
way of compensation for their sufferings.
' The Kafirs were expelled ', so invariable tradition has it,
but presently ' crept back '—as often on later occasions, and
in other parts of the country. But in a wide, almost trackless
bush country, with a very sparse and scattered population, no

[1] *Cape Col. Qn.*, p. 144.
[2] Theal, *History before* 1795, iii, p. 128.

expulsion could have been so thorough as to necessitate any stealthy ' creeping back '. Even in 1921 the density of the population in the Somerset-Cradock-Bedford-Albany area was no more than from four or five to twelve to the square mile ; in those days it must have been far less. The adventures of General Christiaan de Wet in the war of 1899–1902 are sufficient proof of the extreme difficulty, even with modern facilities— roads, railways, and the telegraph or even the heliograph—of making a clean sweep of (or by) columns operating in wide African spaces. It is quite obvious that while in this first war the Xosa were sharply punished, the Zuurveld must have been only temporarily and very partially ' cleared ' of its Xosa popula- tion. The Company Government, indeed, was in no position to take strong firm action for the holding of its new boundary, and in 1789 a ' second ' war had begun, still for the most part *west* of the Fish River. This time the Government in making peace agreed to allow the Xosa to remain in the Zuurveld, ' without prejudice to the ownership of Europeans '.[1]

In 1793 again there were both Kafir attacks and a formidable counter-attack. The Government for its part was inclined to regard the encroachment of its own Boers as the prime cause of the trouble, and in 1793 General Sluysken, the last of the Company Governors, showed his disapprobation of the warring commandos of that year by a formidable proclamation, which recapitulated all the penalties threatened by earlier edicts, and forbade trade and all intercourse with the tribes beyond the Baviaans River (a tributary this time slightly *east* of the Fish River proper). Five years later, in 1798, the British Governor, Earl Macartney, followed this up with a proclamation defining the Fish River boundary a little more precisely and forbidding ' elephant-hunters ' or others to cross the line except with an express permit. Neither the Company nor its immediate successors (British after 1795) were disposed to take the steps necessary for the security of frontier colonists, but in spite of Government frowns, the struggle had fairly begun for possession of the country ' unto the Konab, or it may be even unto the Kat ' [2] —and beyond it, indeed, to the Kei. The time was not far distant when, as one General Vandeleur prophesied, ' either the Boers and British together must drive the Kafirs from the Zuurveld or the British must build a fort and watch the Boers and the

---

[1] Theal, iii, 181.
[2] Petition of the Burghers for land, to General Craig, in 1796.

Natives fight it out '.[1]   The frontier Boers, that is to say, though
they suffered constant raids and losses—more than once farms
east of Uitenhage were left deserted—never dreamt of abandoning
all hope of potentially fat farms for fear of a parcel of Ama-Xosa
barbarians.

The failure of the old Dutch Government to afford the
frontiersmen the protection and security which they thought
their unquestionable right, together with the practical humanitarianism of a Dutch official, the Landdrost Maynier of Graaff-
Reinet, had consequences of permanent significance.   In 1795
a party of malcontents took forcible possession of the *drostdy*
(Residency) at Graaff-Reinet, expelled the unpopular Maynier,
who had done his best to restrain them from dealing with natives
and native opposition in their own way, and proceeded to elect
officials of their own.   A few months later, Boers at Swellendam
following this example established their own ' republic '.   Both
Graaff-Reinet and Swellendam were apparently far from the
Kafir frontier, but in those days they were also the most distant
outposts of Government, and the double outbreak was in large
part due to the Company's utter failure to govern its dependency.
In the seven years immediately following (1795–1803, the time
of the first British Occupation), years of fair progress and prosperity in the west, the interior and the eastern frontier continued
disturbed enough, and the cleavage between the Colony and
the frontier deepened.   In Graaff-Reinet there was still overt
rebellion ; farther east, Kafirs, and even Hottentots, raided
and plundered and learnt the art of war from their white masters
—the Xosa by 1803 being probably more firmly established
than ever in the Zuurveld from the Fish to the Sundays River.
The continuing state of insecurity, due as it seemed to the weakness of Cape Town, confirmed a section of the frontier Boers
in a lasting tradition that the only remedy for grievances was
to take the law into their own hands and establish a ' republic ';
and so separatism was the last of the legacies of the Dutch East
Indian Company.   That it was bound up from its earliest
beginnings with a peculiarly self-confident view of the only
way to deal with Native races, may in part account for the
truculent, sometimes merely petulant, aloofness of much latter-day
republicanism.

After a few more years the authorities of the second British
Occupation (1806) woke up to realize that the state of the frontier

[1] Quoted by Walker, p. 138.

demanded serious attention. The pressure of the farmers clamouring for land, and the insecurity of legally occupied farms to the east of Uitenhage, led Earl Caledon to send a certain Colonel Collins round the borders, like van Plettenberg before him, to report; and in 1809, Collins recommended [1] that the best hope of peace was to extend the border to the Koonap, to increase the number of the magistrates, to strengthen the European population, and more immediately, to drive the chief Ndhlambi and his people out of the Zuurveld. Earl Caledon seems to have hesitated to use force—fearing the disapproval of Downing Street; on 16 October 1809 he reported to Lord Castlereagh against the proposal to clear the Zuurveld, and in June 1810 that the frontier was ' quiet '. But in 1811 his successor, Sir John Cradock, inclining to more vigorous measures, first deplored to Lord Liverpool the abandonment of farms near Algoa Bay, then on 8 October ordered the landdrosts to call out the burghers, and finally on 18 October gave Colonel Graham, the frontier commandant, a free hand to deal with the situation —using ' persuasion if possible '. In the early months of 1812 Colonel Graham came to blows with Ndhlambi near Coega on the Sundays River, and Ndhlambi and many followers were forcibly driven across the Fish River. In March, according to Dr. Theal, ' the war was over ', but in spite of the foundation of Grahamstown and lesser strong places to hold the line of the new-old Fish River frontier, there was very little difference between ' peace ' and ' war ' in those parts, and the burghers called up in October 1811 were disbanded only in the July of 1814.[2]

The significance of all this is perpetually missed. It is preposterous to pronounce as if it were the righting of a wrong that ' 20,000 Ndhlambis and Gunakwebis ' were ' driven out of the Zuurveld across the Fish River '. Ndhlambi's protest, reported from the Sundays River in 1811—' This land is mine. I won it in war, and intend to keep it ' [3]—shows clearly that land and not cattle-stealing was always the Kafirs' first concern. A boundary which banishes and excludes all the original inhabitants of a district is an anomaly. Annexation of the country carried with it an obligation towards existing occupiers. But now the Ndhlambis who had obviously been in occupation of the Zuur-

---

[1] *Records*, vii, 101 ff.   [2] *Ibid.*, *passim*.
[3] *C.C. Records*, viii, p. 235.

veld for many years, having no other home, were only driven on top of their rivals, the Gaikas, who were neither able nor willing forthwith to make room for 20,000 'immigrants'. This long-deferred and strong-handed clearing of the Zuurveld, therefore, did little or nothing to bring peace and security on the frontier.

The advent of European colonists on the borders of Bantu Ethiopia would in itself have accounted for a good deal of tribal commotion. If the early conflict of colonists and Bantu, even in those days of outposts and of small things, left its indelible mark on the spirit and structure of white South African society, it is not to be supposed that things remained the same as before for the Bantu. They had population and land questions of their own, and were themselves probably the result of a great 'migration' ultimately caused by economic pressure. Any check to their front line on the Fish River was likely to have its repercussions in the rear. Influences at work in the troubled country of the Amaxosa must have been felt far beyond the Colony, to add to the tumult of the wars in the north.

The tribal system of the Bantu readily lent itself to dissensions like those which, for example, rent the Empire of Charlemagne in ninth-century Europe. The chiefs were a royal family, but neither were the chiefs 'absolute' nor was there any salutary rule of primogeniture or direct hereditary succession. The 'heir' was the son of the 'great' wife, not of the 'right hand' wife nor of the 'left'. But as the 'great' wife was commonly married late in life, the heir was often an infant, whose elder brothers were themselves the leaders of a strong interest or 'clan' of their own, and possibly even regents during the 'paramount's' minority. There was, therefore, a multitude of chiefs of the blood royal. This readily explains the bewildering number of 'tribes'. On the Cape frontier, for example, the Amaxosa were a tribal group rather than a unity in any real sense, who, till about 1775, recognized a common allegiance to one Palo. Early in the period of contact, however, two groups had emerged, one, east of the Kei, adhering to Palo's 'great' son Gcaleka, the other, or western branch, following Rarabe. It was now the turn of the 'Rarabes' (as the western Xosa are sometimes called) to break up, and even in the seventeen-nineties there are ominous signs of divisions and of rivalry in their own ranks, some clans adhering to Gaika, others to his uncle Ndhlambi—Gaika being

the heir and grandson, by the ' great ' wife, of the widely acknowledged chief Rarabe, while Ndhlambi was the ' wicked uncle ',
an older and more experienced man, the son by a less important
wife of Rarabe himself.[1]   When to their own domestic quarrels
(their faction fights and ' beer ' fights are still common enough)
there was added the struggle for land about the Fish River,
with the driving in of tribe upon tribe, the disturbance was
manifestly increased.   Moreover, European intrigues for Kafir
support [2]—even if it was only by adventurers like one notorious
Coenrad Buijs, with his Xosa wives, in the Graaff-Reinet troubles
following 1795—must have further stimulated and intensified
the divisions among tribes.

The internal dissensions of the Bantu soon reached a climax
which materially affected the unity and disposition of the tribes
in the Fish River area.   The irruption of the Zuurveld refugees
brought lively disorders, and a great sharpening of the old feud
between Gaika and Ndhlambi.   The feuds of the Bantu were
obviously not unconnected with the menacing proximity of the
white man, for it was Ndhlambi, the chief of the newly conquered
Zuurveld, who was the source of disturbance.   The more distant
Gaika, being less directly involved in the colonial advance and
having, as it chanced also, the better hereditary title, was the
recognized ally of the white man.   As early as 1803, for example,
he agreed with General Janssens to acknowledge the Fish River
as the boundary, it being convenient to ' recognize ' his para-
mountcy, in spite of his practical inability to answer for Ndhlambi
and the Western clans whose interests were primarily concerned.
In 1815 again Gaika found recognition of another sort, flattering
no doubt to his sense of dignity, when twice over he was
approached with requests for help by Boer malcontents then
engaged in the episode known as the Slagter's Nek rebellion—
a protest against the legal protection now being given to Hottentot
servants.[3]   In later years this was not forgotten by Gaika's
son Maqomo, who complained in 1835 that despite his loyalty
in 1815, Gaika, when his turn came, like Ndhlambi before him
lost his country.[4]

---

[1] For genealogy, see Theal, iii, p. 93.   In later times, the chief
Maqomo played a somewhat similar part by his younger brother, Gaika's
' great ' son, Sandile.

[2] *Records*, ii, pp. 148, 333, 349, 364.

[3] *Cape Col. Qn.*, p. 91.

[4] Journal of Capt. Stretch, September, 1835.

At the time, Gaika's weakness, and his eventual overthrow in 1818 by Ndhlambi in a large-scale battle on the Amalinde Flats, near the later King William's Town, were traceable in no small measure to what seemed his partiality for the white man and his failure to rally the Xosa peoples for the defence of their Fish River borderlands. The leadership of the Bantu in what was unmistakably a primitive nationalist movement passed into other hands, and their hero between 1812 and 1819 was an Elisha, at once soldier and prophet, by name Makana,[1] evidently a remarkable personality. Makana's aim seems to have been to restore Xosa unity, and the danger from the white man who had already ' cleared the Zuurveld ' gave him his rallying cry. In 1818, Makana's influence thrown on to the side of the fighter Ndhlambi was decisive in the overthrow of the waverer, Gaika. When, moreover, Gaika's appeal for Government help brought a European force raiding beyond the Fish, Makana it was who, on 22 April 1819, led a counter-attack on the Colony, and, from an eminence still known as Makana's Kop, and at close quarters, directed wave upon wave of warriors against the very gates of the barracks at Fort England in Grahamstown. The attack was, of course, in vain ; Makana soon after was compelled to surrender,[2] and it was left for Lord Charles Somerset to patch up with the restored Gaika a continuance of the *pax bellicosa* by the establishment of a ' Neutral Belt ', in a vain attempt to place a vacant strip of land, ' from the Fish to the Keiskama ', as a barrier between the mutual encroachments of European and Bantu.

[1] For details, see Theal, i, 269 ff. The missionary Williams writes of the prophet as *McKannah*, his bellicosity perhaps suggesting a Hibernian connexion.

[2] He died by drowning in attempting to escape from his prison on Robben Island ; but for long years, according to Dr. Theal, his people looked for Makana's return—like that of a hero of the Middle Ages.

CHAPTER IV

THE NORTHERN FRONTIER—THE GRIQUA 'STATES'—EXPANSION CHECKED, 1834

EVEN in the sparsely peopled North the ' clash of colour ' was not to be deferred much longer. The advancing colonists soon began to find their occupation of land and fountains disputed not only by remnants of the helpless Bushmen, as at Tooverberg (Colesberg),[1] but also by various Mixed-Breeds, refugees from the Colony itself. In numbers and in organization these people were weak and insignificant enough ; but some of them having an admixture of European blood, they were, perhaps, more sophisticated than the older Hottentots, and, as protégés of the London Missionary Society, had champions to put up a strong defence of their rights. First to arrive, they had taken possession of land about the Orange River and of the none too numerous fountains. From the eighteen-twenties, therefore, there was trouble in store for Boers looking for farms even on this secondary front of the Cape Colony.

These Mixed-Breeds, themselves comparative new-comers, owed any little coherence they had to the organization and discipline of missionaries of the London Society. According to a fragment of missionary history, Messrs. Wm. Anderson and Kramer—two of the missionaries who arrived soon after Dr. van der Kemp, about 1800—directed their attention to Bushmen on the Zak River (north of Beaufort West). There they soon ' collected a number of people belonging to different tribes, Korannas, Namaquas, Hottentots, Bastard Hottentots and Bushmen, who ultimately formed what is now called the *Griqua* people '[2] For six years or more Mr. Anderson and his colleague

---

[1] *Cape Col. Qn.*, pp. 128 ff.

[2] These tribes were all closely allied—none of them Bantu. Colonists significantly tended to rank them all together as ' Bastards ' ; though at least one missionary distinguishes between ' Bastards ' and ' Griquas '. (Fragment in handwriting of Mrs. Philip.)

lived a semi-nomadic life with this ' motley group of scattered remnants till they were able to induce their flock to settle in villages '. By about 1820 there seem to have been three such village centres, at Klaar-water (Griquatown), Campbell, and, a little later, at Philippolis, with Andries Waterboer, Cornelius Kok, and Adam Kok respectively as ' captains ', appointed under missionary influence, and vaguely recognized by the Cape Government. It must have been heart-breaking work for the missionaries to build up the so-called Griqua ' States '; that there were three—in a population estimated in 1823 at no more than 3,000 in all—is the measure of their ultimate insignificance.

The difficulties were, indeed, immense. The character of the country made close settlement impossible. The Griquas retained some of the primitive nomadic traditions of the aboriginal Koranna or Hottentot tribes, while the more sophisticated ' Bastards ', cherishing resentment against the labour conditions in the Colony from which they had fled, were likely to be intractable. Even the advent of white colonists brought little agricultural development, so that there was no serious local demand for labour which would have provided wages, however poor, to supplement the bareness of life in these rather arid northern districts, where, even in later times, only the diamonds of Kimberley have made some little progress possible. In those early times, therefore, the Griquas easily fell into bad ways, not without prompting from runagate Europeans.[1] A very old native once described to me how, in his early days, there were ' only lions and Bushmen ' in that country. The Griquas seem to have thought, similarly, of the unfortunate Bushmen, that they were there to be harried, not infrequently pursuing them with ' commandos '.

The presence on the frontier of an even rudely organized body of coloured people, closely related to the ' free ' coloured inhabitants of the Colony, would have seemed to necessitate some attempt to define their official and legal relations with the Colony. The Government was not anxious to incur new responsibilities, but from time to time stepped in to remind the Griquas of their obligations. The first instance of interference, however, was not calculated to promote harmony, or to give the Griquas confidence in the benevolence of the Government. When in 1814 it was proposed to strengthen the Cape Corps (of ' Hottentots ') for the defence of the Kafir frontier, the colonial

[1] Walker, p. 158.

origin of the 'Bastards' was the warranty for ordering Mr.
Anderson to furnish twenty recruits from Griquatown to make
up the quota to be 'commandeered' from the nearest, and
yet far distant, *drostdy* of Tulbagh. Not unnaturally the missionary failed, or refused, to make himself responsible for doing
duty as a recruiting sergeant.

As a direct consequence of this incident the official view
now came to be that it was undesirable to have such communities
of coloured people near, and yet beyond, the frontiers, imperfectly 'controlled' by missionaries; they would only serve,
it was alleged, as 'rendezvous' for runaway servants; and two
Bushman stations of the L.M.S. were actually suppressed in
1818. This question of 'control' beyond the frontiers was
still a burning one during the first two years of Dr. Philip's
superintendency. The Rev. John Campbell, a visiting Director
of the L.M.S., agreed, in 1820, that there was need for firm
'control'; but meantime, in 1819, Governor Somerset went so
far as to complain to London that the mission stations 'subtracted
that useful class of labourers from those useful occupations to
which they were best suited', and told Dr. Philip that 'Griquatown should be broke up'.[1] Griquatown, in fact, was not so
treated; but the threat did much mischief. For when in 1822
its chief was so far 'recognized' as to have Mr. John Melville
sent to him as a resident Government Agent, Waterboer and
the Agent were continually hampered by the fear of the people
that one main object of Government control was to draw on the
military resources of the Griquas and 'make them soldiers'.

In the early 'twenties anarchy in the Griqua country was
intensified by the reactions of the Chaka Wars. With three
chiefs contesting the supremacy in the villages, malcontents
broke away altogether and took to the 'mountains', whence
there came and went small bands of *Bergenaars*,[2] obtaining all

[1] *Cape Col. Qn.*, ch. x.
[2] 'The spirit of independence among the Griquas, with the strong
prejudice in the minds of some against the Colony, appears to me to be
occasioned in great measure by their connexion with the "Bastards"
of the Colony, who live all along the Orange River, and in different
parts of the country, and who seem at present to acknowledge no authority whatever. . . . The obstruction to the introduction of suitable
regulations and the preservation of good order is the want of power
in the chiefs. . . . That the banditti (e.g. plunderers of the Bechuana)
should have such facilities in trading with the farmers on the frontier
favours their independence and is an inducement to others to join
them' (Melville to Col. Bird, 22 Jan. 1824).

the guns and powder they needed by illicit traffic with white colonists, and too often paying for them with cattle stolen from neighbours like the Bechuana. In 1822 Dr. Philip wrote :

> ' The Boers began to visit the Griquas and trade with them in guns, gunpowder and brandy ; whereupon they soon got tired of depending on their own efforts to increase their herds, (and, becoming more daring, went further afield and) attacked the herds of the more helpless Bechuanas with guns.'

One influence alone promised to check Griqua dissensions. Early in 1823 Mr. Moffat reported from Lattakoo, or Kuruman, the menacing advance of the Mantatees—a ' fierce nation from the south-east, who lay everything low before them '. ' Kureechane ', where in 1820 John Campbell had attended a vast *Pitso*, or folk-moot, of 16,000 or 20,000 Bechuana, (so he estimated), was said to be a heap of ruins. Three months later, in June, Mr. Moffat found it necessary to ride post-haste to Griquatown for help, and, towards the end of the month, a body of Griquas, temporarily united, made effective use of their possession of guns and utterly broke the invaders in the neighbourhood of Lattakoo. The Mantatees, vanquished in a few hours by something under 200 Griquas, with only fifteen rounds of ammunition apiece, were probably never much more than a fugitive rabble. The weak and unwarlike character of the Bechuanas, on whom they had made their onslaught, made them formidable ; but the lack of unity and the disorder of the Griquas themselves were in the end merely increased by the confusion and the opportunities of plunder afforded by the comings and goings, for years after, both of Mantatees and of the Bechuana tribes broken by this invasion.

But the importance of these small and inherently weak Griqua States was their strategical position. Dry and difficult as it was their country commanded two main lines of advance into the centre of Africa and was, therefore, directly and vitally involved in the developments of the next twenty or thirty years. Griquatown was early recognized by travellers like the Rev. John Campbell, and after him by his colleague, Dr. Philip, as the ' gate ' to the far interior. The chief of Griquatown was from the beginning in close touch with the Bechuana tribes [1], who reached as far south as Taungs and Kuruman, but occupied also a great part of what is now the Western Transvaal. Later,

---

[1] E.g. tribes such as the Batlapin, Barolong, Bapedi, Baharutsi, Bamangwato, Bakwena, Bangwaketsi.

Griquatown and Kuruman became the recognized starting points of the ' Missionary Road ' into the interior—a road favoured as being at once more central, and avoiding some of the ups and downs of any route which had to climb the High Veld ridge of the Transvaal only to descend again to the malarial valley of the Limpopo. This was the road, first followed by Moffat and Livingstone, which ultimately figured largely in the Cape to Cairo plans and dreams of Cecil Rhodes.

Immediately, however, these continental considerations mattered almost less than the local South African significance of the Griqua country. While Waterboer held the gate to the interior, the Kok family round Philippolis were so unfortunate as to lie at the point of convergence of four of the main *drifts* or fords across the great Orange River, right across the main or High Veld line of advance, first of the old colonial Boers, and ultimately of the Great Trek itself. The Griquas, therefore, who had fled from the Colony with ideas of ' independence ' not unlike those of some later Boers, were destined not long to remain undisturbed. In 1826 the Colonial boundary was extended to the Orange River, and, before many more years had passed, their claims to the land and the fountains they had occupied on its northern bank were sharply challenged. In the late 'twenties Philippolis was already torn by dissensions due to the close approach of the Boers. In the 'thirties and 'forties Philippolis became even more acutely the storm centre of disputes between Boers and missionaries, the latter seeking to defend the prior rights of the coloured people. The greater part of the Griqua country was soon so completely absorbed by the dominant Europeans that the important part it once played is apt to be forgotten to-day. The virtual disappearance of the Griquas who, however feeble, were in a position to bar the way to the north, at a moment when the Bantu threatened to close the road to the east, has a significance out of all proportion to their numbers and quality.

As early as 1820 Dr. Philip had begun to plan for political reform and general reconstruction in Griqualand. He proposed to strengthen the missionary personnel, urging also that ' by increasing their artificial wants, you increase the dependence of the Griquas on the Colony, and make for the preservation of peace '.[1] In criticizing Mr. Melville's appointment as Agent

[1] Dr. Philip to Sir Rufane Donkin, 12 May 1820.

in 1822, he put his finger on the weak spot when he insisted
that 'such an Agent should have effective Government power
behind him, and Government ought to *accompany the appointment
with sufficient power to enforce its authority*.[1] But the pre-1828
disabilities of the Hottentots [2] within the Colony brought Nemesis
in their reactions even on trans-frontier problems. The semi-
civilized Griquas had fled from the amenities of farm service
in the Colony, and such stout champions of the Rule of Law as
Dr. Philip himself were at first chary of bringing them too
directly under the control of the Colonial Government. To
Robert Moffat he wrote on 31 January 1822 (a letter of which
the then newly appointed Mr. Melville was the bearer) :

'The present situation of our stations within the Colony gives us
very little to hope from the extension of the Colony. . . . Look at
Bethelsdorp, Theopolis and Zuurbraak. While the greater part of
the able-bodied men are serving the Government, and receiving nothing
but rations, the women and children are perishing at home for want
of the necessaries of life, and the missionaries are teased to death about
every trifle the local authorities think proper to impose upon them.'

As it was, Mr. Melville's letters, both to the Governor and
to Dr. Philip, make it clear that with little or no effective support
behind him, the more Waterboer tried to get control and to
keep order in the country in a natural and evidently sincere
desire to stand well with the Government, the more the *Bergenaars* continued to attract recruits by trading on the general
'fear of being made soldiers'.[3] Waterboer's reward, indeed,
was to have Andries Stockenstrom, Landdrost of Graaff-Reinet,
writing to warn and advise the Governor against assisting him
on the ground that he 'is unpopular with his own people'.[4]
If he was unpopular it was undoubtedly because of his attempt
to suppress gun-running and lawlessness.

'After four years' discouraging work'[5] the Government
Agent resigned in despair in April 1826. The depredations of
the *Bergenaars* continued, though they do not seem to have been
so serious as to prevent a good deal of coming and going by

[1] Letter from Griquatown, to some unnamed official, in September
1825, when Philip reviewed the whole history of the Griqua frontier
from which he had just returned.
[2] *Cape Col. Qn., passim.*
[3] Letter of J. Melville to Col. Secretary, Dec. 1824.
[4] Report from Landdrost of Graaff-Reinet, 22 Oct. 1824.
[5] Cory, ii, p. 229.

solitary travellers.[1] Under the guidance of a new and capable
missionary (Mr. P. Wright) Waterboer, indeed, seems gradually
to have established order in his own immediate neighbourhood.
For when, about 1832, a new and serious danger arose through
the advent of the formidable Zulu (or Matabele) Moselekatze,
Waterboer was one comparatively stable protection to those whom
Dr. Philip described (after a tour in 1832) as the 'peaceful
and unwarlike Frontier Boers'.[2] All this time partial Government recognition had continued ; for example, a note survives,
dated 7 August 1827, in which Captain Stockenstrom requests
'Captain' Waterboer to apprehend a burgher called Karel
Kruger, who had crossed the border with a false pass, and to
'hand him over, a prisoner', to any one of the field-cornets
on the frontier. Many later difficulties, both in the days of
the Trek and at the time when diamonds were discovered,
might have been prevented had the highly elastic boundaries
of the Cape Colony been extended at that early time to include
definitely this Griqua country.

So long as intercourse between the Colony and Griqualand
was so slight, the failure of the Government to follow any strong
or consistent policy in the north was hardly to be wondered
at. Where the population was so scanty, fifteen or twenty
horsemen constituted a 'robber band' and the advance of such
a party against Griquatown a 'battle'. But now, just when
the anarchy of the Griqua bands was beginning to yield in some
small measure to discipline and missionary organization, the
economic distress of the colonial farmers, with their chronic
land-hunger intensified by droughts, brought increasingly large
numbers of Boers to sow fresh discord.

The 'First Great Trek' which had gone on almost uninterruptedly through the later eighteenth century now pressed
in upon the Philippolis Griquas. Actual annexation, though

---

[1] Mr. Miles, Dr. Philip's substitute, visited Griquatown on the
eve of a *Bergenaar* 'attack' in Dec. 1827, while Messrs. Moffat, Hamilton and Hughes seem to have moved freely between Griquatown and
Kuruman.

[2] In face of Moselekatze, Waterboer kept his head better than his
neighbours. To one panic-stricken appeal from a Bechuana chief,
he replied, with characteristic shrewdness, advising the chief not to
show his alarm, but 'blij dood stil' (keep perfectly quiet) ; while
his preparedness, and comparative efficiency, kept him and his immediate
neighbours from suffering any serious interference.

hitherto it had never been long delayed, tended to linger behind occupation, and the years following the boundary proclamation of 1825 were marked by great activity on the part of trekking Boers along the newly defined boundary. Unlike earlier movements the trek in this part of the country had eye-witnesses and is described, especially in reports to their superintendent, Dr. Philip, by the London missionary champions of the Griquas who, with remnants of the Bushmen, were now in danger of being dispossessed and, in the classical sense of the word, ' exterminated '. Not only was the eighteenth-century ' trek ' prolonged into the nineteenth century without any pause, but the Great Trek itself was taking fairly definite shape for some years before 1836.

As early as 1825 a missionary artisan named James Clark, who had the Bushmen as his special charge, wrote from Philippolis describing a journey he had made ' to the east ' ; he had difficulty, he said, in getting into touch with the wild Bushmen, who fled at the approach of his party ; one old man, however, explained that ' they thought we were Boers, that their native kraals were near the boundary of the Colony, but that in consequence of Boers coming over the boundary . . . they had left their kraals and gone farther into the country '. That is to say, at a station well beyond the Colony, ' Boers who come over the Cradock (i.e., Orange) to pasture ' (Mr. Clark's words) were a matter of course and no new phenomenon. Throughout the year 1826 Mr. Clark's Journal is full of complaints that the Bushmen were leaving him in consequence of the numbers of Boers pressing into the district, apparently with Government permits, and that Boers were petitioning the Government for leave to occupy the (Bushman) fountains beyond the Orange River, which had been fixed as the boundary one year before. In December 1828 he writes :

' I beg to mention that in consequence of *hundreds* of the Boers having been over the boundary this, *as in former years*, with their cattle, (they have been since last June in the Bushman country), they are not only driving the Bushmen from their fountains, and the wild game, their principal support, but they have thus reduced them to the necessity either to steal the farmers' cattle, or perish of hunger.'

About this time, indeed, the pressure became too great for the shy Bushmen, and Mr. Clark was obliged to remove to a new ' Bushman Station ' (at or near the later Bethulie), leaving

Philippolis entirely to the Griquas whose numbers, it seems, were being recruited from among the newly freed Hottentots of the Cape Colony.[1]

While it must be said that the Griquas themselves were as like as the Boers to harry the unfortunate Bushmen—even in 1833 Dr. Philip was still censuring Kok for the behaviour of his people towards them—Mr. Clark's Journal is illuminating as evidence that as early as 1826 the Boers had made their presence felt. Mr. Clark mentions also attacks by ' Caffres ', presumably remnants of the Mantatees, and refers to the Boer habit of leaving cattle and ' cattle places ' (farms used for grazing only) in charge of ' Caffre ' herdsmen. This practice, remarked on also by Captain Stockenstrom, was complained of by Mr. Clark as depriving the Bushmen of their only hope of employment, and tending, therefore, to drive them to live by theft. But the ' Trek ' was as yet primarily a search for grazing rather than a wholesale migration of families. Mr. Clark, indeed, attributed some of the Boer unsettlement to the new quit-rent tenure of farms,[2] as if the increased Government charge for land forced a choice between over-stocking the farms and a trek ; habitually, he added, they spared and increased their herds by living on the game which still abounded.

But for whatever reason, the Boers had come to stay. ' Captain ' Adam Kok's solemn restrictions on the sale or exchange of the farms he ' granted ' to his burghers were utterly futile.[3] Repeated references by missionaries clearly indicate that in return for waggons, oxen, or possibly even brandy, the unstable Griquas readily enough gave the encroaching Boers extensive rights to lease or occupy both lands and fountains. Their leaders appealed in vain to the people to put ultimate security before the chances of immediate profit. In the end of 1829 a copy of a petition signed by Adam Kok, Hendriks, and others, begging the Governor to deal with Boer encroachments

[1] ' Hottentots were glad to leave the Colony because the Boers left no land for them there ' (Clark to Philip, 2 April 1830).
[2] The quit-rent introduced after 1813 was a charge that varied according to the quality of the land—the charge for the older *leeningsplaats* being an invariable annual amount (Walker, p. 204).
[3] Philippolis, 5 May 1828. ' By this the place called Witkrans is given to the Burgher Manels as lawful property to him and his heirs, under this condition that the said Manels shall not sell or exchange this place to any colonial Burgher.' ' Given by Captain Adam Kok and his council.' (Sgd. Capt. Adam Kok). (Translation.)

on 'land that belonged to their fore-fathers', was sent to Dr. Philip by Mr. Melville, now turned missionary, and confidential secretary to Adam Kok.[1] The petition urged that the Griquas had always been a defence to the Colony, recalled with alarm the 'oppression' their fathers had suffered, and begged that the farmers be forbidden to cross the frontier. Significantly, they also asked for a ban on 'hawkers' who supplied Korannas and others with ammunition (this last being a hint that they were not responsible for alleged robberies). Some eighteen months later, May 1831, Kok was writing to Philip, still protesting rather lamely, against a charge that his Griquas had attacked the Bechuana. Mr. Wright had some reason to fear (in August 1833) that 'it is so easy to steal cattle, and then to exchange cattle for ammunition from traders and horses from Boers, that it is difficult for " good men " to remain " good " in that country'. Griqua depredations, however, were without terrors for the Boers, and in the same letter of 1831 Kok protests that his people are about to move, since they 'love freedom and fear the Boers'. The Boers, moreover, are too strong to be resisted ; and though they encroach on their lands and fountains, the Government does not protect them ; they mean to go, therefore, they 'know not whither', but 'will take a missionary with them'.

Of the steady Boer encroachment there is no doubt, and being wholly without government, the country was thrown into greater confusion than ever by disputes between masterful land-hungry Boer colonists and feeble Griquas who, first in the field, had taken possession of the most eligible farm-sites. In 1831 Kok was thinking of removing 'he knew not whither'. In [October 1832 Dr. Philip wrote from Cradock : 'there are 1,500 Boers (the numbers are probably travellers' guess work) across that boundary, depasturing the Bushman country and contending with the Griquas'. Two years later—in what were really the initial moves in the 'Great Trek'—there were said to be 1,600 Boers beyond the Orange River, half of them on the 'grounds of the Philippolis mission station' (a 60- or 70-mile

---

[1] At first, 31 Dec. 1828, Mr. Melville remarked that he was received with hostility or suspicion at Philippolis, because he brought no supply of the gunpowder which as Agent he secured for Waterboer, and also because of his previous holding of a Government position. In Oct. 1830, he had settled down, and tells Dr. Philip he 'will see that the chief writes nothing but what will bear examination'.

stretch). They were, however, still so much 'of' the Colony that they came to Colesberg annually to pay their taxes.[1]

In face of this now permanent complication in what was still sometimes called Bushmanland, the Government, like its predecessors, was inconsistent in its attitude. Economic forces were in any case too strong. On 25 April 1828, Major Dundas, Civil Commissioner of Albany, suggested to the Government the expediency of relieving the distress of the farmers through drought by granting them permission to pass the frontier. This was refused, the letter being endorsed with the Governor's minute in pencil : ' Acquaint the Civil Commissioner that His Honour cannot approve of this suggestion. It would lead to the unlimited extension of the Colony.' [2] Notwithstanding the Acting Governor's disapproval, however, or before it had reached him, Major Dundas seems to have acted on his own responsibility, issuing the following Notice,[3] which was freely acted on for years to come in spite of a long series of earlier prohibitive proclamations :

' The inhabitants of the sub-division of Tarka are hereby informed that the undersigned has been apprised by the Field Cornet, J. H. Steenkamp, that the cattle belonging to the inhabitants of his division suffer much by the drought for want of good pasturage.

' The Field Cornet is, therefore, hereby empowered to allow the cattle to be sent to graze beyond the boundary, in such places as are not occupied by Tambookies, or other natives.

' He will also be vigilant to prevent as much as possible all intercourse with the said natives.

' Civil Commissioner's Office, Cradock,
' April 14th, 1828.
' (Sgd.) W. B. DUNDAS,
' Civil Commissioner for Albany and Somerset.

There is an undated copy of another Government notice bound up with Mr. Clark's letters, which obviously belongs to this period :

[1] Dispatch No. 40, 1 June 1834, and Chase, *History of South Africa*, ii, 35, 255. In October 1834, Philip wrote to Miss Buxton, ' When I was on my Northern Tour in 1832 there were not 15 Boers, where there are now 1,100. I was then apprised of their intentions, and warned the Government of the danger, but nothing was done.'

[2] *Cape Town Archives*, Vol. Albany, No. 588.

[3] There is a doubt about the date, but none about the fact of this notice. Sir B. D'Urban, in the discussions of Sept. or Oct. 1834, refers specifically to Dundas's notice of 14 April 1828, annulled in *Gazette* of 12 Sept. 1834, which also recapitulated earlier prohibitions, now to be enforced, against trekking.

' (Griqua Country) : And whereas many memorials have been presented, praying for grants of land situated beyond the boundaries of the Colony, and even beyond the Great Orange River, it is hereby notified that no attention will be paid to such Memorials.'

In spite of the frowns of the Government memorials persisted[1] and land was occupied, even without regular legal sanction. Dr. Philip, when discussing later frontier questions with Sir Benjamin D'Urban, blamed ' the imbecile administration of Sir Lowry Cole '[2] for much of the trouble in the north, and hinted that the contradictions were deliberately designed, the prohibitions and restrictions for the consumption and solace of uneasy Secretaries of State, and possibly of Humanitarians—the concessions, like that of Major Dundas, as expedients to meet the local situation. But the weakness lay rather in the Government's inability to cope with the situation. With no legal authority, few troops and no police, the Government was nearly helpless even to maintain order beyond the frontiers, where, as Earl Goderich (Colonial Secretary) reminded Governor Sir Lowry Cole on 3 December 1831, colonial judges had no jurisdiction unless with express Parliamentary sanction.[3] Only strong administration could really have availed. But now, in spite of the confusion across the frontier, the Government which so lately as 1825 had extended the Colony to the Orange River, refused any further responsibility. It neither attempted to limit Boer expansion nor brought the Griquas under its protection and control.

The Colony and Governor, had they chosen to attend, might have been guided by the good sense and moderation of one travelled and well-informed statesman, their bugbear Dr. Philip. On his first trip to the north, back in 1825, he summed up the position in a sentence : ' The Landdrosts of the Frontier districts are too far removed from the scene of action. What would Scotland be like were there no magistrate north of Edinburgh ? ' Returned from England in 1829, Dr Philip was on tour again in 1830, though on this occasion he did not go north of Kafirland. Armed with frontier impressions, however, and letters from the spot, in his report for 1830 he wrote :

[1] See, for example, reference by the Trekker, Sarel Celliers, Bird, i, 252.

[2] Letter to Miss Buxton, 7 Oct. 1834.

[3] Such powers were sanctioned only in terms of the Cape of Good Hope Punishment Act of 1836, extending jurisdiction to Latitude 25 degrees South, and even then proved so unsatisfactory in practice that the Act was seldom applied, and did nothing to control the Trek. (See below, ch. xii.)

'Things cannot remain long as they are now. The farmers have *for some years past* been in the habit of crossing the Colonial Boundary and oppressing the Griquas in their own country. The Griquas have hitherto borne all this with admirable patience, waiting for the Colonial Government to put a stop to the cause of their grievances. . . . The Griquas are to a man attached to the English Government, and are willing to make sacrifices to remain in connexion with it.'

And again :

. . . . 'such has been the beneficial influence of missionary institutions among them that the Griquas might be more formidable than the Caffres, but it has not been necessary to have *one* soldier on the more extended Frontier of the Griquas, to defend that part of the Colony.'

To this Philip added a note on the trekking habits of the Boers. Their numbers, he says, it is impossible to calculate, for at eleven fords they are continually passing and repassing, some of them coming 'even from within an hour of Graaff-Reinet':

'Last year ('29) a Veld Cornet had only one old man left, and asked permission to recall some farmers for the protection of the Colony. Farmers generally go with three, five, or ten, or even more, waggons to a great distance up the Caledon, Orange, Riet and Modder Rivers. . . . Each brings nearly his whole stock of cattle, including often the herds of one or two friends who have remained at home. . . . In return to the Bushmen for a little tobacco and garbage, the farmers fatten more cattle, get a better price, and large quantities of game. . . . They organize shooting parties ; one farmer and son went for ten long days to the source of the Modder, got eighteen hippos, sold for skins a load of sjamboks even with the sides of their waggon, the large at 3 R.D.s., the smaller at 4 skillings, besides 180 lbs. of bacon, at 4s. per lb. ; and besides all this, wood for building. In three weeks, seven waggons passed at one spot, and returned almost immediately well laden.'

Again in 1832 Dr. Philip set off on tour, spending the whole summer (September to February) in the interior, November and December in the far north—returning to Cape Town by Graaff-Reinet, the Kat River and Bethelsdorp, the road he had gone. By this time, for his share in freeing the Hottentots and pressing for the (now imminent) emancipation of the slaves, Dr. Philip's name was a hissing to the Colonists. His travels were not without anxiety : the Governor thought he was 'mad' to make the venture. Sometimes to the Boers he met he was merely 'a *sendeling*' (missionary), for when known to be 'Dr. Philip' he was repeatedly refused leave even to 'out-span'; 'on some occasions, I believe the Boers came together to do me injury, but the moment I went up to them in a friendly manner, offered them a pinch of snuff, and talked with them a little, I had them all as civil as possible.' Even so, by the end of October, he was relieved to reach peace and security . . . ' amid savages . . . in the lion country ' at Philippolis.

After a long tour Dr. Philip returned to Cape Town in March 1833 and began to press upon the Government the importance of a settled policy on this frontier.[1] In Griqualand he had seen the first-fruits of ordered missionary instruction, so that a people who, as he said, were till at least 1811 mere nomads completely ignorant of tillage, had made most notable progress even since the time of his first visit to them in 1825. Now by the efforts of Mr. Wright, aided by one of themselves, Willem Fortuin by name, the Orange River had been utilized for irrigation. This suggested the practical comment :

In a country like this the mechanic may do as much for the Kingdom of God as the missionary, and the man who subscribes money to purchase a pump to raise the water of a river at a missionary station does a service as truly acceptable to God as the man who lays out his money sending missionaries and Bibles to the heathen ; for what can a missionary do for the salvation of such a people if he has no means of bringing them together to receive the first elements of Christian instruction or of keeping them together till those instructions give rise to the formation of a society which will give a permanent footing for the Gospel, with all the apparatus of printing and schools that must follow in the train of the missionary before he can have any security for the effects of his labours ?

Both by letter and in conversation Dr. Philip pointed to the economic consequences of unrestrained trekking, ' with no villages forming,' and no markets. ' The system is ruinous to the Colony. The extension of the boundary adds greatly to the expense of defending it.' Yet there is no expansion of the colonial revenues, ' since all are producers and there are no consumers '. Now, to stop all trekking would have been to run counter to natural forces and attempt to change the essential character of the country, but the Trek need not have gone on all unheeded. Dr. Philip pressed two alternatives on the Gover-

---

[1] The Civil Commissioner of Graaff-Reinet got little encouragement in trying to take a serious view of the situation. Early in 1832, he was informed by the Colonial Secretary : ' The Governor laments the continuance of atrocities by Griquas. . . . *In calling the attention of the chiefs to these outrages you have already done all that can be done* in such distressing cases ' (Col. Bell to van Ryneveld, 16 Jan. 1832).

nor.[1] As by this time the reforming Ordinance 50 of 1828 had secured the legal position of the free people of colour in the Colony, he now came down definitely in favour of closer relations between Colony and Griquas. Failing 'incorporation' of the Griquas in the Colony—'on the same footing as the Kat River Settlement'—he suggested that they arm the one capable ruler, Waterboer, with effective authority, and supersede the weaker Koks (who owed their position to the L.M.S.). The Koks, he agreed, failed to restrain, if they did not even encourage, free-booters and banditti, like one Stuurman, who was then raiding Northern farmers from his base on islands of the Orange River. To 'incorporate' the Griquas might be a strengthening of the frontier; with a small garrison of thirty men at Philippolis to represent the colonial authority, and with regular salaries for the chiefs, the Griquas might serve as a defence against both the Matabele and the Orange River banditti along the whole of a 300- or 400-, if not a 700-mile frontier. Unless some such action was taken, the country would fall to the Boers, who even then were 'casting their eyes on the territories of the Griquas'; these territories, however, 'would not satisfy fifty families of Boers', who would, moreover, be 'unable to protect either themselves or the Colony against Moselekatze'. As in many other instances, Dr. Philip was too far-seeing for his contemporaries, but on this occasion he was too late. There were difficulties in placing Boers indefinitely under the jurisdiction even of Waterboer, whose ultimate survival was due less to his authority than to the fact that the Griquatown area offered fewer attractions to settlers than the country behind Philippolis. 'Incorporation', therefore, Dr. Philip's first alternative would have been wiser, for the first essential was to establish a strong civilized government, capable of dealing with land and other disputes by ordinary legal process.

Now, not a little by Dr. Philip's prompting, the authorities were not ill-informed. They were apt, however, to stress the incidental lawlessness, rather than the need for general legal control. Thus Colonel Wade, the Acting Governor, reported to Mr. Stanley on 14 January 1834 :

'It is not pretended that there has been of late years any increased demand for powder, for the usual purposes within the Colony itself, and there is not the slightest doubt, that, from these places, it finds

---

[1] These suggestions, the substance of conversations, were embodied, apparently by request, in a long letter to Colonel Wade in Oct. 1833.

its way across to Bastards or Korannas, and other native tribes. . . .
Having sought information on this important subject from the magistrates, missionaries, and all others who could best inform me, I cannot
hesitate to assert that to the hourly traffic in arms and ammunition
must mainly be attributed the increased boldness of the banditti. . . .
But besides these there are the farmers, who, in defiance of the law
and the severity of its penalties [*sic*], emigrate beyond the boundaries,
and at the same time that they supply the natives with the means of
attacking the Colony, unfortunately furnish them also with something
of a reasonable pretext for doing so, by dispossessing the weak and
unarmed, and occupying all the fertile spots and springs. In my
opinion, there is no part of the frontier affairs that requires more decided
and prompt measures than this one. In the country between the
frontier line and the upper Orange River, there are at this moment
upwards of a hundred families . . . having seized upon the district
that best suited them without any regard whatever to the rights of the
natives. . . . But to oppose the banditti, measures of a more decided
nature must at length be had recourse to. They are ever increasing
in number and in daring, and yet, strange to say, whilst a regiment of
British Infantry, &c., are permanently posted on the Eastern frontier,
there is not one soldier or any organized means of defence . . . that
can be depended upon to oppose the merciless invaders of the districts
of Somerset, Graaff-Reinet, Beaufort and Clanwilliam.'

Immediately after this, Colonel Wade was superseded by
Sir Benjamin D'Urban, who, as later events were to show, was
not distinguished for prompt and courageous decisions. When
at last he roused himself to action, in the end of 1834, he was,
no doubt, forced by the attitude of Downing Street to lean towards
Dr. Philip's second alternative. So in December, Waterboer
came to Cape Town, to return fortified by a ' Treaty '.[1] Had
only Waterboer and Griquatown been concerned, all might have
been well ; the treaty with Waterboer might have been a preliminary step to a final settlement, and to ultimate incorporation. But
by this time the centre of interest had shifted to Philippolis,
now in the line of the main Boer advance, and a scene of dire
confusion, far beyond the power of any petty local chief to

[1] Waterboer was pledged to keep order in his district and to send
back fugitives and criminals to the Colony; he was to protect the
frontiers from invaders or marauders, and generally to co-operate with
the Colonial Government. In return he was to receive a salary of £150
per annum, and adequate supplies of ammunition. Mr. Wright,
moreover, by a letter from the Governor, dated 15 Dec. 1834, was
appointed *confidential organ* of communication between Governor
and Chief, being required to obtain all possible information about
surrounding tribes, and to make a report at least once monthly through
the Field Commandant of Graaff-Reinet. In Mr. Wright's absence,
Waterboer was to report direct, £50 being set aside for expenses.

control. About this time, and independently, Adam Kok of
Philippolis set out in the hope of concluding a treaty with the
Governor on the Kafir frontier, where he was expected in
September 1834. Shortly afterwards, Adam Kok died, to be
succeeded by a son Abram (who indeed seems to have belied the
faith the missionaries put in his powers as a ruler). The Government, failing entirely to grasp that the situation in Philippolis
was the crux of the matter, 'recognized' Waterboer, whose
authority hardly ran in Philippolis, while Kok was left to be
dealt with separately. For, in October 1834, the Civil Commissioner of Graaff-Reinet had written to

'afford His Excellency opportunity to judge how far Adam Kok is
to be depended on. Almost all the representations and complaints
about illicit traffic in gunpowder, &c., have come through Philippolis,
and notwithstanding all possible exertions on the part of the Clerk
of the Peace, he has never been able to succeed in getting Captain
Adam Kok to co-operate with him in trying to prevent it.'

The result was that, if only because of more immediately serious
complications on the Kafir frontier, there was not even a treaty
with Philippolis. Its chaotic disorder was the warrant for leaving
it utterly alone, and the Government did just nothing.

Before the days of a considered policy of Native ' Reserves ',
even incorporation in the Colony might have resulted in the
swallowing up of the Griquas' land. In the end, economic
pressure has had this result in any case. As it was, the Griquas
were ' recognized ', without effective government, to the extent
that in the north, as in the east, Boer appeals for grants of land,
and for the opening up of new country, were now firmly refused.
The check on the Kafir frontier at the same time made land-
hunger especially acute, and pent-up energies were likely to
produce an explosion against the scruples or fears of a Government that refused to maintain ' proper ' relations between masters
and servants, and hesitated also to take a high hand either with
Griquas or Bantu. Nor were the Boers allowed to take the law
into their own hand for the forcible expulsion of the Amalekites
who possessed the chosen land. The utterly ineffective treatment
by the Government of the less complex Griqua problem failed
to save or protect the Griquas' lands, and merely engendered
violent Boer antagonism. The Griqua territories remained for
some years longer a feeble barrier, forcing the Great Trek even
further afield—more rapidly and superficially than need have
been—to the infinite complication of South African problems.

CHAPTER V

FRONTIER POLICY AND MILITARY RULE IN THE EAST—THE NEUTRAL BELT

AFTER 1834 the attention of the Government, wavering as it had been, was for several years completely withdrawn from Griqua affairs. So long as there was room for comparatively unchecked expansion to the north, the unsettlement on the Kafir frontier mattered very little. But now that there was a check in the north, pressure in the east was intensified, and until at least 1842 the Kafirs and their neighbours absorbed all the attention of the Government. When Griqualand again came into the picture its affairs were much more complex. By this time the country lying between the two fronts (Griqualand and Kafirland), and a good deal beyond it, had filled up; it was as if a ' salient ' in the old line had been ' straightened out ', and contact established on one unbroken front from east to north.

The question of Frontiers was the earliest phase of the South African Native Problem. The actual fixing of a boundary was the least part of it. The real difficulty was to make any line secure and peaceable. The Bantu were so long a real danger, in a military sense, that South Africans from the beginning have thought in terms, if not of armies, then at least of a quasi-military police force as the first essential of safe and sound Native ' policy '. That, even from the earliest days, frontier ' settlements ' affected the whole social and economic life of the Bantu themselves almost more than that of their much-harassed colonial neighbours, was habitually lost sight of. As colonists advanced upon the Bantu there came first a period of unsettlement, with cattle-thieving, raids, and counter-raids, till some more than usually serious ' incident ' culminated in a ' war '. The war was followed by a fixing of boundaries, usually a little farther east than before; for since some action must be taken against a tribe guilty of murder, or even ' theft ', the obvious punish-

52

ment was to seize cattle and confiscate land. But the more land the Europeans thus annexed at Bantu expense, the more the Bantu were driven into precisely those straitened conditions from which the Colonists were striving to escape. Colonial Governors, soldiers almost all of them, habitually ignored this fact—thinking perhaps that, as one account has it, ' Bantu agriculture does as much for the soil as the caterpillar for the cabbage it lives on '. Time after time, to secure a suitable military frontier, whole tribes were transplanted, or tribe hurled back upon tribe ; and when, in consequence, the Bantu were driven to war among themselves, as at Amalinde in 1818 (p. 34), or to retaliatory raids on the Colonists' cattle, or even to attacks on the Colony itself, the inevitable specific was to drive off more cattle, confiscate more land, and fix yet another boundary, so beginning the process all over again.

In spite of occasional official and missionary protests,[1] the military fallacy of the all-sufficiency of mere frontier-fixing as a rule of Native ' policy ' persisted, and has done its disastrous work. That there were other aspects of the Frontier Question was further obscured by the prevalent notion that the less land the Bantu had to abuse by their wasteful methods the more they would be available to increase the supply of cheap labour for the farmers. But the continued growth at the expense of the Bantu, instead of making for more adequate agricultural use of the land by Europeans, intensified rather the disposition to never-ending trek, and the superficial methods of cultivation which have, in the fullness of time, reduced the untrained, undisciplined ' Poor White ' to fierce competition with landless and over-crowded Natives. The impact of the European upon the Bantu was a steady process of depression and mutual impoverishment.

The Frontier story has invariably been presented as nothing more than a long series of raids by ' thieving ' Kafirs on the fat herds of hard-working, inoffensive white farmers. The wide difference between European and Bantu ideas of law, property, and government made friction inevitable ; but in the first instance

[1] Administrative officials, bound as they were to secrecy, could not always express themselves openly, but their letters and journals, now available, make it clear that they gave many warnings to the authorities. Captain Charles Lennox Stretch, for example, frequently cited below, and later a member of the Cape Parliament, who for long served as a Resident Agent among the Xosa tribes, was typical of many who have done more than can ever be known to preserve, in spite of everything, Native belief in the white man's justice.

the Bantu had just as good a ' right ' as their rivals to be where
they were. It is not that Bantu law and government were no
government at all. The tribes had well-established institutions
and customs, but they were those of tribal Europe before the
days even of feudal land laws. Though the Colonists, too,
were pastoral, the higher standards of the white man made an
even more formidable demand on the land, on which all equally
depended ; while tribal institutions kept the Bantu together in
groups, the Colonists, with confidence in themselves and in their
guns, spread far and wide, taking to themselves *property* in land
in a way foreign to all Bantu thinking. It was an unsocial and
exclusive claim not merely to use land, but to appropriate it,
and to bar all others from a share in its enjoyment. The limits
of tribal lands being *ex hypothesi* ill-defined, and all land unfenced,
the individualist farmers planted themselves down wherever
there seemed to be room, with no nice inquiry about the grazing
or hunting habits, or ' rights ', of the Bantu. At the same time,
by their isolation and dispersal, the farmers made themselves
an obvious prey to retaliatory attacks by the tribes whom they
thus, often no doubt inadvertently, but sometimes overtly, dispossessed.

A clash was unavoidable ; but the position is not explained
when the Kafirs have been written down as irreclaimable barbarians and thieves. The Bantu were called upon to accept a
very one-sided application of ' civilized ' standards ; and to
make history turn on Bantu cattle-stealing is one-sided and
false.[1] Before ever the Bantu became a factor to reckon with,
the resistance offered by the Bushmen had taught the frontiersmen
to unite for mutual defence. The burghers fully recognized
the obligation of their ' commando ' system, and in time of
danger readily stood together to chastise refractory Natives.
In the earliest Kafir Wars the ' commandos ' sometimes took
the law into their own hands without waiting for instructions
from Cape Town, sometimes in defiance of the authorities,[2]
and, as on the Spanish Main, there was ' no peace beyond the
line '—wherever the ' line ' may have been. The greater resources

[1] P. 8. It has a certain significance that the earliest conflict of
Europeans with Bantu in 1702 was due to a cattle ' trading ' expedition
of colonists, who may or may not have been attacked ' without provocation ' by the ' Kafirs ', but were admittedly guilty of ' plundering '
the weaker Hottentots. Fouche's *Adam Tas*, p. 335.

[2] Walker, *History*, pp. 121-3.

of the British Government, which took over in 1806, made no real difference, unless it was to make cattle-driving and kraal-burning more frequent and incessant—the ' strong ' action in ' clearing the Zuurveld ' in 1812 being an incitement to further cattle-stealing and ' depredations ' by the ' Kafirs '.

Little significance attaches to minor differences in frontier practice. In 1817 Lord Charles Somerset came to an agreement with Gaika to apply to the disease of cattle-stealing the well-known primitive practice known in South Africa as the ' spoor-law ' and equally familiar to the early English.[1] It now became the practice for owners, accompanied by ' patrols ' of troops, to follow the ' spoor ' of stolen cattle to the kraal at which it ended, and there ' either to retake the cattle or recoup themselves at the expense of the kraal.'[2] Sometimes an equivalent number of beasts sufficed, sometimes an equivalent (and arbitrary) value[3]; further, if one visit obtained satisfaction, good and well, but this, says Dr. Theal, ' seldom happened '; whereupon a ' reprisal ' was deemed necessary—that is to say, 'a joint force of burghers and soldiers marched to the kraal *suspected* of being most deeply implicated in the robberies, and *secured* compensation'.[4] As appears from later discussions, there was no effective check on the number of beasts alleged to be stolen, and without doubt, as Theopolis Hottentots once complained, ' the sins of jackals, wolves and tigers ' were often ' laid on the backs ' of the Kafirs.[5] Little wonder, as Dr. Theal agrees, the system was ' not free of abuses '.[6] General Bourke, therefore, seeking some better

---

[1] Stubbs' Charters : ' We have ordained,' says Edgar's *Ordinance of the Hundred* (959-75), ' concerning unknown cattle, that no one should possess it without the testimonial of the men of the hundred, or of the tithing men . . . also if the hundred pursue a track into another hundred, that notice be given to the hundred man and then he shall go with him. If he neglects this let him pay xxx shillings to the king ', &c., &c.

[2] Walker, p. 161.

[3] Cory, iii, p. 55, *note*, for a glaring example of frontier ' valuation '.

[4] Theal, ii, p. 3.

[5] *Cape Col. Qn.*, p. 239.

[6] Dr. Theal (ii, 4, *note*) qualifies this admission, suggesting from his own personal experience in 1877 that old men who had lived on the frontiers in the 'twenties entertained no grievance about the activities of patrols. ' Taking the district between the Keiskama and Fish River from Gaika was regarded very differently, and in their view real injustice.' In other words, surely, cattle-stealing was a mere incident in the war for possession of the *land*.

way, decreed in 1828 that patrols must not enter Kafirland unless the stolen cattle were in sight. Sir Lowry Cole, on the other hand, faced by an apparent increase of stealing—for which there were other reasons (below, p. 68)—stiffened the practice once more, allowing patrols to follow the spoor wherever they could, though they were ' not to seize Kafir cattle as compensation '.

The Spoor Law may have been according to Bantu custom, but it was applied without the necessary qualifications or safeguards which accompanied it in Bantu practice. For example, with the Bantu as with the Anglo-Saxons, it was usual to halt on the frontier and send for the nearest headman (as it were the English ' hundredman ') and throw on him the onus of proving that the ' spoor ' led through or away from his area; moreover, ' any attempt to obliterate the spoor would be sufficient proof of guilt '. Then, with guilt reasonably established, there was a further all-important safeguard, by which the nearest kraals were made *collectively* responsible over an ' area taken according to the value of the property stolen '. ' The usual course is to include a sufficient number of kraals for the number of cattle paid not to exceed one or two for each kraal ' (i.e. household). In the last resort ' the tribe as a whole is responsible '.[1]

The difficulties in the way of European authorities applying Bantu law from the outside are obvious. It was, for example, permissible for those following the spoor to question men, women or children, and information might easily be given in order to save the ' nearest kraal ' from the penalty. But where the theft was one of tribe from tribe, still more of a tribe from the Colony, the patrols met a combined conspiracy of silence. Nice but relevant distinctions, therefore, got little attention from the colonial authorities, distracted as no doubt they often were by the vagaries of the Bantu on one side, and the complaints of farmers on the other. The ' Kafirs ' were undoubtedly awkward neighbours, but as a resident missionary put it in 1830 :

' It is highly desirable that a better understanding should be established between the Colony and the Caffre nation. The custom is still maintained by some colonists of making reprisals for cattle stolen from the Colony by sending armed patrols into Caffre-land, attacking and plundering different sections of the country for the supposed guilt

---

[1] The Spoor Law is described in a *Memo.* drafted by Mr. (now Sir) W. E. Stanford, in 1882, shown me by the late Mr. W. Carmichael, when R.M. of Tsolo.

of one or more kraals. *In most cases the guilty escape with impunity, while the innocent are deprived of the means of support and reduced to want and misery.'* [1]

The quite inevitable result of the practice of ' patrols ', varied by the more intensive ' commandos ' or ' reprisals ',[2] was the state of incessant war and chaos that makes up the story, as usually detailed, of the frontier in the 'twenties and 'thirties. It is usual to speak of the ' policy ' of these years in particular as ' vacillating '. But an examination of frontier history reveals no real variation of principle or method. From the very beginning the Frontier Problem was dealt with only by the rule of force. The ' vacillation ', therefore, was in the degree of vigour with which successive Governors applied the military policy to which they all pinned their faith. Only in the 'thirties, after the missionaries had won a great fight for Hottentot rights within the Colony, Humanitarian criticism began to be turned to the Bantu Question, and ventured to put it to the authorities that mere force would settle nothing.

Those who had to deal with the situation on the old Cape frontier had some excuse for being absorbed by the mere task of trying to keep the peace. With slender and inadequate forces at their disposal, and a distant Home Government watchful and impatient of new and expensive ventures in a wild and rather useless and unprofitable country, they were in no position to take risks, or to incur responsibility by any departure from the course that seemed simple and obvious at the moment. Slavery itself was still part of the established order, and in the nature of things, frontier duty fell to soldiers who had little eye, and less mind, to weigh the ultimate social consequences of their actions. In early days the Dutch East India Company, which had consistently refused to recognize the legal existence of the Hottentots, would fain have left the Bantu alone, and the two ' wars ' thrust upon it by the clamant demand of its

---

[1] J. Brownlee's Report to L.M.S. for 1830.

[2] Contemporary accounts distinguish between ' patrols ' (where the owner, accompanied by troops, tried to follow the spoor of his own stolen beasts) and the more elaborate expeditions where troops combined with a burgher ' commando ' to make ' reprisals '—possibly for a series of alleged thefts. Frontier tradition suggests that the theoretically less objectionable ' patrol ' was liable to abuse, since in practice the farmer's friends joined together to hunt the spoor without waiting for the troops, and virtually levied private war.

frontiersmen for ' security ' were small affairs, conducted almost entirely by commandos of burghers whose interests were directly concerned. The Company, however, by its well-meant but very casual 'treaty' in 1778, gave the Colony a legal (if not rather legalistic) claim to the country up to the Fish River, and served to establish one all-important tradition. It is true that eleven years later, when the Bantu proved themselves still a factor on the colonial side of this boundary, the Company forbore to expel the culprits, and ' allowed ' them to remain where they were—' without prejudice to the *ownership* of Europeans '. But after 1806, when the stronger British Government turned its attention to the eastern frontier, its officers, without over-scrupulous inquiry into all the circumstances, were readily per-suaded that the Bantu were responsible for disorders in the Zuurveld, and were in a part of the Colony where they had no right to be. In extending the boundary to the Fish River, the Government had never extended its administrative functions to include the Bantu as subjects within the sphere of its juris-diction and protection ; and even now, instead of adhering to this first principle of government, Sir John Cradock, with more resources behind him, all too faithfully imitated his Company predecessors in refusing to think of the native people as an integral part of the Colony, took the obvious short-cut, and had the Zuurveld forcibly ' cleared ' of its Bantu population—this being the first overt act in a long drama.

In the years that followed, some such clear-cut plan of ' keeping the races apart ' has often had its champions ; it appeals as the obvious way of escaping the entanglements of a mixed community in which advanced and backward peoples are thrown together. Had the segregation adumbrated in frontier policy at this early stage been realized in 1812 or 1819, it might have cost us much of the light as well as the shade in the story of the last hundred years. But the plan broke down at its first attempt because it ignored the fact that relationships had already been established. Even in those days of small things, the problem that the segrega-tionists evaded was the whole crux of the matter, that fitting relationships must be maintained between white and coloured people in so far as they have already come to live and work together.

The clearing of the Zuurveld in 1812 merely transferred the dispute to the region of the Fish River and the Keiskama, where some of the tribes hankered after land they had lost,

while others went in fear for their own. Not only was there
the old struggle for possession of the land—however disguised
by the allegations of historians as to the Kafir ' propensity for
thieving '. Points of contact were developing. Trade was
beginning, and in 1817 the Governor arranged a system of ' passes '
to allow natives to visit a ' fair ', to be held twice a year, first
in Grahamstown, later at Fort Willshire on the Keiskama. In
the 'twenties, also, as colonial development increased the demand
for cheap labour, frontier officials found farmers torn between
fear of the ' thieving propensities ' of the Kafirs, and a desire
to make use of them as servants—and the economic need tended
to prevail to bring more and more Kafirs into the Colony and keep
them there.[1]

These years saw the beginning also of regular missionary
work in Kafirland. The London Missionary Society was, as
elsewhere, the first in the field, and Mr. Joseph Williams, their
pioneer, who settled with Gaika near the later Fort Beaufort,
has left a journal which throws glimpses of light on frontier
conditions. His missionary venture, it may be believed, met
with some opposition, and probably more ridicule—the ' general
opinion ', so he writes, ' both of Boers and of officers being that
nothing but powder and ball would do to bring such savages to
their senses '. The Kafirs, too, had their suspicions, so he says,
' because Boers had circulated the report that the missionaries
had come for the Caffres' destruction '. Nor was Mr. Williams
altogether favourably impressed by the Kafir character, which
was, of course, to him new and strange : ' The chiefs are very
anxious and greedy over presents—they continually ask for
them '. Witchcraft, he found, was a serious factor in native
life. Just then a certain ' prophetess ' was active in ' smelling
out ' culprits, and he describes how ' they think nothing of
murder if the prophetess ascribes any calamity to the poison of
a particular individual '. Here the missionary touched an
important feature of life on the frontier. Even Gaika and
Makana, both of whom ' are anxious to profess Christianity '
were remonstrated with ; ' but they do not see the wrong of
committing murder when a person is accused, for example,

[1] As early as October 1823 the missionary Brownlee wrote to Mrs.
Williams of how natives were being ' induced into the service of Boers ',
sometimes, he says, ' with threats of Robben Island ' (the convict
station) if they refused. See also Cory, ii, 382, and *Cape Col. Qn.*,
pp. 252–3.

of withholding rain. . . . In fact life is of little value. One human life is reckoned as equal to three beasts'. But when the attempt was made to bring the Bantu under European law (and even in Anglo-Saxon England the *wer-gild* of a *ceorl* was doubtfully of more than the value of 'three beasts') not many administrators had the wisdom to explain their innovations with the carefulness of Theophilus Shepstone, who, in 1850, introduced a new code into Natal, with the preamble : ' Know ye, therefore, all Chiefs, Petty Chieftains, Heads of Kraals and Common People, *a man's life has no price ; no cattle can pay for it* '.[1]

Questions of men and of cattle claimed a good deal of the attention of the earliest missionary, and one of Williams' great worries was that the Colonial authorities could see little justification for any missionary to the Kafirs who was not also at least a semi-official Government Agent in Kafirland. Colonel Cuyler, for example, the Landdrost of Uitenhage, had written demanding information about thefts by Kafirs, expressing at the same time his willingness to hear complaints against Colonists ; he even suggested a weekly letter ; whereupon Williams protested that he had no secular authority, and could not afford the expense of such regular communications. In the end, Cuyler, losing patience, seems to have written saying that he could not see that Williams was serving any useful purpose if he did not help to ' control ' thefts, and ' reported ' him to the Governor as ' harbouring' runaway Hottentots from the Colony : ' He is not to be allowed to do as Mr. Read and Mr. Anderson do.' About the time of his death, therefore, in 1818, Mr. Williams' station was included in the criticism then being levelled against all missions ' beyond the Colony '.[2] For two or three years new stations were prohibited altogether, though, in the hope of keeping missions under control, Mr. J. Brownlee was appointed by Lord Charles Somerset to succeed Williams as a ' Government ' missionary, remaining in official service till 1825 when he returned to the L.M.S. Meantime Dr. Philip, whose experience led him to oppose the tying of missionaries to the Government, had won his battle for the removal of the embargo on extracolonial stations, and in the early 'twenties representatives of the Wesleyan, Glasgow, and London Societies established themselves throughout Kafirland. The missionaries were one more link in the chain of influences that were fast binding together the interests of the Bantu and the Colony.

[1] Quoted by Professor E. Brookes, p. 52.   [2] *Cape Col. Qn.*, p. 128.

This period of growing interdependence was chosen by Lord Charles Somerset for a designed attempt to put a definite barrier between the Colony and the Bantu peoples beyond the frontier, official opinion naturally desiring to reduce intercourse to a minimum. The Company having set the fashion of running away from the difficulties, the Report of the Circuit Commission in 1813, together with many of the letters of frontier officers about the same time, show that for some years before its deliberate adoption in 1819, the plan of a ' neutral belt ' was taking shape. The experiment may have been worth a trial. The ' impossibility of promiscuous intercourse ', with ' Kafirs coming freely into the Colony ', was generally felt.[1] After the war of 1819, Lord Charles Somerset seems to have had an idea of setting patrols to keep the land between the Fish and the Keiskama empty of both black and white. But his settlement was imperfectly conceived, and so cavalierly executed that there was never any real hope of its permanence. From the nature of the case a ' treaty ' with a barbarian chief rests on an insecure foundation. The agreement should, therefore, have been drafted in very clear and definite terms ; but the Governor obviously acted on the contrary assumption that, for a savage, any form of words would suffice. To begin with, in spite of Gaika's overwhelming defeat at the hands of Ndhlambi in 1818, the Governor persisted, as he had done previously, in refusing to treat with any but Gaika, who himself protested that he could not speak for other chiefs. It was thus not even a dictated peace made with a vanquished enemy ; it was a peace dictated to a potentate of straw set up for the occasion by the victor. It was not even a written bond, but a verbal arrangement, and Somerset's own evidence is by no means clear as to its terms. On the day of the treaty Somerset announced in the *Cape Gazette* that, by a bargain with Gaika, the country between the Fish and Keiskama was to be thoroughly cleared, and expressed the hope that ' as the boundary is completely

---

[1] Quoted from a ' Review ' of S.A. Missions by Dr. Philip, a document intended ' for publication ' but cancelled at the end of 1821 (*Cape Col. Qn.*, p. 134).

Dr. Philip, whose first trip to Grahamstown and Theopolis was made within three months of the Battle of Grahamstown, in July 1819, was impressed by the havoc wrought by war. On his journey he ' saw no Caffres and did not wish to see any '. ' The farmers ' he wrote on his return to Bethelsdorp ' have been stripped of everything, and unless the commando shall recover their cattle they must be ruined.'

freed from Kafirs, repose and security will be the results of the
late operations '. On the same day he reported to London,
by way of comment on the treaty—what he had not said to
Gaika—' The country thus *ceded* is as fine a portion of ground
as is to be found, and, together with the still unappropriated lands
in the Zuurveld, it might perhaps be worthy of consideration
with a view to systematic colonization '.[1]

Even the definition of the boundaries was vague. Gaika indeed,
having given away land belonging to tribes whom he did not
control, was ' allowed ' to remain where he was, in the Chumie
Valley. But before very long, in spite of the alleged stipulation
that it ' was to be occupied only by soldiers,[2] the ' neutral '
territory filled up with farmers and came to be described, almost
habitually, as the ' Ceded ' territory. As early as 1820 the
Acting Governor, Sir Rufane Donkin, having gone to the trouble
of getting Gaika's consent—as if to a departure from the bargain
of 1819—supported a short-lived scheme for a military settlement
at Fredericksburg, near the Keiskama.[3] About the same time
a party of Highland settlers was destined for the Kat River
Valley, and, as they failed to come, Thomas Pringle, then settled
near the frontier and enthusiastic about the quality of the land,
made suggestions for the strengthening of the frontier by planting
a settlement of Hottentots there.[4] His proposal shows, indeed,
how little people on the frontier itself were aware of the idea
of a ' neutral ' belt. Next, with Donkin's encroachment for
precedent, the chief Maqomo, elder son of Gaika, ' crept back '
into the upper part of the Kat River Valley, to be followed by
his brother Tyali, and it was felt politic to leave them alone so
long as they behaved themselves.[5] In 1822, a blockhouse, the
nucleus of the later Fort Beaufort, was established on the lower
Kat River, a little north of its junction with the Fish, ' to act
as a check upon Maqomo '.[6] Three years later, the missionary
Brownlee,[7] casting about for a sphere of work on his return to
the L.M.S., reported mournfully that the site of Williams'

---

[1] *Records*, vol. xii, 15 Oct. 1819. In 1824 the Commissioners of
Inquiry, sent out to review the whole state of the Cape Colony, found
conflict of opinion about the terms of the treaty even between Somerset
and his Secretary, Col. Bird.

[2] Theal, i, p. 283.

[3] Cf. evidence of Stockenstrom, *Records*, 8 Aug. 1825.

[4] Letter to Philip, 15 Jan. 1821.

[5] Cory, ii, p. 343.   [6] Cory, ii, p. 147.

[7] To Philip, from the Chumie, 3 July 1825.

former station was now ' for ever separated from Caffre Territory ', for the reason that in the years before 1826 the Colonial Government had systematically been making grants of farms between the Fish River and the Koonap, not only to British Settlers, but to Colonial Boers. In 1825 the Governor had expressed an intention ' not to permit the Territory to be inhabited until our endeavours to civilize the Kafirs had been successful ',[1] Somerset, in this, showing himself a more incorrigible optimist than any of the missionaries. But the clamour of the colonists for farms, and more farms, made short work of his intention, and an important part of the country was soon broken up to supply their demand. In 1825 the district of Somerset was extended to include the modern Bedford; in 1827 the only discussion seems to have been whether or not the regulations which forbade British settlers in Albany to keep slaves ought to be enforced upon Boers in the ' Ceded ' Territory. What never seems to have crossed the mind of those responsible for law and order was that the Kafirs had as good a right to return to their own homes in the Neutral Belt as colonists to have it portioned out to them in farms. Though it is true that in 1829 the Kat River Settlement was established for Hottentots, whose claims had been pressed by Brownlee in 1825,[2] and that the chiefs Pato and Congo were now given permission to graze west of the Keiskama, by Proclamation of 17 April, in that very year, 1829, the colonial boundary was definitely extended to the ' heights west of the Chumie'.[3] This was the end of the ' Neutral ' Belt.

[1] Somerset's second thoughts in reply to Crown Commissioners, C.C. Records, 4 Jan. 1825.

[2] ' From the late arrangements in enlarging the colonial boundary by colonizing a portion of the Neutral Territory between the Fish River and the Gonappe, I think the Hottentots have a strong claim.' He therefore urges ' a new Institution ' in those parts as a better buffer than white men who cross the boundary and traffic with Kafirs more than the Hottentots do (Brownlee to Philip, 28 March 1825).

On the 29th Sept. 1828 the Commissioner General was given authority to inspect the Kat River lands for this purpose (Cape Archives, Sundry Letters, vol. 261). Dr. Philip at this time was away in England, but missionary letters suggest that the establishment of the Kat River was a move in the war for Hottentot rights, and deliberately designed to weaken the ' dangerous ' influence of the L.M.S. (See Theal, ii, p. 10, and Cape Col. Qn., p. 241).

[3] Walker's Atlas, Map. 10.

CHAPTER VI

PROBLEMS OF THE FRONTIER—TRADE AND LABOUR—UNREST AFTER 1829

THESE ten years of half-hearted experiment with a ' neutral ' belt were an interval of at least comparative peace, in which there was some growth of almost normal intercourse on the frontier. The Grahamstown fairs of 1817, continuing at Fort Willshire in the 'twenties, were so far successful that in 1827 General Bourke increased their number. Thereupon, plucking up courage, a few traders got permission to enter the country north of the Winterberg, where the tribes were supposed to be more peaceable ; till presently, in 1830, restrictions were removed, and the fairs proved superfluous. Persons ' of assured good character ' [1] were now permitted to pass and to trade freely anywhere in the Native Territories, carrying some of the custom of civilization far into the heart of Kafirland. In itself, no doubt, the trade was small enough. All the Bantu had to offer were skins and hides, with a diminishing quantity of ivory (the latter the original cause of a ' boom ' on the eastern frontier [2] in the 'twenties) ; yet in the five years, 1831–5, the value of skins and hides exported from the Colony doubled in value, till they accounted for fully one-quarter of the total exports ; the open roadstead of Port Elizabeth, moreover, now accounted for 19 per cent. of this total, indicating partly the relative importance of the native trade, and partly the faint beginnings of prosperity for the Settlers, in spite of the Native ' menace '.[3] As for the traders themselves, their free and adventurous life was probably as great an attraction as the hope of large profits. In the 1835 war the natives for their part seem to have made a dead set

---

[1] Cory, ii, 342. [2] Cory, ii, 174.
[3] Theal, ii, p. 43, gives the annual value of hides and skins and of total exports as £37,454 and £218,412 respectively from 1826 to 1830, and £62,829 and £243,646 from 1831 to 1835.

against a class they hated ;[1] but in time, the trader came to play a regular and established part in the life of every tribal community. In many of the territories to-day the largest share of the trade seems to be still in the hands of families who have succeeded to the business of fathers and of grandfathers. This seems to show both that native trading offers a good living rather than a great fortune, and that a strong mutual attachment has often grown up between the good trader, who is at pains to understand the life and ways of his customers, the natives among whom he makes his home.[2] It has usually been easy for Europeans who choose to live among them to maintain good relations with the naturally patient and friendly Bantu.

The other side of the problem of the 'twenties, as of our own day, was far more difficult. If isolated traders, like missionaries, readily enough adapted themselves to life among the Bantu, it was a very different matter for members of the Bantu race to fit into the much more complex structure of colonial society. The ' neutral belt ' policy, had it been given a proper trial, might have kept the Bantu at a distance from the Colony, and reduced the pressure upon them, thus ensuring that, so far as they came to better their fortunes in European areas, they would have come in more easily manageable numbers. Although officials and missionaries perhaps continued to look askance at the growth of intercourse, as appears from the hesitant encouragement given even to trade, the colonists themselves were in two minds. These ' Kafirs ' were still ' incorrigible thieves ' (a charge, incidentally, in flat contradiction of wide later experience of natives as domestic servants) ; it was dangerous to have many of them—at least on the farms of one's neighbours. In the 'twenties, however, owing to the new slave laws, and the prohibition of slaves in Albany and in the ' Ceded ' Territory, the labour shortage was acute. In spite of the risks, therefore, colonists often met their needs by the employment of Xosas, as well as refugees (Bechuana or Fingos). These Bantu were cheaper even than Hottentots, and in spite of the risks, there was a steadily increasing demand for their services. Wiseacres

[1] Cory, iii, 73. Many traders were murdered, and Read's letters especially emphasize their misdeeds and their unpopularity.

[2] I suspect there is reason to add that the steady impoverishment of the Bantu generally has added considerably to the difficulties of traders, and that this, rather than keener competition, has in these days somewhat reduced the traders' prosperity. (Articles in *Cape Times*, 12 April 1926, ff.)

might shake their heads, or write to the papers about it,[1] but it was not only the weak-kneed humanitarianism of the Acting Governor, General Bourke, that was responsible for an Ordinance (No. 49 of 1828) definitely providing for the admission of Kafirs to the Colony. The law authorized the nearest border field-cornet to grant ' passes ' to any natives who desired to enter the service of colonial farmers.

Now the tradition of South African history still tends to classify its governors after the fashion of *Kings* and *Chronicles* in old Bibles ; poor General Bourke's term, for his share in the emancipation of the Hottentots by the Fiftieth Ordinance, and for the evils supposed to flow from this new frontier law (No. 49) tends to rank almost as ' Bourke's wicked reign ' ; his very ordinary and uninspired successors, on the contrary, Sir Lowry Cole and Sir Benjamin D'Urban, did what seemed well-pleasing in the sight of colonial opinion—and were, therefore, ' good ' and ' right '. In this instance we are given to understand that the Forty-ninth Ordinance was never more than a wrong-headed law, notable for its effect in facilitating ' thieving '.

The later history of this Ordinance is on any showing extra-ordinary. Immediately after its promulgation, the outcry against increased ' thieving ' was so lusty [2] that on 25 August 1829 the Ordinance was ' suspended ', by Dr. Theal's account, or ' repealed ', according to Sir George Cory ; Dr. Theal explains that at this date Sir Lowry Cole ' instructed officials to apprehend all who were wandering about without *proper* passes ', recognizing, in fact, that the object was to facilitate the employment of natives. But how their engagement was regulated thereafter is not so clear. For a time the question lapsed. At the end of 1836 the Ordinance was sometimes referred to, and on 13 February 1837, Stockenstrom acknowledged a letter from Sir B. D'Urban assuring him of the legality of Ordinance 49. In the 'forties the use of native labour was an established custom ; on 20 September 1844, for example, H. Fynn, Government Agent with the Tambookies under the treaty of 1836, complained of the conflict between the terms of the Treaty, which he had to

---

[1] Among many examples, ' W. G.' in the *Grahamstown Journal*, 14 Feb. 1833, describes the ' scarcity of labour ' as the ' cause of all our troubles '. ' Yet ' he adds ' Kafirs are not to be trusted as servants in the Colony.'

[2] Theal, ii, 11.   Cory, ii, 341, 350–361, 367–382.   Other letters cited are in Cape Town Archives.

administer, and of the Forty-ninth Ordinance, pointing out that when he, as Agent, refused passes, his natives were able to get them freely from frontier officials *under Ordinance* 49. On 27 September 1849 Colonel Mackinnon complained in the same terms, from the newly created British Kaffraria, that passes were being given by missionaries and traders ' apparently under Ordinance 49, though regulations under that Ordinance were never made '. Thereupon, on 3 October 1849, Attorney-General Porter minuted that a new Proclamation could only be made under the Forty-ninth Ordinance which, though marked in ' Harding's *Ordinances* ' as ' allowed ' by the Home Government, had not really been so allowed. It, therefore, fell under a clause of the Royal Instructions, and *lapsed after three years*. Yet, he concludes, ' The cessation of the 49th Ordinance it is not desirable to proclaim '.

There could hardly be a better illustration of the slackness of colonial frontier administration. The subsequent interpretation of the Forty-ninth Ordinance as a mere humanitarian blunder is equally indicative of the failure of historians to apprehend the inwardness of the problems that were even then shaping themselves. Like the relaxation of trade restrictions about the same time, the Ordinance was *prima facie* evidence of increasing ' normalcy ' on the frontier. It was first and last a labour law, intended to meet a loudly voiced need. This was especially acute at the moment, if complaints of shortage due to the emancipation of the Hottentots are to be taken at their face value ;[1] the Ordinance was designed to bring in a reserve of native labourers, not, as hitherto, almost by stealth, but under some kind of legal regulation. For the military-minded Government this was an unwonted excursion into the field of labour legislation, as the extraordinary fate of the measure was to show. The Government's later conduct admits perhaps some excuse ; for from 1829 onwards, to the war climax of 1835, and in the general upheaval that followed, it had little enough leisure for constructive social policy and planning. Tradition, however, engrossed by the anxieties of Government and Colony, and in its obsession with ' thieving ', has been blind to the real significance of the Labour Ordinance of 1828.

The ten years of the Neutral Belt allowed time at least for the British settlers, planted in 1820, to get over their first difficul-

---

[1] *Cape Col. Qn.*, pp. 219 ff.

ties,[1] thus considerably strengthening the Colony on the old Fish River Line. But to create and maintain a vacuum on such a wide frontier was an all but impossible task in the circumstances of the time, and the peace was by no means unbroken. All this time there were cattle-stealings enough, with ' reprisals ', and ' patrols ', and ' commandos ', making the frontier farmer's life highly dangerous. From 1822 patrols were active once more, and the example of Colonel Somerset's ' blundering commando ' in 1825, when twice in succession the ' wrong ' village was destroyed, with loss of life, deserves to be noticed.[2] The neutral territory, having been treated as the ' ceded ' territory, gradually filled up—from both sides, it is true. Xosa chiefs reoccupied parts of the Kat River area, where, though it makes little showing on a map, the country is exceedingly attractive —being not one confined valley, but rather a *strath* with a whole series of ' glens ' running off it. Farms were granted to colonists in equally attractive country about the Koonap, the ' predatory habits ' of the Kafirs being the warrant for fresh European encroachments, till by 1829 the idea of a neutral belt died, by the definitive annexation of the more important part of the area to the Colony. With this there came a very climax of unrest, with ' renewed ' and ' extensive depredations ', in which all thought of constructive regulations for the establishment of law and order gave place to the more immediately pressing considerations of a state of virtual war. By 1829 it was clear that all other matters would have to await the firmer establishment of some kind of settled order on the frontier, where direct contact of the races was fully renewed; conditions were much the same as before 1819.

In this new crisis Maqomo, the regent for Gaika's heir, Sandile, appeared as the arch-enemy. It was now the turn of Gaika's people to be broken like those of Ndhlambi, whereas he himself had served as a protégé and make-weight against the Colony's more immediate neighbour ; there was none now to fill Gaika's old rôle as the Colony's ally. It was by no means only that the new European farms offered wider opportunities for the Kafirs to ' indulge ' in cattle-stealing, still less, as is always suggested, that General Bourke's milder measures proved too strong a temptation to lawlessness. Though Maqomo, for example, had been ' allowed to creep back ' into the Kat River country, his position was highly insecure, whereas the European

---

[1] See *Cape Col. Qn.*, ch. ix.   [2] Cory, ii, 237–8.

annexations were sufficiently definite to confirm the Kafirs in the belief that, as a later missionary put it, the white man ' conquered only in order to dispossess '.

It tends to be forgotten, also, that at this time the Kafirs were suffering increased pressure on two fronts. To the northeast the Chaka wars had the whole country in a ferment, the Xosas being directly involved in the disorder by the irruption among them of refugees like the Tembus and Fingos. Against their raids—supposed to be by Chaka himself—British troops and colonial commandos penetrated between 1826 and 1828 far beyond the Keiskama, to the Kei and the Umtata.[1] Significantly enough, the immediate occasion of decisive action against Maqomo, who had earned grace to be left unmolested for nine years, was a raid he made, not on the Colony itself, but on certain newcomers, the Tambookies. No doubt it was inconvenient to have the Bantu fighting each other so near the colonial frontier, but this clearly was an internal feud among themselves. It was natural enough for Maqomo, doubtful as his tenure was in face of the Colony, to seize on quarrels among the refugee Tambookies to strike a blow against these fresh invaders of his shrinking pasture-lands.[2] Now the cup was full. For when, in 1828, colonial expeditions entered Kafirland to forestall the danger of attack by the Zulus, the unfortunate Tambookies,[3] in flight before the ' Fetcani ', who in turn were victims of Chaka himself, had thrown themselves upon the colonial protection. The dignity of the Government was involved, and, on 6 February 1829, the Colonial Secretary instructed Colonel Somerset to punish the ' atrocity and insolence of Maqomo's proceedings, the well-grounded conviction that he has long forfeited any claim to favourable consideration having at length determined His Excellency to take steps for ridding the Colony of the neighbourhood of this most troublesome and dishonest chief '.[4] Early in May the necessary steps were taken, with the inevitable kraalburnings, and impounding of cattle, and Maqomo was driven out, to find new homes for his people as best he might, among his friends and neighbours farther east.

[1] Cory, ii, 344–363.
[2] ' The Tambookie Chief had planted some kraals near the sources of the Koonap ' (Cory, ii, 380).
[3] In July 1825 the missionary Brownlee writes of a ' third ' attack on the Tambookies, either by Mantatees or ' Fetcani '.
[4] Cory, ii, 380.

This chief, Maqomo, who figures largely in frontier history for many years to come, was by all the evidence one of 'nature's gentlemen', with a great faculty for gaining goodwill, if not respect and esteem. In his misfortunes, his first stalwart champion was the nearest missionary, the Rev. John Ross, of the Glasgow Missionary Society, some of whose pleadings are extant.[1] In 1832 he returned for a time to his 'old haunts', with the surprising but express permission of Colonel Somerset, 'who had always been indulgent towards Maqomo'.[2] In later years bluff and good-hearted Harry Smith agreed for once with Somerset, and was obviously fond of this 'most troublesome and dishonest chief', frequently treating him with marked indulgence.[3] When in 1835 Sir B. D'Urban pronounced Maqomo, and many more, 'irreclaimable savages', one of the missionaries' ladies protested: 'If only he could meet Maqomo!' Still later, even after, like so many of the chiefs, Maqomo had taken badly to the white man's fire-water, Captain Stretch was known in the Cape Parliament for his devoted attempts to redress some of his wrongs. Finally, among his own people his memory is still green, and Xosa bards make invocation, to this day, 'By Maqomo!'

But, whatever his personal qualities, Maqomo's star was an unlucky one, and it is abundantly clear that the cause of all his trouble was the natural desire to keep his land. It may well be that it was from his senior, Maqomo, that the younger Paramount Sandile learnt to pronounce: 'The patrimony of a chief is not cattle. It is land and men.'[4] Though his plea, on the eve of ejection in 1829, to be taken under colonial orders, need not be taken seriously,[5] Maqomo clearly had reason for desperation like that which drove Gaika, before him, to beg, quaintly, to be given lands—and peace—*in England*.[6] As his missionary, Mr. Ross, pointed out in an interview with Sir Lowry Cole, colonial commandos often 'recovered' more cattle than they had lost, and by making one tribe pay for the theft of another, set tribe against tribe. Though the Government constantly demanded that the chiefs should punish raiders, Maqomo was

---

[1] Copies of Notes and Letters in Philip MSS.   [2] Cory, ii, 451.
[3] E.g. Cory, iii, 228. Captain Stretch in 1836 once says, 'Smith can refuse Maqomo nothing'.
[4] Quoted by Walker, p. 119.
[5] Mr. Ross wrote on 23 April 1829, to Colonel Somerset, on Maqomo's behalf, requesting 'a section of land where he may be under your hand and receive orders in all affairs from yourself'.
[6] Cory, ii, 350.

chastised for punishing the Tambookies. With Bantu logic, Maqomo retorted that magistrates were not punished when colonial wrong-doers escaped.

Above all, the disingenous treaty of 1819 was now bearing its fruit. When on the expulsion of Maqomo the Governor and Captain Stockenstrom hit on the plan of filling up the vacant Kat River lands with Hottentots—thus doing a tardy measure of justice to the Hottentots at Kafir expense, while at the same time planning to make them a ' buffer ' against the Bantu—it was not to be wondered at that the idea of three thousand Hottentots exhausting the carrying capacity of the district seemed extravagant to the overcrowded tribes beyond. The belt had never really been ' neutral ' to the colonial authorities, and it was precisely in this area that the boundary was left ill-defined.[1] Maqomo had been undisturbed for nine years, but the uncertainty about the frontier line was sufficient, on the one hand, to give the Government a pretext for his ejection, on the other to give Maqomo a very real sense of grievance. According to Mr. Ross, moreover, those expelled included fragments also of Gaika's people, and since Gaika was in 1819 the ally of the Colony, Maqomo had further reason to complain that, if indeed this land was forfeit—which he refused to understand—then, ' though his father Gaika, and his chiefs, had accompanied the colonial forces against Ndhlambi, after Ndhlambi was defeated they deprived them of their country as if they had been the offenders '.[2] A missionary sums up :

' We used Gaika as long as he served us. When he failed to conquer Ndhlambi we did so ourselves and *then took Gaika's country.*' [3]

Finally in 1833, Maqomo was once more ejected from a corner of the Kat River valleys, whither he had returned with the sanction of Colonel Somerset—even though it was admitted that

[1] Of the establishment of Fort Beaufort to guard the ' frontier ' (and to ' watch ' Maqomo) Dr. Philip writes from the spot in 1830, that it is as much use to protect the alleged frontier ' as Perth would be as a fort to protect Blair in Atholl from invasions from the north '. Following the definition which annexed a large part of the ' Neutral ' Territory in 1829, Colonel Wade in 1833 made a further ' rectification ' which ' cut off from Kafirland the beautiful site of the present Lovedale missionary institution, and several square miles of fertile land now in possession of the Fingos ' (Theal, ii, 55). It was not only Maqomo who suited himself about the line of the boundary.

[2] MS. report by J. Fairbairn of an interview with Maqomo, 1830.

[3] MS. notes on Ross's negotiations.

his faithful dealing with thieves ' gave no ground for complaint '. Not without reason, ' Maqomo's heart was very sore about the land ; the subject always set him on fire '. [1]

Meantime, the expulsion of Maqomo did little to bring peace —as how could it ?   On 2 January 1830, Sir Lowry Cole, writing to Sir George Murray in Downing Street, regretted that Kafirs were ever allowed to re-enter the ' Ceded ' Territory ;   having been allowed back, they have ' gradually occupied the best part of it ', and ' have claimed the occupation more as a matter of right than of sufferance '.   In recent months, moreover, of 5,000 cattle stolen not more than 1,500 were recovered by patrols.[2] Hence, to bar further encroachments, the Government had tried the experiment of planting Hottentots in the ' vacant ' land.[3] To this Murray replied on 6 May 1830, regretting the presence of the Kafirs, but definitely discountenancing forceful expulsion, though ' misconduct ' was ' to be punished immediately '.   To this Lord Goderich added (26 May 1831) a suggestion that the territory be used ' for the general purposes of settlement ', farms to be *sold*, not granted, only to Englishmen and Hottentots, and on no account ' to the boers of the Colony '.

[1] Evidence of Chief Botman in 1836, quoted Cory, ii, 398, *note* ; also Cory, ii, 451, and iii, 52.

[2] These allegations of numbers stolen must be taken *cum grano salis*.   In an unfenced country, full of wild beasts, all losses were habitually ascribed to ' Kafirs '.   See also p. 242, *note*.

[3] The Kat River Settlement was entirely a Government venture, unprompted by missionaries.   In this connexion, indeed, Cole made his well-known attack on Dr. Philip, who was to be ' kept out ' of the Kat River as ' it is to be feared, more a politician than a missionary '. The Hottentots themselves, however, ' called ', and brought in James Read and the L.M.S., obliging the Governor to send his own nominee as an afterthought.   Mr. Read's appointment was confirmed by Philip, on his return from England, on the ground that ' the hatred of the colonists against him was not from the moral obliquity into which he had been led (before his suspension 10 years earlier), but for his uncompromising stand against Oppression '.   Read, on this account, was *persona grata* also with the Kafirs—an important consideration in a settlement planted in ' Kafir ' land.   The Hottentots, thus ' reinstated to the rights of British subjects, and to a place of residence denied them within the limits of the old colonial boundary ', (Brownlee's Report, Dec. 1830) did very well.   Missionaries described the foundation of the settlement not only as a blow aimed against the L.M.S. but also as a ' popular ' act to disarm critics of the Government's treatment of Maqomo.   It succeeded, however, both in keeping peace with the Kafirs, and also in retaining Hottentot loyalty to the Colony in 1835 (*Cape Col. Qn.*, pp 239–42).

Measures and precautions were equally vain. Depredations continued, and lost nothing in the telling by frontiersmen. The result of firmer action was, indeed, some bad attacks of ' nerves '. In September 1829 the Governor had to dash to the frontier, only to reach the conclusion that ' a coalition to invade the Colony never entered into the contemplation of the chiefs '.[1] On New Year's Day, 1832, a Sunday, Colonel Somerset rode hurriedly to the Kat River to find the Hottentots quietly at church, whereas the Boers, hearing that the Hottentots were about to attack them, were mobilizing and preparing to ' get in first '.[2] The position of the tribes themselves was pitiable. In their unsettled state, one chief complained, they ' had no security that the place they were in to-day would be theirs to-morrow '.[3] In 1832 an L.M.S. missionary, Kayser, was ' sent to be near Maqomo, though the way Maqomo is moved from pillar to post by the Government makes it impossible yet to establish a regular mission in his country, as he desires),[4]—and impossible, it may be added, to make any serious advance in the task of education and of civilization. A year later, 2 November 1833, the missionary James Clark, now moved to the Keiskama, wrote of the effect of the expulsions from the ' Ceded ' Territory :

' There is no doubt they will be quarrelling among themselves about the want of pasture ; as they are now thronged upon each other, their cattle will be in such great numbers that the first drought they will find themselves poor and dying with hunger.'[5]

In all these years there is really no hint of measures calculated in any way to further the essential problem of how to govern this frontier. Patrols, commandos, and the ' clearing ' of any number of Zuurvelds, did nothing whatever to establish the authority of law and ordinary civil government. At this time the Cape was feeling the full force of the anti-Slavery Movement, and old-fashioned Boer farmers were unwilling to submit tamely

[1] Cory, ii, 393.
[2] Read to Philip, 3 Jan. 1832.
[3] Philip's Notes on Conversation with ' one of Gaika's sons ' in 1830.
[4] Philip's Report to L.M.S., Sept. 1832.
[5] It has some significance that this extract is from the mass of evidence, much of it from the L.M.S., that reached the Colonial Office in 1835 (P.R.O. *Papers relating to the Kafir War*, 1835). There is evidence, not sufficiently complete to detail, that years of unusual, perhaps despairing, unrest on the frontier were often also years of drought—1834 for one.

to the ' reform ' and eventual abolition of slavery, resenting even more laws which threatened to make Hottentots their legal equals.[1] The Bantu themselves feared that they would be ' broke up as the Hottentots were '.   No society could long stand such a state of tension.

[1] *Cape Col. Qn.*, cc. xv, xvi.

CHAPTER VII

THE PHILANTHROPISTS TAKE A HAND

A T the eleventh hour an attempt was made to avert the impending disaster. The drive towards some real policy for a settlement on the frontier came originally not from governors, or from colonists, but from the ' Philanthropists '. The missionaries had good reason to fear that the Bantu would suffer the fate of the Hottentots before them, and be reduced to landless serfdom like that of Fingos and other refugees who, even then, were competing with their Hottentot converts and ' under-cutting ' wages.[1] The missionaries knew also that the restlessness of the tribes was due to the pressure they were suffering. After his first journey through ' Kafirland ' proper, in 1830, Dr. Philip wrote advising the Paris Missionary Society to avoid Kafirland :

' The Caffre frontier has been for some years in a very troublous state. Since 1812, three districts have been taken from that nation and added to the Colony (the last not later than 1828). In consequence of these curtailments the Caffres have been driven back upon the territory that is still left to them, and several of the chiefs, with their people, are without any fixed residence ; and while they profess themselves willing to receive missionaries they profess they cannot protect them nor afford them the opportunity of instructing their children by settling in any one place.' [2]

More generally Philip commented later :

' Individually, savages may be as rational (as far as their observation goes) as Europeans, but it is in union and government that they

---

[1] *Cape Col. Qn.*, p. 253.

[2] In the first instance the Frenchmen went to the Bechuana, but on the advent of Moselekatze transferred to Basutoland. In 1833 Dr. Philip was similarly called upon to advise the American Board of Missions, and it was on his suggestion that the Americans shortly after settled in Natal.

lack the justice and lawfulness of civilized nations. The power of
the chief . . . tends to express force rather than justice. But without
a religious basis for their civilization they use their knowledge only
to rob their neighbours and then lose all again in marauding expeditions.
When men have no settled homes . . . it is easy for them to desert the
means of instruction on any provocation.'

The first hint that Dr. Philip, the guiding and ruling spirit
of the Philanthropists in South Africa, was to transfer some of
his vigilance to Bantu affairs, came very soon after his long visit
to England, whither he had gone, in 1826, to put the case for the
legal protection of the Hottentots before British rulers and
people. Returning to Cape Town on 7 September 1829, he
found news awaiting him from the inland stations which led
him, on 4 January 1830, to set off on a five months' journey
to the interior. With his trial for libel pending, he was now no
longer *persona grata* in the Colony, and to Fowell Buxton he
wrote confidentially (5 January) noting the change in public
feeling from the days when he had been a protagonist in the fight
with Lord Charles Somerset.[1]   About the same time he wrote to
Mrs. Buxton (24 December) : ' Our great people here know that
everything is not yet just as it should be on that (eastern) frontier
and have some dread of an exposure. My journey, however,
is purely missionary, and beyond the duties of a missionary it
is not my intention to go.' Certainly he adhered to his intention
of moving cautiously. Two years later, in September 1832, he
set out once more, to spend a long hot summer travelling, this
time both east and north, and it was only after his return to Cape
Town in March 1833, that, armed with fuller knowledge, Dr.
Philip entered the fray in real earnest.

Even on the earlier journey, in 1830, his observations are
far more than a mere tourist's impressions ; four times already he
had been in Albany (in 1819, 1821, 1823 and 1825), and in 1825
far beyond it to the north. Very few officials or colonists, and
no governor of them all, had seen as much of South Africa,
and few had a wider range of correspondents. Entering Kafirland, his traveller's instinct led him at once to appreciate the
significance and the beauty of the land itself—the country towards
the Katberg and the Amatolas.

' Since I left Fort Willshire I have been travelling in the finest country
I have ever seen. I do not know how to describe it better than by
requesting you to fancy to yourself all the riches and beauty of the

---

[1] *Cape Col. Qn.*, cc. xiv and xv.

finest English scenery spread over the barren mountains, deep valleys and picturesque ravines of the Scotch Highlands. I do not wonder that the Caffres are a cheerful people, their mountains and valleys are quite inspiring. Everything in this country is divine, except the habitations of the human race.'

Of the Bantu themselves he wrote :

' The Caffres are not the savages one reads about in books. They are intelligent and are not afraid of conversing with strangers ; they are, moreover, well acquainted with their own history and study mankind, if not books ; at ten years old, they are politicians ! . . . They have humour and are clever at giving characteristic nicknames ; they are not generous, but they say they are poor. They acknowledge the white man's superiority in science and arts, but do not individually feel inferior to those they meet ; though they despise the contempt of the colonists, yet it rankles in their minds and degrades them in their own estimation.'

Like the ' Victorians ' after him, Dr. Philip attached a deal of importance to dress, going so far as to make the adoption of European clothing a mark and test of civilization. The men in general, he finds, go almost naked, but ' they have their points of delicacy '. Of the many chiefs he saw, he remarks : ' They do not all adopt European dress entirely, because all their people could not afford to do so, and they would alienate their sympathy.'[1]

The ' romantics ', Dr. Philip admits, may have ' exaggerated Caffre virtues ', and ' between the world of the European and the world of the Caffre there is a great gulf ', which neither can cross without a thorough knowledge of the other's language. Yet Philip and his party go unarmed, and ' the Caffres have made no attempt to steal our oxen though they were left untied '. This suggests the missionary's comment : [2]

[1] ' It is customary for them ' Dr. Philip notes ' to dress when they dine with British officers or people. Then they are immaculate. At interviews they wear skins '. Referring to the first missionary and to Dr. van der Kemp's having ' gone amongst the Caffres, wearing their clothes and eating their food ', Philip thinks this did ' great good '. ' You might expect criticism of this practice from colonists ', but he is surprised at Lichtenstein in the *Quarterly Review* being so ' unphilosophical '. Van der Kemp's ' successor ' he adds 'made a fool of himself by wearing skins when the Caffre chiefs themselves would have worn black coats '.

[2] Dr. Philip's custom on tours was to write a full account of his doings and impressions and send these to Mrs. Philip to be kept for future use and reference. From stations in the Colony he posted instalments as letters ; when he left posts behind him he kept a ' Journal '.

'The Caffres have not only gained nothing by their intercourse with the colony but they have greatly deteriorated. In the earliest contact in the Zuurveld there were no commandos to rescue stolen cattle . . . only petty thefts. They have acquired no arts from us, they have borrowed none of our agricultural processes. . . . The farmers have done nothing for them. . . . Their manner of life and their superstitions are the same. But stealing is more common. . . . Many of them, particularly their chiefs, have been ruined by violent spirits. They have had the vices of civilization grafted on. . . . Only the missionaries have done them any good, trying to civilize them by understanding them . . . and they have so far been limited. The value of missionary labour begins to be appreciated. The missionaries are respected, but they have been more useful as a protection than as seminaries. . . . On the other hand, nine-tenths of the settlers are opposed to the civilization of the Caffres.'

So far Dr. Philip shows himself the observant traveller. But there are glimpses in the Journal also of the missionary statesman who applied what he saw to his judgment of official policy. As he travelled he interviewed a large number of chiefs including the Queen Mother, Sutu, with her minor heir Sandile, and the big brothers (or wicked uncles) Maqomo and Tyali. The burden of their complaint was almost exclusively of the loss of their lands, of the wrong done by the treaty of 1819, and of faulty or corrupt interpreters ; Gaika neither had the power, nor dared, to give away the land of other chiefs—no more right, Philip comments, than the King of England to cede the property of his subjects—and in the end he was bereft of his own land. ' At the end of the conversation Maqomo and Tyali told us they hoped the missionaries would help them by representing their grievances to the Government, but we refused to interfere.' Dr. Philip, however, drew his own conclusions. Gaika had been a mere tool in the hands of the Government. ' The borders were modified at the caprice of military men. . . . What Boer would stand it ? ' More emphatically, though of this the chiefs seem to have said little, by the evidence of his own eyes he was moved to indignant condemnation of the effect of commandos, in which ' the love of enterprise among the soldiers who would otherwise die of ennui has found an outlet ' :[1]

' The thieves on the borders have been represented as those who have been robbed in the interior and brought down to the frontier by their necessities. This is not the fact. The people who infest the bush

---

[1] He seems to vouch for one official by whom the Kat River was ' discovered ' to flow into the Fish, not, as was supposed, into the Keiskama.

on the frontier are those who have been robbed by the colonial commandos. This was the case with the Bechuanas I met at the Cradock (Orange) in 1825, and it is now the case on the Eastern frontier. . . . Some of these commandos have taken ten or sixteen thousand head of cattle from the Caffres. . . . Nineteen out of twenty who have been plundered were innocent. . . . .

' Stockenstrom stated [1] that he could mention fifty cases when Boers had gone on commando *having lost no cattle* . . . says, too, it is exceedingly difficult to trace spoors, but Somerset and others can do it in any quantity when they lead to a *kraal* that has good cattle in it.'

This statement is taken from a private letter and was never submitted as a public charge. Making some allowance for exaggeration, it is still a heavy indictment.

Some two years later, September 1832, while Dr. Philip was himself once more at the Kat River Settlement, some horses were reported ' stolen by Caffres '. Spoor-finders followed into Kafirland without success. Three or four days later the animals were found grazing in a corner of the location—not stolen at all. ' What ', he asks, ' if Boers had made the same mistake ? ' . . . 'All losses ', he continues, ' tend to be made good at the expense of the first Caffre cattle met with ' . . . but, ' Caffres thus losing property have no remedy at all '—and, as he had pointed out many years earlier, in 1824,[2] a pastoral people, deprived of their herds, ' have no resources left and inevitably betake themselves to the thickets and attempt to live by plunder '. Yet, and so Dr. Philip summarizes the impression left by the tour in 1830 :

' Such is the system that is now followed, that I can see nothing before the Caffres but slavery or extermination (meaning, as usual, extrusion from their lands) if they are not educated. Education would teach them that their true interest is to be at peace with the colony and the folly of resistance, raise them above stealing, and fit them for coming under the colonial Government. Such as have been at the mission stations prefer the Government of the colony to that of their chiefs. Many are now leaving Lovedale and the Chumie to settle in the neutral territory and among the farmers. . . . Their country is already courted. There are numbers of rapacious individuals who have set their hearts upon it.

' Slander and defamation, and the injuries done them by the Colonists, have already done their work, and their slanderers are now waiting an opportunity to excite a quarrel that will furnish a pretext to the Government to drive them from their lands, when they hope to share their cattle and their land. In such a colony there are numbers of toadeaters, civil servants who want estates. These men are on the very borders, from them the Government secures all its information

---

[1] Cf. Cory, ii, 398.   [2] *Cape Col. Qn.*, p. 114.

respecting the Caffres, and they are incessant in their exertions to accomplish their objects. Frontier Boers, Field Cornets, magistrates, friends of magistrates want new grants of land, and these grants must be taken from the Caffres.'

' The English ' he remarks further ' have never pursued a wise and liberal policy in their colonies '. They have been too much guided by ' monopolists '. Painting an over-idyllic picture of Native life, he concludes :

' Why not leave them ? Let the military come to the Keiskama and no farther. . . . Were there but one man in Caffreland to tell the wrongs these people have suffered for the last thirty years from the British Government, he would rouse a spirit in England which would do more for them than all the assegais of their country from the Keiskama to Port Natal. . . .'

As a good citizen Dr. Philip was zealous in obtaining first-hand knowledge of his country's problems, but for a long time he kept these observations on the state of the eastern frontier to himself. For two years after this journey his trial for libel, and the Theopolis land dispute, were sufficient pre-occupation.[1] Occasionally, in private letters, he made some allusion to ' the bloody commandos ' (as to his friend Thomas Pringle in January 1831) ; but till his next tour at the end of 1832 there is little more about the Kafirs. By this time (September 1832) the Hottentots on the Kat River had learned to attribute their new-found freedom to Dr. Philip's championship ; now the Kafirs also looked to him ' to *get land* and redress of grievances for us '.[2] Dr. Philip for his part in his interview with Maqomo, Botman, and others, kept to safer topics, taking the occasion of their visit to an Infant School to read them a lesson on the importance of knowledge as the ' true source of English power and greatness '. ' The Gospel ' he comments ' is the same ', but in England it has a thousand years of growth and development behind it.

On 11 October 1832, in a letter to Miss Priscilla Buxton [3] from ' Buxton ', a village on the Kat River, Dr. Philip returned at last to the ' horrors ' of the commando system :

' The pretence is the predatory habits of the Caffres, stealing the cattle of the colonists. Any lying Boer has only to go to a military post and

---

[1] *Cape Col. Qn.*, c. xv.

[2] Maqomo, Philip says, wanted ' a missionary, but not a fool or a child '.

[3] Most of Dr. Philip's correspondence with Fowell Buxton was made through other members of the family.

say he has lost so many cattle. A commando is immediately got up. No affidavit is required, no proof as to the number said to be stolen. . . . . The first Caffre cattle the commando comes to, upon the *spoor* of the cattle, are seized. . . . If the Caffres resist they are shot dead upon the spot, as if they were dogs. On such *evidence* they have been declared to be a nation of thieves, robbed of their cattle, their only means of support, and from time to time of their country.'

Continuing, he points the contrast with the Hottentots, settled on the most exposed part of the frontier to protect the Colony from the Kafirs, who have no difficulty in recovering stolen cattle through and by the chiefs themselves :

' This is a fact which speaks volumes, which will fill the Government with astonishment . . . but to which *no* reply can be made. The Government at Home, after this *fact* is known will be wholly without excuse if a stop is not immediately put to the nefarious system of commandos.'

Indignation breaks out in this still quite private letter at the blatant one-sidedness with which the Frontier Problem was so continually regarded. Dr. Philip had been one of the first to stress for European farmers the economic evils of dispersion, and was never lacking in sympathy for their losses and sufferings. The fierceness of his criticism was directed against the only remedy hitherto attempted, and its utter disregard of elementary safeguards of justice,[1] the failure, for example, to require reasonable proof of losses sustained. There was neither civil control nor legal check upon the exclusively military treatment of what was in essence a social disorder, and unhappily events were soon to prove that it needed no Philanthropist to give the Bantu a sense of grievance.

Even after the tour of 1832, the Humanitarian protest was first made public, not by Dr. Philip himself, but by an eager though inexperienced fellow-traveller who knew less how to walk warily. Early in 1833, Dr. Philip returned from the far north to find the heather set on fire by articles contributed to the *Commercial Advertiser* by the Hon. Alex. Bruce (a ' descendant of the Kings of Scotland ') who had returned to the Colony

---

[1] Philip's Journal for October 1832 vouches for a story that in 1828 a commando under Colonel Somerset, finding three branded cattle with one of the chiefs, confiscated the whole herd. The ' three ' were afterwards ' proved ' to have been obtained by an exchange with a trader.

B.B.B.

G

from the Kat River some months earlier. Dr. Philip had learned in his struggle on behalf of the Hottentots that the case must rest ' on generals rather than on particulars ',[1] but his aristocratic colleague, ' a stranger who had merely galloped round the country for three weeks ', plunging into controversy, only succeeded in raising a storm as a ' maligner ' of the colonists. In Grahamstown on his way back in January, Dr. Philip supported the *Grahamstown Journal* in its demand for a ' full investigation ' of Bruce's charges ; he would have evidence from missionaries on the spot, as well as from discharged soldiers of the Cape Corps (Hottentots), on the ' whole trend of policy since 1819 '. Sir Lowry Cole decided that ' the case scarcely called for an investigation '; ' it had been refuted ' already, and, coming from such a source, could command no serious attention.[2]

What the next steps were is not clear in detail. When Dr. Philip was thinking hardest, he seems to have written least [3] —but of the trend of his activities there is no doubt. There was obviously little to be done with or through Sir Lowry Cole, and, as Frontier policy was the special concern rather of the Secretary of State, Philip made his appeal to Fowell Buxton. In any case a change of Governor was in the wind,[4] and now was the time to get the ear of Downing Street. On 7 March, Andries Stockenstrom [5] sailed for England, taking with him

[1] *Cape Col. Qn.*, p. 163.
[2] Cory, ii, 424.
[3] Cf. *Cape Col. Qn.*, p. 138, for a similar lull in correspondence after Philip's Bethelsdorp discoveries in the end of 1821. Some letters he must have written in 1833 are missing from the Philip MSS.
[4] Philip writes to Stockenstrom as early as 13 January 1833 hoping for fuller co-operation with the ' next governor '.
[5] The relations of Philip and Stockenstrom at this stage are curious. In 1825 the two had made friends and come to an ' understanding ' on Native policy (*Cape Col. Qn.*, p. 213). After Philip's return from England he seems to make only one, unkind, reference to Stockenstrom—warning Pringle against him (Jan. 1831). Now Stockenstrom was thinking of resigning and of a trip to England, and in October 1832 Philip wrote indicating that ' an introduction to Mr. Buxton would be undesirable. In England he should be independent.' Stockenstrom was quick to take a hint, and in November replied agreeing that as he and Buxton might be in agreement it would be well to avoid the appearance of ' collusion ' for the defeat of those who differed from them. On his Northern trip Philip seems to have mellowed, and on 13 January 1833 wrote cordially hoping to be in time to talk things over before he sailed. Finally on 7 March Stockenstrom sailed, armed both with his introduction from Philip to Buxton, and with a bundle of letters ' for 55 Devonshire Street '.

letters and an introduction to Buxton. In June and July 1833 there was some excitement in Cape Town about Cole's new *Commando Ordinance* (the 99th) ; on 10 July Miss Buxton is promised more documents bearing on the Commando system ; and in a letter begun on 21 September but finished only on 5 December, Miss Buxton replied to Philip :

' My father has been very well this year, and gained twelve pounds weight in the first twelve weeks after the Abolition of Slavery. He has taken a great holiday, I must say, but is now turning his mind a little to your part of the world, and your horrid commandos. *He has been with Mr. Stanley several times about them*, but begins to fear that little will be done without open war, and public opinion. Therefore, he is very anxious to make himself master of the subject before another session, and begs you to send him all the facts and authentic documents you can, without any delay.

The Governor's Ordinance was designed to deal with raids and disorders on the scattered Northern front of the Colony. Distances there were so great that farmers proved unwilling to serve on commando, and Cole felt it necessary to stiffen the law with penalties. Though it had been designed less for the East than for the North, the Ordinance alarmed the critics of commandos against the Kafirs, especially by its second clause which authorized any official, from the Civil Commissioner down to the provisional field-cornet, ' at all times of actual or threatened invasion, or for the protection of the colonists or their property, or when they shall otherwise deem it absolutely necessary ', to summon or, in effect, ' commandeer ' men for military service. It may be that Cole, who, by the time the Ordinance reached Downing Street, was himself in England, failed to distinguish between the needs of the Eastern and Northern frontiers. The evidence, however, with which Dr. Philip armed Mr. Buxton, was sufficient to warn Mr. Stanley of the danger of increasing the efficiency of the military machine.

In a memorandum, undated, but obviously, from its references, belonging to 1833, Dr. Philip reviewed the situation. The farmers' requests for the help of patrols, he pointed out, were unchecked by any need to make affidavit or furnish proof of the extent of their losses : the frequent patrols were impoverishing the Kafirs and therefore had the effect of provoking more of the thefts so much complained of. The experience of the Kat River showed the system to be as ' unnecessary as it is impolitic and unjust '. Indian parallels do not hold : ' From what parts of our Indian territory have the Indians been exterminated? . . . The friends of humanity will have no objection to the annexation of the Caffre country to-morrow, provided the people are not robbed of their cattle and deprived of their country'. He remarked further on the fact that there were so many traders (up to two hundred) in Kafirland, and that these went unprotected without suffering harm. Finally, a point forgotten by Sir B. D'Urban and others who complained that missionaries failed to give any warning of the outbreak a year later, Dr. Philip clearly foreshadowed ultimate resistance by the Kafirs, and inevitable war, 'since they will feel they may as well fall by the sword' if the present system is to continue.

These arguments seem to have prevailed. Commando service might be unpopular in the North, but the patrols on the Eastern frontier were active enough. On 9 November Mr. Stanley informed the Governor that the Commando Ordinance 'has been reserved for further consideration'[1]. On 15 November Sir Lowry Cole submitted his defence and explanation, but on 27 November the point was decided against him, and the Ordinance disallowed as from the 1 August 1834. This was not all. In his dispatch of 27 November to the new Governor, Sir Benjamin D'Urban, Stanley expressed the view 'that there may be something in the allegations' against the 'commando' system, which he considered 'brutal'. In consequence: 'It will now, of course, be incumbent upon you to devise such other measures as may appear calculated to protect colonists against unprovoked aggression.' To this end—and here Dr. Philip's constructive proposals are in evidence[2]—D'Urban was instructed to consider the propriety of stationing Government 'agents' on the frontier, with the practicability of annual presents, or salaries, for the chiefs, as a means to regulate and improve intercourse with the Bantu tribes, and a first step towards reform.

The onus was now upon Sir Benjamin D'Urban. The system was inherently vicious and already almost beyond reasonable

[1] The Secretary of State also asks for more information about Crown Lands, 'more particularly those in the Ceded Territory, which are understood to be better adapted for cultivation than the unappropriated land within the limits of the colony'.

[2] Cf. letter of 19 July (below, p. 90, note) and also D'Urban's dispatch of '9 June 1836', referring to the idea of 'an establishment' suggested as early as dispatch of 27 November 1833, and discussed with Dr. Philip 'as one versed in the subject of that dispatch and of its bearings and intentions'.

control ; but the Humanitarian contention which had moved
Stanley was eminently sound. It was not that innocent ' Kafirs '
were habitually wronged by cruel and vindictive reprisals ; but
that the whole policy of the frontier was stupid. Purely military
as it was, it could not in any case attain the only real end   a
well-ordered, settled *Society*.

CHAPTER VIII

THE NEGOTIATIONS OF PHILIP AND D'URBAN IN 1834

SIR BENJAMIN D'URBAN began his fateful term of office on 16 January 1834 by no means with the ' plaudits ' of the philanthropists.[1] Though he had been slow to take up the Kafir Question, from this point onwards Dr. Philip was industrious in following up what had been gained by Buxton's intervention. Throughout the critical year 1834, he laboured to keep the new Governor to the task of reconstruction assigned to him, but D'Urban's dilatoriness in action was fatal to his plans and hopes. On 20 January, within four days of the Governor's landing, Philip wrote to ask favourable consideration for the Griquas who ' with scarcely any exceptions are desirous of being included within the limits of the colony '. He respectfully asked D'Urban to give his attention to the full *memorandum* which he had submitted to the Acting Governor Colonel Wade in October 1833 (Ch. IV above). On 17 February he wrote to the L.M.S. :

' I am busy preparing notes for the governor, to assist him in coming to an opinion on the frontier system. He proposes to leave Cape Town next April to see and hear with his own eyes and ears, and to form a plan to remedy the evils so much deprecated. I sincerely hope he will be kept free of any colonial bias. All our hopes depend on the introduction of a different frontier system.'

A month later, on 13 March, Dr. Philip's notes were completed and submitted to the Governor in a memorandum of

[1] Dr. Philip wrote in dismay to Buxton : ' I see by the papers to-day (1 Sept. 1833) that our new Governor has left Demarara amidst the regrets of the colonists. I am almost in despair at this circumstance. Had they had public rejoicings on the occasion, I should have had more hope of him. " Oh, Lord ! how long " are we to have such men sent us as governors ? ' For Dr. Philip's comfort, however, the Governor's instructions (8 Nov.) expressly enjoined him at least ' not to propose or assent to any Ordinance whatever ' imposing on non-Europeans ' any disabilities or restrictions ' not equally applying to Europeans.

86

great length, recapitulating and elaborating with detail the
arguments already outlined in his letters to Mr. Buxton. The
effect of commandos and of patrols as hitherto practised, was,
in short, to create a constant state of alarm in the Kafir villages ;
instead of putting down ' thieving ', it made fresh robbers. At
the same time, the system was a temptation to unscrupulous
colonists, and bad men were attracted to the frontier by the
opportunities of plunder ; worthless horses were sometimes
purposely lost, and the indemnity for stolen animals was quite
oppressively heavy. Tribes in the immediate neighbourhood
might be the first to suffer, but the ' repercussions ' reached
far into the interior—adding to the commotion already caused
among the tribes generally by the ravages of the slave-trade.
Having detailed, further, the disputes about the lands beyond
the Fish River, Philip argued that these arose inevitably out of
Somerset's treaty with Gaika in 1819, and concluded with suggesting remedies. He would require an affidavit or other certificate
of the number of animals alleged to be stolen, and of their value
—with a penalty for deception.[1] More Hottentots might be
placed ' on land that would not satisfy 50 Boers ', so that a strong
force of Hottentots might easily be rushed to any point of disturbance. Finally, whatever might be done should be reduced
to ' something written '—that chiefs might know to what they
were committed, and that there might be an end to the ' fluctu-
ations ' of frontier policy universally complained of,[2] by which
the natives never knew from one Governor to another what was
the policy of the day.

To this long statement the Governor replied quite promptly ;
but, with an apparent desire for secrecy which is evident in all
his dealings with Dr. Philip, this note, with the whole of a series
of seven, extant, was written with his own hand :

Sir Benjamin D'Urban presents his compliments to Dr. Philip,
and is very much obliged by his communication of to-day.
Sir Benjamin D'Urban has for some time been grieved at the drought,

---

[1] In a letter to D'Urban in July, Philip maintains that ' depredations '
were ' much exaggerated '. Many farmers even then were ' in Kafirland itself ' and one, he instances, ' claimed double the number of
cattle he ever possessed ', as was ' proved by a reference to the landdrost's books : when detected, the man confessed his mistake, without
appearing in the slightest degree ashamed of his conduct '.
[2] Cf. Theal and Cory, *passim* : Philip elaborated this point in a
letter of 27 October 1834.

which has occasioned such distress along the frontier line ; but he has to-day more favourable news—and he hopes that the rains which have hitherto been but partial may have been more general.

Thursday, 20th March.

To the Rev. Dr. Philip

A long pause followed, of which Philip took advantage to prepare a further formidable series of documents with which to arm Mr. Buxton, who for his part made a fruitless endeavour in the same year to secure a Select Committee to investigate the policy pursued towards the native races of the Cape frontier.[1] Then at last the Governor woke up to remember the charge laid upon him by Mr. Stanley in the previous November :

Private

GOVERNMENT HOUSE
Saturday, 31 *May* 1834

SIR,

The time is now come for me to take into my most serious consideration the whole of the frontier system, and I have accordingly been for some days past devoting it to that important subject. In the process of this, the Memoir with which you had the kindness to favour me, has demanded my careful attention ; and thereupon I will request you (if it be not inconvenient to you) to call upon me on Monday next at half past one o'clock.

The enclosed was addressed to me the day after I had had the honour of an interview with Mr. Stanley and Mr. Ellis immediately before I left England.

In your Memoir you advert to a Paper which had been published in the ' Commercial Advertiser ', as deserving notice. I have not seen it ; if you can readily lay your hands on it, perhaps you will take the trouble to send it me for perusal.

Believe me to remain,
With great respect and esteem,
Sir,
Your very faithful, humble servant,
B. D'URBAN

---

[1] A mass of documents including Ross's evidence on Maqomo, a letter ascribed to the Chief Tzatzoe, and a long letter of his own to the American Board of Missions was posted apparently on 5 May, the postal charge being originally no less than £5 (*Cape Col. Qn.,* p. 58). Mr. Buxton got his Committee in 1835, and several of these papers are printed in the volume of *Evidence* (1836). In his own letter Philip distinguishes between ' patrols ' and ' commandos '. The patrol is purely military, with possibly a farmer guide, the commando is primarily a much larger mixed force of soldiers and burghers, bent usually on reprisals ; the term commando, however, is also used for small expeditions, seemingly well known and common, where farmers themselves acted together, without the formality of getting military help.

The interview that followed this letter was the first of a good many, and for two or three months relations between D'Urban and Philip were intimate, with much passing to and fro of letters, and even of private official documents. But the period of intimacy was very short—it was interrupted when Dr. Philip set out for the frontier on 13 August, to return only after Christmas within a few days of D'Urban's setting out to conduct the war, and it is clear that the two men never reached any real understanding. Discussion began on the question of the proposed new frontier ' system '. D'Urban's instructions (from Stanley, November 1833) had not only suggested the propriety of establishing ' agents ' on the frontier, but had authorized expenditure for the purpose—the rather inadequate sum of £600 for the payment of ' prudent and intelligent men '. Further consideration of the names of the proposed agents passed between the Governor and Philip.

Private and Confidential

18*th June* 1834

My dear Sir,

I am very much obliged by your letter of the 12th which I should earlier have acknowledged, but for much pressing public business.

Your remarks are, I am certain, very valuable, and you may rest assured that they are not—and will not be lost upon me.

You mentioned, the other day, the Name of a Person on the Eastern (or North Eastern) side of the Colony, whom you thought eligible for a *resident agent*, in Kafirland, and I made a note of his name at the time, but I cannot lay my hand upon it now, and it has escaped my memory. Be so good to inform me of his name and description. It was a person who you said was likely to have applied for some grant of land ?

I shall go to the Frontier (many thanks for your anxiety about me personally) as soon as I have disposed of two or three very important matters of business here, which I *must* see to myself before I quit the seat of Government. When that is done, the Weather and the Rains will be but secondary considerations (as such things ought to be where duty is to be done).

In the meantime I think I have instructed the authorities in that quarter cautiously, but effectually, so that they can get on for the present without me.

Very faithfully,
My dear Sir,
Yours,

B. D'Urban

In his reply next day Dr. Philip suggested that the new plan would meet with opposition not only from colonists but from ' higher quarters ' (meaning probably Colonel Somerset and the military authorities). An agent, he says, to gain the necessary respect, must be ' broad, educated, and a gentleman '. The Governor, Philip tells Mrs. Buxton about this time, ' has received my suggestions favourably, but nothing can be done till the Governor visits the frontier ',[1] action being delayed till the Governor should see conditions for himself.[2]

In these months of 1834, D'Urban freely consulted Dr. Philip about other points of the highest importance that were now forcing themselves upon his attention. One of these was the threatened modification of the Hottentot reforms of 1828 by a ' Vagrant Law ' which was introduced in the Council in May. In June Dr. Philip had an opportunity of calling the Governor's attention to a great influx of alarmed farm Hottentots to the Kat River. D'Urban on 22 June was able to report a favourable intervention in their behalf.[3] It is significant also that on 31 July D'Urban took an opportunity of delaying the

---

[1] Undated letter in Mr. J. G. Gubbins' collection.

[2] A month later (19 July), when wider issues had been opened— Dr. Philip returned to this point and suggested in detail that in Kafirland there would be *three* Agents, one with the Pato-Congo tribes in the South, one with the Gaikas (Maqomo) in the centre, and one with the Tambookies in the North. Of these one should be chief, with a salary of £500, two of them subordinates with £250 each ; £154 suggested by the Commandant is inadequate, but a total expenditure even of £3,000 would cost much less than ' armies '. The essentials of this plan were adopted a year or two later, when Dr. Philip's own name had become anathema to the Governor.

[3] A letter written by D'Urban 22 June 1834 :

Private   22 *June* 1834

MY DEAR SIR,
    The circumstances of the Hottentot families of Rudolff van Ender, Andries Andries and Hans Battercense (I . . . *words illegible* . . . Rennie of Hans Hans) who had migrated from Graaf Reynet to the Kat River in consequence of orders, real or supposed, attributed to two Field Cornets of the former district, were brought under my notice in the end of April by Capt. Campbell and Capt. Armstrong—and a strict Inquiry into this alleged proceeding which had caused so much distress to these unfortunate People, was immediately directed to be instituted, the result of which I am every post expecting, from the Civil Commissioner Mr. van Ryneveld.
    Capt. Campbell and Capt. Armstrong stated at that time that ' the whole of the land at the sources of the Kat River, intended for the free Coloured Inhabitants, had been already appropriated to them, and generally in small allotments, so that the whole Population was as dense as could be admitted '.
    He has, however, doubtless suffered these families to remain, and,

' Vagrant Law ' by asking for the opinions of the judges.[1] In the end he decided against the law, probably as a result of Dr. Philip's representations ; [2] it was an inestimable advantage to ' have the ear of the Governor ', as he put it, at this crisis in the fortunes of his particular protégés, the Hottentots.

The most engrossing subject at this time was, however, the increasingly serious discontent among the frontier Boers. Not only were they full of natural complaint about the insecurity of the frontier, but now, on top of the (alleged) ' vagrancy ' of the lately emancipated Hottentots and the Governor's hesitation about the ' Vagrant Law ', came the announcement that on 31 December 1834 all slaves were to be set free. As early as February the resident J.P. at Cradock reported ' ferment ' in his district, and that farmers were leaving the Colony, taking slaves with them.[3] Hardly had D'Urban and Philip parted after their first interview when D'Urban followed it up with a note :

Private and Confidential

Thurs. Mg., 12 *June* 1834

My dear Sir,

You will have in recollection my conversation of the other day with you ?

With reference to it, be so good to read this, and afterwards send it to me again.

Very sincerely yours,
B. D'Urban

' This ' was a letter of 7 June from Colonel Somerset, Commandant on the frontier. Its purport seems to have been the insecurity of the frontier, the ' contempt ' inspired in the Boers by the failure of the British Government to give protection, the impera-

as they do not seem to have been followed by others (which was at the time to be apprehended) I dare say there will be no difficulty about their being located.

I shall write about it immediately, as well as about relief being afforded them. But I expect to hear in the interim that all this has been already done under the orders of Capt. Campbell, and the Justice of Peace on the Kat River. I am much obliged to you for this, as I shall always be for any, information which you give, or may give me, and you may be assured that it will be held confidential.

Believe me,
Very sincerely yours,
B. D'Urban

To the Rev. John Philip, D.D.

[1] Theal, ii, 81. [2] *Cape Col. Qn.*, p. 243. [3] Cory, ii, 461.

tive need to strengthen the Cape Corps, and the threat of the
Boers that they ' would be obliged to leave that part of the
Colony unless they are protected '.

The same day (12 June) Philip returned Somerset's letter,
commenting that the complaints were not supported by detailed
evidence, pointing out also that Maqomo, already punished for
interfering with the Tambookies, could not in any case be concerned in troubles on the upper Koonap. The frontier is so
ill-defined that ' excuse me saying I have my suspicions that
they (complainants) are themselves in the Caffre country ';
there are ' disaffected ' Boers, he adds, ' occupying farms on
the Kye '. The tail of Philip's letter had a sting, a hint that
His Excellency warn colonists that a stranger was already on the
frontier collecting information for a Select Committee of the
House of Commons.[1]

The very day after he received this reply D'Urban wrote
off post haste to Somerset and to others on the borders. He
does not want, he says, to go himself to the frontier till August.
' There appears to exist a great alarm and excitement for which
I am at a loss to account.' He hopes it is not ' got up by the
Boers or others interested ' in discussions in the British Parliament, for which, he hears, *agents* are *now* collecting information.
' Be sure ', he concludes, ' that alleged robberies are *within the
proper and well-understood boundary of the colony* '. Within a
month, which was prompt for those days of no roads, reports
came back from the frontier, and D'Urban wrote to Philip :

Private and Confidential   14*th July* 1834
My dear Sir,

I told you the other day that I had some papers to send for your
perusal. They are herewith, and I will request you to return them to
me as soon as you shall have read them, because I want to have reference
to them in the course of the week (indeed on Wednesday).

No. 1 has reference to the subject of Mr. Read's letter to you of
10 June, returned herewith, being in original, and contains the result
of an investigation which I had directed to be made in April as to the
causes of the removal of Hottentot families from Graaf Reynet to the
Kat River.

No. 2 has reference to Mr. Read's other letter of which you were
so good to send me an extract, upon the ' emigration of inhabitants
beyond the border carrying with them slaves '.

The papers marked (*a*) in this packet will give you the result of
the inquiries set on foot by the Civil Commissioner thereon. (*b*)
will show you that this subject had my early consideration after my

---

[1] Who this was does not appear.

arrival. I am at a loss to conceive the cause of the alarm expressed
by the Rev. Mr. Munro and the Rev. Mr. Read in the extracts sent to
me in your letter of the 27th June. There is no official measure pending
inimical to the Caffres. A formal communication was made to their
assembled chiefs on 17th June from me, which I trust may have a good
effect—and the instructions which I have sent to the Civil Commissioner,
Commandant and Magistrates, are assuredly of a nature not at all to
warrant any such alarm, the tenour of them being to repress all violence
on the part of our own inhabitants, while, at the same time, due and
legal protection must be afforded to the persons and property of His
Majesty's un . . . and unoffending subjects living *within the proper
boundary* of the colony.

I must, however, apprise you that the amount of stolen cattle from
farmers in the districts of Albany and Somerset within the six months
preceding the middle of June has been in round numbers 900 head,
and of horses 100, and that by my last months (?) reports I see that
the robberies have been latterly attended with more than one attempt
at murder and great ill-usage of women.

I have not failed to avail myself of several of the suggestions in your
letters, where they have been applicable to the existing state of things
and you will always oblige me very much by giving me the advantage
of your future views.

Believe me ever, dear Sir,
Very sincerely yours,
B. D'URBAN

To the Rev. John Philip, D.D.

The enclosures included a report from a Mr. Rennie, a farmer
on the Baviaans River, who had just returned (29 June) from the
White Kei, and a letter of 27 June from the Civil Commissioner
(Campbell) of Albany. From these certain facts stand out
clearly. There were depredations, especially in Albany and
Lower Somerset, and, says Campbell, 'the idea that these are
fabricated for any purpose is absurd ; they are increasing if
anything', and extend to Grahamstown and Lower Albany,
'both of which have been free for some years'. On the other
hand, possibly as a result of the combined effect of these 'depredations', of shortage of farms in the Colony, and of Hottentot and
slave legislation, a good many farmers had undoubtedly taken
the risk of the 'Kafirs' and gone 'beyond the border'. Mr.
Rennie had heard that '1,200' Boers had crossed the Orange
River owing to severe drought in the Tarka ; more definitely,
he had found thirty-one families between the Swart and Wit
Kei, and twenty-one, he gathered, had crossed the boundary
for pasture—'eleven of them to form a permanent settlement'.[1]

[1] Obviously the 'trekker' Louis Trigardt and his friends. Cf.
Cory, ii, 461.

These Boers, moreover, had fifteen slaves with them, and one, to ' mak siccar ', had put his slaves in irons.

In more general terms this state of affairs is confirmed by the Civil Commissioner. There is and has been ' trekking ', and farmers could not survive the dry season without it—nor *will* they when the land beyond is taken up ; therefore the authorities wink at it, and in any case could not prevent it because on the border there are neither troops nor field cornets—the latter being chosen for their central position in the wards—and ' because ' (for what mad reason does not appear) notices warning farmers against trekking ' had to be sent in English which very few read or understand '. In the last two years, he adds, permanent emigrants have been filtering out from *western* districts—whether to evade the slave law he does not know.

The Governor's communication, which shows that even at this time he was not ' in Philip's pocket ', at once had Philip busy writing—obviously with great care ; so many drafts survive of letters dated between 15 and 22 July, that it is not clear which or how many of them reached Government House ; but the trend of his argument is quite clear. On 15 July Philip thanked the Governor for the opportunity given him of supplying information ' on the important matters now engaging Your Excellency's attention ', and asked for another day ' to look up his files '. Then he got to work, and at once seized on essentials commonly missed by both colonists and their historians : he puts no reliance on exact numbers, such as the ' 1,200 ' trekkers beyond the Orange River, but quotes a letter from the missionary Kolbe, (from Philippolis on 13 May), in support of the view that their numbers are certainly relatively large. In the north, he points out, the Griquas are peaceable and inoffensive, whatever the ' Caffres ' may be, and the troubles and difficulties are due ' solely to the advance of the Boers '. The only thing needed is to ' secure to the Griquas the possession of their country, freed from the annoyance and injuries they are now suffering '. ' Drought ', he holds, is no warrant or excuse for the Boer exodus ; ' I know of no *unoccupied* country on the borders of our Colony ', and drought hits the native inhabitants just as hard as the colonists ; farmers, in any case, ' have no business to keep 2,500 beasts while they pay the *opgaaf* tax on only 250 '. Let them, if they must habitually overstock, provide themselves with reserves ' *behind them* ' ; but ' for this they must have *paid*, and this is the sole reason for their present unjust and disgraceful practice—avarice is the motive . . .' Farms said now to be inadequate were granted quite recently, many of them only in 1828. A draft of 18 July continues :

The invasion of peaceable countries and the progressive extermination of their inhabitants cannot be connived at, much less sanctioned. Britain which has extinguished her Slave Trade and recently given twenty millions to procure freedom for her slaves, will no longer suffer her national honour to be tarnished, as it has been, by the system which has been so long pursued in this colony to gratify the avarice of the Frontier Boers. . . .

In 1809, and 1810, the Boers complained of the Caffres as they are now doing, and to gratify them the Zuurveld or Albany was taken from the Caffres. . . . In a few years the Caffres became as troublesome on the Fish River as they had been on the Zondag River. . . . It was next found that the Keiskama (was as bad) . . . and Maqomo and Gaika's Caffres were driven in 1829 from the Kat River and from behind the Gonap. All these invasions and those also on the Northern frontier were in the first instance preceded by permitting the Boers to cross the colonial boundary under the pretext that it was necessary to preserve their cattle from perishing. . . . After being allowed to roam about in the country of our neighbours for a few years—to make room for their children they found the actual possession of those countries necessary, and they were gratified in their wishes. . . .

When I was at the Caco (Gaga) Post in 1830 some hundreds of Boers had been applying for land in that district. Scarcely had they settled but they must have liberty to cross the boundary in dry seasons . . . that is, every season ; and if the Key was the boundary to-morrow, in seven years they would be on the Umtata.

From the whole of the Civil Commissioner's letter your Excellency must perceive that the laws are not enforced. One cannot, therefore, wonder at the contempt into which the British Government is *said* to have fallen among the Boers. That having sent a Government Order on so important a subject in the English language only, to men whom we *know to be ignorant of that language,* is no extraordinary instance of Frontier management. . . .

When your Excellency shall have time to settle the affairs of the Frontier on an equitable basis and when it shall be known that faithful men will be appointed over them, and supported in the discharge of their duty . . . when proper agents shall be appointed and proper relations entered into with the Frontier nations . . . and your Excellency already perceives what is to be done to remedy the evils of the old system . . . every difficulty will be overcome . . .

The Boers, like all ignorant people, just take as much as is given them. They acknowledge no other limit. When Government assumes a commanding aspect, no people on earth are more submissive. And it is lamentable to observe how for so many years their ruinous encroachments have been winked at, and even encouraged by the Frontier authorities. It is to this we are to look as to the spring of all the mischief. Your Excellency has a great work upon your hands, a work which involves, in it, the prosperity of the Colony and the preservation of the Tribes to a great extent beyond it, and I sincerely hope that Your Excellency, under the blessing of God, will be instrumental in effecting both.

This analysis of the fundamental causes of frontier troubles defies serious challenge. It may be that Dr. Philip tended to be more right in what he affirmed than in what he denied, and that at least he did not gauge the strength of the farmers' absorption in their own grievances. In picking out flaws and ' discrepancies ' in the reports from the frontier Philip may have been dialectically over-subtle. For example, he reiterated that figures of losses went all unchecked, taking no account of ' strays ' or of ' restored ' animals ; and that Somerset put the ' thieving ' in Upper Somerset, while Campbell put it in Lower Somerset or Albany ; yet the very discrepancies were evidence of sorts that there was general stealing and unrest. But making every allowance for the justness of the complaint of long-established European farmers that life on the frontier generally was intolerably difficult and dangerous, it remains that in seeing further and deeper into the causes of the unrest, and in his consistent emphasis on the need for civil administration rather than military (and militarist) ' handling ' of the Frontier Problem, Dr. Philip was a lonely prophet and pioneer. Most of the trouble, he insisted, arose from the weakness of a distant Government in Cape Town attempting to control a frontier where there was scarcely any civil administration at all.

But his case for a constructive policy broke down before the opposition of men who could not see beyond their own very real sufferings. Discontent was already so great that their movements were no mere casual migrations of a semi-nomadic people, but the beginning of a deliberate and voluntary exile. As Philip himself wrote a little later : [1] ' When I was on the Frontier in August and September all the talk was about *Boers leaving the Colony* '—with the addition, certainly, that they had hopes that ' the Governor would come and give them new farms beyond the Frontier '. This was the time of the so-called *Commissie* Treks (expeditions like that of Piet Uys, who in 1834 spied out the land towards Natal and brought back favourable reports), while other famous leaders of 1836, like Piet Retief, were known to be even then contemplating their great removal.[2] Only the diversion caused by the outbreak of war

[1] To Buxton, 1 January 1835.
[2] Walker, p. 181. Letters of Stockenstrom and others in 1836 and 1837.

in December 1834 has obscured the significance of events that were clearly the definite beginnings of the ' Great ' Trek itself.[1] In face of Dr. Philip's representations,[2] the Governor was much exercised about the emigration, and, having on 5 September drafted a memorandum himself, on the 10th he got a not too hopeful opinion from the Attorney-General, with a list of the laws nominally in force imposing penalties on emigration. On 12 September a Proclamation in the *Gazette* called attention to these old laws and expressly cancelled the temporary permission granted by Dundas in his Notice of April 1828 (above, p. 45).

But now the preparations for the Great Trek sank out of sight for a time, being overshadowed by a crisis in relations with the ' Kafirs '. The misinterpretation of events that preceded the war of December 1834 may be attributed to the almost congenital blindness of many South Africans to the possibility that ' Kafirs ' can have grievances, if misguided Europeans are not so foolish as to draw their attention to them. It is still an article of faith (to be quoted like the Bible against modern Churchmen critics of a reactionary measure like the ' Colour Bar ' Act of 1926) that the war of 1834–5, *a fortiori* the Great Trek and all the fatal divisions of later South African history, were due, never for a moment to the crudeness of a whole generation of frontier policy, but primarily to the ' interference ' of ' missionaries '. Words written by Colonel Somerset in the end of 1834 were quoted with complete satisfaction in the ' Colour Bar ' controversy of 1926, in denunciation of ' A New Philip Party '[3]:

' As a result of the pains taken lately by evilly disposed persons to put into the minds of the Kafir chiefs the idea that they are oppressed by the Government, a feeling of enmity has been aroused in them which must be seen to be believed.'

Now, Colonel Somerset, as Commandant on the Frontier, and virtually second-in-command in the Colony, ought to have been taken into the Governor's confidence in his plans for reform. Owing, however, to the extraordinary secretiveness of D'Urban in his intercourse with Dr. Philip in these fateful months, neither Somerset nor anyone else knew that Philip's expedition was a

[1] See references in Eybers, p. 145. The actual documents of 1834 were not available in Cape Town Archives some time ago.
[2] In letter of July 1834, and *via* Buxton as early as 1832 or 1833.
[3] *Die Burger*, May 1926.

B.B.B.   H

definite ' mission ' authorized by the Governor himself to prepare
the way for his own coming : ' My proposal ' (to go ahead of
the Governor to gather fuller information), Dr. Philip wrote
in a later ' Narrative ', ' was warmly embraced, and being told
that the Governor would certainly leave Cape Town by mid-
September, according to agreement I left Cape Town on 13
August 1834 '. Philip, therefore, far from ' interfering ', was
so much in the Governor's confidence that on 12 August, ' in
the bustle of leaving ', he was still receiving highly confidential
documents to keep him apprised of all that was going forward.[1]
Dr. Philip himself was reserved about the important part he
played, letting himself go only to those at a safe distance.[2]
To the L.M.S. on August 13, very near if not on the day
of his departure (and to a Director in the same words), he
wrote :

' I am setting off (early) that I may meet the Governor on the Kat
River, to try, if possible, to introduce a new system. . . . I am the
only person in the Colony who knows the Governor's mind on this
subject, but this is a circumstance that *must not be known here*, and I
must not anticipate too much till I see how he will be able to stand in
the midst of all his civil and military authorities, who will do all in their
power to shake his personal resolution and (. . .) do everything to
defeat us in our object.'

James Read, too, was unaware of Philip's rôle as adviser to the
Governor. Knowing as early as April of D'Urban's intended
visit, Read wrote both on 5 and 13 August, welcoming Philip
to Kafirland, but utterly preoccupied with the question of
Hottentot ' vagrancy ' and never mentioning the Kafirs, as he
must have done had he had reason to imagine that Philip was
coming on a semi-official, though informal, embassy.

Philip's letters from the frontier, both to D'Urban himself

---

[1] News of an alarming murder in Hintza's country having reached
him, D'Urban at once wrote :

Tuesday, 12 Aug.

MY DEAR SIR,
I send these for your perusal, when you have read them be so good
as to return them, for I have not (as I intended) second copies of them.
Very sincerely yours,

To the Rev. John Philip, D.D. B. D'URBAN.

[2] The L.M.S. in London got impatient at times. On 21 July
1834 Philip was told by Ellis the Secretary : ' You will not allow your
correspondence with that respectable individual (T. F. Buxton !) to
interfere with your communications with the Directors.'

and to Buxton, Pringle,[1] and others in England, show that while
there he was conscientiously gleaning information about frontier
conditions, but keeping very ' dark ' to all parties. ' If the
missionaries were left in ignorance on the subject (of any connexion with the Governor) ', he writes later, when D'Urban
himself was taking credit that the chiefs knew, through Philip,
of his ' favourable intentions ', ' I could not have made it known
to the chiefs, as the missionaries were my interpreters '. Philip
was hopeful of the reform that was to come ; but except that
the Governor contemplated, or even recognized, the need for a
' new system ', there was, of course, nothing definite for him
to ' communicate '. It may be that, under the circumstances,
he travelled with a consequential air ; and the chiefs, being full
of real grievances, may have been led to conclude that it was not
for nothing that an important visitor of this kind came talking,
as he was bidden, of the prospects of a changed frontier system.
They naturally welcomed him, and were for some time after
his visit on their very best behaviour. Perhaps Dr. Philip himself
under-estimated rather than exceeded his warrant, and from
first to last regarded his mission as an informal attempt to ' prepare
a way ' for the Governor by getting more complete information.
D'Urban's own later account [2] gives the journey more official
significance than Philip himself ever attached to it :

'I had in the middle of last year caused communications to be
made to the chiefs [3] . . . expressive of my disposition to enter into a
new order of relations with them, upon a footing which could not but
be advantageous to them . . . (though) its carrying out must mainly
depend on themselves . . . I afterwards availed myself of a tour which
Dr. Philip, the Head of the London Mission, made through those tribes
later in the year—to explain to them more fully, and in detail, the nature
of the agreements which I should be prepared to enter with them,
provided that meantime they abided by the line of conduct suggested.'

This (January) dispatch must have been inspired by the prickings
of a bad conscience ; the ' detail ' of the ' new order ' depended
on his own constantly deferred visit—' to see for himself '.

Sir Benjamin's faculty for delay is astounding. In January
1834 he arrived with definite instructions to attend to the frontier,
the condition of which was obviously of vital importance to the

---

[1] Thomas Pringle was now Secretary of the anti-Slavery Society.
Even to him Philip says only that ' the present Governor appears to
be willing to do what is right '.
[2] P.R.O., C.O. 48/49, Dispatches of 5 January 1835.
[3] Cf. D'Urban's letter of 14 July 1834, above, p. 92.

life of the Colony. By April his impending visit had been
announced to the Kafir chiefs ; but only on 31 May (above,
p. 88) ' the time has *now* come ' to give the matter his august
attention. Then, indeed, he hoped to go in August. In August
Mrs. Philip was given a definite date, 15 September. On 12
September, he tells Somerset that he is coming ' early next
month ' ; the same day Lady D'Urban ' called ' on Mrs. Philip,
for the third time in three weeks, to ask for ' news from the
Frontier ' for the Governor, who is ' certainly going ' early
next month. By 3 October Mrs. Philip began at last to despair :
' I really hope Sir Benjamin means to go,' she writes to her
husband. ' Lady D'Urban says now about the middle of the
month, although the Town report is that he is not going at all.'
At that very minute a note arrived from Government House
announcing the appointment to Uitenhage of one Hudson, who
is ' to meet us on the frontier when I go thither '. (Another
note followed immediately telling Philip, through her, of his
plans for meeting the Griqua Waterboer, who, it had been
intended, was to meet him at Graaff-Reinet, but was now to wait
his ' return ' to Cape Town.) Mrs. Philip then adds :

' I shall say nothing about it in town, for it seems to be a secret
that he is going at all, and perhaps he wishes to come upon the people
in the interior unexpectedly. I find that the people here are quite
annoyed at him, he is so particular, so close. . . . For my part I think
there is a great deal more in him than many are willing to allow and
from experience we see that he is very attentive to business.'

On 17 October, and again on the 20th, Mrs. Philip has ' no
certain news ' of the Governor's plans. She now ' hears it may
be 15 November ', but he has to be back for ' Emancipation
Day ' on 1 December. Unfortunately, she thinks, Colonel
Wade (ex-Acting Governor, and hero of the ' Vagrant Law ')
will be his forerunner on the frontier. Finally on 31 October,
Lady D'Urban says ' about the 10th. I shall believe when he
is off ! '

In an enclosure in a dispatch of 10 November, to Mr. R. W.
Hay in Downing Street, D'Urban himself throws one faint
gleam of light on all this procrastination, showing incidentally
that Philip's reports from Kafirland had not been lost on him.[1]

[1] About 22 September Philip began to ' report ', and with the
secrecy preferred by D'Urban, sent this and later letters under cover
to Mrs. Philip ' lest a letter addressed to Your Excellency from this
place (Philipton) should cause " surmises ".'

The Governor explained how the discontent of chiefs like Maqomo arose from their expulsion from the Ceded Territory; but ' communication which I caused to be made ' to chiefs both east and north have, he thinks, had a good effect—and he hopes for still better results from a personal visit to the frontier *where he would have gone two months ago* but for his waiting for instructions about the regulation of slave-apprentices (due to be freed on 1 December). Meantime, he had reason to believe that good had been done by the visit of an (unnamed) ' resident of fourteen years standing '. The tribes were at present quiet and friendly,[1] and the prospects good for the conclusion of a ' political and commercial treaty ', with regular Agents to represent the Government in Kafirland. He thinks also that he will need probably £1,800 rather than £600 for the new frontier ' Agents ' and goes on to suggest that Colonel Wade, who ' has ill endured the loss of consequence ' in his new position of subordination, ' had better not come back from his leave '—especially as ' there are certain points in the system that preceded me which I have not been disposed to adopt '.[2] Even after this, in November, when Philip was on his way back, D'Urban having had Waterboer to dinner [3] and concluded a treaty with him, Mrs. Philip wrote again (on 21 November) : ' Wade is coming by sea and will get the first word of the Governor ' . . . but the Governor, who is now ' waiting for important dispatches ', will ' probably make up his own mind *when he visits the frontier* '.

The Governor's dalliance rendered all Philip's efforts on the frontier vain. On his visits to the chiefs in September, Philip was accompanied apparently by the Reads, father and son, and by a Hottentot, Stoffles, but there seems to be no written record of their doings. In October, however, he settled down on the Kat River to sort out his impressions while he waited for D'Urban ; and seldom in his busy life did he do more writing. So far was he from having ' details ' of the Governor's scheme that his own ideas were just beginning to mature ; for example,

[1] All accounts agree that ' thieving ' was less prevalent during the time of Philip's visit, cf. Cory, iii, 47.

[2] Wade had offended in particular by acting in Council on ' Vagrant Law ' so as to ' place the Governor in the position of explaining and justifying his official acts at the bar of the Legislative Council '.

[3] On this episode Mrs. Philip comments : ' well may the Dutch people say the world is at an end, and the Bible not true,' adding, however, ' I hope the poor man's head (Waterboer) will not be turned '.

to T. Pringle (7 October) he writes of having a tentative plan now clearer in his own mind, and this he will submit to the Governor ; and to Mrs. Philip (14th) he is ' not sorry the Governor is delayed as he is now ready for him with a grip of the whole situation '.[1] To D'Urban himself he wrote at frequent intervals. Sometimes it was on points of detail ; on 22 September, for example, he anticipated later practice by suggesting the Chumie Post as headquarters for the Agent, who ' could not very suitably live in a Kafir Kraal '. Another letter, on 9 October, is a recital of ' cases ', but goes on to describe how—in spite of ' thieving '—' where on my tour in 1832 there were not 15 Boers, there are now 1,100 '. Confirming this statement by a reference to evidence from the mission station at Philippolis, he takes occasion to emphasize the oneness of the Frontier Problem in the east and in the much simpler north, urging a ' treaty ' and, essentially, ' protection ' for the Griquas against the encroachments of the Boers.[2] As for the Kafir frontier, the very foundation of his plan was, he told Pringle, to *substitute political commissioners for military officials* ; and to D'Urban himself (14 October) he emphasized how he would find that the ' exceptional difficulties were due to the neglect by his predecessors of any *system of Justice* '.

Though Philip never seems to have taken offence or alarm at the Governor's delays, he presently bethought him also of Fowell Buxton, who for the moment was only a second string to his bow ; as in the 'twenties and again in the 'forties he had resort to English political aid only when direct dealings with the Colonial Government seemed hopeless.[3] About this time, however, there was some prospect of a Select Committee of the House, and in August, Pringle, agitating in London, sent Philip a reminder : ' By the way, you should stir up Buxton. . . . He **is** a most excellent man, but dilatory, and somewhat irresolute when he has to deal with *civil* men like Spring-Rice (then Colonial

---

[1] His Kat River experience, also, inspired another vigorous letter in denunciation of Colonel Wade's Hottentot ' Vagrant Law '.

[2] ' A fortnight ago,' he had told Pringle on 7 October, a ' Proclamation appeared prohibiting Boers from crossing the boundaries of the Colony under a penalty of ten pounds. In face of that, twelve Boers have passed through this Settlement, in front of the chain of posts, into Caffreland. Another party crossed last week behind the Winterberg, refusing to obey the Field Cornet who ordered them to return.'

[3] Cf *Cape Col. Qn.*, p. 185.

Secretary), trusting to their good *intentions*'. Mrs. Philip also
reported Pringle as saying that Buxton had to speak, ' as members
were leaving in shoals ', and that he was lucky to get a quorum
for an ' Address '. Buxton, in consequence, began to get very
full letters from the Kat River ; [1] this important evidence he
used with effect in the following year when he came to press,
successfully at last, for the well-known ' Aborigines ' Select
Committee, whose functions included an inquiry into the causes
of the outbreak of the Frontier war.

At length, about 27 October, Dr. Philip began to think of
returning. In the prevailing air of ' suspicion ' about his long
visit, which he told Colonel Wade was prolonged by his hope of
seeing Adam Kok, he had come to think the Governor had
' better see the chiefs *alone* '. He sent, however, a statement
on frontier policy to meet D'Urban in Grahamstown. In this
document he avowedly paid more attention to existing evils
than to the possible remedy. Colonel Somerset, for example,
had just demanded from Maqomo 480 cattle—more than the
chief had already returned—and more, the chief protested,
than were ever taken by natives. Philip urged ' investigation '
of this ' claim ': ' First ascertain the *facts* ' before Somerset
carries out his threat of an ' expedition into Caffreland '. The
Patrol System, he insisted once again, was ' unjust and indis-
criminate '. There must, further, be *written* agreements about
boundaries. ' Passes ' for traders were too freely given.
Maqomo, on the other hand, was lately arrested, at a missionary
meeting, for having no ' pass '. In this connexion (diagnosing
an evil that persisted) he urged that natives should be treated
by officials ' with ordinary civility and respect '. Any new
system, finally, would require a strong hand to cope with the
prejudice of the colonists, and, ' as in India ', it must be *civil*
administration. If the Colony, he said, got no military help
from Europe they would find themselves compelled to live
closer together, and amicably with their neighbours. As it
was, he reiterated, ' even on the Eastern frontier you will find
many Boers living in Caffre territory '—1,500 by some accounts
he had heard. Thefts, therefore, could not be so bad as alleged,
but the present method of dealing with them was demoralizing
the natives. Following this, in a private letter :

[1] One was drafted on a huge closely written *folio* sheet. Then
remembering that this had to serve to congratulate Miss Buxton on
her marriage, he ' took a smaller sheet ' and began again !

'Having done this (i.e. drafted what he calls an appeal, based on "justice", and sent it to meet the Governor) I consider my work in this place done. Nothing is now left to accident. I can leave the frontier, should the Governor not come at this time, without caring whether I am at a public meeting of the chiefs or not. The principle of my scheme (and that is all I care for) is now no longer an experiment that may fail, but a law that must be enforced. God commands it. The thing is practicable . . . I stand as on a rock'.

Then, indeed, in a moment of misgiving (showing again that he was not blind to the losses of the farmers) Philip wrote to Miss Buxton (now Mrs. Johnston) on 21 October : 'What is to happen if the Caffres shall continue to steal from the Colony, and if lies and perjury shall be employed as they have been to aggravate the evil, and if the colonial spirit shall again prevail ? '

Shortly afterwards (24 November), Philip's friend, the astronomer—Sir John Herschel—welcoming news from Philip of a probable restriction of ' commandos ', and pleased with Waterboer, who ' dined ', and was shown the stars—put the philanthropist case in a sentence, emphasizing the ' ill effect of the increasing *bellum ad internecionem* on the colonists themselves, who presumably approve, *thinking by long use that it is essential to their welfare and safety* '. In their zeal for the material welfare of the colonists, however, they forgot how little any people like what is ' for their good '. The fault of the Humanitarians was that in the essentials of frontier policy they were too enlightened and advanced for their time.

Philip's last memorandum from the frontier seems to have reached D'Urban only in the middle of January, when his preoccupations with the new sufferings of the frontier farmers blinded him finally to the constructive and more important part of Philip's work and writing. While Philip was on his way back, travelling, in face of colonial hostility, with the escort of a friendly field-cornet, D'Urban tarried in Cape Town. The frontier, therefore, remained in the unrestricted control of Colonel Somerset, who was now bent on cattle and ' reprisals '; and Somerset's action, with D'Urban's inertia, precipitated the crisis. The Governor had been warned repeatedly of the dangers ; and, after the event, colonists themselves were wise about the comings and goings of (drought-stricken) Kafirs, and a great ' meeting ' of ' Gaikas ' and ' Ndhlambis ' in August, [1] as foreboding a ' long premeditated onslaught '; yet as there was

[1] Cory, iii, 47.

relative peace and quiet at the time of Philip's communications in September, it may be that an outbreak was not so ' inevitable ' as is suggested. Nearly thirty years of Border ' Law ', leading up to such a month of harrying as Sir George Cory graphically describes,[1] sufficiently explain both the genuineness of Kafir grievances, and the likelihood of their subsequent resistance, with violence. On 20 November, while Somerset was contemplating action for the recovery of his ' 480 cattle from Maqomo', a farmer named Joubert was robbed in the bush near the Koonap of ' three horses and a foal '.[2] The farmer and his friends set out and tracked the spoor to a kraal on the Keiskama, where presently they got the chief Eno to admit the liability of his people, and to promise redress. ' After waiting five days and nights ' nothing happened, so the farmers applied to Fort Willshire, whence on 2 December Ensign Sparks, an ' inexperienced youth ' (' spectacled, and fond of mathematics ', says Dr. Theal) set out with an orthodox ' patrol ', to investigate. Arrived at the alleged guilty kraal, and getting no reply from the ' sullen ' occupant, ' they dismounted and seized *forty head of cattle* '. Here Sir George Cory hesitates, and explains [3] in a note, that the relative market price of (any ?) horse and Kafir cattle being what they were, ' no injustice was done in this reprisal '. But now—as if the chief more than agreed about market prices—the Kafir told Sparks that ' Eno had already taken sixty from him for his offence '. This certainly suggests a very wealthy ' kraal ', if the number is to be believed ; but, without any investigation, ' Sparks advised him to get them back from Eno '. After this exploit it is hardly surprising that the patrol was sharply challenged within a mile, being saved from attack only by the intervention of Eno's son, called Stock. Near Fort Willshire, however, they were attacked again, and this time Sparks was wounded in the arm by an assegai. ' Thus the Kafirs drew first blood ', comments Sir George Cory.

Now in all these years of patrols there is little or no evidence of such forcible resistance as this, and before taking the action such unwonted violence seemed to demand Colonel Somerset might well have looked to the state of his armaments. ' Ammunition in the Government magazine ' was, however, ' at its lowest ebb ', and the troops ' barely sufficient for the defence of the

[1] Cory, iii, 54 ff. [2] Cory, iii, 54.
[3] Cory, iii, 55, *note.*

outposts of Grahamstown '.[1] Unconsidering, or nothing daunted, Somerset set out with a stronger force, and though he ' scoured the bush ' one day, when ' not a Kafir was to be found ', on the next Eno arrived with a large retinue for a parley. Eno was then told that he ' had forfeited the indulgence of residing west of the Keiskama ', and was required also to ' restore ' 150 head of cattle ' and the horses already stolen ' (and paid for by the cattle ?). Eno proved submissive. In two days 137 cattle and 13 horses were ' captured '; and within a week the number ' sent in ' by him was 237 cattle and 18 horses.[2] ' Stealing ', however, continued, as did reprisals—cattle taken for more stolen horses, and ' some other cattle ' being seen to emerge into the open, men were ' sent to take them also '. Somerset, in fact, was out to ' drive the last man over the Keiskama '. It was war, and inevitably serious incidents followed. The cattle ' seen to emerge ', and ' seized ', were the personal property of a chief; and, by Bantu custom, to seize the cattle of a chief was to declare war upon him. A Kafir slightly wounded in a skirmish turned out to be a petty chief, Xoxo, and this was ' an insult to the memory of their ancestor Rarabe '.[3] Sir George Cory comments : ' The continued stealing of cattle and horses had long, too long, been a regular feature of the life of a frontier farmer, and in this respect there was *nothing particularly exceptional* in the fateful month of December 1834 '—nor, it is to be feared, was the manner of treating the disease out of the usual.

From a different angle, James Read looked on in despair. On 9 December he wrote from the Kat River to Dr. Philip :

' Somerset is now clearing the country from Willshire to the sea, all Eno's people and Congo's people. The old thing over again ; for the act of one man punish hundreds, and now again just in the time of harvest while the corn is in the fields. Can this be Sir Benjamin's order ? or would they dare take such a step without orders ? I am sorry for the case at the moment, as the chiefs will think we have deceived them.'[4]

It needs no elaborate theory of ' long premeditation ' and preparation to account for the explosion that followed. Before Christmas the Xosa tribes had hurled themselves upon the Colony, devastating whole districts, up to Grahamstown and beyond, with fire and assegai.[5] The organization of the Bantu

[1] Cory, iii, 64.
[2] Cory, iii, 57.
[3] Cory, iii, 57–9.
[4] P.R.O., 1835, ' Papers '.
[5] Even then the evidence is that women and children were uniformly gently treated. Theal, ii, 91, and Cory, iii, 73.

was, indeed, far too loose for long and secret planning, even under stress of a common feeling of reckless desperation. Twice, early in the year, D'Urban himself had ' caused communications to be made ' to the chiefs, promising them changes—so that it did not need Philip to suggest to them that reform was due. Instead of a friendly visit from D'Urban to hear what they had to say, and to originate a new order, Colonel Somerset followed hard upon Dr. Philip's embassy with almost unprecedentedly violent application of the old.

When at last D'Urban reached the frontier in January, after it had been devastated by actual war, he promptly forgot his earlier doubts, suffered a violent revulsion of feeling, and— soldier that he was—came down heavily on the side of those whose chief faith was in ' powder and ball '. Dr. Philip's warnings [1] went unheard in the clamour of European discontents, and his attempt to initiate a new order was defeated by the forces of prejudice and intransigeance now let loose. The ' mystery ' [2] in which, from the beginning, D'Urban's relations with Philip were wrapped has led to gross misrepresentation of what the missionary leader said and did at that time, as in 1835 and after (below, cc. ix, x). For his ' interference ', both on behalf of Hottentots and Kafirs, Philip has filled the bill as a very *diabolus ex machina* in South African history. But the real responsibility rests on Sir Benjamin D'Urban for his fatal procrastination, and on officials and colonists who alike pinned their faith, through thick and thin, to a mere crude application of the remedy of brute force. In the ruin and chaos that followed, Sir Benjamin D'Urban turned with peculiar violence against his quondam adviser and all that was wisest in his counsel.

[1] D'Urban complained, 5 January 1835, that missionaries gave no ' warning ' of an outbreak.
[2] Theal, ii, 50.

CHAPTER IX

THE WAR OF 1835—D'URBAN AND HIS PHILANTHROPIST CRITICS

By the Christmas Eve of 1834 a generation of militarist frontier policy had done its work. Instead of the Kafirs being driven beyond the Keiskama, the frontier farms of the white colonists were given over to fire and plunder. The hard lessons of 1819, when the tribes ventured a massed attack on Grahamstown itself, were not lost now on the Kafirs. In the new war, by operating in quite small bands, the Xosa were able to make the most of the physical features of the country, and, while in the first few days the scattered and undefended homesteads of the colonists were ravished over a wide area—with relatively small toll of European lives—the tribes, for their part, almost completely evaded any decisive conflict with the columns presently sent out against them. The final conquest of the Bantu was not quite yet.

In the last days of the year news of the invasion reached Cape Town. Early on the morning of New Year's Day, Colonel Harry Smith set off alone on a famous six-day ride of six hundred miles to bring order out of chaos in the east. This breezy soldier was to have a long experience of the Cape frontier. Impetuous he always was—he had saved and won a young Spanish bride at the sack of Badajoz in 1812—and always theatrical, whether storming at the City Fathers of Grahamstown, or dressing up Kafir chiefs, or firing off charges of gunpowder to impress them. Almost sentimentally pious, he was at the same time essentially kind and human. In many ways he was a complete contrast to his slow-going, slow-thinking superior, Sir Benjamin D'Urban, who followed, as befitted his dignity, more at leisure. Thus, while Smith, as early as 6 January, got busy putting the Grahamstown Committee of Safety in its place, D'Urban had to arrange his affairs in the capital, and only set sail from Simonstown on the 8th, arriving in Grahamstown on the 20th.

The Governor's long-deferred visit to the eastern districts had now come about, under very difficult circumstances. Sir Benjamin was, naturally enough, ' horrified ' at the ruin he found in Albany. But, with little power of thinking things together for himself, he was not slow, like some other responsible but muddled men of affairs, to take impressions ready-made from those nearest at the moment ; so that now, throwing to the wind all promises of reform and forgetting all he had learned in 1834, he was at once satisfied that the war was ' the result of long combination '—' so well have the wily savages masqued their purposes that neither missionaries nor traders suspected anything '.[1] Missionaries, at least, had given him ample warning that things could not long continue as they were ; and even now, had he stopped to consider which of the chiefs were most implicated, he might have drawn some significant conclusions for himself. By all accounts the most truculent of the chiefs was Tyali, whose cattle had been seized during Colonel Somerset's recent clearing of the country, and whose brother Xoxo had been wounded in December. Another was Eno, the hero of the Sparks episode (p. 105 above). By some accounts, Maqomo, more important than either of these, at first hung back ; but he was in it too, and had his own very real grievances ; according to a missionary version of a comment by one Major Cox, he was indeed ' a much wronged man '. Pato, on the other hand, was quiet—a testimony, as it may be, to the pacific influence of the Wesleyan missionaries. But Pato had also been for years in peaceable occupation of the lower and less attractive part of the Ceded Territory, in Peddie, and being little troubled by commandos had less cause for complaint.[2] (The same Pato, none the less, was out fighting in the last ditch in the later war of 1847.)[3]

Farther afield there was a greater chief than any of these, the Transkeian Xosa Paramount, Hintza. That he sympathized with his western kinsmen's troubles there need be no doubt ; nor that when either Kafir or colonial cattle were to be had, he received them gladly, for ' safe keeping ', beyond the Kei. But the assertion that he was the ' chief instigator of all the mischief '[4] rests on the flimsiest evidence of panic-stricken traders, and is,

---

[1] Letter of 21 January, to his Secretary, Colonel Bell, who was left in charge in Cape Town.
[2] Evidence of Rev. W. Shaw and S. Young. Cory, iii, 304, 307.
[3] Cory, iv, 514. [4] Cory, iii, 116.

on the face of it, an unnecessary assumption. One of D'Urban's
first actions, however, seems to have been to authorize a ' mission '
to Hintza to obtain his ' neutrality or co-operation '—in effect,
to compel his co-operation—thus almost wantonly extending the
scope of military operations for the not very adequate colonial
forces. Within a week of his arrival in Grahamstown, Sir
Benjamin had apparently quite thoroughly absorbed the traditional
yet rather bankrupt precepts of frontier policy. Discarding all
ideas of a constructive policy for the control of black and white
relationships, he seems at once to have inclined towards an enterprise that would reproduce all the successive troubles of past
years—the demarcation of a new and more distant line of frontier.
Thus, as early as 28 January, D'Urban had begun to toy with
the idea of pushing the colonial boundary back from the Fish
River to the, possibly, shorter and more easily defended line of
the Kei.[1] To this plan he adhered consistently in the months
that followed ; though just how he proposed to deal with the
immediate problem presented by the Gaika tribes between the
Keiskama and the Kei is never quite so clear.

The course of the short campaign, that was virtually over
by the beginning of May, confirms the view that the Governor,
concentrating on the military needs of the moment, had little
eye for the troublesome details of an administrative system that
might have established permanent peace. The first task was to
re-occupy Fort Willshire and other posts abandoned in the rush
of war. With some delay, due to the flooding of the rivers by
the summer rains, this was done ; and in February and March
the troops carried the war into the enemy's country. The
tribes had merited punishment, but were now by no means
eager to show themselves in force. It was not Colonel Smith's
fault that, as he complained, the only possible warfare was a
kind of ' Smithfield Market cattle-driving '. ' You gallop in,'
he said, ' and half by force, half by stratagem, pounce upon
(the Kafirs) wherever you find them, frighten their wives, burn
their homes, lift their cattle, and then return home in triumph.'[2]
The country so lent itself to guerrilla tactics that there was little

---

[1] D'Urban has noted and marked a Memo by one Campbell, dated
28 January 1835, which claims that the Kei is safer and shorter, and
argues also for the occupation of Natal. Rough notes indicate that
the Surveyor-General was called in, and questioned the 80-mile estimate
of the length of the line. D'Urban, however, advocated the Kei line
as being ' considerably less than 100 miles ' (Cape Town Archives).

[2] Quoted, Cory, iii, 130.

obvious advantage in carrying the campaign still farther afield. (In June, and even in September, the Kafirs were still active in their ' old haunts ', in Albany and on the Koonap,[1] in spite of the ' conquest ' of the country up to the Kei.) With Maqomo and his friends by no means broken, and the essential frontier still unpacified, D'Urban about the end of March started his greater enterprise of a march against the distant Hintza. Throughout April the troops pushed forward, collecting much cattle, but still with little serious resistance ; till at last, at the end of the month, after repeated ' summons ', Hintza himself arrived in D'Urban's camp in the neighbourhood of Butterworth, having come, of his own free will, to negotiate.

There followed a sorry imitation of Lord Charles Somerset's ' peace ' of 1819. The ' Paramount ', Hintza, was required to ' order ' Tyali, Maqomo, Eno and company to make peace, and himself to find surety in some 50,000 cattle and 1,000 horses. The Kafir ambassador now filled the rôle of hostage—as a prisoner, royally and kindly entertained by his ' father ', Harry Smith. He could thus hardly be called a consenting party to the ' treaty ' imposed upon him. The new Province of Queen Adelaide was, however, formally proclaimed on Sunday, 10 May. Tragedy followed quickly. The very next day the troops set out on their return march to occupy their new conquest—Hintza, full of suspicions and fears, being taken along with them to guide them to the cattle he was to restore. On a difficult part of the road, Hintza, like an ill-fated Rob Roy, made a dash for freedom, was quickly pursued and shot ; unhappily, his body was also mutilated. Though the circumstances of this tragedy gained immediate notoriety, and became the occasion of a formal inquiry which honourably absolved all the officers immediately concerned, yet the episode remains a mystery.[2] As early as 2 June Sir John Herschel wrote in this vein to Dr. Philip, who seems to have accepted the same view : ' As I now view it, Hintza's death is a most untoward event, but a mere chance-medley affair brought about by his own conduct.' It was indeed highly ' untoward ', and had a profound and unfortunate influence on Native opinion. According to frontier tradition it was a long

[1] Cory, iii, 175, 216.
[2] Sensational evidence was collected by one Dr. Ambrose Campbell, a somewhat eccentric or ' cranky ' Grahamstown doctor, and sent by him to Dr. Philip, who forwarded the letters, with little comment, to the L.M.S., whence they reached Lord Glenelg.

time before chiefs would again willingly trust themselves to British officers.[1] It is significant, moreover, that among the Natives themselves the war of 1835 is known to this day as the ' War of Hintza ' ; though his share in or responsibiilty for the outbreak is only remote and indirect, its tragic denouement made him a hero.

Another apparently minor incident of the campaign against Hintza was fraught with consequences as long-lived as those of the ' peace ' with which this expedition was supposed to end. There were scattered among Hintza's people a good many thousands of refugees from Chaka's Reign of Terror in Natal, the so-called Fingos. About the origins of these people both record and tradition are confusing, oppressors and oppressed being sometimes indistinguishable. There would seem to have been two main waves of ' destroyers '—the ' Baca ', about 1820, and one Matiwana's people, the Fetcani, in 1828. The Baca still survive as a separate tribe (in Mount Frere and Umzimkulu) ; other remnants, refugees from Chaka, destroyers and again refugees, according to circumstances, would seem to make up the ' Fingos '. Their sufferings as refugees were probably remembered and charged somewhat indiscriminately against Hintza's people. Thus by some accounts these people were treated by the Amaxosa as ' slaves '. That they were still too newly arrived to be fully absorbed as good Xosas, and that they were subjected to many disabilities in their new home, may be true ; but they probably suffered something a good deal short of ' slavery '.[2] The mere fact of their being where they were shows that they had enjoyed protection of a sort. They were apparently even beginning to be able to acquire cattle of their own.[3] The advent of the powerful white man, however, seems to have suggested to them either the possibility of escape from thraldom, if such it was, or else the advisability of being on the

[1] The incident is also said to account for the quite unusual mutilation by Kafirs of European victims of the war of 1850 (Theal, iii, 89).

[2] Stretch writes to Fairbairn on 22 March 1836 : ' Ayliff (Wesleyan missionary) is returning to Hintza's country to collect more Fingos seeing that many have gone back to their oppressors.'

[3] Frontier tradition, from a Fingo source, boasts of a Fingo who, being trusted by a Xosa chief as ' milkman ' (in effect King's cup-bearer), betrayed his benefactor and slew him, fled to Colonel Smith, and persuaded the good Colonel that the Xosa were the aggressors. Smith, without inquiry, is said to have taken this man's story as a warrant for threatening Hintza and his people with dire penalties for their alleged ill-treatment of the Fingos.

side of the big battalions. Sir Benjamin D'Urban now found the Fingos not only ready allies but anxious to secure protection. Tempted by the prospect of making use of them as a buffer to protect the frontier, he was perhaps even too ready to apply the principle *divide et impera*, and take them under his wing.

On 24 April, before Hintza's surrender, D'Urban had given them their wish and proclaimed them British subjects. Thereafter, these new subjects, some 16,000 all told,[1] collected much cattle—their own and Hintza's—and set off in a long procession to seek asylum nearer the Colony. The defection of the Fingos was naturally enough a sore blow to the Xosa, then and long afterwards. Even then Xosa violence against Hintza's ' dogs ' was made a warrant for keeping Hintza himself under closer surveillance ; on the other hand, the cattle lifted by the Fingos from Hintza were ignored in the reckoning of the 50,000 for which the chief was held responsible.[2] This was far from being the end. In the months and years following the Xosa had the mortification of seeing these ' deserters ' planted on old Xosa country, grown comparatively rich with Xosa cattle, and basking in the sunshine of official favour. This was too much even for the chief Pato who, loyal in 1834, tried in 1846 to drive the Fingos out of ' his ' country.[3] In later times the Fingos, increased far beyond their original 16,000 or 17,000, became a very considerable factor in frontier life. Originally, perhaps, a less warlike people, they have shown themselves both shrewd and capable. Their prolonged feud with the Xosa kept them distinct, and served also to keep them loyal. Over and over again, therefore, Fingos were brought in to act as a protection or buffer against warring or rebel tribes, and rewarded for their services with ' rebel ' lands—beginning with old Gaika lands about Alice and Peddie in 1836.[4]

With the unfortunate death of Hintza left to rankle in the minds of the Xosa, and with the Fingos thus brought in as a new complication of the frontier, an embarrassment rather than a source of strength, Sir Benjamin's definitive peace would need

---

[1] Cory, iii, 145.   [2] Cory, iii, 141, 148.
[3] Cory, iv, 437.

[4] The feud with the Xosa is not quite dead yet ; in these days when outside pressure is rapidly obliterating tribal distinctions, at least among the more educated Natives, discussions about Bantu leadership still occasionally reveal the latent rivalry of Amaxosa and Fingo (Articles and Correspondence, e.g. in Johannesburg Native paper, *Umteteli wa Bantu*, 1928).

to have had great merits to atone for its unfortunate accompaniments. It was not even as if the death of Hintza meant the removal of a powerful or astute enemy. The terms of peace professed indeed to depend on Hintza as Paramount ; but if Hintza was little likely to be able to control Maqomo, still less was his young heir Kreli equal to the task, supposing him disposed to make the effort. The peace was announced in a Proclamation, made with some pomp and ceremony in the presence of the unhappy Hintza on 10 May, and gazetted on the 29th. By this precious edict Tyali, Maqomo, and others, having ' without provocation or declaration of war ' invaded and plundered the Colony, having now been ' defeated, chastised and dispersed ', were sentenced, as ' treacherous and irreclaimable savages ', to be ' for ever expelled ' from the country west of the Kei River —all this in terms of agreement with Hintza the ' paramount chief of Kafirland ', with whose ' concurrence and countenance ' these crimes were committed, who had now been ' compelled to sue for peace and accept the terms of it '. But the bottom fell out of such a settlement since Tyali, Maqomo and company, though they may have been dispersed, were certainly not yet ' expelled ' from their country ; driven by hunger,[1] they were still making occasional raids on colonial farms and property. There was as yet neither peace and order, nor even ' conquest ' ; there was the prospect only of a prolonged campaign of ' expulsion ', against an embittered enemy—a task far beyond the power of the available forces. Sir Benjamin D'Urban was giving away the skin before he had caught his lion.

Now D'Urban was a painstaking Governor confronted with a singularly difficult task. But the strength of the D'Urban tradition, and abiding belief in the beneficent wisdom of the ' policy ' he is supposed to have pursued in spite and in face of supposedly bitter and wrong-headed Philanthropic opposition, make it needful to lay some stress on the weak points of his attempt to bring peace and settlement to a distracted frontier. The letters of Dr. Philip, the head and brain of this opposition, tell their own tale, but the excitement of 1835 was so intense and the sequel so momentous—involving as it soon did the disruption of South African unity—that the prejudices then roused still survive to warp historical judgment.

In the Colony itself criticism came chiefly from the *Com-*

[1] Missionary letters, e.g. from Mr. Munro, Grahamstown, emphasize the distress.

mercial Advertiser, edited in Cape Town by Dr. Philip's son-in-law, John Fairbairn. Dr. Philip personally had nothing to do with the newspaper, but his communications to his own Society in London, and to Fowell Buxton, gained some notoriety for their supposed influence at headquarters in Downing Street. The *Commercial Advertiser* made an unlucky beginning. On 24 December 1834, when only the news of Colonel Somerset's earlier activities could have reached Cape Town, the paper made unfavourable but hardly unjustified comments on the high-handed treatment the frontier tribes had received. This issue of the paper, as it happened, reached Grahamstown on 2 January at the height of the worst panic of actual war. Thereupon 479 infuriated frontiersmen signed their names to a declaration denouncing these and former ' false statements ', alleging ' the visit of its Editor to the frontier as among the causes of a confederacy among the Caffre chiefs which threatens the total ruin of a large portion of the Colony ', and vowing a severe boycott.[1] The colonists were in no mood to distinguish nicely between the criticism of a faulty system of frontier administration, and personal attacks on themselves and their interests. As Fairbairn, for his part, did little to mollify their wounded feelings, in their continued rage they could thereafter see in the Philanthropists only a clique of fanatics who were obsessed with an idea of outrages on defenceless natives.

Grahamstown, indeed, went one better and began to elaborate counter-accusations which have stuck. There was, for example, the preposterous charge, embodied in this January declaration, that Fairbairn's tour of Kafirland in 1830 had so inflamed a sense of grievance in the chiefs as to pave the way for their outbreak four and a half years later. And had not the arch-plotter, Dr. Philip, been intriguing with the chiefs even in the last months of 1834 ? In the light of after events the agitation against the Hottentot Vagrant Law, and a ' missionary meeting ' on the Kat River in September, assumed a new and sinister significance ; on 13 February, though the Hottentots had already proved their loyalty, ' An English Settler ' wrote to the *Grahamstown Journal* to say how the chiefs had been impressed at that September meeting by the importance of this visitor, who ' had the ear of the Governor ', and an ear also for their grievances.[2]

[1] Cory, iii, 90.
[2] In July 1835 Dr. Philip's friend, Captain Alexander, then an officer on D'Urban's staff, better known later as the traveller Sir James

There were two main phases in Dr. Philip's campaign. Originally he had attacked the impolicy and crudity of the old frontier system, as practised, *in excelsis*, by Colonel Somerset in the end of 1834 : later he directed his criticism against the unwisdom of D'Urban's May policy, not for its proposal to annex Kafirland, but because the project was to drive the offending chiefs out of their homes : in the interval between January and May, when and so long as the colony was in actual danger, he refrained completely from any kind of opposition. On 1 January, the very day the news of the invasion reached Cape Town, Dr. Philip wrote and signed a circular to all the L.M.S. stations, calling on the missionaries to see that the Hottentots ' obey His Excellency's summons, as no doubt they will ', and give all the service required of them in the ' dreadful state ' to which the Colony has been reduced in this sudden crisis—an injunction the Hottentots fully obeyed. But the course events had taken was no surprise, and while D'Urban reported the ' extraordinary fact ' [1] that the outbreak befell ' without arousing the suspicion ' either of missionaries or of traders, Philip at once wrote to London, on 2 January :

' The irruption of the Kafirs has not come upon us without warning. The Government has been told for years that this crisis was unavoidable if the old system should be persisted in.'

Alexander, having absorbed on the frontier D'Urban's official view of events, suggested that the chiefs had ' deceived Philip when he went among them as a negotiator ', and that severe measures were now necessary against them. On 21 August Dr. Philip replied insisting that he went in 1834 merely to ' collect information ' for the Governor, with no authority whatever to ' negotiate '. He was all the more ' secret ' about his hopes of a ' change ' of policy for fear of rousing frontier opposition ; and even James Read, he claims, knew nothing of the Governor's direct interest in the inquiries that Philip directed Read to make, till Read heard of it in Grahamstown in 1835 from the Governor himself.

Further, ' I am perfectly sensible of the truth of all you say about the Governor's urbanity . . . and the readiness he always manifested to hear everything I had to tell him. . . . The affection I bear to him gives poignancy to the grief I feel at the difficulties in which I now see him involved in the attempt he is making to expel the hostile tribes from their native soil. If their expulsion is just and absolutely necessary you are correct as to the necessity of shooting the Caffres, burning their corn, and taking from them their women even their wild goats ; but the necessity and policy of the first measure must be determined before the second can be defended.' (See also *Cape Col. Qn.*, p. 240.)

[1] To the Secretary of State on 5 January and again to Colonel Bell from Grahamstown on 21 January.

The Philanthropists generally, having had such a clear anticipation of the dangers of the old policy,[1] could not now share the common feelings of the Colony. To Philip it was ' this catastrophe ', as contrasted with ' what might have been ' had the Governor's visit not been deferred,[2] though till late in 1835 there is no suggestion of censure on D'Urban even for his fatal delay.[3] More than once, indeed, he hints somewhat wildly that the war was not unwelcome to those who were determined to get Kafirland given out as sheep farms—or even that had Colonel Somerest desired war he could not have gone a better way about it. Not without reason he was angered by the boast of an eastern official that ' powder and lead ' would now ' put an end to the march of humbug '—that is of Philanthropy—in frontier policy. The most despairing (and characteristic) comment for these months comes on 16 February from Mrs. Philip :

' The Caffre War has put an end to cheering hopes that another nation might have been saved from extermination by their Christian neighbours. Alas, I fear, the poor infatuated wretches, goaded by oppression, appear to have put it out of the power of the missionaries to plead their cause.'

For the rest, in letters to Fowell Buxton at this period Dr. Philip was content to ' point out the cause of this catastrophe and to give you suggestions as to the course to be followed at home to close the wounds . . . and to gain the object we have had so long in contemplation '. His own sentiments he sums up in a letter quoted from a Mr. Fleming of Uitenhage : [4]

' I have come to these conclusions about this disastrous state of things . . . that the *system* has engendered a bad feeling, that the recent patrols caused it to burst forth, that the Caffres—" all the tribes " —have not combined, and if they had they might, if guided by an intel-

[1] E.g. as early as 12 April 1834, Read wrote to Fairbairn : ' It is a wonder that under all provocation during the last eight months the Kafirs have not attempted to retaliate.'
[2] To Thos. Fowell Buxton, 19 and 23 January.
[3] At great length, on 9 January, to Buxton, Dr. Philip excused D'Urban for staying in Cape Town : ' Had he, for example, left Cape Town while the Vagrant Law was pending in the Council, with Colonel Wade, the father of that Act in his chair, our situation might have been worse than it is . . . with the whole coloured population alienated. . . . Thousands of Hottentots would have left the Colony. . . . (There were also) the foolish fears of the Cape Town people about the 1st December, the day on which slavery was to cease. . . .'
[4] To T. F. Buxton, 23 January 1835.

ligent person, have destroyed every town from this to Cape Town
and ravished the country at the same time. It required but boldness
and celerity during the *Panic*. . . . No one ever seems to have apprehended that the power of the Caffres to blast the Colony was hanging
over our heads like a drawn sword suspended by a thread . . . I must
confess this fact is alarming. Our contiguity to such formidable
enemies shows the necessity of basing our intercourse on principles
of justice if we wish to avoid future causes of war, as well as maintaining a strong attitude on the frontier line to defend the Colony.
We must be the masters, but rule as we do in India, making the interests
of the natives the grand policy of our conduct. Our very existence
in India is a miracle of God for that object, and when we neglect it
the Kingdom will depart from us—and it is such views I am inclined
to take of our rule and of our duty in this quarter of the world.'

Thus, nearly a century earlier, an unknown Uitenhage merchant
used language—preserved by chance in this letter from the
best-hated South African Philanthropist of his day—prophetic
of the ' sacred trust of civilization ' doctrine of the Covenant
of the League of Nations. This doctrine, startling even in 1923
when echoed in the famous Kenya Declaration of the Duke
of Devonshire, was too much for the suffering Cape Colony of
1835, and served only to bring upon its chief sponsor the charge
laid against Jeremiah of old :

' This man weakeneth the hands of the men of war that remain in
the city, and the hands of all the people ; but this man seeketh not
the welfare of his people, but the hurt.'

Abuse was the natural weapon of the more extreme of those
who could see no further than that the Colony was in mortal
danger. ' We have all manner of stories ', Dr. Philip writes on
5 February, ' about the missionaries being the cause of the war,
and how they got out whole boxes of assegais from Austin Friars
(L.M.S. headquarters) to distribute among the Caffres before
war commenced.' Again, to James Read on 13 February :
' The Grahamstown people are throwing much dust, but it blinds
no one but themselves.' His chief concern with this ' dust '
was its possible effect on the Governor :

' With his conduct, so far as it is yet known, I am satisfied, but as
he is now upon his trial we must be reserved in what we say about the
future. No man who ever came to the Colony had to encounter one-
tenth of his difficulties. . . . If he is not supported from home, he
may make the same complaint as General Janssens made to van der
Kemp, that he was required to " break iron with wood ". He has
not now on the frontier a single man about him who has any other
notion of settling the affairs of the Caffres but by powder and lead.

The frontier colonists have long set their hearts upon Caffreland—they already calculate upon having it given them for sheep-farms and the general cry is " blood ! blood ! " . . . The war is ascribed to Pringle's poem " Makanna's Gathering " (which no Caffre ever saw), or to Fairbairn and his paper : we are told by the *Zuid Afrikaan* of yesterday that " as for Dr. Philip and his crew, the inhabitants ought to extirpate them forthwith ". Here we have all the venom engendered by the Slave Question, the Hottentot Question, the Vagrant Act, and their fear of having their expectations with regard to Caffraria disappointed, concentrated and pouring out all its energies like the lava from the crater of an active volcano. . . . But my object is not to fix your attention upon Fairbairn and myself, but to show you what the Governor will have to contend against. . . . It is obvious that he can do nothing efficiently to effect the introduction of a mild and equitable system on the Caffre frontier unless he is supported from Home.' [1]

Even if the Governor was ' on his trial ', Dr. Philip was still loyal to him. ' There is a party here hoping that the Governor will fall, but we have put the saddle on the right horse ', he writes on 27 February, ' and Sir Benjamin has nothing to fear from what has yet taken place '. His letters, therefore, deal with general questions. To his view of the causes of the war he adds a warning against the expansion of the Colony :

' The Colony is nearly all just farms and families, no villages are forming and the distant Boers, having no markets, never think of producing more than for their own consumption. Therefore, they contribute nothing towards defraying the expenses of defence. . . The Colony, since the British got possession, is already doubled in its extent. The English Government has robbed the Natives of a territory as large in thirty years as was taken by the Dutch in 150 years. . . .

Expansion is actually dangerous :

' since it may drive the Kafirs back into the more savage interior, from the frontier where they have been in contact with more humane standards. The Cape will then have Dingaan and Moselekatze as still worse neighbours.'

A few months later he was to advocate an extension at least of colonial law and institutions ; and now, in urging the return of Stockenstrom, a capable civilian whose removal in 1833 he held to be a main cause of the war, he again stressed the essential of all reform : ' The affairs of the frontier must be consigned entirely to a *civil* agency ; exclude the military in all ordinary circumstances from meddling with the affairs of the Caffres.[2]

[1] To T. Fowell Buxton, 23 January 1835.
[2] To Buxton, 23 and 27 January, and 17 February Colonel Smith later reached the earlier conclusion.

This was the burden of all Dr. Philip's letters to Fowell Buxton,
with the further proposal : ' In any case there should be a
Committee of the House of Commons to take into consideration
the whole of the frontier system '. By 12 March the January
news had reached England, and Priscilla Buxton wrote at once
to say that her father had given notice to move on 19 May for
such an inquiry ; by that time he ' hoped to have facts ' to go
upon. This time Mr. Buxton ' got a capital good Committee ',
and the so-called ' Aborigines Committee ' of 1835–7 was
presently instrumental in bringing South African affairs into
unusual prominence.

On 10 May the war had drawn to an end of sorts, and Sir
Benjamin D'Urban made his great Proclamation. At once
there is a new note in Philip's letters : ' The Kafirs have been
subdued ', he begins on 23 May :

' In former communications I informed you I considered it my
duty to support the Governor in what he had done and was doing in
relation to the Kafirs, but that I then considered him upon his trial,
and that we should be called upon to decide on his conduct in this
affair by the manner in which the war might be carried on and concluded.'

Dr. Philip now let himself go on the general state of Kafirland
as he had seen it, taking as his text the terms of the Governor's
Proclamation.[1] In view of his repeated warnings, the initial
suggestion that the Kafir invasion was ' without provocation
in a time of undisturbed peace ' moved him almost to scorn,
driving him back to recapitulate—with fresh evidence—his view
of the fundamental causes of the war. ' It is true ', he says,
that when he reached the frontier in the previous August the
chief excitement was about the ' Boers leaving the Colony, in
the hope that the Governor when he came would give them all
new farms beyond '. It is true also that things were sufficiently
settled for ' 200 traders ' to pursue their activities in Kafirland,
and that, as the Scottish missionary Ross pointed out, the Kafirs

[1] Between February and May Dr. Philip seems to have worked
at a long Memo. on ' The Causes of the War ', which was still in preparation as late as 1 May. Quotations following are from this document
and from a long series of letters written between 23 May and 15 July,
dispatched apparently, in two or three great bundles, before the middle
of July. These exist, some in draft MSS., some at the L.M.S. rooms
in London. Long passages in the L.M.S. copies are marked in red,
' To be sent to Mr. Buxton and Lord Glenelg,' and may be seen also
in the volume *Papers on Kafir War of* 1835 (C.O., 48/165).

had that spring planted ' immense gardens and cornfields ' ;
' what abundant crops ' (certain officers) saw, as did Ross himself
and Read (above, p. 106), giving the prospect of a good harvest
after the notoriously heavy drought of 1834. These signs of
peace, however, suggest not that the war was a ' long premeditated ' onslaught, but the very reverse ; that, as Ross and others
agree, all was calm, with no serious excitement, till December.
Then, when instead of the Governor coming to make reforms
Somerset, Sparks, and Sutton (another patrol leader) were ' let
loose ', their ' patrols ', more active than ever, ' kindled the
flame '.

'The harassing conduct of the frontier authorities ', Dr.
Philip himself continues, ' and the refusal to allow the Kafirs
to occupy a small part of the country taken from them, and of
which we made no use, was a constant source of irritation.'
On the other hand, ' wherever this rule has been relaxed and
grazing allowed, the colonists have been least molested and
thefts by Kafirs checked '. The only chiefs left unmolested
were Pato and others who had grazing in what the Governor
himself had described as ' an uninhabited and worse than useless '
part of the Ceded Territory. But, ' not only were the Kafirs
driven from what no one could deny to have been part of the
Neutral Territory ; they had at the same time the mortification
to see their kraals and huts burned on ground which had always
been regarded as part of Caffreland '. Philip himself found
only ' destruction ' ; ' for 20 miles west of the Chumie there
were no huts standing ', and below the junction of the Chumie
and the Keiskama, on 5 November, he had ' seen kraals burning '.
This destruction went on till December, and the wounding of
Tyali's brother was the last straw. ' What an abuse ' to term
this a period of ' profound peace '. ' It was impossible for the
Kafirs to see their country taken from them piecemeal for
fifteen years, and not to ask how to save themselves. But there
was no plan among them to attack the Colony before the Sparks
and Sutton affairs.' ' Then indeed ', writes Ross on 5 June,
' the Kafirs took fire, and the last communication I had with
Sutu (the Queen-Mother) before leaving, was that they were
stirred up and encouraged by Hottentots and some Boers to
attack the Colony.' December, at least, when the storm broke,
was ' no time of undisturbed peace and amity '.

A second phrase of D'Urban's roused Philip's ire—the
suggestion that he had ' long and maturely ' considered his

change of plan, from the ' new system ' of 1834, with civil law
in the place of ' commandos ', to the ' sentence of extermination '[1]
pronounced in the May Proclamation.   In all, D'Urban had been
only a matter of weeks on the frontier.   On 18 January Philip
had written to him, still in the manner of a trusted adviser, calling
his attention to the state of Hottentot families left without their
soldier bread-winners, and begging him to ' discriminate between
the innocent and the guilty ' in Kafirland.   There is no evidence
of any reply, or of any further exchanges between them, though
at that time Philip clearly was still most willing to believe in
the Governor's benevolent intentions.[2]   As late as 17 April
Captain Alexander had written to Philip from the Kei expressing
the hope that ' you will shortly see a new and better order of
things introduced on the borders of Ethopia '.   But now, still
without a word to Philip himself, D'Urban—having on 19 June
brought himself after the usual delay to frame a dispatch to
London reporting his ' long matured ' May ' settlement '—
seems to go out of his way to give warning that ' Dr. Philip
and his party ' are sure to attack ' this important measure of
extension as unjust in itself, and very probably as severe in execution '.   At the same time, as if by way of counterblast, he expressly
claims that he has the full support of the Wesleyans.[3]   The
emphatic change that took place in the Governor's attitude
when he reached the frontier must indeed have been prompted
as much by the tales he heard from the colonists as by the light
of his own judgment.[4]

[1] Much misunderstanding has probably arisen because Philip
and others habitually use the word ' extermination ' in its strict classical
sense, meaning in effect ' depriving of land '.

[2] Philip begins to be a little guarded, as on 1 June : ' Fairbairn
has not said all he might on the war on the ground that we think it
desirable to leave a retreat open to the Governor.'   It should be remembered that letters travelled slowly.   Events on the Kei on 10 May
were known in Cape Town only after the 20th, so that little Cape Town
criticism can have been known to the Governor when he wrote on
19 June.   Captain Beresford, however, who left with D'Urban's
dispatches about 26 June, writes to the Governor on the 12th to say
that his policy is welcomed by ' all except the Saints ', whose influence
soon came to be feared.

[3] Dr. Philip wrote a great deal about the attitude of the Wesleyans,
pointing out to Buxton (20 June) that several leading Wesleyans were
settled in European charges, shared the Albany panic, and ' knew nothing
of the commando system which goaded the Caffres to desperation '.

[4] Philip and others suggest that the change was due to the advent
to power of the short-lived Tory ministry under Sir Robert Peel from

Two things particularly galled the Philanthropists—one the Governor's use, chance and rhetorical as it probably was, of the phrase ' irreclaimable savages ',[1] the other and more important, the ' sentence of extermination ' implied in the words ' expelled for ever '. The suggestion that the Bantu were ' irreclaimable ' was a direct challenge to the missionaries, and to the first principle of all their work. Even at that time Dr. Philip was able to point to a good deal of evidence of their progress. In twelve years, he claims, the frontier trade of Grahamstown had grown to as much as £35,000 per annum. In the war itself women and children were invariably spared.[2] One native carried a child to safety in Grahamstown, only to be made a prisoner for his pains ; the missionaries, moreover, ' enjoyed almost absolute security '—Brownlee had made the journey *on foot* to Burns' Hill and the Colony, even interviewing Maqomo *en route*, and some stations were abandoned only by express command of the military authorities. Finally, he contrasts the free movements of Major Cox and other officers, who visited the chiefs in Kafir-land, with the forcible detention and death of Hintza.

The decree of ' extermination ' was, however, of more importance, and on this point the Philanthropists' attitude, straightforward enough, has been even more than usually misrepresented. The earliest reference is, perhaps, on 29 May :

' We have twelve missionaries in Grahamstown at this moment, and others of our Kafir missions in other places, and if things go on as they appear to be doing, and *if the Kafir country is to be given to white settlers*, all our labours in Kafirland must be lost.'

As Dr. Philip had been urging all along, the problem was to *govern and administer* the frontier as it existed, not to create a new frontier and begin all over again on the old plan.

November 1834 to April 1835. ' The news was conveyed to him (D'Urban) before any change in his purpose was avowed. . . . Whatever the Tory ministers may do for England, it is indicated pretty clearly what he expected from the effects of their administration in the colonies.'

[1] This phrase is echoed and denounced in the letters of the time by Philip and Fairbairn, by missionaries and their wives, as well as by Dr. Ambrose Campbell and also by Sir John Herschel. Mrs. Philip writes on 23 June : ' Oh ! our Governor from whom we expected so much has preached us such a practical lesson from Isaiah ii. 22 ("Cease ye from man," &c.). The Caffres have been pronounced "irreclaimable savages " and are to be driven from their country.'

[2] Cory, iii, 72, 73.

'You will recollect (he continues on the same date) that I have said *I do not object to any of the countries beyond us becoming part of the Colony, provided the Natives have their lands secured to them* and are governed as the Hindus are, and that it is the system of extermination to which I am opposed. . . . (No decision is yet announced, but) it is the opinion of the Colonists [1] that they are to have the territory divided among them, and the treatment of the Caffres (their " expulsion ") gives but too much countenance to the supposition.'

Again, on 4 June, still to Buxton :

'Had the Governor taken Caffraria under British protection, or had he added it to the Colony, reserving at the same time the country to the Caffres, the result might have been in the end favourable to the success of our missionary labours. England, like the Romans, by spreading her institutions over such provinces as Caffraria, might have made her dominion a blessing to this ill-fated Continent.'

This clear statement of the only ultimately sound policy has been entirely lost because Philip's antagonists fastened rather on what they felt to be exaggeration, as, for example, the next sentences of the same letter :

'England (he continues) has the abolition of the Slave Trade and of Slavery to her glory, but if the extermination of the Natives is permitted . . . no credit can be given to the Government for abolishing the slavery of Africans while it leaves the Natives, whom she makes it a felony to transport, to be massacred wholesale by her troops to gratify the cupidity of men who have been turned into monsters by the brutalizing effects of one of the most unjust and bloody systems that ever disgraced any country. The error into which Sir Benjamin D'Urban has been led by the ascendancy gained over him by those who have been long the abettors and the life of this system may to a certain extent be relieved ; but if the sentence of expulsion be sanctioned by the British Government, our hope of saving and civilizing the nations from the border of our Colony to Delagoa Bay are at an end.'

The ' colonial party ' not unnaturally took to themselves the strictures on the ' brutalizing effects of an unjust system '. The Colonial Office (and the Treasury) shied at the expense of the administrative responsibility which alone offered any real solution of the problem. At the same time Philanthropists in England fell in with the official desire to avoid responsibility and expense ; missing the point that civil administration in

[1] Cf. *Grahamstown Journal*, early in June : ' Anyone who ventured to predict at Christmas that before midsummer Sir D'Urban would seize as a colonial possession a larger tract of country than all the former encroachments, as they have been called, of all the former governors put together ' . . . would have been ' a fit subject for a lunatic asylum '.

Kafirland was a necessity, in their utter abhorrence of the old
' system ', they threw their weight on the side of complete withdrawal. Dr. Philip himself evidently was afraid of this ; for
on 28 June, when he heard that one Captain Beresford was to
go to England that week ' to try to get sanction for the annexation
of Caffreland to the Colony ', he returned to the theme, concluding
a thirty-six page letter to the L.M.S. with a postscript :

' I wish it to be understood that I do not object to the extension of
the colonial boundary to the Kei River *provided the lands are secured
to the Caffres* as has been the case in all our conquests in India. It
is to the extermination of the Caffres that I object, and that is a measure
Parliament can never sanction. The people exempted from the exterminating decree form a very small part of the Caffre nation, and if
Caffreland is given to the colonists they will not be allowed to enjoy
long what may be left to them. Should the news of the change of
Minister lead the Governor to show mercy to the proscribed chiefs
and peoples I shall write you immediately ; in the meantime Mr.
Buxton should be in direct communication with the Colonial Office
to prevent, if possible, the plan proposed by the Governor of giving
Caffreland to the colonists. Should that measure be approved at Home
our hopes are at an end. Nothing (will remain) but a continuance
and extension of the system of desolation so long carried on in South
Africa. O that the wickedness of wicked men were come to an end.'

A reiteration of the same point in evidence before the Select
Committee a year later [1] still made no impression.

While these 1835 letters were on their way, D'Urban's own
action was in the end such as to vindicate the chief contentions
of the critics. On 4 June, within three weeks of the peace, Dr.
Philip had heard of negotiations between Major Cox and the
chief Maqomo.[2] When Cox said the war must continue, Maqomo
replied : ' Very well, you may fight, but I will not '. Whereupon
Philip comments :

' But no ! the submission of the chiefs would have spoiled the idea
of the new order of things which had *long* been considered, and determined for *weighty* reasons. . . . The itching ears of the projectors
of these measures of spoliation (must be) gratified with the magical
sounds of " Province of Queen Adelaide ",' &c.

In other words, the chiefs were ready for peace, but the ' decree
of expulsion ' meant prolonging the war indefinitely.
To make ' expulsion ' effective was, however, beyond the

[1] Aborigines Committee, Evidence, p. 625.
[2] Maqomo, it seems, protested that he had no confidence in the
English people as Hintza was a prisoner and two of his men (Hintza's)
had told him to be on his guard.

Governor's powers, and impracticable. The force at his disposal
was inadequate for the task of 'clearing' the country, even to
the Kei River. As soon as the May 'peace' was proclaimed
the colonial burghers became impatient to get back to their
farms and homes, and were disbanded, the services of the Hottentots being, however, retained, apparently to the distress of
their dependants in the Grahamstown location and on the mission
stations. The Governor seems to have taken no steps to secure
reinforcements for his garrison of regular troops ; nor had he
really counted the cost of the task he had set himself.[1] The
Fingos whom he had taken under his wing were a considerable
addition to his embarrassments. There was considerable delay
in getting them placed in a ' location ', so that they soon dispersed
themselves in disorderly groups over the eastern districts ; and
the mere fact of their presence on the frontier—some of them
on old Kafir lands—was a chronic irritant to the enemy Kafirs.
The Fingos not only provoked Kafir attacks and cattle-raiding,
under the very guns of the frontier posts,[2] but also strengthened
the will to resistance ; so much so that in the middle of August
some of the burgher forces had to be recalled to arms.

The Governor now protested that ' the fire was nearly
extinguished when it was lighted again by the unnatural invectives
. . . of Dr. Philip and his party '.[3] But in fact his own difficulties, the counsels of his new advisers the Wesleyan missionaries,
and probably also the military experience and the humanity of
Colonel Smith, were bringing about a modification of his views,
and a will to a less Carthaginian peace.[4] On 18 August Colonel

[1] P. 19. Cory, iii, 272.

[2] P. 19. Cory, iii, 194 ff. In later peace negotiations the chiefs
' protested ' against bringing Fingos ' across the Kye '. Captain
C. L. Stretch's ' Journal ', 15 August.

[3] To Mr. Borcherds, 16 August (D'Urban's MSS. copied in South
African Library). Dr. Philip had some word of what was going on,
and for the first time gave vent to mild personal criticism of D'Urban
in a letter of 14 August. ' Poor man, if his head were but as good as
his feelings. He is just like some good-natured parent who, having
lost authority in his family, works himself into a frenzy.'

[4] These new influences are reflected in a note from young Theophilus
Shepstone, suggesting, as early as 28 July, that hints of the Governor's
intended clemency be circulated stealthily by the agency of Kafir
women. Shepstone, at this stage an interpreter, was the son of a Wesleyan missionary, one of the first of a long and honourable line of Native
administrators born and brought up on frontier mission stations among
the natives themselves.

Smith, in a ' Confidential P.S. ', told the Governor he thought that if he could get hold of Maqomo he could get the chief to agree to, and to recommend, a British occupation, which would ' protect and provide for them (the Kafirs) by equitable laws and just magistrates '—adding, ' with no Moultries or Bowkers '.[1] D'Urban in reply, on the 21st, speaks of ' overtures ' from Maqomo, who begged that he be not ' sent beyond the Kei '. Another month of cautious and delicate negotiations, with Major Cox, Captain Stretch, and others seeking out and reasoning with Maqomo in his own haunts—and on 17 September a new peace was signed at Fort Willshire. By the new treaty Maqomo and his friends, so far from being ' expelled for ever ', were left to stay pretty much where they had been.

That the Xosa were now to be British subjects was so far to the good, and an important advance. Responsible opinion was converging to the view that the civilized government must take control of the frontier as a whole ; and here, for the first time since the conflict had begun in 1779, the Bantu were recognized as subjects, and part of the frontier population, under Government care—presumably, therefore, as having the right to be protected in their lawful interests. Within a few months D'Urban and Smith proceeded to the appointment of Resident Agents with each of the principal tribal groups, and to the recognition of the chiefs as ' magistrates '.[2] In the task of administering justice, with primitive chiefs as magistrates, Colonel Smith and his colleagues had no experience to guide them. It was a good many years before administrators hit upon the plan, now almost universal,[3] of recognizing the legal authority of Native Custom, in so far as it does not conflict with the ' general principles of humanity recognized throughout the civilized world '. In practice, Colonel Smith carried on, with the utmost kindliness and goodwill, and considerable success, as ' Inkosinkulu ', or Great Chief. Smith might be fond of ' acting a passion ', but he soon made friends with Maqomo, granting him the use of land he coveted on the Keiskama, and urging on him the sowing of corn. Were they not now ' our

---

[1] I.e. Settler magistrates (D'Urban MSS.).

[2] The tribes concerned were the Gaikas, the Ndhlambis, the Amagunukwebe (Pato and Co.), and later, the Tembu or Tambookies to the north. The chief Magistrate was one Hougham Hudson, whose name was suggested by Dr. Philip in 1834.

[3] Cf. Transvaal Law 4 of 1885, and Union Native Administration Act of 1927.

subjects ', even ' our Kafirs ? '[1] Maqomo, he says, wants schools, and teaching, and money, and ' missionaries, who do not pray more than one day in seven, but who teach us to be useful to each other '. Smith, indeed, was ardent for ' policy ', and a ' new system ' ; and, as was his wont, more single-hearted than the Governor. Smith could even learn to write : ' The old colonial system tended to promote plunder, the punishment was inefficient though most unjust '.[2]

D'Urban, with more responsibility no doubt, was worried, and clung to the old ways. To Colonel Hare he wrote (19 September 1835) bidding him ' keep the country well scoured and shoot all Kafirs found in it. . . . The whole is an experiment never tried before and we must give it a fair trial. . . . But even if it succeeds it must be *bellum in pace* for some time.' To Armstrong a week later : ' Keep the district clear. You have still the right to shoot them ; this is an absolute necessity.' On the other hand, on 6 October, there being ' now no more war ', Smith deprecated making ' bandits ' of the Kafirs by ' driving them across the Kei '. Again, a few days later, the Wesleyan missionary Boyce, who succeeded Dr. Philip as the Governor's confidential adviser, was urging strong measures for the ' security ' of the colonists : Kafir custom, he pointed out, sanctioned a fine of ten head of cattle for every one stolen, and to exact only one might be taken by the Kafirs for weakness or stupidity ; yet, as such severity might not be practicable on a large scale, the Government ought to make up the deficiency in the compensation paid to suffering colonists by grants of land between the Keiskama and the Kei. On this and other suggestions Colonel Smith expressed his disappointment with Boyce as ' more full of dragooning our new subjects than a hundred soldiers '. ' The Man of the Gospel is, after all, a worldly fellow '.[3]

On one highly important point D'Urban's original plans for his new Province were open to serious question. From the beginning he resolved to restrict and define the Kafirs' right to remain in occupation of their old homes. Maqomo is, indeed, ' to be a British subject ' ; but ' if this is so ', D'Urban writes to Smith on 21 August,

' he may be placed in a *location* in His Majesty's Colony, provided he becomes responsible for certain main points in his people's conduct.

---

[1] To D'Urban on 27 September.
[2] D'Urban MSS., September 1836.
[3] D'Urban MSS. in South African Library : Memo. of 12 October.

This location must be made with a careful limitation. There must be sufficient intermediate space, *to be filled as soon as practicable with British locations*, between the Gaika's Western boundaries and the Western banks of the Chumie and Keiskama.'

This is one of the earliest appearances of the ill-omened word ' Location ', now inevitably suggesting the cramped and neglected fragments, like flotsam and jetsam in a flood tide of white settlement, that have become the normal portion of the Bantu population all over South Africa. Yet just this all too familiar congestion was likely to be the outcome of such a policy, conceived as it was by Sir Benjamin D'Urban with a sole eye to immediate military security—with no thought for the social consequences, and no provision even for the natural growth of the native population. So far from advocating the policy of segregation, for which experience has raised many modern advocates, D'Urban's hope was that ' thus alone it must be, if by any device these savages are to be at length (at any rate the rising generation) assimilated with the mass of old colonists '.[1] Raw blacks and white settlers were to be deliberately mixed up. Thus interspersed among the natives, the dominant whites must inevitably bar the expansion of the natives and reduce them from the status of a free people to economic dependence, converting their homes in time to the semblance of rural slum areas—at the same time putting it beyond the wit of man to devise a system of local administration capable of harmonizing the conflicting interests of farmers and natives so as to secure the needs of the district as a whole.

At a very early stage Dr. Philip had heard what was in the wind, probably from Captain Alexander of the Governor's staff, to whom he wrote from Cape Town the same 21 August 1835 :

' I have always thought it would be a good thing to take the Caffres as subjects under the British Government provided their country is secured to them ; but the dispersion of English or Dutch settlers among them in present circumstances is a scheme that cannot succeed, and one that the Home Government will never sanction.'

In fifty years, he concludes, ' perhaps '.

As it turned out, D'Urban's plans miscarried and his white settlements were not begun. Some twelve years later, unhappily,

[1] In dispatch of 9 June 1836 D'Urban again expressed his belief in the benefits of ' intermixture ', from ' locations judiciously introduced '.

B.B.B.   K

the good Sir Harry Smith, now guided by considerations of purely military expediency, was destined to begin the long process of planting settlers in among ' locations ', which in time converted the fair districts of Kaffraria into a chess-board of black and white areas, and the congested slums which disfigure the ' Cis-Kei ' of to-day are the result.

But the D'Urban experiment soon came to an end. As Judge Menzies at once warned the Governor (in October 1835), only the Crown could authorize him to naturalize aliens ; Kafirs, as aliens, could not legally own land ; and chiefs could be made legal magistrates only by Charter ; the treaties, in short, were of no effect till ratified by the Crown. In the last resort, therefore, Smith's authority as ' Great Chief ' depended on the bayonets of the troops and on Martial Law. Colonel Smith very well understood his position. When, owing to the frowns of Downing Street, D'Urban in August 1836 took fright and deproclaimed Martial Law, Smith protested : ' The sooner we march out of the Province the better, for how am I to " eat up " Kafirs, according to Blackstone ? ' How it happened that the decision of Downing Street was so unfavourable to D'Urban's fond schemes is, however, a story by itself.

CHAPTER X

THE D'URBAN SETTLEMENT 1835-6

THE reversal of the D'Urban Settlement, synchronizing with the Great Trek, is often said to have been its main cause. But the facts about the Settlement itself and about its reversal are not all that they seem. It is habitually overlooked, for example, that in the year 1835 D'Urban himself made almost a *volte-face*, what he actually tried to carry out in September being fundamentally different from what he had first intimated. D'Urban's pride, or it may be his constitutional dilatoriness in dispatch writing, was such that this radical change of plan was hardly so much as reported to Downing Street. Such account as he sent of the September Settlement, written in November, reached London only in January 1836 ; so that Lord Glenelg's famous dispatch of 26 December 1835 was written in condemnation of the May policy which D'Urban himself had found it necessary to modify. These May plans, and the causes of the war in which they had their origin, had set Lord Glenelg asking so many questions that he had ears for nothing else until his doubts were satisfied ; and the weight and asperity of his dispatch so overwhelmed the Governor that he, for his part, left Glenelg's questions all unanswered, in effect, for more than a year.[1] All this time, therefore, left with the bad impression made by D'Urban's ill-considered first thoughts on how to handle his Frontier Problem, the attitude of Downing Street was hardening.

In May, in fact, D'Urban's plan had been to annex his new Province, and to clear it entirely of those Xosa clans which had been responsible for the outbreak, replacing the expelled Xosas

[1] Glenelg's dispatch was sent off in December 1835. Its receipt was formally acknowledged on 23 March 1836. But the full reply, dated June, was dispatched only in December 1836, or even January 1837, and received only in March 1837. For over fifteen months, therefore, Glenelg had practically no news from the scene of war.

by white settlers.   By August he had come to see that wholesale
expulsion was impracticable, and, in private at least, that this
involved a radical change of policy.   On 21 August, in the
private letter in which he expounded to Colonel Smith his
plan of interspersing ' locations ' of blacks with Europeans
instead of expelling them altogether, he ends with the words :
' I have come to the conclusion, trampling underfoot my preconceived opinions, and sacrificing also some prejudices . . . to
open a door to the course of proceedings above adverted to '
(i.e. to make peace without driving the Kafirs beyond the Kei).
But later, and in his official letters, D'Urban's cue seems to
have been, for some reason, to minimize the importance of the
change.   Thus in a confidential note of 17 September, which
was presently embodied in his report to Downing Street, he
writes of a ' new system, long and anxiously deliberated ', whose
terms were

' *in conformity with those I held out to them* (the Kafirs) *in my overtures
of 12 May, but with a little extension as to the numbers to be entertained*,
arising from the supplication of these people, their expressed contrition,
their professions and, however justly deserved, their sufferings '.

Now there is no doubt that ordinary colonial opinion wanted
nothing more ardently than the May policy of total expulsion.
Several times, in September and October, the *Grahamstown
Journal* recorded its objection to having any of the Kafirs left
in the Amatolas (whence depredations, said to be more numerous
than ever, might easily be made) ; on 8 October it knew of ' no
solitary instance in which those (September) treaties have been
spoken of with unqualified approbation '.   The vocal displeasure
of the Grahamstown people is proof enough of the difference
they, at least, saw between the plans of May and those of September, and it may be that it was to soothe these ruffled feelings
that D'Urban now insensibly made light of the change, stressing
the fact that while Kafirs would be ' settled in a portion of the
land conquered from them ', yet of this land ' *large tracts are
still left vacant for the occupation and speculations of Europeans* '.[1]
But an emphasis thus calculated to win colonial support was
the very thing likely to rouse the ire of the Colonial Office in
London.   As late as 17 March 1836 the *Grahamstown Journal*
protested again that it ' never admired ' the Settlement of Sep-

---

[1] In a Confidential Note on the Treaties, 17 September ; to Bell
on 25 September ; and again in November to Glenelg.

tember, but added that ' the whole frontier is in a ferment at the news ' that Downing Street was unfavourable : ' Not that they want the land for farms, but for protection. . . . To give it to (the Kafirs) would increase robbery and cause the frontier to be deserted '. For this reason they would not have ' any part ' of the land revert to the aborigines. Two weeks later, on 31 March, alarm changed to consternation at an ' incredible report ' that Stockenstrom was to be made Lieutenant-Governor, and even the modified September policy reversed. It was only in face of this dire threat—from a feeling that the September treaties, even with their concessions to the Kafirs, were better than this—that colonial opinion now gave D'Urban whole-hearted support. In the end D'Urban hero-worship became so ardent as to cover up his delinquencies, and the inefficient negligence that marked his whole conduct of affairs.

It was only after deliberate delay, in order that his report ' might conclusively embrace this series of measures and events ', that D'Urban at last, on 7 November, detailed the (September) proposals, ' which appear satisfactory with regard to present effects and future prospects—for which I humbly trust to His Majesty's gracious approval '. Colonel Bell, at least, in Cape Town, realized that the Governor had made the Kafirs concessions which, he trusted, would close the mouths of *the Saints* ; but the light in which these were presented to Downing Street was ill designed to allay uneasiness :

' Our losses ', D'Urban reported, ' were under 1,000, theirs over 4,000 of their warriors. There have been taken from them also—besides the conquest and alienation of their country—about 60,000 head of cattle, and almost all their goats ; their habitations are everywhere destroyed and their gardens and cornfields laid waste. They have been, therefore, chastised—not extremely but perhaps sufficiently, and will, I think, have such a salutary recollection of what they have suffered as to prevent a recurrence.'

Then follow details of the new experiment, with hopes that ' the gentlemen to be selected as Resident Agents, in the spirit of the Secretary of State's dispatch No. 13 of 17 November 1833 ', will prove efficient, at a cost ' somewhat less ' than he had esti-mated in his dispatch of 28 October 1834. ' It was indeed high time to devise measures differing in character from those after former wars, since these invariably ' left conditions on the Border as bad as, or worse, than before '. It is ' worth a trial ' ; but ' it is obvious that for a considerable time to come Law Martial

must continue in force. . . .   The terms, in short, of becoming
His Majesty's subjects, settled by His Majesty's grace in a portion
of the land conquered from them—of which, meanwhile, large
tracts are still left vacant for the occupation and speculations of
Europeans—instead of expelling them beyond the Kye, whence
they might return ', are such that ' their system of clan chiefs
will be at once broken up and its spirit rapidly subdued and
forgotten—and the whole will be brought under the power of
the general colonial laws '.   These will be easily enforced as
' the military power is ever at hand '.

The original copy of this dispatch, preserved in the Public
Record Office, shows what an impression it made in the Colonial
Office.   Significant words are scored and underlined in pencil :
' the Kafirs have been " *Chastised—not extremely* " ; to enforce
the laws, " *the military power is ever at hand* " ' : and as for the
hint that ' large tracts of Kafirland are still vacant ', a pencilled
note in the margin exclaims ' *European speculations ! !* '   There
is not much doubt that if D'Urban's language, emphasizing the
chastisement of the Kafirs and the hope of planting settlers in
the conquered territory, was designed to allay colonial feeling,
it could hardly have been more nicely calculated to touch a
sore spot in the conscience of Lord Glenelg and his permanent
advisers.   It must be remembered that D'Urban had gone out
in the end of 1833 with express orders to devise a ' new system ',
and the report that war had broken out followed hard on the
dispatch of 28 October 1834, in which D'Urban himself, clearly
recognizing that the old order was intolerable, was sketching
plans of reform.   Though the Governor was ' taken by surprise ',
permanent officials, like James Stephen, who did not change so
often as Governors or Secretaries of State, can hardly have been
astonished to hear that the bad old system had produced an
outbreak.   Throughout 1835, both during the conduct of the
war and in attempting a settlement, D'Urban was quite extra-
ordinarily reticent, giving London no hint of any need for reinforcements, or of the additional expenditure likely to be involved,
and omitting to clear the ground by full and clear explanation
either of the causes of the war, or of the necessity for remedies
so much more drastic than those contemplated in 1834.   D'Urban
was sparing even of ordinary news.   His own task was heavy ;
but he seems to have ignored the greater weight of responsibility
resting on his superiors in London, whom he asked, in effect,
to approve the annexation of a whole Province on the strength

of a single dispatch.[1] In the whole of 1835, apart from almost formal intimation in January that war had begun, with short notes in February and March, the only detailed news he sent was in the dispatch of 19 June which reported the May Settlement ; that of 7 November with its modified proposals arrived only in January 1836.[2]

With such very scanty official information to work upon it was natural for the officials at the Colonial Office to welcome any available supplementary evidence, such as soon began to reach them from one obvious source, ' Exeter Hall '. The Philanthropists had a ready spokesman in Mr. Fowell Buxton, whose representations about the ' commando ' system on the frontier had already borne fruit in the instructions given to D'Urban when he was appointed Governor. As Chairman of the Select Committee appointed in May 1835 to inquire into the treatment of ' aborigines ' in all the British Colonies, Mr. Buxton was now in close touch with the Colonial Office. He was also, as we have seen, ' well informed ' by Dr. Philip of what was passing at the Cape. From his own point of view, therefore, D'Urban would have been well advised to anticipate, and meet if he could, the criticisms that were thus likely to reach London, rather than vent his spleen, as he did afterwards, in pencilled notes [3] on the unwelcome dispatches, inspired by his critics, that presently reached him.

It is not to be supposed or suggested either that Buxton made officious or hasty use of Philip's evidence, or that the Colonial Office received it except with due caution. Buxton deferred even his motion for an inquiry from March till May (above, p. 120) till he should receive ' further information '. For some time longer he adopted Dr. Philip's waiting attitude—busying himself with his ' capital good Committee ', getting the evidence of

[1] Glenelg himself complained that, having heard in London early in 1835 of an invasion of the Colony, he got his next report six months later : ' I (then) for the first time became aware that the war was to end not in the repulse of the invaders, but in the acquisition of a new and extensive province.'

[2] See Cory, iii, 272. The June dispatch was carried, with verbal evidence to back it, by one Captain Beresford, son of Lord Beresford.

[3] E.g. on the dispatch of 20 October 1835 D'Urban's very first remark is : ' Philip's insinuations have been working their will here.' There are many more notes, mostly quite illegible, on that of 26 December, such as ' This is all Philip '.

Stockenstrom, with which he was ' delighted ', and of Mr.
Shaw, Wesleyan missionary, ' who has given better evidence
than we expected '.[1]   According to a letter of 28 August from
his Secretary, Miss Gurney, to Dr. Philip, Mr. Buxton

' has spent much time over your letters though not in answering them,
and he means during the recess to get the subject thoroughly up.   He
has a doubt whether it would not be advisable to summon yourself
and Mr. Fairbairn to give your important evidence personally next
session.   On the subject he would be much obliged to you to write
him *immediately* your own views and opinions.   For the present he has
thoughts of going to the Government and of urging them to suspend
the ratification of the arrangements with respect to the new Province
of Caffreland till the origin and cause of the war be investigated.'

Though news of events in May had thus reached England, Mr.
Buxton, according to Thomas Pringle in 1834, was rather slow
to move, and though, in the end, the action of the Government
was precisely ' to suspend the ratification ' of D'Urban's treaties,
it is evident that up to this point none of Philip's comments had
found their way to Downing Street.   Dr. Philip, it will be
remembered, then regarded D'Urban as still on trial and held
back as long as the country was in danger.   Even his weighty
Memo. on the ' Causes of the War ' was still in preparation about
the time of the May ' Proclamation '.   Then, for the first time,
he felt himself bound to strike at his old friend the Governor ;
and on 23 September, as an endorsement shows, a great mass
of his communications arrived simultaneously at L.M.S. headquarters, supplying far more detailed information than any
D'Urban had yet seen fit to send, with closely reasoned criticisms
of the course of policy which the Governor was proposing to
follow.   These documents arrived opportunely, just in time for
one of the missionary society's regular Committee meetings,
and at once made a profound impression.   Mr. Ellis, Secretary
of the L.M.S., got busy—possibly even without fully digesting
Dr. Philip's letters.   Mr. Buxton, whose ' thoughts of going
to the Government ' on 28 August had not yet matured, now
roused himself, and only three days later, on 26 September, Mr.
W. A. Hankey, the retired treasurer of the Society, to whom the
news quickly spread, reported : ' Ellis and Buxton are at this
moment at the Colonial Office '.   On the day of this first
momentous interview Ellis himself still found time to write

----

[1] Colonel Wade also ' attended all the meetings ' of the Committee,
and letters suggest that it was through him that news leaked out to the
Cape.

to Dr. Philip, officially, about Buxton's project of summoning him to England,[1] and ' privately ', as follows :

LONDON, *Sept. 26th*, 1835
Private

MY DEAR SIR,

My official letter to you of this day's date will convey to you the views generally of the Directors on the question proposed to them by Mr. Buxton, viz. their inviting your return to give evidence before the Committee of the House of Commons on the general question of the treatment the Aborigines of South Africa have received at the hands of the Colonists, and the best means of preventing the recurrence of the evils complained of.

Since the interview with Mr. Buxton on 2nd Sept. all your letters have come to hand, and all of them within the present week. Part of them I had the opportunity of laying before the Committee on the day of their arrival, and received instructions to see Mr. Buxton on the following morning. On the next morning your long letter of 4 June came to hand, and without summoning a Committee, I took them all to Mr. Buxton. He instantly wrote to Lord Glenelg requesting an interview on the subject of the seizure of the Caffre Territory, the expulsion of the Chiefs, death of Hintza, etc. To this interview he requested me to accompany him, I having furnished him with copies of your letters as far as the time would admit. I breakfasted with him and Mr. Johnston this morning, and at 12 met with him and Lord Glenelg at the Foreign Office. His Lordship's attention was called to the origin of the War, the increase of the Commando System in the close of 1834, the conduct of Sparks, the fine levied on account of his being wounded, the assault of Lt. Sutton, the wounding of Macomo's brother, the murder of the Caffres as having urged the people to desperation, the honourable manner in which the Caffres had conducted the war : Macomo's conduct to Sparks, the Chiefs' conduct to Major Cox and Lieut. Grant, the circumstances of the arrival of Hintza, his detention as a prisoner and the savage manner of his death, the subsequent proceedings of Col. Smith—especially his dispatch as published in Fairbairn's Paper of the 1st July ; the injustice of expelling the people from the country and the inevitable destruction that must follow : with a request that he would restore the country to the Caffers, or if it must be part of the Colony, not to give it to the Colonists, but preserve it for the Caffers, bringing them under the laws of the Colony.

---

[1] Letters passing between Buxton, Sir George Grey, Under-Secretary for the Colonies, and the Treasury, show that the move to have Philip officially ' summoned ' to give evidence was too late for that session. The Treasury could meet the expenses of his visit only with express authority from House or Committee. The onus, therefore, was on himself, and shortly after receiving this and other letters of August and September, he sailed for England on his own responsibility (January 1836), with only an implied promise that Buxton and others would help to defray expenses if official help was not forthcoming.

To this Lord Glenelg replied that he had a different version [1] of the cause of the war, the conduct of the Caffers, the circumstances of Hintza's death, and the necessity for extending the Colony to the Kei. The cause of War, he said, was, secretly, Hintza's disaffection to the English, the refusal of Macomo to restrain his cattle from prohibited territory, the frequent inroads of the Caffers to the Colony, their plunder and outrages, the increasing complaints of the Colonists of the loss of property and insecurity of life, which had rendered military protection necessary, and which led to the breaking out of the war at a time when it was evident no apprehension was entertained in any place of its taking place ; as the Frontier had never been in a more unprepared and unprotected state. To meet this the evidence of Mr. Ross and others was adduced as to the extensive cultivation etc. and your own evidence as to what you saw of the vigour with which the Commando System was pursued when you were on the Frontiers : the statements of Macomo in his letter to the Governor, and his pointing you to the smoking huts, together with a full detail of the affair of Sparks and Lt. Sutton.

In regard to Hintza's coming to the British camp, and his death, the letter of Dr. Campbell of the Glasgow Missionary Society, with the evidence of Glass, were read to his Lordship, and evidently produced a deep impression. He inquired, ' Where is that man ? ' and was told ' in Dr. C.'s keeping '. His Lordship then said that he understood the missionaries had been in great jeopardy until the arrival of the Governor. Our evidence of the kindness and protection of the Caffers was then fully brought under his notice, and also the treatment of the Caffer Chiefs ; as to the necessity of extending the Frontier in order to protect the Colony,—the good understanding between the Hottentots at the Kat River Settlement and the Caffers, until the former were brought under the Commando System, was adduced, together with Capt. Stockenstrom's evidence that for this purpose no extension of the boundary was necessary.

His Lordship then wished Mr. Buxton to furnish him with all the information he possessed, and Mr. Buxton is to forward to him your letters with a digest of their contents. He then expressed his wishes to receive any information the Directors might possess, as it was his desire to be fully acquainted with all the circumstances, and he promised to give the whole case his best attention. Here the matter rests for the present. What I have done in communicating with the Secretary for the Colonies has been on my own responsibility with the sanction of one or two of the Directors. I was most anxious to prevent any pledge being given to the party (which is) anxious to secure the sanction of the Government to the expulsion—or rather extermination—of the Caffers, and therefore, communicated instantly with Mr. Buxton and the Colonial Office. I shall bring the whole of the documents before the Board on Monday, and shall be able to write you more fully as to the views and proceedings the Directors may adopt, by the next conveyance. The conduct of Macomo in refusing to withdraw his cattle from the prohibited Territory, the great increase of

---

[1] In addition to D'Urban's scant dispatches, there was the *verbal* evidence of Captain Beresford, the bearer of the dispatch of 19 June.

the depredations of the Caffers, which occasioned the more urgent complaints of the Colonists, appeared to be regarded by Lord Glenelg as the causes of the War, not the increased aggressions of the Colonists. On this point and on Hintza's conduct, whether he secretly prompted the War, and as secretly urged the Chiefs to continue it, and not to comply with the terms or wishes of the Government, the fullest and strongest evidence should be supplied.

Lord Glenelg referred to a pamphlet which he had ; it was entitled, I think, ' Narrative of events which preceded the irruption of the Caffers '. It appeared about 60 pages, and was printed at Grahamstown. Neither Mr. Buxton nor myself had heard of it. Send copies if you can. We have not all Mr. Fairbairn's papers you mention. It would be well in cases of importance always to send duplicates, and then if one is lost, the other may come.

I mentioned to Mr. Buxton this morning the desirableness of your bringing over a sensible intelligent Caffer should you come,— he said it would be an excellent plan. Should you determine to come, you will think of this ; it might be of the utmost benefit to his nation.

I have just returned from the Colonial Office—the time for the vessel's departure has arrived, and I must close with assurances of sincere sympathy with you and deep interest in the preservation of the people in whose behalf you have made such persevering exertions.

Believe me,
Yours very truly,
W. ELLIS

The tone of this letter suggests fairly clearly what happened. Ellis, enjoying a sense of importance, closely maintained the touch with Lord Glenelg that was thus established. Finding that the Colonial Office was ' kept in surprising ignorance ', his first step was to send copies of Philip's chief communications,[1] with others as they arrived, these being followed up by letters and requests, ' repeatedly enforced in personal audiences ' (for example, on 25 November—' I have just returned from the Colonial Office where I have been for *the last four hours* '). But Ellis had not Philip's grasp of affairs, and his emphasis tended to be on the wrongs suffered by the Kafirs for years past, on the tragedy of Hintza, and generally on the emotional side. He stressed the case for the restitution of forfeited lands, but missed Philip's understanding of how necessary it was that the British Government should take full responsibility and control by

---

[1] Usually the names of writers were suppressed, Ellis explaining that the letters were so frank because they were obviously meant to be private. It seems to have weighed with Glenelg that Philip had been D'Urban's ' negotiator ' with the Kafirs in 1834. Examination of the volume C.O. 48/165 shows that the greatest part of its contents is of L.M.S. origin, including letters from missionaries like Read and Ross, who wrote from the front to Philip.

acknowledging the Kafirs as British subjects.   At this very time,
on 19 October, far away at the Cape, Philip embodied his maturer
views—more clearly and emphatically than in any letter that
reached Glenelg—in a striking letter to the younger James
Read at Bethelsdorp :

On the subject of it being desirable that the Caffres should be
retained as British subjects, I have long made up my mind.   The
question is not with me what might be, had we such men as Governor
as William Penn, but what kind of Governor we have to expect in the
ordinary course of things, and as the affairs of our Colony have been
managed, and will be managed for a long time to come.   *The Caffres
cannot otherwise be saved from annihilation.*   Were the Colony surrounded by belts of Native Tribes under the British Government,
nations would get time to form beyond us, but no Tribes will be allowed
time to rise into civilization and independence on our borders, if they
are in immediate contact with our colonists.   We never could have
done anything with the Griquas, if it had not been that our work had
arrived at a certain point before the Colony was extended to the Great
River, and even notwithstanding their distance from us, nothing but
a peculiar combination of circumstances could have saved, or can even
now save, them. . .
Contiguous nations never can be independent of each other without
a balance of power, and there can be no such balance betwixt this Colony
and the uncivilized tribes upon our borders.   This fact must be obvious
to any man acquainted with the Philosophy of History, and may be seen
with half an eye by any one who is accustomed to look at men and
things in the Colony as they are. . . .   Barbarous nations may rise
to civilization and independence situated in the midst of nations in
similar circumstances with themselves, and even in that case it must
require long periods of time, and they must work their way to those
points through great difficulties and much bloodshed ; but in immediate
contact with civilized nations—never !   It may do very well to produce
a momentary excitement on an English platform to talk of raising up
civil Governments in Africa, as a man would light one candle by the
gleam of another ; but woe to the cause of missions and humanity
in Africa if our missionaries beyond a certain point have no better light
to guide them in their labours.   When Mr. Campbell one day told me
that Kok and the Griquas promised to keep his laws, and he wondered
that they did not keep their promise, I asked him how long the Israelites
kept their promise made at the foot of Mount Sinai—' all these things
will we do.' . . .
The more silent we are on the present state of things on the frontier
the better ; the question has become now so complicated that it will
require more evidence than certain persons possess to know what
should be done.   Your wisdom now is to be careful to note down
facts, and to avoid giving opinions.   An experiment has been set up,
and we must confine our attention to the results. . .

Yours very truly,
JOHN PHILIP

Here, at least, Dr. Philip, far from ' unwarrantable interference ', was most unfortunately and unduly ' silent '.

It is to Glenelg's credit, and to the honour of British Imperialism, that annexation was not to be lightly and greedily sanctioned for the sake of acquiring territory. The fate of D'Urban's experiment now hung in the balance, and much was to depend on how the Governor himself satisfied his critics. During the summer Stockenstrom's evidence to the Aborigines Committee told against D'Urban's plans, his stress being all on the shortcomings of the old frontier system, and generally in favour of greater leniency. Beyond this the Committee does not seem to have had much serious influence on the actual course of events, either now or later.[1] The immediately decisive criticism probably came through Mr. Ellis of the L.M.S. For example, though the Committee took evidence all the summer, Glenelg still had a ' different version ' on 26 September. But by the 20 October, under the influence of Ellis and Buxton, his opinion about the justice of the annexation had decisively changed, and he warned D'Urban : ' His Majesty's Government ', while ' anxiously bestowing consideration ' on the question, are ' as yet unable to apprise you ' of their decision in regard to ' the territorial acquisition which has been the result of your aggression upon Caffreland '. The ' present inclination is to doubt in some measure the justice, and in a larger degree the necessity, or the policy, of that acquisition '. D'Urban is not to ' anticipate the decision of His Majesty's Government upon the question of retaining or rejecting that acquisition ', but he is ' *not to make a single grant of land*, build forts, or commit His Majesty's Government any further '. At last, after more ' anxious consideration ', and still somewhat tentatively, on 26 December he launched

---

[1] The huge Blue-book of 1836, containing the evidence taken by this Committee, together with earlier ' leakages ', was a mine for Cape journalists at the time, and has been invaluable to historians since. This has somewhat disguised the fact that its Report (see below) was hardly even a damp squib. But the existence and composition of the Committee seriously offended the Colonists and their private friends in England. Captain Beresford, for example, D'Urban's dispatch-bearer, reported on 8 December that the Committee would certainly meet again next session, commenting : ' It is disgraceful the way this Government truckles to the Radicals, Saints and agitators.' Colonel Bell in Cape Town writes about the same time, on hearing that Philip was to proceed to England : ' He and Stockenstrom will be heavy odds against the Colony ', with a ' packed ' Committee, and ' with its president '.

perhaps the most momentous dispatch in South African history.

While the blow of 26 December was preparing, D'Urban and his colleagues continued to grapple with their South African problems. Colonel Smith, in particular, was busy and enthusiastic in his efforts to discipline the frontier. There was still some word of measures of mere repression ; on 10 November Smith wrote from King William's Town of beautiful land reserved for Settlers in the Amatolas, where, ' within the last three weeks I have burned 2,700 huts '. In the same breath, however, he adds : ' Again I say 100,000 men would not have kept the people over the Kye ', and for the next three months he carefully and generously pushed on with plans for the ' location ' of the Xosa population, with some regard to facts as he found them. Three days later the Glasgow missionary, Ross, reported from Grahamstown to Dr. Philip :

' Everyone is beginning to *see* that the statements of a few missionaries, as to the ground or country given in the Treaty to the Kafirs being inadequate for the population, were true. The Commissioners are (now) urging grants permanent and inalienable.'

The Gaikas alone were found to number over 55,000, and before February, Captain Stretch, one of the Commissioners, reported : ' as the ground defined in the treaty of peace is by far too limited, we have recommended most of their former territory being restored '.[1] On 4 February Smith ' thanks God the great subject *location* is now finally settled ; and on the 6th D'Urban himself dated a letter to Glenelg saying that he had taken a census of the Gaika and Ndhlambi tribes and ' enlarged their locations to their great satisfaction—they being *more numerous than he thought* '. ' All ' is now ' peaceable '—on the new borders and on the old.

An equitable land settlement, which incidentally left less room for the ' European speculations ' feared of Glenelg, paved the way also for administrative measures calculated to establish the frontier on something more permanent than ' Martial Law according to Smith '. It would appear that one Major Maclean, at this early date, came very near to the plan that has often been

---

[1] This was to Fairbairn, who as editor of the *Commercial Advertiser* would seem to have arranged an authoritative news service. Stretch, and later Stockenstrom, were for long in the habit of sending him a fortnightly bulletin.

successfully applied in later times. Writing ' with due deference ' of Smith as ' Great Chief,' he comments :

' It is not a time for experiments. . . . Radical changes can only be effected by imperceptible degrees. . . . No, No ! a spark could ignite the whole fevered body '. (With) ' tact and firmness ' (by all means,) ' in the interim all coercive measures necessary should appear at least to emanate from their own judges and tribunals. (In a particular case under discussion) I would advise a meeting of the Councillors of Sutu, submit to them the cause of complaint, let them decide and enforce the law, the " Great Chief " reserving to himself the right supreme to approve, confirm or revise their proceedings and verdict.' [1]

Colonel Smith himself had some grasp of the needs of the situation. ' That (the old) Border policy was insufficient, unjust and imperfect is well known ', he writes to the Governor,[2] but it was unjust ' not alone to the Kafirs, but also to the colonists ', who had ' embarked their capital ' in expectation of protection and reasonable security. He would now have religious establishments, with schools and schoolmasters to train the Kafirs in ' mechanical arts '. With prohibition of ' ardent spirits ', he would encourage the use of money, and the growth of towns and villages as the ' nuclei of civilized life '. In the last days of the experiment, in July 1836, Smith drafted a simple Code of laws—perhaps somewhat on the lines hinted by Major Maclean —which would make salaried chiefs, with Kafir police, primarily responsible for the maintenance of peace and order.[3]

Meantime, though a section of the Boer colonists were almost restive (before ever Glenelg's dispatch arrived there was continuous outward pressure of the kind that culminated in the ' Great Trek '[4]), yet, in Albany, in spite of occasional ' depredations ', there were not wanting signs of prosperity. Military expenditure, it is just possible, had something to do with this, and Captain Stretch, for one, anticipated Stockenstrom in accusing Grahamstown merchants of ' profiteering '.[5] There is

[1] Copied in letter of February 1836, from Stretch to Fairbairn (or Philip), apparently reaching Philip in London, and marked ' For Lord Glenelg '.
[2] On 10 April 1836, and other letters in D'Urban MSS.
[3] Sir George Cory (iii, 330–1) suggests that this was on lines afterwards followed in the Stockenstrom treaties ; but there was the essential difference that Smith's chiefs were to be ' British subjects '.
[4] Cory, iii, 259 ff. Cf. especially Colonel Somerset's Memo. of October 1835, and the Attorney-General's opinion in August 1836.
[5] Captain Stretch alleges in January 1836 that ' in a few weeks ' D'Urban was involved in heavier expenditure than the whole cost of

also less challengeable evidence of prosperity, in the columns of
the *Grahamstown Journal*,[1] where, in March and April, discussion
was renewed on the old question of shortage of labour. ' Much
as we may want servants,' writes ' A. B.' on 7 April, ' Kafirs
cannot be safely employed ' ; and yet, though employers of
' passless ' Kafirs incur a fine of £5, the law is ' practically a
dead letter '. In May, moreover, a ' Juvenile Emigration Ordinance ' was introduced in the Legislative Council to help to ' meet
the urgent need for labour '.

On the whole, therefore, ' the System '—as D'Urban and
Smith called it—was promising well ; [2] but it remained that
some effective substitute for Martial Law would have to be
found. The credit for what success there was must be given
rather to Smith than to the Governor, who appears all this
time to have been nervous and uncertain, like one whose task
was too heavy for him. Smith, though impulsive, could not
have been more loyal as a subordinate ; yet D'Urban's trust
even in him was by no means unqualified—he not only dallied
in Port Elizabeth in November 1835 for fear of leaving Smith
alone in the east with full discretionary power, but was not

Colonel Willshire's campaign in 1819, Grahamstown merchants con-
triving, for example, to get the Hottentot levies dressed in ' Caffre
baize from Tom Wood's store '—' rubbish ' costing ' thousands '
instead of ' hundreds ', which was recommended because it would be
needed ' only for two or three months '. So much, he says, for this
' stricken people, where £ s. d. are concerned '. (For Stockenstrom,
see Cory, iii, 370, 398, and *Cape Col. Qn.*, pp. 79, 80.)

[1] The *Journal's* suggestions at this time favoured treating the
Hottentots as ' colonists ', with ordinary ' title ' to land ; this being
calculated, so critics objected, soon enough to disperse them among
the farmers as servants. One R. M. Burnley, quoting the *Journal's*
account of a Wesleyan meeting in February 1836, breaks out against
' this Gazette of Methodism—the voice of a tiger-cat from behind the
cowl of a monk ! '

[2] Captain Stretch gives favourable evidence to the Governor on 17
May, ' The new order is progressing with every prospect of success '.
Even the ' new colonists ' (Kafirs) say ' we cannot revert to the way
we have lived. . . . To give up (the new Province) would be ruin
both to Colonists and to Caffres, and this opinion prevails among the
latter to a considerable degree.' On the other hand, in August, missionary Brownlee returned to Kingwilliamstown, but hesitated to
' show tacit approval ' by building a new station. His old place was
now Government headquarters, and, so he understood, ' nearly half
the country was reserved and intended to be given to colonists ' ;
therefore, for missionaries to accept such grants ' would prejudice the
Kafirs against them '.

above letting his doubts on the subject be known.[1] Nor, where he made his own decisions, were the Governor's interventions happy or helpful. He was usually little more than a restraining influence on Smith's more energetic reforms. Like a mere soldier, he pressed for greater stringency (above, p. 128) towards the King's new subjects, the Kafirs. Of those older subjects, the Hottentots, who owed him gratitude for his disallowance of the Vagrant Law, he was now unjustly distrustful. At a time when the Hottentot levies, and their missionaries on their behalf, were urging that, having lost a whole planting season, they should, like the burghers, be released from their prolonged military service, D'Urban wrote to Smith (8 January 1836) : ' I have every reason to believe that the *Unnatural Party* (the London Mission) are straining every nerve to disaffect the Hottentots.' To this, Colonel Smith, who had more than once expressed his thanks for the loyal service rendered by the Hottentots, returned (on the 26th) a laconic ' I doubt it '.[2] D'Urban's hostility to the London Missionaries became an obsession, and led him into petty persecution of James Read and others ; he ' can't think ' of Read's returning to his charge on the Kat River —' the demon is not to stalk again in the Settlement '.[3] Philip counselled Read to have patience—though himself at last impatient :

' Since his arrival on the Frontier the Governor appears to have no mind to keep him out of difficulties or to extricate himself when he gets into them, and he suffers no one to approach him who has any more mind than he has himself.'

[1] E.g. to Captain Armstrong on 17 November and to Colonel Bell on 27 (D'Urban MSS.).

[2] E.g. to Stretch on 11 January Smith wrote : ' If you will express your desire for those (Hottentots) who have faithfully and bravely served, I shall have pleasure in laying the same before the Government.' More precisely, to Rev. G. Barker in August 1835 : ' It is evident the wily Kafir built much on being joined by the Hottentot community in his late acts of perfidy . . . in which expectation he has not only been disappointed in a friend but has found a bitter and vigorous enemy.' Fairbairn put the case in a letter to Philip (25 October 1836) : ' There is no doubt that the alarm and agitation caused by Wade's Vagrant Law induced the Kafirs to believe that the Hottentots would not be very hearty in the colony's defence.' In this instance D'Urban's own action in vetoing the Vagrant Law saved the country from a Hottentot rebellion (*Cape Col. Qn.*, p. 240). To meet their distress, Stockenstrom in 1837 planted Hottentot settlements on the Fish River, but the site proved totally unsuitable.

[3] To Colonel Bell in November 1835.

B.B.B.   L

And for once Read had a revenge. As he could not return to his station he was left free in 1836 to make his almost notorious British tour with Dr. Philip, accompanied by the Hottentot Stoffles and the chief Tzatzoe. Neither his meetings, nor even his evidence before the Select Committee, were of any particular importance ; but they quite seriously annoyed both ' the colonists ' and D'Urban himself, whose action had thus driven Read from his regular mission work.

The lack of balance manifest in D'Urban's actions at this period is in keeping with the remissness of his dispatch writing. Such dispatches as he did send conform to one type—usually a somewhat perfunctory explanatory letter, always with scores (and even hundreds) of ' enclosures ',[1] from which the Secretary of State and his officials were left to draw their own conclusions. D'Urban, it would seem, had a mind only for details, with little or no grasp of the situation as a whole—or, as Fairbairn once put it, ' no power of reaching a clear decision based on principle '.[2] In the early months of 1836 frequent rumours reached him [3] that his policy was little favoured, and presumably ill-understood ; but even when, in March, Glenelg's great December dispatch arrived to prove this, D'Urban was content to await a reply to his own November letter.

[1] 254 ' enclosures ' on 9 June 1836 (sent off only in January 1837), 125 of Stockenstrom's letters in June 1837, followed by 120 in July. In the delayed dispatch of ' 9 June ', the Governor actually seems to congratulate himself that he ' now ' had the advantage of being able to forward Smith's report on the successful administration of the already abandoned Province.

[2] To Philip at the very time, 28 March 1836, of the arrival of Glenelg's dispatch.

[3] Repeatedly from Captain Beresford (e.g. about November 1835) and from one of the Cloetes, then in London.

CHAPTER XI

LORD GLENELG AND THE REVERSAL OF THE SETTLEMENT

THE mere length of the Glenelg Dispatch (150 folio pages) made it the more portentous for poor Sir Benjamin D'Urban, and for most of a year had him groping even after its meaning—as the, often illegible, pencilled notes on the Cape Town copy show. Even the generalities with which the dispatch begins are somewhat mordant. D'Urban's military success is ' grateful ', but 'success against such an enemy would bring little accession to the military distinction which you have acquired in other parts of the world '. Then comes the first point : ' I still find myself impeded, (in my) anxious desire (to reach a decision) at a much earlier period, by the want of official information for the guidance of His Majesty's Government (as to) the origin, progress and result of your hostility with the Kafirs. . . . With the most ample details of all your military operations you have not combined any clear and comprehensive [1] explanation of causes . . .' (On this D'Urban notes : ' I thought it had been well enough known '.) Having deferred a decision ' to the latest possible moment ', Glenelg continues, and though he began ' with a predisposition in favour of the measures adopted by yourself,' when D'Urban's dispatches never came he felt ' at last reluctantly compelled to draw many conclusions from less authentic sources of information '.[2]

Glenelg agrees with his predecessor, Lord Aberdeen, that it was D'Urban's duty to meet the necessities of the situation, namely : (a) to repel invasion, (b) to do so possibly even within

---

[1] The words ' clear and comprehensive ' seem to be set in and added to the original text as an afterthought by an editor.

[2] These documents ' from various sources ' are ' carefully recorded in this office . . . to remain here in vindication of the opinions deduced from them '—presumably C.O. 48/165, ' Papers relating to the War of 1835 '.

Kafirland itself by counter-invasion, and (c) to ensure against a recurrence. But, he adds, with an eye on the campaign against Hintza, ' hostilities might have been more limited in their range '. The Kafirs, he goes on to observe, in words deeply galling to colonial opinion, had ' *ample justification* ' in the ' conduct towards (them) through a long series of years, and which the short period of your administration could not have enabled you to correct . . .' ' I had begun and the Kafirs knew it,' D'Urban comments.[1] (Unhappily he had not continued.)

Glenelg then deals at length with the alleged ' ample justification ' for Kafir unrest and retaliation—always, it should be remembered, in the light of D'Urban's May Proclamation, which threatened merely to reproduce on the new Kei boundary the troubles of many years on the Fish and the Keiskama. Going back to the treaty with Gaika in 1819, he criticizes the attempt to bind other chiefs by an agreement made with a paramount of straw—a futility repeated with Hintza—the occupation of ' Neutral ' territory, and the dispossession of Kafirs who ' endeavoured to resume possession of some part of their lost country . . . but were at times driven back at the point of the bayonet '. The commando system it is ' impossible to condemn too strongly or lament too deeply as productive of calamitous results ', including ' extremities ' like ' the burning of huts ' and the punishment, as by Sutton and Sparks in 1834, of resistance made by Kafirs in defence of their ' ancient and lawful possessions '. D'Urban's comments on all these points show how touchy he was about his own honour, and how little real comprehension he had of the situation as a whole. Of Kafirs and the Neutral Territory he notes : ' They lived in it by sufferance ' : expulsion by bayonet was ' Not in my time ' : of commandos, ' What have I to do with this ? ' ' Burning of huts ' was ' Not latterly '. As to Kafir rights of possession, D'Urban missed the essential point that not only were the Kafirs in effective occupation, but that Kafirland was their only possible ' home '—having resort to a well-seasoned ' red herring ' : ' I differ. They were not their ancient possession. They had taken them from the Hottentots . . . (the rest illegible).'

[1] Glenelg disputes, apparently, that Dr. Philip in 1834 ever negotiated or delivered any message ' from D'Urban to the chiefs '. On this D'Urban who, like Philip, had hitherto rather minimized the formal significance of this embassy, now retorts : ' He did both Fortunately I have his own handwriting to prove it.'

The 'irreclaimable savages' passage in the Proclamation gave Glenelg 'pain'; as did a Wesleyan Memo. of 10 January, which went further (than ' you ') in severity. Even the smallness of the casualties was evidence against the theory of Kafir 'savagery.' —' Is this a reproach ? ' D'Urban asks, ' There seems to be no feeling for the losses and wrongs of the colonists.' D'Urban indeed —dimly realizing in his September policy that the only Government capable of maintaining the equal justice, or the ' equal punishment ' of black and white, so eagerly desired by Glenelg, was one that made the Kafirs ' British subjects '—had laid an unfortunate emphasis on land for ' European speculations '. Lord Glenelg's instructions at this time—tentative though they may have been—were almost unique in South African history in over-stressing the Natives' case, missing the problem of *control*, and crediting tribal institutions with some of the permanence and stability of a settled government. He now laid it down as a first guiding principle that, on grounds both of ' justice ' to the Kafirs, and of ' expense ' [1], ' any extension of His Majesty's dominions by conquest or cession is diligently and anxiously to be avoided '. To keep the peace there should be a local militia, a ' wise Border policy ' (D'Urban : ' What is that ? '), with a Lieutenant-Governor, a ' Protector of Native Tribes ', ' Agents ' in Kafirland, and ' Treaties '. Finally, though sovereignty between the Fish and Keiskama rested on no foundation of International Law, its relinquishment was impossible. But the claims of sovereignty over the new Province must be renounced—' right being on the side of the invaded ' —and D'Urban was to have till the end of 1836 ' to prepare the public mind ' for this abandonment. The onus, therefore, was on D'Urban to convince the Home Government that his was the better way. Without making the effort D'Urban dropped his experiment.

In this it has been questioned whether D'Urban was allowed any real discretion. ' All his deductions ', Glenelg expressly states, are based on a view of the Origins which must be disproved. . . . I cannot, I repeat, hazard the experiment of laying upon you peremptory

---

[1] Moreover, none but Kafirs (and Fingos) were to be settled east of the Great Fish River. D'Urban had already suggested that ' this accession of territory will be some indemnity against the expense of the war '. Glenelg agrees that it contrasts with the ' prevailing sterility of our own possessions ', but inveighs against the already excessive extension and expense of the Colony.

and inflexible instructions for your guidance in these affairs. . . .
It will become your duty to assume to yourself the responsibility of
suspending, until further directions, the execution of any part of the
following instructions which you may be convinced had its origin in
any such misconception. . . . (And at the end) His Majesty's Government will await with solicitude the report you will transmit to me in
answer to this dispatch. That (report) will contain as full explanation
as you can on every topic on which I have stated doubts and difficulties.
After deliberate consideration of (the reply) . . . final instructions.'

On the other hand, the evidence of Lord Howick, a member
of the Cabinet, suggests that this discretion, rather curiously
at variance as it was with the peremptory order to abandon
the new province, was only a Cabinet gesture to mollify King
William IV :

' It appears that the King has most strenuously objected to that part
of it which peremptorily orders the relinquishment of the newly acquired
territory. Lord Glenelg obviously thought that this alteration would
be decidedly wrong. Spring-Rice concurred with him . . . I said
that I was willing for the sake of soothing His Majesty to consent to
the Governor's being allowed some latitude as to the time and mode
of surrendering the territory, but that nothing should induce me to agree
to the dispatch being delayed or to the orders for the surrender of
the territory so unjustly acquired being rendered even a degree less
peremptory.' [1]

D'Urban's marginal comments on the dispatch seem to
show that he was thrown into some pardonable confusion. His
first remark is : ' From p. 102 I am authorized to suspend until
further directions ' . . . ' The case was so widely different
when I reported in June . . .' (remainder of sentence illegible).
' His Lordship seems to have written at any rate in ignorance
of the peace and the terms of (?) the treaties '. Now surely
D'Urban's business was to make this essential change perfectly
clear. There is a small episode which suggests that Glenelg
was not immovable. In March, on representations made by
Stockenstrom, the Lieutenant-Governor designate, he at once
modified his ban on settlement beyond the Fish River in favour
of colonists already established there. Later, according to
Stockenstrom, Glenelg himself was to speak of ' this premature
abandonment '. But D'Urban delayed incredibly even to answer
this letter. For a time, indeed, even while thus dallying, he used
the discretion to carry on his ' system '. To Smith he wrote in
May : ' If I do not err, he (Glenelg) is not at present prepared

---

[1] From Howick's *Journal* : an excerpt sent me by W. P. Morrell,
Esq., of Balliol College, Oxford.

to order me to withdraw from the Province.' But at the point where Glenelg closes the dispatch with His Majesty's *personal* demand for proofs of the establishment of a ' Border System advantageous alike for Kafirs and for Colony ', D'Urban's comment seems to suggest that he regarded the issue as settled : ' I have done this. What those may do who alter it, time will show.'

It must be admitted that in spite of the discretion wrung from him, ' for the soothing of His Majesty ', Lord Glenelg proceeded to act as if ' abandonment ' was fixed policy. On 5 February he appointed Andries Stockenstrom to be Lieutenant-Governor of the Eastern Districts, with express authority to make ' treaties ' with the Kafir chiefs. The Governor remained the supreme power and the only channel of communication with London ; [1] but the new officer was to be primarily responsible for the Natives, it being felt that, with the Governor so far distant as Cape Town, ' the tribes were almost permanently under martial law, the administration of justice being left to the Commandant and his soldiers,' and the latter ' sheltered from all real control '. Even so, though Stockenstrom received a copy of the 26 December Dispatch showing ' H.M.'s strong disposition to abandon the conquest ' . . . ' final decision is suspended. . . . You are not to proceed to treat with the Kafirs till the Governor's final report is received ; meantime it is your duty to administer the law as it actually stands.'

Glenelg, that is to say, continued under the influence of the impressions that went to the drafting of the December dispatch.

[1] In this matter Dr. Philip's advice did not affect the issue, except possibly that, in several of the letters which had reached Glenelg, Stockenstrom was mentioned as the only man capable of carrying through a more enlightened frontier policy. On the other hand, on 17 December, in a letter that can have arrived only when the appointment was settled, he wrote : ' The proposal of Phillips (a " Settler ") to send out a Lieutenant-Governor is a Grahamstown opinion and one that should not be acted upon, which is likely to make things worse. The people on the Frontier want a little Court among themselves, and a man whom they hope to influence by having him in their midst. The only public man fit for the introduction of the New System that I know personally is Stockenstrom, and it would be sufficient in the meantime to send him back as Commissioner General with full and well-defined powers to introduce the new system and watch over its workings for a time.' In the same letter, he says also : ' I believe I formerly intimated to the Directors that as matters stand it would be well to retain the Kei River as the boundary of the Colony—but no English or Dutch should be allowed to settle or have land among the Caffres.'

This had cost him so much effort that, till its wide general questions were answered, there was—he felt—no more to be said. D'Urban's November dispatch, therefore, reporting his modified plans, arriving at this moment, received short shrift. The treaties ' scarcely demand a very studious consideration ', wrote Glenelg on 17 February, since ' the King is not disposed to accept the allegiance of the Kafirs ', and ' I regret that His Majesty's ratification was not declared essential to their validity '.[1] ' It remains to be seen what will be their fate ', he concludes, and, cutting out polite phrases about ' confidence in your humanity ' (which appears in the original draft), he asks bluntly for ' further explanations '. Thus far Glenelg ; he had made up his mind according to the light he had. He got no more material for his ' final decision ' for over a year, and before that time D'Urban himself, with Glenelg's deputy, Stockenstrom, had between them taken the final steps and abandoned the conquests of 1835. On 23 March, indeed, D'Urban briefly acknowledged Glenelg's outburst, speaking unrepentantly, but without elaboration, of the importance of the newly acquired territory and of the ' colony in a position so improving '. In April he was in correspondence with Smith about it, Smith sympathizing : ' It is evident Lord Glenelg is shuffling every responsibility upon Your Excellency ', and adding : ' That canting crouching jesuitical dispatch is really (for) the House of Commons.' On 13 May the lion roused himself : ' I am now in a condition to overthrow every assumption and every argument and inference put forth by Lord Glenelg by the stubborn power of facts and *I shall send off my dispatch in a few days.*'[2] Though notes went in the interval, this essential reply, dated 9 June, reached London only on 15 March 1837.[3]

One initial excuse for this astounding delay was that Captain Stockenstrom, the new Lieutenant-Governor, was expected to arrive very shortly after the dispatch, bringing with him fuller and later instructions from the Secretary of State. His arrival was delayed by three weeks in quarantine, till 23 July. It

---

[1] The original draft, thus modified, reads : ' They will probably be abrogated ' (Public Record Office Copy).

[2] D'Urban MSS. to Smith, 13.

[3] What minor dispatches reached Glenelg is not quite clear. On 13 November 1837 Glenelg complained to Napier that he was ' nearly 18 months in office without news '.

cannot be said that Stockenstrom was welcome. D'Urban, indeed, agreed with Smith (1 May) that ' His Majesty's Commission must be respected ', whether or not with Smith's further remark that Stockenstrom possessed ' a very considerable share of common understanding '. But there was never any real hope of friendly co-operation between Sir Benjamin D'Urban and this man of strongly marked and independent character, who was expressly commissioned to carry out a reversal of the Governor's frontier policy. The appointment indeed was unwise. Lord Glenelg had almost better have anticipated his dismissal of D'Urban and made an entirely fresh start.

Captain Stockenstrom has been spoken of as an enigma. His twenty years' previous service, however, when he was in virtually unchecked control of the immense lonely frontier district of Graaff-Reinet, largely explains his later attitude and conduct. Stockenstrom was in origin a colonial frontiersman ; latterly, and even more particularly, a keen and zealous official. His official duties brought him to see, increasingly clearly, that the interests of Bantu, Hottentots, and even Bushmen, did not always get full justice where they clashed with those of their conquerors, the white colonists. Keenly interested in his work, he must have been lonely enough on the frontier, and, like other officials thus placed, delighted to get rare opportunities of ' talking shop ' with intelligent ' philanthropic ' visitors. But he was never an Evangelical Philanthropist, and probably no one was more surprised than he was himself to find how much he had in common, even in 1820, with a new-comer like Dr. Philip.[1] An intimacy thus begun slowly developed—Stockenstrom glad to talk things over when he got a chance of doing so—Philip and others being much impressed both by Stockenstrom's inside knowledge, and by his sympathy with measures for the common good alike of colonists and of natives. Stockenstrom's latest term of office, moreover, as Commissioner-General on the eastern frontier, had been unfortunate, when his authority had conflicted with that especially of the military commandant ; rather than continue as the ' fifth wheel to a waggon ' he had thrown up his post early in 1833, and left the Colony, as if for good—somewhat embittered, and full of contempt for the methods of the frontier administration. The news of the Kafir War reached him in London in 1835, and, being a proud man with

[1] As in 1820 and again five years later (*Cape Col. Qn.*, pp. 129, 214).

absolute confidence in his own capacity as an administrator, he was all too ready, when consulted, to support Glenelg in the view that, for the control of colonists and natives, annexation of territory was superfluous.[1] If only he could have a free hand, he was confident of his own ability to bring order out of chaos ; and going out again with the more emphatic title of Lieutenant-Governor, he believed that his new commission was sufficiently clearly defined to save him from his earlier embarrassments. He was doomed to early disappointment. Sir Benjamin D'Urban, who was of a no more yielding disposition than Stockenstrom himself, started with a prejudice against the man deputed to undo his own work, consulted him no more than he was compelled to do, kept him in the dark about at least one vital decision (the repeal of Martial Law), and in the last resort held up his communications with London.

Nor were these the least of the Lieutenant-Governor's trials. Before ever his new appointment was in question, in the summer of 1835, Captain Stockenstrom had been called to give evidence before the Aborigines Committee ; and there, free from the cares of office, but with an official's consciousness of having inside information for an important audience—probably also nursing a grievance that he was an official no longer—he certainly ' let himself go '. In the main, his evidence had been a critical review of frontier policy—his impression that the prevalence of cattle-stealing was largely due to the carelessness of the farmers themselves, and that ' punishment in ninety-nine cases out of a hundred falls upon the innocent ', leading him in the end to a round condemnation of the commando system. Now frontier life being by no means safe or easy, a young colonial community was likely to be highly sensitive to blows of criticism which would glance lightly off the thicker skin of an old settled Mother Country. In 1835 the Eastern Province was smarting under the fresh wounds of a war that cost it more than cattle. Before ever it was known that this culprit critic was to be Lieutenant-Governor, there was a howl of rage at his evidence in London. Characteristically enough, ignoring Stockenstrom's comprehensive criticisms of the frontier system, the leaders in Grahamstown, fastening on incidentals, furnished Colonel Wade, before March

---

[1] See also pp. 182–3 and chap. xiii, below. Stockenstrom seems to have believed, not unwarrantably, that while, in the end, annexation was desirable, it might, if applied without such a period of preparation as ' treaties ' would make, lead to opposition and open resistance.

1836, with affidavits to prove his exaggerations in the details of one particular episode [1] of five years back.

And now this ' maligner ' of the good name of the frontier colonists was to be their ruler. Grahamstown was up in arms, and ' welcomed ' their Lieutenant-Governor with a ' loyal ' address,[2] challenging him, in Sir George Cory's words, ' to say to their faces what he had said behind their backs '. Such was the civic rage that, though Stockenstrom was only a Captain, and an irregular at that, the officers of the garrison were indignant and went out of their way to do him honour. Sir Benjamin D'Urban quite truthfully reported to Glenelg on 23 August that while, officially, Stockenstrom was ' studiously ' paid every attention and honour, he had ' as Your Lordship is aware, from some circumstances past, come out under the disadvantage of being personally unacceptable to a large proportion of the inhabitants of the districts he is destined to govern '. The ' address ' was but a foretaste of what he was to suffer during some twenty-three months of personal wrangling and strife ; which left him neither time nor mind to turn his constructive administrative abilities to the work he had taken in hand.[3]

It had needed something more than ' studious ' attentions and honour to keep Governor and Lieutenant-Governor on good terms. On 12 July, reporting that the Lieutenant-Governor was delayed in quarantine, D'Urban had protested once more, still without any detailed supporting argument, that his own frontier system ' even surpasses my expectations ', being ' calculated to ensure the security of the frontier and the speedy civilization and happiness of the Native tribes beyond it '.

' Nevertheless ', he continued, ' it is my duty to obey your Lordship's commands, and I shall proceed to do so with as little mischief to the Colony as may be compatible with that obedience unless I shall find on conference with the Lieut. Governor (who may have a later opinion than 28th March) that there remain any reasonable grounds for my continuing to take upon myself the heavy responsibility of further delay '.

On 23 August, with a note on the ' excitement caused by the prospect of renunciation ' of a ' system whose efficiency has proved it equally beneficial to colonists and tribes ', he added

[1] Cory, iii, 286 ff.   [2] Cory, iii, 341 ff.
[3] This is strikingly suggested by a series of almost fortnightly letters of 1837–8 to Fairbairn, in Mr. J. G. Gubbins' collection (below, chap. xvi).

that, after a ' confidential conference ', the Lieutenant-Governor had agreed to their taking ' the still remaining chance of Your Lordship's determination having undergone a change '. Meantime, on 5 August, the Governor had sent Colonel Smith detailed instructions for the abandonment of the new province,[1] but— presumably as the result of this consultation with Stockenstrom, who ' seems a straightforward man of business enough '—he added a note suspending these orders : ' Although I have scant ground I am decided to continue to hold the Province upon my own responsibility . . . (till) further positive orders.'[2] On 17 August Stockenstrom left for the frontier, apparently under the impression that for the present ' the system ' was to continue.

D'Urban's next action gives the measure of his would-be co-operation with Stockenstrom. By general consent, the efficiency of ' the system ', however hopeful it might seem, depended in the last resort on the power of the frontier authorities to enforce their decisions without the inconvenient interference of the ordinary courts, under Martial Law. But the Law Courts of those days were more jealous than they have always been since of the executive's use of emergency powers ; at the very outset (in October 1835) Judge Menzies had warned D'Urban of legal difficulties, suggesting that the new territory should be treated as a conquered province, ' to be ruled as the Crown should think fit ' rather than as an integral part of the Cape Colony. Now, as the upshot of discussions with the Judges, on 18 August, the very day after Stockenstrom's departure, like a bolt from the blue, came the Governor's Proclamation that as ' peace, order and good government ' prevail in Queen Adelaide, *Martial Law should cease.*[3]

Stockenstrom, that is to say, in spite of his private ' conference ' with the Governor, had had no warning of a step that made ' the system ' finally impossible. D'Urban's action in this matter was also disingenuous.[4] To Stockenstrom he wrote on

---

[1] Detailed in Cory, iii, 327 ff.

[2] ' Although ', also, ' by waiting I may forfeit the advantage of their execution under your able auspices '. The ' instructions ' were apparently intended to draw Smith's comments.

[3] The debate with the Judges had been known to Colonel Smith, at least, fully a month before ; in August he had expressed concern at Sir John Wylde's opinion that the jurisdiction of the Colonial Courts ran in ' Adelaide ' as in the Colony.

[4] Or, according to Fairbairn (to Philip on 10 September), merely ' stupid ' : ' When will they spare us a man with intellect—who can comprehend a thing and know his own thoughts ? '

19 August that he had deproclaimed Martial Law ' rather
reluctantly ', having ' no alternative ' ; on 7 September he was
not above boasting to Lord Glenelg that his ' system ' had brought
such ' tranquillity ' as to make this deproclamation of Martial
Law possible. As ' all agreed ' that without Martial Law the
' system ' was impossible, the Governor's conduct in this matter
was some warrant for Stockenstrom to protest in later years that
the decisive step in the policy of retrocession was D'Urban's own.

Stockenstrom could now (5 September) only protest that his
advice had not been asked. A week later he took over from
Smith, and as soon as he faced the hard facts of the Frontier
Problem he seems to have come down decisively in favour of
Lord Glenelg's policy. On 22 September he wrote to Fairbairn :

> ' As for keeping this territory, it is quite out of the question. Even
> Smith and his party admit that it cannot be done without Martial Law,
> and I even believe they feel that it can neither be done with or *without*.
> I only wish we had Lord Glenelg's final decision '. And again : ' If
> Dr. Philip succeed in keeping the new territory we shall be in a pretty
> scrape unless he can get Joseph Hume to allow us a few extra regi-
> ments.' [1]

Stockenstrom, the Governor wrote on the 13 October, having
seen conditions for himself, was satisfied that abandonment
was expedient. There was ' nothing left for the Governor to
do but to issue the necessary instructions '. [2] In October accordingly D'Urban took the law into his own hands and resolved

---

[1] This is quoted in a letter to Dr. Philip from his daughter, Mrs.
Fairbairn, who adds : ' *Supposing that you approve of keeping it.*' From
a letter of the same date (Captain Stretch to Fairbairn) it appears that
Stockenstrom and Fairbairn favoured evacuation, while Stretch, like
Dr. Philip, thought : ' More can be done for the happiness of the Caffres
if they remain under the British Government than is possible under
their own.' Mrs. Philip writes of the end, on 22 December : ' Mr.
Fairbairn feels rather troubled at your letter to him about the giving
back of the Caffre territory to them as it is actually done and proclaimed
last week. How it will answer I know not. I confess I should have
been glad for the people to be under equal laws with ourselves, but
Stockenstrom wrote to Fairbairn that he found it would be impossible
to retain the country without a much greater force than he could command, so he thought it would be better to give it to them than to have
it wrenched from us by another overwhelming war.' Finally, a letter
from Mrs. Johnston (Priscilla Buxton) in August 1837 (see below, p. 161)
seems to indicate that Dr. Philip in England gave way on annexation
in the belief that Stockenstrom was capable of carrying through a
' new system '.

[2] Cory, iii, 366.

to 'put an end to the suspense' both of colonists and of natives by ordering the evacuations to begin.

From this point the two men were hopelessly at loggerheads,[1] and Stockenstrom for his part, having made up his mind, did not stick at half measures. Even Lord Glenelg, in his December dispatch, had contemplated treating the old 'Ceded Territory', from the Fish to Keiskama, as part of the Colony. Stockenstrom, however, decided that, to control the dense bush on the Fish River, a strong line of forts on the Fish Fiver itself would be more efficient than smaller posts scattered amongst the tribes beyond it. To this end he used his wide discretion as Lieutenant-Governor to abandon forts which D'Urban would fain have maintained, and, ultimately, in the treaties he concluded on 5 December, to make over the Ceded Territory, as a 'loan in perpetuity', to certain Bantu chiefs—*quamdiu se bene gesserint*. These treaties, indeed, were Stockenstrom's work entirely, since, as D'Urban himself had reminded him (13 October), Lord Glenelg had laid on him the responsibility for 'framing, consolidating and carrying into effect such a system as may ensure the maintenance of peace, good order and strict justice' in frontier relations. Following Glenelg's instructions to the letter, Stockenstrom went the length of withdrawing completely from Kafirland. Abrogating anything resembling the old 'commando system', the treaties threw on the chiefs the onus of keeping the peace and of checking cattle-thieving, British authority being represented in Kafirland no longer by magistrates, but by mere Agents, armed only with 'diplomatic' powers. On 2 February 1837, a Proclamation formally renounced British sovereignty in Kafirland.

[1] Stockenstrom (to D'Urban on 18 January 1837) 'regrets that he is seldom able to make his acts intelligible to, or to get them approved by, His Excellency'. To Glenelg on 15 March D'Urban complained of the division of powers 'when there is a Lieutenant-Governor like the present one, self-confident, impatient of control and jealous to a degree' for his own authority. His independent military power, in particular, is 'an encroachment on the duties of the General Officer Commanding, who cannot honestly be held responsible'. D'Urban of course had a case, but the methods he chose to remedy the position were dubious. Presently, in June, he sent home Stockenstrom's dispatches 'for a year', to show the difficulty of their relations. Later, a 'confidential' letter of 11 August, to Bowker, a frontier official, asks him to 'keep me acquainted immediately and directly with all that may occur under your observation . . . by every post'—suggesting that the Governor was not above dealing with and through subordinates.

Now that the issue was settled, Sir Benjamin D'Urban turned at last to his long-deferred reply to Lord Glenelg. On 3 November he had resumed the dispatch officially dated 9 June :

'This delay can be of little consequence as in my dispatches from 7th November to June and July the position would have been shown to be so changed that my answer (to 26th Dec.) could no longer have been necessary to Your Lordship's decision. . . .'

On 2 December he starts off once more :

'The time has at length arrived when I may no longer delay the execution of Your Lordship's will.'

He is very sore that ' even after six months practical experience of the system ' adopted in September 1835, that decision should remain unchanged. 'The determination to renounce the Province of Adelaide ', he continues,

' had been made known long before *I* had given it publicity, and in truth the state of uncertainty on both sides of the border had at length assumed a dangerous aspect and could have been endured no longer. . . . . Hence the execution of Your Lordship's deliberately projected renunciation of the acquired territory admitted of no longer delay and it will thus have been effected (as you designed) by the end of the present year.'

D'Urban had made no use of the interval of discretion allowed him to explain himself and get a more favourable verdict on his ' system '. But now the deed was done ; the responsibility lay with Glenelg and his ' anonymous ' advisers. At the same time he could not refrain from harping rather childishly on the excellencies of his ' system '. The main dispatch, dated ' 9 June ', was now of little relevance to a closed issue.[1] D'Urban's main attempt was to explode ' assumptions, arguments and inter-ferences, the same as those which appeared here during the last year in a colonial paper, the organ of Dr. Philip of the L.M.S., whose relative is the editor '. Like Lord Chas. Somerset in 1824 [2] D'Urban put the blame for all his troubles on the doughty Dr. Philip, and to this day D'Urban's allegations pass for definitive history.

To give colour to the picture there are dark allusions to Dr. Philip's ' machinations ' in London, where the Aborigines Committee was at work during three sessions, 1835 to 1837.

[1] For a detailed summary, see Cory, iii, 315 ff.
[2] *Cape Col. Qn.*, xiv.

The missionary campaign of Philip and his companions [1] has been given undue political importance. While Lord Glenelg was waiting in vain for D'Urban to supply material for his ' final decision ', there is no hint in any of Philip's letters that Philip so much as met the Secretary of State. For political influence he trusted wholly to Fowell Buxton, the Chairman of the Aborigines Committee ; and even here he never had the success he looked for. Buxton's first concern, throughout, was with the more general question of West African and West Indian slavery, and even his *Memoirs* make singularly little reference to the Cape in the most critical years of its history. His services to the Humanitarian Movement, which is supposed to have stirred public opinion so deeply, did not suffice to save his seat at Weymouth in the election of July 1837.

In 1836, however, and part of 1837, Dr. Philip undoubtedly hoped for great things from Buxton's Committee. In the early summer of 1836 he crossed swords with his old acquaintance, Sir Rufane Donkin (now an M.P. and a minority member of the Committee), as well as with Colonel Wade, Acting Governor in 1833, and flattered himself that he had ' blown their evidence to pieces '.[2] For his own part he adhered, in his evidence, to

[1] Philip and his party reached England in the spring of 1836. Philip's visit was urged by Fowell Buxton. The suggestion that he should bring ' a Caffre ' came from the L.M.S. and was designed for purely missionary propagandist purposes. Dr. Philip seems to have thought for a moment of getting the chief Maqomo. In the end he took Jan Tzatzoe, a lesser chief who was also a mission teacher, not without friction due to Martial Law restrictions, and to the fact that Tzatzoe was one of Colonel Smith's ' Magistrates '. The common theory that all England was roused to indignation by ' horrid tales ' of the wickedness of the colonists rests on a very frail foundation. ' Exeter Hall ' has never been more than a well-organized body of enthusiasts, influential out of proportion to their numbers just because so few people were likely to bother their heads seriously about happenings in a remote and rather insignificant colony. In the country generally, ' Exeter Hall ' depended for support on those who were enthusiastic for ' foreign missions ', chiefly the keener sort of Nonconformists. It was to these—and primarily to raise funds for mission work—that Dr. Philip and his companions addressed themselves at missionary meetings throughout England, in Scotland, and even as far afield as Cork.

[2] Dr. Philip was not above ' diplomacy '. To Fairbairn, June 1836, he describes how, on Mr. Buxton's advice, he ' out-generalled ' Wade and Co. : ' I wrote an introduction to my papers on the Kafir affairs, and I made it long to tire them, and when it had done as I anticipated, to avoid hearing the whole they agreed to print all before they were read.'

the advice that ' the recent treaty (annexing Kafirland), with such modifications as may be deemed necessary, should be confirmed by the British Government '. In the winter his hopes and his activity mounted even higher. ' I can do here what I can't do at the Cape,' he writes in February. Mrs. Philip, indeed, sent him a ' scolding ' for neglecting his home letters,[1] and began to insist quite strongly on his return. Throughout the winter, especially in January at Northrepps Hall, Buxton's home near Cromer, he was excited and preoccupied, helping the Chairman to draft—or even himself drafting—the ' Aborigines Report '. By April the draft was completed and Dr. Philip set off in high spirits on another missionary tour—satisfied, among other things, that ' the Tories and the King must give way to the Report, and D'Urban's recall must follow as a matter of course '.

But D'Urban, whom Philip now regarded as impossible, was not yet finished with. Unknown to Philip apparently till August, when bad news reached him on his return from Scotland, D'Urban's belated reply—' a bundle of papers a yard high ', says Miss Gurney later—had at last arrived, and certain Buxton letters in the Philip MSS. only now clear up the mystery of the really rather colourless and innocuous Report that issued from the famous Aborigines Committee. The following extracts from a letter to Philip from Priscilla Johnston (Buxton) explain its history :

We have been longing for some communication with you. . . . Surely the events of the last few weeks have been matter of common and deep interest—and then *the report* ! Our dear report, alas ! you will have to behold *sore* gashes in it and especially in *your* part—I mean the Caffre War. Anna Gurney says it is like a table without a leg— and I feel for you when you first have to look upon it. As to us, we have become by this time tolerably reconciled considering *how much* is gained, and that after all, if words are restrained, *deeds* have not been—Adelaide restored and the Government apparently enforcing the right system. I have just been looking over the letters which passed at the time between the Cottage ladies and ourselves, and as I believe I should have been faithful to my old correspondent had you been in Africa, I think I will copy a few extracts from them which will interest you. My father wrote to Anna Gurney June 17th thus : ' At the last meeting on Wednesday week, when I began in a good audible voice to read our South Africa, Gladstone and Bagshaw proposed to omit the whole of it. This did not disturb me. I had no fear that my troops would consent to such slaughter and it proved on a division that they had but their own two votes. But then Sir George Grey did

---

[1] Philip protests at her urging a friend to send him back, ' as if I were a little boy playing truant '.

alarm me, he said they had received and answered a Dispatch from Sir Benjamin D'Urban that it was absolutely necessary for the Committee to read it before they agreed on their report—and that it was gigantic in size. He was pleased to think, however, that if we were lucky and the printers industrious, it might be in print in two months! At the same time we received intelligence that the King was dying— and I was told on authority that immediately on his death there would be a Dissolution. So the least toil was postponement for the Session —to which very probably, was to be added my being turned out. No wonder I was alarmed and took to being sulky. I went, however, soon to Grey and after a good deal of poking at his conscience, we agreed that I should consent to hack away at South Africa, all that related to the late War, and that then he should not insist on the destruction of the whole. I have given him leave to mark all offensive passages for suppression—subject to my approval. These I hope to get on Monday, and I mean to sacrifice much rather than lose the Session—but it is hard work—it would have made you laugh or cry or both, to have watched the coolness with which he set his mark against our tit-bits. I bore it well at first, but when I saw him put his ugly scratch against our most stinging morsels, I almost fainted with horror. Still, I think we shall retain *almost all that is necessary*—though the ornamental will surely perish. Such gashes and ghastly wounds as he had the heart to make! . . . While I am writing, down comes a packet from Andrews containing Grey's alterations—tho' dreadful they are bearable, even if we have to submit to them all. . . . But South Africa, shorn of its beams, and dull as an advertisement as he has made it, will do the *main job*.'

On June 24th he writes : ' Dearest ladies, I thank God the Report is through the Committee—and I report it on Monday to the House —that is but form, the thing is done.'

June 28th, my mother writes from Weymouth whither she had accompanied him : ' Monday saw the happy conclusion of this dear Report—presented and done with. We waited, though very anxious to go to Weymouth. I persuaded him to wait and do it himself—and it was well—for the clerk said it could not be printed, it was so much interlined—but he made him get over the difficulty, one which might have been a sad obstruction, by saying he would himself correct the press. He was next told it was impossible to have it presented till after the private business, which would last for hours, but he mastered this too, went to the Speaker and said his sick wife was waiting at the door of the House, all packed for Weymouth, if he would allow him to come on *first* ;—and by his pathetic pleading he obtained leave, was instantly called, in one minute his precious report was carried up, presented, and ordered to be printed—he was out of the House—and we drove off in Triumph.'

I am sure I need make no apologies for sending you these letters for I am certain they will interest you. They must be kept private of course. We have never seen the report, they corrected the proof of the parliamentary copy, but it is not yet printed ; you cannot, however, expect too much devastation of the Caffre War, Hintza's death, etc., for you will find scarcely a trace of it.

Finally [1], Anna Gurney writes on 15 October 1837, with many underlinings :

He (Buxton) thinks after all he *forgot* to explain to you *the* point on which the great omission turned. The fact was this. In the very last days of the session Sir George Grey brought down to the Committee a heap of fresh documents—papers from Sir Benjamin D'Urban, etc.—a pile standing a yard in height. It was a physical impossibility that these should have been *printed* within four months—and yet, as they *were* given in, it would have been manifestly unjust to give the summons of the case, without the other members of the Committee examining, or at least having the *power* of examining them. Mr. Buxton *did*, I believe, turn them over—and saw *nothing* to invalidate our statement—but that would not have been done for all the Committee—and to have delayed for the sake of *completing the* Report would at that late period have lost the whole of it—and he thought the ' principles ' were worth preserving, though the hiatus is *terrible*. *I* said at the time it was like tearing the *heart out* of our creature !

As Mrs. Johnston comments later : ' Sir Benjamin D'Urban's reply to Lord Glenelg's dispatch was *pert* to an excess, no other word describes it.' Glenelg needed no prompting to object to ' passages which I must be permitted to regard as of a declamatory nature and upon which it can scarcely be incumbent on me to dwell '. Directly but quite restrainedly on 1 May, in a letter received by D'Urban on 26 August 1837, Glenelg wrote that it was clear they could not work together and that he was ' left no alternative ' but to announce the Governor's recall. In a personal letter of 16 August the Governor's friend, Sir Henry Taylor, agreed that the King had no option but to agree to recall because of ' expressions you used, not in a hasty effusion, but as the result of deliberate reflection '.[2] Without Philip's ' machinations ', there were grounds enough for recall, which took effect, in January 1838, on the arrival of Sir George Napier.

While the order for recall was pending, D'Urban and Stockenstrom were left to get on each other's nerves for the whole of

[1] This letter (Priscilla Johnston to Philip, 25 August 1837) throws an illuminating side-light on how the cheap penny postage of 1840 was so long delayed ; expensive postal charges mattered little to those who, having friends at Court or in Parliament, used ' franks ' as a matter of course. Mr. Buxton having lost his seat—' Now we have no franks it is rare to me to write so much, but I must beg one from a friend, the first frank I have asked for almost in my life.'

Dr. Philip seems to have got the Aborigines Protection Society to publish an ' edition ', ' with comments ', which probably embodies some of the discarded ' Report ' (London 1838).

[2] D'Urban MSS., Cape Town.

one unhappy year, 1837. Never was a new experiment for the
control of the difficult Cape frontier launched under conditions
more unfavourable. The relations between the two officials
went steadily from bad to worse. One cause of dispute was
D'Urban's legacy of special obligations to the Fingos whom
he had accepted as British subjects back in April 1835. Being
a homeless people, the Fingos had to be provided with land ;
but when all land east of the Fish River reverted to the Xosa
chiefs they were little disposed to tolerate these ' traitors ', and
even in the old Ceded Territory the Fingos were a constant
source of annoyance to the Xosa, to whose cattle they had liberally
helped themselves. It was largely for fear that the Fingos would
be unprotected that D'Urban had quarrelled in the beginning
(October 1836) with Stockenstrom's plans for withdrawing to
the back line of the Fish River. When the Treaties took effect,
the problem of the Fingos, with Xosa attacks on them, was a
continual embarrassment to Stockenstrom and Stretch on the
frontier, while away in Cape Town the Governor naturally felt
his honour to be involved in giving them ample protection.

There were other causes of conflict in plenty, if only because,
while the Lieutenant-Governor was responsible for the welfare
of the Eastern Province, the Governor remained Commander-in-
Chief of the forces. Throughout the year 1837 there was a
wordy war between the two principals, with the colonists overwhelmingly on the side of the Governor. Grahamstown, seething
with discontent and disappointment, was convinced that no
good could possibly come of Stockenstrom's administration.
Stockenstrom and his officials were equally emphatic that
Grahamstown alarm was the work of a ' war ' party, not borne
out by the facts of ' depredations ' ; they went on to contrast
the existing ' tranquillity ' of the frontier with the conditions
prevailing before August, under Colonel Smith's policy of Martial
Law [1]—to the further annoyance of D'Urban, whose resentment
reached a climax in August when he reported, on the 12th, to
Glenelg, that ' the treaties are nothing but waste paper '. The
truth of the matter would seem to be that it was the strong
feeling of resentment at the policy of ' abandonment ', intensified

[1] See, e.g., letters of 15 January, 13 February, 24 February, 18 May,
and Frontier reports generally. Stockenstrom on occasion took the
offensive, as when he hinted that all was peace except so far as D'Urban
himself had set ' Kafirs ' and Fingos against each other, whereas under
Hintza there was no feud.

by war losses,[1] that found vent in personal attacks on Stockenstrom.[2]

Stockenstrom for his part was far from tactful in his treatment of the colonists, especially of the Boer leader, Piet Retief, and in the midst of the personal wrangles between D'Urban and Stockenstrom, and between Stockenstrom and the colonists, while D'Urban became more and more concerned at the development of the ' Great Trek ', the last thing to receive the consideration it demanded was the proper administration of the frontier. In August 1838 Stockenstrom was driven by the persecution he suffered to go on leave. In the following year Lord Normanby decided that his unpopularity made it inadvisable that the Lieutenant-Governor should return to his post, trying to console him by the conferment of a baronetcy, and eight or nine years of virtual ' drift ' followed, even the attention of the Philanthropists being all but completely diverted from the Kafir frontier. For with the Glenelg policy the resentment of the Boer colonists, who had long looked askance at the growing manifestations of a new attitude to the coloured races, had reached a climax. By 1838 thousands of Boers had sought to renounce altogether their allegiance to the British Government. The natural expansion of the Colony, heavily and apparently finally checked in the east, turned now in full force to the north, and the next years saw the old Cape Colony broken up to become the new and long-divided South Africa.

[1] Stockenstrom himself consistently favoured compensation for ' real ' losses, and since D'Urban, even as late as his reply of ' 9 June ', not only urged effective protection and security, but hinted that the grant of ' farms ', presumably in Kafirland, might help to meet the need, the abandonment was a double disappointment to frontiersmen.

[2] Cf. Cory. These attacks, culminating in the publication of highly offensive cartoons, led to his unsuccessful libel action, *Stockenstrom vs. Campbell*, originating in a charge against Stockenstrom of misconduct in an early frontier campaign, till at last an official inquiry was needed to clear his character and conduct.

CHAPTER XII

THE GREAT TREK AND THE TURNING OF THE BANTU FLANK, 1836-42—BRITISH INTERVENTION IN NATAL

THE significance of the Great Trek is not exhausted when we have described the fortunes of the Boer pioneers and laid stress on the momentous political consequences of their exodus. Its roots were deeply laid in the past, and, being essentially a conservative movement, the Trek served to carry on into a later generation elements of the life of the eighteenth century that had better have died, accentuating and perpetuating the dispersal and the isolation of South African life, which have made the backwardness of the Back Veld. In colour policy it meant in the end the substantial defeat of the enlightened liberalism that triumphed in the Cape in the emancipation of the Hottentots in 1828 and of the slaves in 1833 (even at the same time that the withdrawal of the Die-hard Trekkers cleared the way for the legal and political equality which marked the Cape Constitution of 1853). The Trek was the direct means of bringing European colonists for the first time into direct contact with the great scattered mass of the Bantu tribes lying behind the Amaxosa, who had so long held the narrow front between the Winterberg and the sea. A large proportion of the South African Bantu thus began and continued to be dealt with, not in the spirit of liberalism, but on principles that looked backwards to the old days before 1828.

The Great Trek was, in the first place, a good deal less sudden and cataclysmic than is sometimes suggested. The year 1836 is invariably given as its starting-point. A natural reluctance to stigmatize a great national movement as a protest against the emancipation of slaves has obscured the fact that the Trek followed hard upon the Act of 1833, and was in being as early as 1834. Earlier emigration, it is said, was inspired

only by natural land-hunger.   In the early 'thirties the settlers
on the Griqua border still regarded themselves as Cape Colonists,
and even rode from Philippolis to Colesberg to pay their taxes,[1]
while the 1836 trekkers showed a determination to escape altogether from the control of British Government.

But even this separatism was no new phenomenon.   Boer
republicanism had broken out at Swellendam and Graaff-Reinet
in the last days of the Dutch East India Company, and, with
undoubted grievances to feed on, this deeply-rooted intolerance
of authority [2] was growing vigorously for many years before Lord
Glenelg was heard of.   Of all the causes of disaffection the attack
on slavery was perhaps the least, slaves being relatively few
except in the Western Province.   But the principles that inspired
the crusade against slavery struck very deep.   Inevitably the
critics of slavery revolted against the inferior status that was the
lot of all the children of Ham in Southern Africa.   The result
was the prolonged fight on behalf of the so-called ' free ' persons
of colour, the establishment of Circuit Courts and of legal protection, the 50th Ordinance of 1828, and, as the last straw, in
1834, the refusal of Sir Benjamin D'Urban and of Downing
Street to go back upon the Ordinance by passing a Vagrancy
Law sufficiently stringent to secure ' proper ' relations between
masters and servants.[3]

It is usual to minimize the irritation caused by the slave
emancipation—blaming rather the ' manner ' of compensating
trekkers for the slaves they (likewise !) did not possess.   But
there can be no doubt that the Hottentot legislation was bitterly
resented—possibly all the more because the weakness of the
administrative system made it fully more irritating than it was
effective.   Only a few frontiersmen were slave-owners, but none
of them was so poor as to be without some coloured servants.
These new measures, therefore, subjecting the authority of the
master to the sovereignty of the law, brought dismay to almost
every farm-house.   To men whose mentality was of necessity
that of the slave-owner, the maintenance of elementary discipline
seemed impossible under such conditions, and the insistence,
forsooth, on the ' rights ' of coloured persons laid the train for
an explosion.   In a more confined country there might well
have been a general rebellion.   In the wide spaces of South
Africa an obvious alternative suggested itself, and some hundreds

---

[1] Walker, p. 186, and above, chap. vi.
[2] *Cape Col. Qn.*, pp. 84–6.   [3] *Op. cit., passim.*

of the malcontents resolved rather to leave the Colony altogether, and to found new states of their own, where they should be free to pursue a ' colour policy ' more in harmony with their own traditions and prejudices. Their repudiation of British allegiance, first in Natal, and later in the north, very soon showed conclusively that the Trek was in effect a rebellion.

Immediately after the enactment of the 50th Ordinance, before there was any question of a Glenelg policy, one Louis Trigardt, the greatest Die-hard of them all, elected to brave the terrors of Kafirland itself, and settled, with the permission of Hintza, on or about the upper reaches of the Kei River. Trigardt, the son of a Graaff-Reinet republican of 1796, was the leader of a group of essential nomads or trek-Boers. Towards the end of 1834 he came into collision with the law by carrying slaves across the border. Most of the slaves escaped, but he himself presently came under even graver suspicion of intriguing with the enemy Xosa,[1] though to the colour prejudice of later times such a charge seems wellnigh incredible. Thereupon, about April 1835, he finally betook himself across the Orange River to pursue his adventures in the Zoutpansberg and beyond. In the north he was soon joined by kindred spirits,[2] and, by the outstanding bravery and resource with which they all endured hardship and danger in the wilds, the petulance that led many of the discontented frontiersmen to abandon their old home has been forgotten in the admiration which they have won as pioneers and intrepid explorers.

Meantime the idea of an escape from the restrictive laws of the Colony had suggested itself to other more solid and responsible people. In the course of 1834 three parties ('commissions ') went exploring to spy out the prospects for settlers in the land beyond. One party went as far afield as Damaraland, through the *Dorstland* (Thirstland), as they called it, of the far

[1] Theal, *Sketches*, p. 267. Ross to Philip, June 1835. Cory, iii, 53 *note*. The evidence that Trigardt instigated the Xosa to continue the war is inconclusive. But such intrigue had a precedent in the undoubtedly treasonable conspiracy of the Slagter's Nek rebels with the Xosa in 1815. There was also wholesale trade in powder and guns both with Griquas and with Bantu by Grahamstown traders and others, then and long afterwards. The inference is that the modern ' instinct ' for whites to sink their differences and stand together against the black man is not inborn, but a product of the many wars of the nineteenth century.

[2] Notably the Van Rensburg party, who moved to the region of the Limpopo, never to be heard of again.

north-west. A second reached the Zoutpansberg, attractive country in the northern Transvaal, whither Trigardt went ahead, expecting soon to be joined by Hendrik Potgieter and his party. A third ' commission ', under Piet Uys, ventured safely, with fourteen waggons, through the heart of Kafirland to Natal, returning early in 1835 to find the further development of their plans interrupted by the outbreak of the Kafir War—and just possibly, by the hope that after the war farms nearer home might be thrown open for settlement.

In this of course the frontiersmen were doomed to disappointment. The end of the war brought, rather, grave fresh causes of discontent. Early in 1836 the outward movement began again in good earnest. Potgieter, Sarel Celliers, and others from about the Tarka and Colesberg, moved off in February. Meantime Piet Retief, the best known and the most competent of them all, ' swithered ' at his home in the Winterberg. On 11 April 1836 he complained to the Civil Commissioner of Albany of danger from savages (the Xosa), of non-compensation, of distance from the magistracy, of threats to establish a ' militia ', and of lack of servants—adding significantly that the state of the coloured classes in general *under the present regulations* afforded ' little security for them to resume with confidence their agricultural labours '. D'Urban himself reported on ' June 9 ' (probably he actually wrote later) that the farmers had been inclined to emigrate in 1834, that the change in the Commando Law, and the Emancipation Act, increased the dissatisfaction, but that after his annexation of Kafirland in May 1835 they ' relinquished the purpose of emigration and awaited events ', till ' one of the colonial journals, the *Commercial Advertiser*, asserted that this change of boundary would not be confirmed '.

Thereupon there had been a great renewal of restlessness. For now the abrogation of Martial Law in September had removed the last restriction on free movement, the Attorney-General reasserting his two-year-old opinion that the Governor had no legal power to stop migration.[1] In October Piet Retief fell foul of the tactless but harassed Stockenstrom, originally through an attempt on Retief's part to use his authority as field-cornet to enforce security by ' firm ' treatment of passless natives. To the annoyance of D'Urban, Stockenstrom early in 1837 dismissed Retief from office, but even before this he had taken his resolution to be off. By December a meeting of Trekkers at Thaba N'Chu

[1] Eybers, p. 145.

had elected Maritz, a new-comer, as Landdrost, and in the following April they were joined by Retief at their new town of Winburg.

The War settlement may have been the last straw, but there was more to it. Stockenstrom, defending his sharp treatment of Retief, was brutal. He might, he told D'Urban on 25 May 1837, have ' soothed ' Retief with a definite promise that the slaves should not be free, that the 50th Ordinance be repealed, that Kaffraria be divided up as farms, that the missionaries be hanged, and the blacks extirpated. Even so, he thought, Retief was irreconcilable, and the Trek would not have been stopped. Though Stockenstrom's brusqueness can hardly have improved the situation, he was so far right. The original cause of this great dispersal of the strength and energy of young South Africa was horror of the equality between black and white that seemed to be insinuated in the legislation of 1828 and 1833. Nor was Stockenstrom far wrong in his view of the consequences. He ' has it ', he writes, ' from Dutchmen, not from over-sensitive philanthropists, that the Boers are likely to reduce the natives to the condition of the Hottentots lately '. His prophecy was only too accurate. The political divisions that began in 1836 were healed by the Union of 1910. But the decisive social consequences of the Trek are with us yet. The Republics faithfully and rigidly adhered to the pre-1828 system which had entirely satisfied the old Boers, with the result that masses of the Bantu are now a proletariat, reduced to a condition not unlike that of the Hottentots a century ago. The forces of reaction still threaten to dominate the policy of the modern Union, sweeping back from the north with a vigour and a self-confidence born of the glorious achievements of the Great Trek.

Whereas the Great Trek is to be attributed primarily to the new official attitude to the people of colour, it was further induced by the peculiarities of the economic structure of old Cape Society, which gave the movement much of its distinctive character. The Colony, as Dr. Philip was among the first to emphasize,[1] was ' all farms, with no towns forming ', and not very many dorps or villages ; there were, moreover, no markets, no means of transport, other than the ox-wagons which for the most part tramped out their own roads, and consequently no agriculture

[1] There are many references. This quotation is from a letter to Buxton, February 1835.

except in the immediate neighbourhood of Cape Town. As there was no professional or business class, neither were the Boers rich in political administrators. The colonists must needs be pastoralists, growing enough only for their own subsistence, dealing only in kind, with great powers of endurance, but a very low standard of comfort. Such cattle-farming in a dry country, with no intensive winter-feeding, inevitably needed wide spaces, and land hunger was a very real thing. For nearly half a century the resistance of the Bantu had stopped natural expansion to the east, so that in the early 'thirties there were two generations of sons whose demand for farms was clamorous. To make things worse for a poverty-stricken farming population, what farms were still available were made more expensive by the change in 1813 from the system of one-year leasehold (the marking out as one farm of all land ' within half-an-hour ' of a beacon) to a varying annual quit-rent for a surveyed area. Though this was designed to encourage more permanent settlement, and to facilitate regular sale and transfer, not only was the annual charge somewhat higher than under the old system, but farmers had to bear the cost of survey to obtain title-deeds, and delay in the issue of titles was a further grievance. In 1832, moreover, the Government decided to dispose of Crown Lands only by auction.

Land-hunger, therefore, was one motive for the so-called ' Commissie ' treks, the reconnaissances of 1834.[1] Even in the less attractive north, which had for a while relieved the pressure, the farmers were now baulked by the new tenderness of the authorities for coloured rights. The Griquas of those parts, readily enough, exchanged grazing rights for oxen, if not for guns or even brandy ; but in the early 'thirties the Government, on the representations of the missionaries, for the first time decisively refused [2] to make the time-honoured recognition

---

[1] Even the western districts were mildly affected. In 1847 the Civil Commissioner of Swellendam reported that though ' not many were likely to be affected by the proposal to go to the Mooi River (Potchefstroom) or the Vaal ', yet farmers were restless. The reasons he gives are curiously modern—ten or twelve families crowded on to one farm, with consequent shortage of grazing and of water, and over-stocking. At the same time the relatively high price of land made relief by land-purchase difficult.

[2] Bird, i, 272, for Celliers' reference to the refusal of a petition from seventy-two householders. Philip MSS. : *Memo.* on ' Causes of the Boer Emigration '.

of effective Boer occupation by extending the boundary [1] to give
legal title to farms in ' Griqualand '. Shortly afterwards, to
add insult to injury, the Griquas, unlike the Boers, were recognized
as a ' free ' people, though they themselves were only slightly
earlier emigrants from the Colony whose normal expansion they
now barred—and a good deal more was yet to be heard of missionary efforts on their behalf. (See cc. xiii and xiv, below.)

The presence of the Griquas helps in part to explain why
it was that from the very beginning the mass of the trekkers
moved so far away, instead of planting their secession states on
the reputedly ' empty ' land immediately adjoining the parent
Colony. In order to avoid the great mountain knot of the
Drakensberg, lying to the north of Kafirland, the streams of
Trekkers were compelled in the first instance to converge on
Philippolis. To settle there was another matter. Individual
Griquas indeed readily enough granted the Boers leases, but the
' Captains ' disapproved of this practice. Had Griqualand been
fertile and well-watered the Boers might have run the risk of
coming to blows with the only other people in the country armed
like themselves with guns, and even of continued friction with
the British Government. But this arid country was, after all,
not very alluring, and the double risk drove the Boers farther
afield. Once they had taken the further plunge into the beyond,
they found themselves in much more tempting pastures, in the
north-east of the present Orange Free State, across the Vaal,
and above all, in spite or because of Chaka, across the Drakensberg
in Natal.

The firmly-rooted tradition that this country of the trekkers'
choice was ' empty ' calls for drastic revision. For a moment
they themselves thoroughly accepted the reports of the *Com-
missies* of 1834. Trigardt, for example, in the Zoutpansberg,
seems hardly to have realized the extent of the activities of the
formidable Moselekatze, and wondered at the delay of Potgieter
and others, whose intention of joining him there was rudely
interrupted by the Matabele, in the very heart of the ' empty '
High Veld. Nothing, in fact, was more probable than that
chance travellers over that huge inland plateau should get the
impression that they had it all to themselves. Here and there,
after the Chaka wars, they were likely to find human bones,
and the charred ruins of huts and villages, suggesting that the

[1] As had been done so lately as 1826, when the boundary was fixed
at the Orange River.

solitude was due to depopulation wrought by man. But co-
incidence of this kind is unreliable. It depends so much on what
is being looked for. Dr. Philip, for example, concerned to observe
and report upon the facts of Boer emigration, wrote on his 1832
tour of finding 1200 or 1500 Boers ' beyond the Colony '. His
figures, not to be taken as a precise record,[1] are evidence perhaps
that the number of Boers was surprisingly large. On the other
hand, Boers and other prospective settlers were looking for
land unoccupied by potential enemies. They undoubtedly
found what they were looking for. Their evidence does no more
than support the view that the Bantu were relatively few.[2] The
modern traveller by road or rail might equally well get a similar
impression of the emptiness of great stretches of the most highly
developed districts in central South Africa. The great plateau
of the High Veld is most of it very flat, treeless, open, grass
country, with uninterrupted views over immense distances. Its
exposure to cold winter winds, the want of shelter for cattle,
and, in those unsettled times, the difficulty of lying hid from
human enemies, made it very little attractive to the Bantu tribes.
It was likely to be avoided except by refugees, and recent exposures
to raids by Mantatees and Matabele had left only weak and
broken remnants.

Such, however, there undoubtedly were, in as large numbers
—or as few—as the conditions of High Veld life made safe and
comfortable. The open plains, after all, are frequently broken
by low ridges, shallow depressions (*leegtes*) and clefts (or *kloofs*).
The *kloofs* and *leegtes*, especially those with a north exposure,
have patches of sheltering and serviceable bush, and are the
most likely places to have permanent water. In such spots
natives undoubtedly sought refuge and security.[3] And it was

[1] Field-Cornet Ziervogel in 1835 found ' 62 families ' in the same
area (Cory, iii, 257).

[2] The narratives of travellers before the Trek leave a distinct
impression that they were constantly meeting ' natives ' of one sort or
another in a country that was by no means ' empty '. Living tradition
indicates that when the storm had blown over, in the 'sixties and 'seventies,
' danger from Kafirs ' was one of the normal risks of travel even on
the High Veld. (See also p. 294, *note*.)

[3] Strong tradition suggests that native kraals existed at such places
as Heidelberg Kloof, the valley under Aasvogel Kop, near Johannesburg,
and in sheltered parts of Free State River valleys. That there were
also Bushmen and Bushman children to be ' apprenticed ' by the
Trekkers (cf. Walker, 212, 213) certainly indicated that the native
population was sparse.

precisely these scattered spots that were likely to attract the Boer farmers, to the deprivation of such natives as remained. So far from finding the country empty, the trekkers had their first great meeting at Thaba N'Chu, a Wesleyan mission station among Moroko's Barolong; not far off lay ' remnants ' of Mantatees under Sikonyela; and the first trekker capital, Winburg, was planted on land ' ceded ' by a chief of the Bataungs ' in exchange for a troop of cattle and the promise of protection ' against the Matabele.[1] To the east, the Boers were to strive, and frequently to fight, for many years, to clear the eastern Free State of natives professing allegiance to the great Basuto chief, Moshesh, who was strongly ensconced in the foothills of the Drakensberg. Even in the southern Transvaal early Trekker history is one long story of friction with native chiefs from whom the Boers obtained ' title ', by ' treaties '. The open High Veld, therefore, apart from the newly arrived Matabele, was ' empty ' only in the sense that its Bantu were as utterly powerless against the white man as the eighteenth-century Hottentots of the Cape Colony—to whose plight as landless dependants trekker ' protection ' in time reduced the ' remnants '. Their descendants survive to complicate the modern problem of the landless proletariat of ' farm ' natives.

On the High Veld, only the Matabele were at once a real danger, and they were soon disposed of. Trigardt in the first place steered his course wide of Moselekatze, but early in 1836 a party of trekkers known as the Liebenbergs were massacred near the Vaal River; in the same year Sarel Celliers and Potgieter beat the Matabele off at Vechtkop in the northern Free State, at the cost of their food and cattle, and there were other encounters in which more Boer lives were lost. Moselekatze, suspecting that there would be no room in that country for him if the Boers once got a footing, had struck betimes. Early in the next year, however, the Trekkers took steps to teach him a lesson, surprised his kraal at Mosega, inflicted heavy losses without losing any of their own men, and recaptured waggons and cattle. In November of the same year Potgieter and Uys made the running so hot that Moselekatze was presently forced to withdraw from the Marico to beyond the Limpopo, to end his days in ' Matabeleland ' (Southern Rhodesia). The Trekkers remained virtually undisputed masters of the greater part of the High Veld.

[1] Gie, ii, 302.

The scene of the most important activities of the trekkers now changed to Natal, where, they had heard, land was good —and 'cleared' of natives by the inter-tribal wars. Possibly the beginnings of organization, with Retief as Commandant-General, together with their success in chastising Moselekatze, gave the Boers self-confidence, and confirmed their ready belief that the land lay open for the taking. Perhaps the well-watered pastures and genial climate of the coastal province were worth the risk even of a clash with the Zulu power. It may be that some of those who suffered from the Matabele felt that the danger could hardly be greater than that they had already faced in the north. Disputes and rivalry among the leaders themselves helped to decide the issue, and in October 1837, while Potgieter went north to complete the Matabele rout, Piet Retief rode off, trusting to diplomacy to secure from the Zulu chief, Dingaan, a grant of land for the Trekker Republic of Natal

The Zulus soon made it too tragically clear that the Trekkers were unwelcome. When Retief first approached Dingaan with his plaint that the colonial farmers were short of land,[1] the Zulu, with characteristic Bantu evasion, made his negative indirect. Sikonyela, he said, the Mantatee across the mountains, had stolen 900 of the king's cattle ; if the farmers would recover these, then they might talk business. With great rashness, not for the first or last time, the farmers, running counter to modern notions of what is expedient, allowed themselves to take sides in a purely native quarrel. In the fatal February of 1838 Retief and some sixty companions, having fulfilled their side of the bargain, returned to conclude the 'treaty' by which Dingaan 'ceded' them the whole of Natal. The chief, however, had different plans, and to him the treaty was but another piece of temporizing. As the earlier episode of Sikonyela's cattle shows, the Zulus were in touch with the people beyond the mountains and knew of the doings of the Trekkers there ; [2] by Retief's own

[1] 'Our country is small, and we becoming numerous can no longer subsist here . . .' (D. P. Bezuidenhout's account in Bird, i, 368).

[2] From native sources in Basutoland, Dr. Philip, in February 1842, got an incidental sidelight on Dingaan's murder of Retief. Among the witnesses of Retief's 'recovery' of cattle from Sikonyela, in accordance with his bargain with Dingaan, there was, it appears, one of Dingaan's councillors. Having once got Sikonyela into their power, 'the Boers assumed the fact that he had been guilty of the theft and demanded the stolen cattle, with others as a fine . . . forced him into the house of the missionary in which they bound him and threatened to carry

mouth they had news of the defeat of their rebel kinsmen, the Matabele. Now these fellows that were turning the world upside-down were come hither also, Dingaan, as all the world knows, took the shortest way with those who had put themselves in his power and brutally butchered the whole party. Immediately afterwards he sent his *impis* to complete the work by attacks on the Boers in their own camps. The Boers were surprised in laager on the site of Weenen (Weeping), where even women and children were massacred. This, with further losses elsewhere, threw the tenuous Boer organization into utter confusion. Potgieter, who had come to the rescue, but whose first and last love was the Transvaal, withdrew from Natal altogether, the more readily that he could not work with the other leaders and designed to found a state of his own. In the course of the year 1838 Boer losses at the hands of the Zulus were not fewer than 362 men, women and children, besides more than 200 coloured and native servants and 13 English allies—a fearfully high proportion of the very few thousands who had made the Natal venture.[1]

It was impossible that this should be the last word. The British authorities in Cape Town were filled with anxiety about possible reactions on the Xosa front, but, before they could intervene, the Trekkers marshalled their own forces under a new and vigorous leader, Andries Pretorius, with reinforcements come from the Cape to help their fellows in distress, and to share their fortunes. On a famous date, 16 December, now a national holiday, the Trekkers met and routed Dingaan's army, with such heavy punishment that the river ran with blood (whence Blood River to this day). Six months later, with some diplomatic

him to Dingaan ' . . . keeping him bound for three days, to the ' surprise and indignation ' even of the Zulus, whose ' respect for their chiefs was shocked by such treatment. . . . " Is this the way in which you treat the chiefs of the people ? " one asked. Being answered in the affirmative, with coarse and offensive expressions, he asked, " Would you treat Dingaan in this way were he in your power ? " To this they made reply : " We shall treat Dingaan in the same manner should we find him to be a rogue." From that moment Dingaan's councillor became restless and uneasy, and as soon as it became dark he disappeared, proceeded with speed to Dingaan, related his story, along with his own impression ; and the chief, taking fear from his councillor, had made his preparations for the destruction of Maritz (Retief ?) and his party before their arrival with the cattle ' (cf. account in *Owen's Diary*, v. R. Society, p. 170).

[1] Preller's *Voortrekkermense*, ii, 52.

help from a British agent, Pretorius forced Dingaan to accept
a new treaty, by which the Zulus recognized Boer claims in a
very much enlarged Natal, and undertook to pay reparations.
Dingaan was no more to be trusted now than eighteen months
earlier. But like other tyrants he had enemies in his own household, and again the Boers seized their opportunity of applying
the principle *divide et impera*. They now gave their support
to Dingaan's chief rival, Panda, and encouraged civil war. Early
in 1840 Dingaan was defeated, driven into exile in Swaziland,
and there murdered, Panda being recognized as paramount of
the Zulus, but holding as a ' vassal ' of the new Boer republic.
So within three years the Boers had broken the power of the only
two considerable military monarchs in the whole of Bantudom.

Conquest thus threw on the victors a more searching test.
They had now to deal not only with opposition in the field, but
with the problem of governing both old opponents and the weaker
tribes—the ' surplus ' masses—capable only of indirect resistance
by the method of cattle-lifting. The comings and goings in
Zululand, or with the Zulus, were the least of it. The Trekkers
were now to find that Natal was no more than the Transvaal
the ' empty ' Elysium they had pictured. Since 1824 English
traders and adventurers had had a tiny settlement at Port Natal
and occasional dealings with the Zulu potentate Chaka, as well
as with his successor, Dingaan. In 1835 their leader was an
ex-naval officer, Captain Gardiner, but though he got D'Urban's
support, and gave the Governor's name to the port, he was unable
to persuade the Home Government to take them under its
official wing. When Retief arrived at Port Natal in 1837 Gardiner
was established there with a vague magisterial authority ; the
Rev. F. Owen, of the Church Missionary Society, had got a footing
at Dingaan's kraal ; and about the same time American missionaries, advised by Dr. Philip, were preparing for work among
the ' Zoolahs '.

The Zulu centre lay, of course, beyond the Tugela, in districts
that included the present Vryheid. The story goes that, presently,
50,000 to 80,000 natives were found to be ' filtering ' from
Zululand into Natal, though it is difficult to see how the Zulus
in possession, with their large herds,[1] could have made room for
so many dependants. The legend that Natal had been ' cleared '
of its native population probably originated with travellers who,
on their way through Natal, naturally saw only the central and

[1] Cf. Agar Hamilton, 34.

B.B.B.   N northern uplands. Great stretches of the country resemble the High Veld, but at frequent intervals there are secluded bushy valleys. These spots lie for the most part off even modern main roads, and are still, some of them, rather roadless and inaccessible native reserves. In time of stress, and even for choice, natives other than the organized Zulus can never, many of them, have been much farther away than the ' Valley of a Thousand Hills ' (admired afar off by modern travellers between Maritzburg and Durban), the dense bush north of Greytown, the rugged upper valleys of the Mooi and Tugela Rivers, the Umkomaas Valley, and other similar havens of refuge in the very heart of Natal proper.

The overthrow of Dingaan was an undoubted boon to the peaceful natives and these now began to show themselves. The truth would seem to be that as, ultimately, the wars and migrations of the Bantu in general were induced by internal pressure, so now the fall of the tyrants somewhat relieved this pressure in one direction. But this relief, by allowing the weaker tribes once more to range abroad with less restraint, outside the bushy valleys in which they had been forced to seek refuge and lie low, created also a strong demand for land. The Boers, glad enough to have a supply of labourers—even squatters who would, with their women and children, supply their labour needs in return for permission to work a piece of the farm—soon suffered an *embarras de richesse*. As early as 5 August 1840, the new-fledged *Volksraad* passed the first of a long series of *Plakkers' Wetten* (Squatters' Laws), restricting the allowance of squatters on any one farm, other than that of the Commandant General, to *five families*. If restriction was thus found so urgent, clearly then far more than the average of five families were there to be dealt with or provided for. The allowance of five families became a habit. An unrepealed Transvaal Law of 1885 still limits squatters on any one farm to five families, but the limitation has never been enforced. It could not be, for the reason that the ' reserves ' have never yet been adequate for the ' surplus ' native population of any of the republics. In any case, as an American missionary, Mr. Alden Grout, wrote to the Governor of the situation in Natal in February 1844 :

' Whatever may be said of previous occupation, the British Government found the people in the Natal district, or they allowed them to locate themselves there, and I am afraid that the Government will find it necessary to provide for them in one way or another.'

In 1841 the Natal Volksraad, nothing daunted, returned to the charge with a resolution proposing to deal with the ' influx ' by a measure of ' segregation '—though obviously these natives must have been either returning to their homes, or discovered, as soon as the trekkers broke up their commandos and dispersed to their farms, to have been in the country all the time. The ' surplus ' were now to be dumped to the south of the Republic between the Umtamvuna and Umzimvubu Rivers, on territory claimed with reasonable justification by the Pondo chief Faku. The Boers at least did not waste time in investigating Faku's claim. The numbers of the natives in Natal were an unlooked-for embarrassment, and imposed on the Boers a task of government for which they were unprepared, and indeed unfitted. From the very beginning the Trekkers found themselves worse off than in the old Cape. There the thieves were on one side of them only. Here they were surrounded by natives. In 1845, when at last the British Government had definitely intervened and annexed Natal—when, moreover, the tiny European population was again reduced by an exodus of discontented Boers—the Government was faced with the problem of ruling not 20,000 but 100,000 natives.[1]

This old under-estimate of the native population, in the Trekker States generally, probably still tends to vitiate sound thinking on the South African Native Question. The statistics of slaughter in the Chaka wars are little more scientific than Herodotus' fabulous estimate of the size of Xerxes' army. The native troubles in which all the Trekker States were at once involved are proof positive that in the 'thirties the natives were far more numerous than is commonly believed. The pendulum has now swung back. The modern counterpart (and consequence) of the rooted belief in the wiping out of the Bantu by the Chaka wars is the tendency to exaggerate the rate of increase of the native population. The latter day ' increase ' is correspondingly magnified, and the fear that Europeans must soon be ' swamped ' is consequently ' much exaggerated '.

No doubt the Trekkers as a whole wanted only a quiet life. Conquest of the Bantu was no preconceived part of their programme, and what they did was largely for self-protection. The Trekker way with the natives was individual discipline for farm servants (with no legal protection), and the old ' commando system ' for the recalcitrant. An affair with the Baca chief

[1] Cf. Brookes, pp. 24, 25.

Ncapaai illustrates Boer methods. Farmers on the southern border complained of cattle-stealing and traced the spoor to the kraals of this chief, who was a rival of the Pondo, Faku. Thereupon, in January 1841 a commando under Pretorius fell suddenly upon Ncapaai without stopping to investigate the charge against him, and carried off some 3,000 head of cattle,[1] and 17 ' apprentices ', to the alarm even of Faku who, fearing that his own turn might come next, appealed for British protection. In face of such happenings in Natal and the north, the British authorities, with their own responsibilities on the old Kafir frontier heavy upon them, were slow enough to move. It was not as if Natal was a vacuum, where wars and civil wars could proceed for two years without unsettlement and inconvenient reactions elsewhere. In the middle of 1837 Captain Stretch and others indicate that the Cape frontier was at peace.[2] A year later unrest in Natal had the whole of ' Ethiopia ' in a ferment.[3] As early as 1839 there had been ominous rumblings of the quarrels of Ncapaai and Faku on the Cape side of Natal, and in October 1840 Governor Napier found the whole Xosa frontier so disturbed that he feared the worst for the Stockenstrom system.

The British authorities could hardly remain unconcerned spectators. The immense widening of the ' Bantu Question ' is indeed the outstanding consequence of the Great Trek. It is also the aspect most consistently ignored. If most of the difficulty on the old Cape frontier before 1834 arose from the refusal of successive governments to face the problem of setting up a civil administration that might attempt to control both colonists

[1] The 3,000 head, far more than Ncapaai's alleged ' theft ', were designed to ' pay the expenses ' of the expedition (Agar Hamilton, *op. cit.*, p. 142).

[2] To the Rev. James Read (whom he last met on the ' Hottentots Parade ' in Grahamstown) he writes : ' We are quiet and there is less stealing than has been known for many years past, which is convincing evidence that the chiefs can preserve the colony if they are allowed to go on without commandos continually entering their country.'

[3] When Boer fortunes were lowest, Dr. Philip, fresh from England, wrote on 1 June 1838 expressing alarm at ' the discovery of their power and the use to be made of it, by Dingaan and Moselekatze '. Yet, he adds, the Boer emigration continues. ' Compensation money has turned their heads, and they turn it into powder and shot to expel the Canaanite from the Land of Promise. . . . The only part I am taking is that of a spectator, and my only resource is prayer ' (to Dr. Thomas Hodgkin, Anti-Slavery Society).

and natives, the Trek made things immeasurably worse. If the establishment of a settled frontier government was hard even for governors with the might of Great Britain behind them, the task was utterly beyond the power of a scattered community of frontier farmers with nothing but their guns to trust to. The guns sufficed to reduce many tribes to landless impotence ; and Europeans came to settle for the first time among the Bantu, isolated, fearful of remoter stronger tribes, and without any strong government to hold the balance with those they had succeeded in reducing to impotence. The civilization of these subjugated ' heathen ' natives was no part of the plan, and was indeed utterly beyond the Trekker States. The Trekker governments were so feeble that the conquered Bantu were subjected on the contrary to the caprice of individual Boers. It is true that all but irresponsible adventurers among the Trekkers accepted the prohibition of slavery. But the slave-owning mentality remained and could hardly conceive of an educated ' Kafir ' or of an order of society in which the ' Kafir ' should have legally enforceable rights. The argument weighed heavily in 1910 that only a single, united South African Government could hope to deal effectively with the twentieth-century ' Native Problem ' ; but the need for unity of control was still more clamant in 1840. The powers, the coherence, the machinery and resources of the mushroom republics being then, and for a long time to come, utterly contemptible, the British Government at the Cape was the only possible one to attempt to control the relations of black and white throughout South Africa. As the 'forties progressed there was some hope that the British Government would shoulder its responsibilities and attempt to cope with the situation as a whole. Early in the 'fifties Her Majesty's Government, having put its hand to the plough, looked back. The tangled problem of the twentieth century is the direct result.

The dependence of the Cape Governor on Downing Street, and the inevitable difficulty of consultation before the days of cables, hindered the prompt decisions and the effective action that were often needed. The Trekkers, when all is said and done, were British subjects, and only the backwardness and isolation of the Bantu tribes made it possible for H.M. Government to ignore as they did the consequences of Boer emigration. Very early (29 October 1837) even Lord Glenelg scouted the Trekkers' rather naïve plea to be treated as ' a separate colony ' ; the claim was

' so extravagant that I can hardly suppose it serious ; they are subjects of the Queen, who put themselves beyond her protection, and if reports be true, they are no longer useful citizens but freebooters '.

But to bring government and subjects into effective relationship over the wide spaces of South Africa demanded more than pious assertions ; it needed administration, a strong efficient system of magistrates and police such as the Trekkers could not provide, and the British Government would not be at the expense of establishing. Downing Street was not unmindful of its responsibilities, but as, apart from its Kafir wars, even the Cape Colony hardly paid its own way, the Home Government set its face against any extension of responsibility by colonization which would inevitably bring more wars.

At the time of the 1835 war, accordingly, the favoured plan was to conclude treaties, on an Indian model, with native potentates—defining the boundaries of their territories and recognizing them as ' allies ' in the task of preserving something like stability. The first of a long series was the treaty with the Griqua Waterboer in December 1834. Early in 1836 one Dr. Smith gave less formal recognition to the Matabele, Moselekatze —to the great satisfaction of the Secretary of State who (on 3 September) hoped by such treaties to ' cultivate an amicable intercourse with the Colony ', and thus at once to secure peace, and ' to promote civilization among the tribes on our immediate frontier '. The Stockenstrom treaties with the tribes on the eastern frontier were thus not isolated experiments but part of a set policy. Stockenstrom himself advocated treaties on the ground that, while outright annexation was likely to be welcomed by people like the Griquas who were sufficiently advanced to appreciate the advantages of civilized government, it might easily provoke resentment and rebellion if applied prematurely to self-contained Bantu tribes. It had been his intention, he wrote, ' to enter into alliances with all tribes with whom we were likely to come into contact, and who were strong enough to have, or to organize and maintain, a government of their own '—the basis of the agreement to be the ' *acknowledgment of the right to the territory of its then actual possessors* '. Ultimately, he hoped, they would ' see cause and be glad to throw up their independence and embrace British supremacy '.

' Wherever British subjects have already settled,' Stockenstrom continued, ' or the tribes are broken and weak ', the British Government ought to take control. This was likely to be opposed both on the grounds of expense and as appearing to sanction 'dispossession'. But it would be better than the alternative, 'extermination', and in any event, Stockenstrom concluded, till the *system* is settled ' no sort of title (for British subjects) to any of the land ought to be either directly or tacitly admitted . . . and then only by purchase '. Stockenstrom's plans perhaps never had a real chance ; but in spite of the clear warning given by the Aborigines' Committee in 1837 against ' compacts between parties negotiating on terms of such entire disparity ' as likely to prove ' rather the preparatives and the apology for disputes than securities for peace ', treaties were the established policy years before the experiment still commonly put down to Dr. Philip's ' interference ' in the 'forties.

As a complement to the Treaty policy, Downing Street sought, in August 1836, to put some check on its own subjects by enacting the measure known as the Cape of Good Hope Punishment Act. This Act ' for the punishment of crimes ' —and saving the ' sovereign ' rights of tribes or rulers—made the Cape Laws applicable to offences committed by any of His Majesty's subjects in territory adjacent to the Colony ' to the southward of the 25th degree of South latitude ', providing at the same time for the grant of commissions to persons to act as magistrates for the prevention of crimes and the bringing of offenders to justice. In practice the Act seems to have been nearly a dead-letter.[1] Magistrates under the Act were few and far between, their effective power negligible. But the real problem of the Boer advance, their proscriptive colonization of native land, was in no sense a ' crime ', and the first essential remained, to establish some strong authority capable of governing civil intercourse between an advanced and a backward people.

Faced by the consequences of the Great Trek in Natal, D'Urban's successor, Sir George Napier, very soon came to realize that nothing short of annexation and strong government could meet the situation. The Punishment Act had little power or relevance ; and the Trekkers themselves were adepts at ' treaties ' which were really deeds of cession, and tended only to complicate the issues. Lord Glenelg and his successors in office faithfully reflected the opposition of the British Treasury to any assumption of responsibility likely to entail expenditure.

---

[1] Cf. complaint by Rawstorne, the officer in charge at Colesberg : ' I beg to express regret that the Act of 1836 has been allowed to remain unemployed ' (to Government Secretary, 18 September 1840).

Presently, however, the murder of Retief, and the disorders that followed, wrung from Lord Glenelg nervous and qualified permission to intervene, and in the end of 1838 a company of British troops was sent to occupy Port Natal. Just at that moment Trekker fortunes revived. Dingaan was chastised at Blood River, and, as Napier's hands were tied, a year later (December 1839) the troops were withdrawn, leaving Pretorius and his Boers themselves to settle accounts with the Zulus, to establish Panda in place of Dingaan, and to secure from their vassal the cession of an even larger Natal than before.

But now the official British attitude began to stiffen. Lord Normanby and Lord John Russell (1839) were stronger secretaries than Lord Glenelg ; and after 1841, the Tory Ministry, with Mr. Stanley at the Colonial Office, was in the long run no less sensitive where British dignity and interests seemed to be affected. As early as June 1839 Lord Normanby had ordered an investigation of reports of surface coal in Natal, on the ground of its potential importance to ' steam navigation '. In August 1841 an American ship appeared at Port Natal, and in 1842 the intrigues of a Hollander adventurer named Smellekamp, who made various descents upon the coast in a Dutch brig and roused hopes in the minds of the Trekkers of Dutch protection and support, served to remind Downing Street that Natal might be of some importance also as a naval base. Downing Street, moreover, was always concerned for the welfare of the native tribes, and although till the middle of 1842, when Dr. Philip returned from the greatest of his tours—an eleven months' pilgrimage through the lands north of the Orange River—the Humanitarians seem to have been unusually silent,[1] the influence of ' Exeter Hall ' undoubtedly favoured intervention.

In December 1839, just when Sir George Napier had decided to withdraw his skeleton force from Port Natal, Lord John Russell penned the first of a number of dispatches which showed that the determination to resist intervention was weakening. Six months later [2] Russell ordered immediate reoccupation ; but Napier—unwilling to weaken his garrison on the Kafir frontier by the removal of a force of the strength which his earlier experience suggested to be necessary—used his discretion and held

---

[1] The Philip MSS. may be incomplete for the years 1839–41, or Dr. Philip would seem to have been absorbed by the domestic affairs of the missions and of his church in Cape Town.

[2] 18 June 1840 (Bird, i, 605).

his hand. Early in 1841 the affair of Ncapaai, and Faku's appeal, induced him to order a force under Captain Smith to advance into Pondoland for the protection of Faku. In the middle of the year the Volksraad's threatened experiment in ' segregation ' caused further alarm for the security of the Cape frontier, and, armed by yet another dispatch from Lord John Russell, Napier at last ordered the reoccupation of the port. This time the Boers proved less friendly—or more sure of themselves—and in May and June 1842 Captain Smith, who had moved up from Pondoland, was besieged in his camp near Durban—to be relieved in the end by the frigate *Southampton* only after one Dick King had made a famous and desperate cross-country ride to Grahamstown to give the alarm.

The Boer resistance at once collapsed, but even now the Government held back. In January Mr. James Stephen had written a minute for his new Tory chief, Lord Stanley :

' It is very ill policy to enlarge this ill-peopled and unprofitable colony and . . . to make a new settlement at Port Natal where there is not even an accessible port or a safe roadstead . . . (with a danger also of) warfare alike inglorious, unprofitable and afflicting.' [1]

Whereupon Mr. Stanley (10 April) followed Stephen and renewed the offer of amnesty to all Boers who would return. Napier, however, confidentially (25 July) urged the need for the annexation at least of coastal Natal. A month later, by Dr. Philip's report, he pressed for action in the north as well. In December Stanley gave way, decided against the recognition of Boer independence, and agreed to the annexation of Natal. In June 1843 Mr. Cloete proceeded to Maritzburg, armed with a commission to negotiate with the Boers with a view to some definite settlement. Significantly enough, the first condition of annexation was too much for the wavering Boers. They were prepared to agree that slavery must cease, and even that military action against the natives should be undertaken only with Government sanction. But it was also proclaimed :

' There shall not be in the eye of the law any distinction or disqualification whatever founded upon mere distinction of colour, origin, language or creed, but the protection of the law, in letter and in substance, shall be extended impartially to all alike.'

This was too much. Here was the dreaded ' *gelijkstelling* ' (equality) of black and white, inspired by ' negrophilist ' principles,

[1] Colonial Office, 48/214. Public Record Office.

which was the first basic cause of the Trek itself.[1]   Perforce, on 8 August, the Rump of the Volksraad at Maritzburg agreed even to this condition. Not long afterwards the Volksraad ceased to function, and died. Still final decisions were delayed, and, while Commissioner Cloete struggled with problems of land settlement, it was not till August 1845 that Natal received its own Lieutenant-Governor, and entered on a period of eleven years as a separate province dependent on the Governor and Council of the Cape of Good Hope. Meantime a large proportion of the Trekkers had withdrawn to asylum across the Drakensberg, and the centre of interest and activity shifted about 1842 to the country of the Orange and the Vaal.

[1] Cf. comments of Dr. S. F. N. Gie, *Geskiedenis*, ii, p. 341.

CHAPTER XIII

THE TREKKERS IN THE NORTH—GRIQUAS, BASUTO, BECHUANA AND MISSIONARIES—DR. PHILIP'S GRAND TOUR, 1841-2

IN Natal the serious complications caused by the Great Trek made themselves felt very soon. Here was no empty paradise, except, perhaps, in the sense that there was no established government to call in question the actions of these emigrant British subjects who sought to renounce their citizenship, and ' asked only to be left alone '. The Government's difficulty about this simple solution was that the Trekker Boers with their expansive habits left little room, and not so much as a secure legal status, for the native population, whose very existence in fact they ignored. The natives, moreover, were able to make some show of resistance, whether by murder, like Dingaan, or only by cattle-stealing, like Ncapaai ; and with war so near the eastern frontier the Cape Government was rudely awakened to the fact that the doings of its subjects seriously threatened its own internal peace. It is still sometimes asked why the British Government, having ' recognized ' those earlier emigrants, the Griquas, should have denied such recognition to the Boers. The answer is that, whatever their earlier treatment of the Bushman aboriginals, the continuance of the Griquas on their Orange River lands was now the only hope of stability—a mere recognition of the *status quo* ; on the other hand, till the Boers had shown proof of being able to govern—or even some sense of their responsibilities to their prospective subjects—to recognize their government, whether in Natal or beyond the Orange River, was to pronounce a sentence of deprivation on the coloured people who had been there before them. It must have subjected these people to an unorganized body of farmers, who, openly repudiating the laws enacted lately by their own

Government for the protection of the coloured races, were
entirely without efficient law-courts of their own. Even for
Europeans, indeed, it was a long time before the Trekker
Republics were in a position to satisfy the accepted canons
and obligations of 'independence'. These have lately been
summarized as follows :

'Since the Congress of Vienna, it has been the rule that a newly
created State, in order to be recognized as such, should sign with the
Powers which guaranteed its independence a Convention providing for
religious toleration and protection of life and liberty of all its subjects
—or in a phrase of M. Clemenceau, "those elementary rights which
are, as a matter of fact, secured in every civilized state".' [1]

In the 'forties, and even later, it is clear that the Trekker Republics, expressly denying all rights to natives as such, scarcely
even began to satisfy these conditions, and their establishment
was accompanied, in every case, by native resistance and open war.

On the High Veld, the great inland plateau beyond the
Orange River, events were to develop more slowly. Except
perhaps in the foothills of the Drakensberg climatic conditions
made dense population impossible. There was, moreover, no
geographical obstacle to impede free movement, so that Boers
from the Colony began to spread slowly over this area, mere
distance making for the development of distinct communities
almost completely out of touch with one another, and with the
Colony. Before 1836, therefore, and for some years afterwards,
northern developments created little stir—there being here no
danger of international complications—or fear of British naval
interests being compromised as in Natal. Yet in the future of
South Africa this area was to be of the first importance. The
original Bantu population of the High Veld proper—though
habitually much underestimated—was still relatively small, and
the comparative absence of native opposition made this area an
important sphere of white settlement. In time these High Veld
settlers extended their authority over a vast native population
either indigenous or driven to the Transvaal Bush Veld, eventually becoming so strong as to determine in turn the status of
an important part of the native population, and to a great extent
the characteristic outlook upon the 'Native Problem' of a large
and almost predominant part of the European electorate of the
present-day Union.

The earliest colonization of the High Veld was the work of

[1] Article, *New Statesman*, 30 June 1928.

colonial farmers, pushing out, after the manner of the eighteenth century, in search of pasture. Unlike the so-called Voortrekkers of 1836, these men had no violent political bias, and no desire to escape from British control. For a good many years, indeed, the settlers of the Southern ' Free State ', under Michiel Ober-holster, made a distinct party—sharply opposed to the Die-hard Trekkers under Jan Mocke, who pressed on beyond them to Winburgand in greater numbers to the Transvaal (' Loyalists ', they were sometimes called). With them, at least, it might be hoped, a satisfactory and amicable settlement ought to have been possible.

On the face of it, the natives to be considered were few enough and very weak ; with goodwill, and some contrivance, there ought to have been room in those wide spaces for people of both races, black and white. The Griquas of the Orange River were estimated about 1840 at barely 5,000 in all. There were also Barolong and Mantatees in the central area. The Basuto were a good deal more numerous, but even then largely concen-trated in one compact area under one strong chief. In the north and west, however, there was a more considerable sprinkling of Sechuana-speaking tribes than the very sparse modern popula-tion of British Bechuanaland and the Protectorate would suggest ; Sechuana is still the language of the farm natives of the west, particularly of the very considerable native population of the western Transvaal, much of which was conquered from these tribes only in the 'fifties. But the causes of the schism lie be-neath the surface. The first was economic, and sufficiently serious. The Scots artisan and missionary, James Clark, who, even if imperfectly educated, was a shrewd observer, urged on Dr. Philip in 1841 the desirability of instruction in weaving ' as an industry for leisure hours and to teach regular habits '; his motive was that while ' at the colonial stations even the women can get plenty to do ', at such a distance from any market the people were necessarily pastoral, and employment scarce. In other words, even then, as surprising evidence confirms for Bechuana and Basuto,[1] the northern peoples were glad to improve their living by wage-earning.

The immediate effect of the scarcity of employment near

[1] The Moffats' letters from Kuruman in the 'thirties and 'forties often speak of parties of Bechuana going to or returning from work in the Colony. Moshesh, in his talk with Dr. Philip at Thaba Bosigo in February 1842, expressed appreciation of the protection afforded

at hand was that, for present gain, and without any idea of the ultimate cost, Griquas and Bantu alike were very ready to give settlers permission to use their springs and land. The next was that, once they were established, the Boers suffered from the same economic disabilities, absorbed more and more land, and very soon left too little to meet the needs of the original population. Even so the demarcation of native reserves by a strong government might have saved the situation. The farmers, and the whole of South Africa, must have benefited immeasurably had they been thus early forced to more intensive occupation, and, in one missionary's words, to make ' *permanent* settlements '.[1] We might then have begun to learn the truth of the paradox that much of South Africa is ' unable to support a larger population *because* its population is so scanty '. But few were far-seeing enough to seek this solution, and the farmers, at least, had no will to find it.

The needs of the native races who were there before them, and with quite as good right, found no place at all in the farmers' scheme of things. These early Boer settlers, hard beset by difficulties, and in no wise politically malcontent, had to struggle so hard for their own existence that they had no time for new-fangled refinements. To their eighteenth-century traditions and ways of thinking the Griquas were of no more account than the Hottentots and Bushmen whom their fathers had displaced before them. So far as it had views at all, the Dutch East India Company had been of the Boer way of thinking. But now a new factor vitally affected the issue. While the older Hottentots had had no spokesman, the very weakness and unwarlike bearing of the Griquas, the Bechuana and the Basuto, had attracted Humanitarian interest and brought it about that, unlike even

by colonial laws, contrasting the defencelessness of his people in the surrounding country. In the Colony, ' if they enter into a contract for a year they are not detained beyond that period ; if they enter into an agreement their wages are paid ; if they are beaten by their masters they can apply to a magistrate for redress. *They return home with the cattle they have earned.*'

[1] ' The roving disposition so universal among the colonial farmers exerts its influence upon our people . . . who leave their farms on which, with some labour, they could subsist, to go in search of stronger springs, to places, away from the station, where less labour is required and game is more abundant. Could they be induced to build substantial homes this might be checked. . . . It is our constant endeavour to portray the advantages of *permanent* settlements and industrious habits ' (P. Kolbe to Philip, July 1835).

Natal, the lonely High Veld was linked by a solid chain of mission stations. From these stations, in themselves the witness of a newer view, native rights were urged with effect upon a Government now not insensible of its obligation to stand by the principles of its own reforming measures in the parent Cape Colony. The Griqua communities—' states ' they were not—the London missionaries' attempt to fix a nomadic people in villages, stretched from Bethulie to the west of Griquatown, with Colesberg at once as a base and a colonial outpost. Beyond them to the north-west were Robert Moffat and other L.M.S. men among the Bechuana. To the north-east, French missionaries, in close alliance with the L.M.S. through their common local agent, Dr. Philip, had stations among the Basuto—one at Moshesh's kraal, Thaba Bosigo itself. For a while, first Americans, and then Mr. Owen of the Church Missionary Society, the eye-witness of the murder of Retief, worked at Mosega, Moselekatze's kraal on the Marico. Finally the Wesleyans, though somewhat aloof from their brethren, were established as patrons of Moroko and Sikonyela, petty chiefs of the middle east, weaker rivals of Moshesh. It hardly matters that all these missionaries were not always at harmony among themselves. Standing as they all did for freedom, the missionaries, with the important independent evidence they furnished, saw to it that unusual attention was drawn to events in these parts.

Of all these coloured communities that of Waterboer, at Griquatown, strategically perhaps the least important of them all,[1] had alone in 1834 secured official recognition and support. The history of Philippolis, on the other hand, the real storm centre, serves to illustrate at once the economic complexities of the High Veld problem, and in the end the hopelessness of the attempt to leave the control of black and white relations to any petty coloured chieftain. As ill chance had it, the death of the elder Adam Kok in 1835 gave rise to a disputed succession at this most critical juncture, and the rival claims of Abram and a younger Adam Kok—not unconnected with the comings and goings of new-comers in the district—left no settled authority whatever, and no hope of the ' treaty ' still vaguely contemplated by the Government.[2] To make matters worse, the missionary

---

[1] In July 1845 Waterboer reported to Montagu, Colonial Secretary, ' not a single Boer in Griquatown territory '.

[2] (Colonial Secretary Bell to the Civil Commissioner of Graaff-Reinet, 1 April 1836.) According to Stockenstrom (to Jas. Read,

Kolbe fell into disgrace, and was dismissed in 1837. Thereupon a younger man, Atkinson, seems to have divided his time between Philippolis and Colesberg ; a domestic feud with Moffat put out of the question help from that quarter,[1] and only in 1842 the experienced Mr. Wright, for some time Government Agent with Waterboer, transferred to Philippolis to spend the last months of his life in an attempt to restore harmony and order.

This was no mean task. In 1835 Kolbe had written lamenting the action of the Griquas in hiring out land to incoming Boers. In October 1840, Mr. Atkinson, writing from Colesberg, more than confirmed the growth of this practice. The Boers, he says, are ' coming in very fast '. The Griquas [2] are ' leasing their farms to them for six, eight and ten years ', in spite of their own law against such leases, and he fears that ' at this rate the Boers will soon get all the land '. A year later : ' I fear there is no way of helping the Griquas in that district.' Ultimately the Directors were appealed to and pronounced judgement : [3]

' That the Dutch Boers are getting quiet possession of Philippolis seems very manifest, but the Directors do not see how they can prevent it. The Boers have gone there by arrangement with the natives and

---

June 1845) a Griqua treaty, together with a similar project for Moshesh, would in fact have been negotiated ' if I had not left the Colony in 1838 '. Sir George Napier, he adds, intended to act, and " one of the main features was the *acknowledgement of the right to the territory of its then actual possessors* ', with protection for the Bushmen whose actual reinstatement ' had become for ever impossible '.

[1] The great Robert Moffat sulked in his tent rather than co-operate as effectively as the times needed with his ' Superintendent ' Dr. Philip. Moffat was for ' self-government ' by a ' District Committee ', which distances made impracticable, and resented the discipline of one of his colleagues by the Cape Town Agent of the Society. The missionary with Cornelius Kok, at Campbell, proved a failure, and was charged also with flogging a Bushman. Moffat heard that the charge against him was of ' interfering in politics '—a ' ludicrous ' accusation to come from Dr. Philip, who retorted, aptly enough : ' What are politics in the affairs of a chief without subjects, and a missionary without people ? ' —The breach was never really healed. The Directors recognized the Committee (which never functioned), and though the consequent resignation of Dr. Philip in 1843 did not take effect, Moffat neither helped Dr. Philip with first-hand information, nor invoked his help when it might have been of service.

[2] This letter distinguishes between ' Griquas ' and ' Bastards ', the latter being more dependable. Mr. Atkinson also notes ' trouble ' caused by the ' English here ', who wanted ' races ', and were ' naturally ' prevented by the Church-Wardens !

[3] Freeman, L.M.S. to Dr. Philip, 20 April 1841.

on payment of some stipulated amounts. That this occupation may involve the final loss of freedom and territory on the part of the native population is by no means improbable—but no case arises out of the present state of affairs with which the Directors can go up to the Government. We have (nothing) to elucidate or substantiate a charge against the Boers which refers to Philippolis. We are not now speaking as to their general measures to obtain possession of territory beyond the Colonial boundaries, but as to the serious point mentioned in your letter, namely—the restoration of slavery in that part of Africa by the intrusion of the Boers. . . . The Directors are quite ready to appeal to the Home Government, but regret that the Colonial Government is thought to be useless in the matter.'

In September 1841, shortly after receiving this letter, Dr. Philip set off to the north to see things for himself. Arrived on the spot towards the end of the year, he was by no means unreasonable even about Boer needs and claims, and at once began to think of a settlement which would define and perpetuate the *status quo* :

' Let the Boers have guaranteed to them the lands they possess and forbid them to make any addition to them except by *purchasing*, and all that is desirable may be done without bloodshed or confusion.'

In Griqua country, at Glisson's Drift, 90 miles from Colesberg, he wrote again : ' The Boers are masters of this country, and except in Waterboer's and Moshesh's territory as thick as in the Colony itself.' Philip penetrated at once to the importance of the land question, and the social consequences of the Boer occupation. There was, for example, an ominous story from Natal :

' It is a well-known fact that in the late raid on Capai (Ncapaai) the Boers carried off fifty children,[1] and some of these were seen by Mr. —— in families by whom they had been purchased. (Pretorius, indeed) made a proclamation of severe penalties for the practice, but my informant says the price was from 100 to 250 rix-dollars (1 R.D. = 1/6), and the Boers laughed at the proclamation as meant to *gull the English* and never intended to apply amongst the emigrants themselves.'

Second-hand reports of the use made of native children agreed with more immediate evidence of the plight of the Bushmen east of Philippolis :

' Not only has an active slave trade been carried on among the Boers residing at Natal ; but it is well known that an active trade in children has been carried on between them and the Boers spread over the Barotse

---

[1] The number is usually given as only seventeen. On the question of ' apprenticeship ', see Agar Hamilton, chap. ix.

B.B.B. O

country from the Vaal River to the borders of the Colony. Mr. Rolland at Beersheba, and even in the country of Moshesh, is not able to protect the Bushmen in his neighbourhood. (Giving details of a raid . . .) Mr. Rolland is as much feared and respected by them as any missionary in his station can be ; and yet they have taken Bushman children from his kitchen. . . .'

Things were far from satisfactory among the Griquas themselves. At Philippolis he found that a party ' composed of the old *Bergenaars* and those they could influence ' had newly returned from a ' commando in which they have killed many people and taken 20,000 head of cattle and many sheep and goats '. Nothing, in short, Dr. Philip consistently maintained, could meet the situation but effective British Government control.[1]

There was ground enough for apprehension. Beyond Philippolis Philip came into personal touch with Boer extremists —real Trekkers—and noting their hatred against the English expressed the fear that they ' will continue to infuse it into their children from generation to generation '. Unhappily his fears were in some measure realized. But the missionary movement which has been blamed for promoting hostility did no more than call attention to facts as they were. In the light of history it appears that Philip and the missionaries, not their opponents, were substantially right in their foresight of the social consequences of leaving Boer encroachment to run its course.

The issue in the north was the maintenance of those same principles of human justice which inspired Philip's vindication of the equal human rights of the coloured people of the old Cape Colony—admitted more and more to have been the most important cause of the Trek itself.[2] In all the districts affected by the Trek, the Boers, as the stronger party, were in a position to take, or it may even be to acquire, a virtual monopoly of the land. Except under pressure—sometimes by the formidable resistance of the stronger Bantu chiefs, sometimes as a reward for services rendered, and occasionally, as in the later Transvaal, by the direct intervention of the British Government [3]—they showed little disposition to recognize prescriptive native rights, or to provide

[1] After his tour Dr. Philip said little more on the vague general charge that the object of the Trek was to re-establish slavery—though had his travels taken him as far as the Zoutpansberg he might have found practices not entirely at one with responsible Boer professions even in this matter. (See Agar Hamilton, pp. 192 ff, and Walker, p. 290.)

[2] Cf. Gie, ii, 341 ; Walker, p. 207.   [3] Brookes, p. 126.

in any way for the needs of the weaker. They had left the Colony rather than accept the principle that underlay the emancipating 50th Ordinance.[1] Dispossessed natives they left with the old choice between ' vagrancy ' and totally unregulated conditions of labour service ; children, if not dealt in, were ' transferred ' for long periods of unpaid domestic service under the guise of ' apprenticeship '—in either case without the hope of appeal to independent courts of law. In Philippolis, for example —with which as an L.M.S. district Dr. Philip was particularly concerned—the immediate future seemed to threaten a complete undoing of the hard-won rights and freedom of the coloured people. As things stood, all the land must soon be under European control, and the Griquas either driven out or reduced to the status from which the Hottentots had been so lately raised.

Dr. Philip's great tour of 1841-2 [2] was undoubtedly the direct means of forcing at last upon the notice of the British authorities not only the hard case of the Griquas of Philippolis but the hitherto neglected problems of the High Veld and the northern districts generally. For as he travelled Dr. Philip soon came to realize the close relations that existed between the Boers in the north and those in Natal, observing the disturbing effect on the native mind of recent events in that country, which was but a few days' journey away, across a chain of mountains easily and apparently often crossed by men on foot or on horseback. He came to understand, in fact, what the authorities rather missed, the essential unity of the whole trans-frontier question. After some debate, and not without actual obstruction from a party of Boers,[3] he resolved to push on from Philippolis

---

[1] This was substantially embodied in the Transvaal Masters and Servants Law of 1880, enacted by the short-lived British administration (*Cape Col. Qn.*, p. 213).

[2] References following are to a full and carefully kept ' Journal ', which deserves to be edited for publication. His main suggestions were embodied later in letters to the Governor and other officials.

[3] Near Beersheba, in country the Boers themselves acknowledged to belong to Moshesh, Philip's party were ' stopped by some Boers who insisted on our turning back '. With judicious use of his snuffbox, Dr. Philip persuaded them to meet for a ' conference ' at the station of the French missionary, Rolland, who duly sent out invitations to all the farmers in the neighbourhood. Philip himself being the stumbling-block, he left his companions, James Read and Rolland, to begin the interview with sixteen or eighteen of them, and after ' an hour and a half ' was informed that he would be ' allowed ' to proceed,

to pay a visit to the great Basuto chief, Moshesh, at Thaba Bosigo. The Basuto being far and away the most effective chief in a wide area, ' the future peace of the country ', he wrote, appeared to him to be ' involved in the future relations between Moshesh and the Boers '.

The fundamental question everywhere, as he most clearly saw, was the land, since the occupation of the Boers, wherever they got a footing, tended to be so extensive and complete as to raise at once the old, and ever new, problem of the dispossessed. ' So far back as 1828 ', he writes, ' the attention of the Colonial Government was called to the injuries inflicted upon the natives beyond the frontiers by the practice of the Boers who were in the habit of going across the boundaries in the dry season. . . .' Nothing at all was done. At that time the Boers were still mere colonists, taking advantage of official weakness, or connivance, to extend the boundaries of the old colony. Now the difficulty was far greater—to control a movement rooted in disaffection to the Government. The Boers, it is true, were yet by no means at one with each other. ' The immigrant Boers ', Philip writes from Basutoland in February 1842,

' are divided among themselves, the opposing parties are violent against each other, the collisions which arise from differences of opinion make them fear each other. . . . They are in fear from the Colony, and they are in fear from the natives, and this fear will unite them in one body when the time shall arrive to take possession of this country as they have done at Natal.'

' Whether they retain Natal,' he continues cheerlessly, ' or whether ' (as news of the advance of Captain Smith's troops suggests)

on the understanding that should war result within three years he would be held responsible. Thereupon Philip joined them, explained his pacific intentions and left them ' much softened ', after further ' friendly conversation ' in which, incidentally, the visitors ' refused to be convinced that the world was round '. The spokesman of the party, he adds, had told a Mr. Maider in the Colony two years ago that ' he must trek, that Dr. Philip had spoiled the Hottentots, that he had got a law passed which would oblige him to marry his daughter to a Hottentot, that he would rather shoot her than see her so degraded, and that Dr. Philip had taken all his slaves from him and that he wondered at the mercy of God in suffering such a man to live '. Philip ' hopes his views have modified since their late interview'. His conclusion was that ' the real grounds of the Boers' opposition to my journey were not that they were afraid of me and my party, but that they felt they were intruders in the grounds of Moshesh and they trembled for their security if I induced that chief to drive them out '.

' the British Government take possession . . . the result will be the same.' The annexation of Natal is necessary, but ' the Boers who are opposed to the British Government, which many of them are (and these the most ferocious of them) will fall back upon this country (Basutoland). On the other hand, should the Boers be allowed to retain Natal, the only difference in the event will be in regard to time. In the former case the destruction of the native will be more rapid, but *in either case the crisis is near, and inevitable unless prevented by foreign (British) interference*'. A few months later he wrote, almost prophetically :

' If their property and land are not secured to the Griquas, and the protection of the Colonial laws, before ten years there will not be a single Griqua in the country.'

In face of these things Dr. Philip's ideas soon began to crystallize. The one thing needful, he wrote from Basutoland in February, was to ' give the Griquas the protection of the Colonial laws '— that, at the worst, they might continue as free labourers, with adequate and efficient courts to which to appeal. As in 1833, ' incorporation in the Colony ' remained his first specific ; but later, when the British authorities continued to fight shy of annexation as the obvious means of keeping control of the errant Europeans for whose doings as British subjects it was responsible, Dr. Philip fell back on the policy favoured of late years in Downing Street, and suggested that native rights in the land might be secured to them by ' treaty '.

From Thaba Bosigo Dr Philip turned on his tracks and proceeded, by Philippolis again, to the Bechuana mission stations of the north-west. The Bechuana had not at this time begun to feel the full force of the impact of the Boers of Potchefstroom and Rustenburg. Philip's Journal, none the less—though primarily concerned with mission work, and rendered difficult by variant spellings of the names of a bewildering number of small tribes and petty chiefs—throws light on the conditions of the European-Bantu clash beyond the Vaal, where, in the end, things were left to take their own course, almost entirely uncontrolled. This array of insignificant names is indeed of the very essence of the Bechuana problem. In Bechuanaland there was one petty chief at ' Old Lattakoo ', another at Motito, yet another at Taungs, and others equally important (or unimportant) scattered about in all directions—sometimes, like one Mahura, given to troublesome little raids on their neighbours—always hopelessly weak and divided.[1] At this very time, Gottlieb Schreiner, father of a distinguished family, was restlessly seeking a more congenial station than Philippolis, and was warned by Dr. Philip of the difficulties of settling where there was no reliable chief to maintain some kind of stability ; even Robert Moffat, it seems, having made a new venture on his own account when he moved to the great spring at Kuruman, had signally failed to persuade the chiefs Mahura and Matibi (?) to move with him.

At that time also, David Livingston (as he then spelt his name) was seeking a new station in the north,[2] in an area that had been abandoned by the French missionaries ten years before on account of the disturbance of the Baharutse and other tribes by the advent of Moselekatze. As war between Moselekatze and the Boers continued, Philip was apprehensive and sought to discourage this move to an area where French, Americans and Anglicans alike had tried and failed. Moselekatze, he wrote,

[1] Philip notes one feature, probably characteristic of the Bantu generally before the advent of the military and despotic type of chief —' the extreme freedom of speech allowed at their *Pitso* ' (folk-moot). This, he considers, is a ' safety-valve ', and ' a corrective to the extreme absolutism of their chiefs ' (Journal written at kraal of the Batlapin, April 1842).

[2] Dr. Livingstone's opinion of the Superintendent and Mrs. Philip has been preserved (T. Hughes' *Livingstone*, pp. 12, 13—original letter of 13 May 1841, to Mr. Cecil, in Mr. J. G. Gubbins' Collection) : ' I had heard many things calculated to awaken unpleasant feelings. I lived in their house a month. I came to it full of prejudice against them and I left with my prejudice completely thawed, my fears allayed and my mind imbued with great respect for (their) upright Christian character. The charge I had heard reiterated again and again in England that they are spiritual despots, upon all that I can learn, appears decidedly false and calumnious. In all our intercourse I could perceive no attempt to usurp authority . . . or dictate . . . (but) the very reverse. The Dr.'s faculties appear to be now a little impaired by age, but Mrs. Philip is much stronger and very active and energetic. One charge is, therefore, quite true, that she is the chief agent in transacting business ' (i.e. routine business). The letter continues on the troubles of the Cape Town pastorate, amply confirming other evidence that this disturbance was due to the burdens of his official position in the L.M.S. and to the ' active part he has taken in securing the rights of the coloured population '. The activities of the next years suggest that the congregational distractions of 1839–41 (themselves not unconnected with Kafir War disputes) were partly responsible for his faculties then appearing ' a little impaired by age ', though even in 1842–45, it is true, he confined himself more than usual to the matters immediately in hand.

who had thought Moffat useful as a protector, was alienated by the withdrawal of the Americans ; and ' little more than a twelve month ago ' the Boers had already informed the Anglican who tried to reassemble the Baharutse at Mosega :

' that he might continue to teach there for the present but was not to forget that the country belonged to them ; he was to consider himself as occupying their ground by sufferance only until they should require it '.

The Boer account of this episode is that, while they feared to have natives congregated at this station, they were prepared to take the whole tribe under their protection at some point farther afield.[1] According to the missionary Edwards,[2] who early in 1842 had accompanied Livingstone to the north, Dr. Philip exaggerated the dangers. Moselekatze, it seems, had already withdrawn ' 500 or 600 miles farther north than you state ', and the Boers were not likely to want to occupy the country of the Bakwena and the Bangweketsi, which was ' dry and unsuitable for sheep and horses '. But Philip was correctly enough informed, on the Boers' own showing, that ' the Boers lay claim to all that was claimed by Moselekatze ', on the ground that the Bechuana ' retired before the arms of Moselekatze into the desert, where they remain '.[3] As a proof that the Boers ' do not intend the claim to lie dormant ' he cites their pursuit of Griqua hunters, whom they warned that ' the country was theirs and they were never again to visit any part of it to kill game of any kind '. A permanent mission, Dr. Philip concluded, was, therefore, inadvisable :

' Men may look at the eruption of a volcano from a distance, and they may think of one day settling near it, but not till the eruption shall have ceased. . . . Should the Boers prevail to the extent that they meditate, our missionaries will not be allowed to remain in the part of the country under their authority.'

That there was justification for this warning, Edwards himself, with his colleague Inglis, was to learn to his cost ten years later, when, in 1852, with clumsy formality, these two missionaries were expelled by the Volksraad from the newly recognized Republic.

On the Bechuana situation as a whole, Dr. Philip, in fact, saw very clearly the difficulty of preserving the lands of the

[1] Agar Hamilton, pp. 120–1.
[2] Letter of August 1842, on missionary matters ; he also accuses a colleague of ' propagating tittel-tatel ' [sic].
[3] Cf. Agar Hamilton, pp. 50–3.

Bechuana by means of any ' treaty ', since none of the chiefs had any effective authority, and the extent and validity of their land claims were, from the nature of the case, dubious. With possibly rather exaggerated faith in his protégé, Waterboer, strengthened perhaps by the remembrance that the Griquas had actually saved the Bechuana from the raiding Mantatees, back in 1823—and from Moselekatze later—his idea would seem to have been to get them all to acknowledge Waterboer as their leader and protector ; which, indeed, he claims they were ready to do. Robert Moffat was at the moment on leave in England, but this proposed aggrandizement of Waterboer and Griqua-town added fuel to the fires of discontent that had long been burning among the Kuruman missionaries. Remote as they were from the actualities of South African life, and cherishing their ' independence ', they were already chafing at control by Philip and Cape Town, and jealous of Griquatown as being too much of the Cape Town faction. Unmindful, apparently, of the political danger that threatened their natives, they sorely harassed Dr. Philip with trivial domestic missionary feuds, and offered no vestige of an alternative plan for protecting the future of the Bechuana. Rather despairing, he began in June to press back to Cape Town, as fast as oxen could take him, and in the discussions he had there with the Governor, the Bechuana Question, which was really the Transvaal Question, seems to have got less than the notice it deserved.

On the way south he remarked that the country about the *Berg* (north of Graaff-Reinet), had been ' in a great measure forsaken ' :

' The emigration mania still continues. Within about 100 miles of the Orange River we met thirty Boers trekking, and a great proportion of the places they deserted are now used as cattle places by proprietors who do not reside upon them but leave them and their cattle in charge of freedmen, Bechuanas and Bushmen.'

The softening influence of his February interview (above, p. 195 *n*.) momentarily strengthened by the ' great civility ' he received from a Boer at whose house he conducted a Sunday service,[1] was shaken again by the news that met him in the Colony. In the Eastern Province, in July, he got into touch with the Lieutenant-

---

[1] ' My own countrymen ', he comments, ' who were born in a land of liberty I have invariably found to be most virulent in their prejudices against me for my exertions in favour of the rights of the coloured population in this country.'

Governor, Colonel Hare, who was evidently glad of first-hand frontier information, since what news he had at the moment gave cause for anxiety. On 24 June Colonel Hare had reported to the Governor that three or four hundred Boers were said to have left the Mooi River (Potchefstroom) for Natal, where Captain Smith had suffered beleaguerment; from Smith, moreover, news had passed to the Governor[1] of the disturbing influence of the Hollander Smellekamp; about this time Colonel Cloete reported a letter from Pretorius announcing the cession of Natal to the King of Holland.[2] Philip's reports were no more comforting. Alarmed himself at the hostility of the Natal Boers, his tone at once began to harden, since the British action in Natal now made it certain, as he himself had foreseen, that the Griquas and Basutos would be pressed, not merely by moderates, like Oberholster, but by the hostile Trekkers from Natal. In the light of these fresh developments, what he had himself seen acquired indeed a more ominous significance :

'You must be aware', he writes to Colonel Hare, 'that a political organization has already been formed among bodies of the Boers, reaching from the Orange River to Natal, by Pretorius; that they have taken oaths of allegiance to him as president of their republic,[3] and I am credibly informed they boast that they will soon have back by their arms the farms they sold to the English.[4] . . . As it is they occupy the country between the Caledon and the Vaal Rivers, and covet the portion occupied by Moshesh which is small in comparison, but good for breeding horses, because it is high, and horse sickness is unknown. (They have made) tempting offers to Moshesh for part of this land, but finding they have nothing to hope from his goodwill, they are meditating an attack upon him.'

---

[1] Smith to Napier, 14 May, and Napier to Secretary of State, 13 June 1842. And above, p. 184.

[2] Letter of 4 July, sent to Secretary of State in dispatch of 11 November.

[3] An undated letter says Pretorius' tour was 'preparatory to the establishment of the new republic they talk of'.

[4] After his trip through the eastern districts, Dr. Philip writes : 'The agitation caused by the newspapers contributed largely to the emigration of the Boers.' Under the panic thus created, 'they sold their farms much under their value to English settlers, while those who had created the panic became purchasers, and are now selling the farms again at three or four times the prices at which they bought them. They expatriated themselves originally under a delusion created in the first instance by the supineness of the Government, later under the influence of disaffection created by those who wanted (?) their farms at a low price.'

Stressing the danger of allowing the Boers to get too firm a hold on Basutoland and establish their republic on the great stretch of country adjacent to the colonial boundaries, he concludes :

'It would be much easier to keep out the Boers now when a little assistance to the native tribes will enable them to defend themselves against them ',[1] . . . (and in a private letter) ' Since the tribes have no common bond of union, tragedy ', he fears, is ' imminent '.

Philip's solution, at this stage, was ' *annexation up to the Tropics* ',[2] and it was only because the British Government hung back from such a plunge that the plan of ' treaties ' was so prominent in the years that followed. The effect of the troubles in Natal was in every way unfortunate. Even beyond the Drakensberg, the Die-hards, who in the middle of 1842 began to turn north to escape British intervention, had now to be reckoned with, so that when it came to negotiating treaties with the northern tribes, and also with Faku in Pondoland (January 1844) the emphasis was not quite what it might have been a few years earlier. In 1838, under Stockenstrom,[3] the principle underlying the treaties had been ' the acknowledgement of the right to the territory of its then actual possessors '. But the treaties concluded after the hostilities begun by the Boers, in Natal, almost insensibly acquired a sinister aspect, and have been the object of much one-sided criticism. It seemed to the Boers at the time, as it has to too many historians since, that Kok, Moshesh and Co. were taken up by the British Government as military allies against the Boers—which is merely preposterous. On the other hand the scraps of paper recording the ' agreements ' of the Trekkers with the tribes of the interior [4] are treated with solemn respect. The difference between the British and the Trekker treaties is that the former were at least an attempt to preserve the tribes and to prevent their ' extermination '— to prevent indeed the wholesale intermixture of black and white areas ; those concluded by the Trekkers were instruments designed to legalize dispossession.

[1] To Colonel Hare 12 July 1842, asking him to correspond with Mr. Casalis about the possibility of a ' treaty '.

[2] Letter by Major Warden from Somerset East, 18 July, reporting Philip's talk with the Wesleyans as he passed through that place.

[3] In the correspondence of Stockenstrom and Fairbairn in 1838 (J. G. Gubbins' Collection), and again in letters to Dr. Philip in August 1842, and to Jas. Read January to June 1845.

[4] Agar Hamilton, *op. cit.*, p. 21 *et passim.*

The great difficulty in the way of the British policy was that it subjected the Boer farmers to the jurisdiction of a shadowy government of coloured peasants, and that even the strongest of the African potentates was utterly unequal to the task of government when the simplicity of the native ' state ' was complicated by the influx of European settlers. But even Philip's letters of February 1842 still look forward to the consolidation of the *status quo*, including the rights of Boers to land in their actual possession. The wholly justifiable object of the treaties —doubtfully possible of attainment by such means, and certainly attempted too late—was to prevent precisely such intermixture of black and white throughout South Africa as their failure in the end has brought about. They were designed in short to secure the adequate Native Reserves we now deplorably lack.

In July or August 1842, Dr. Philip was in such agitation that for the first time for many years several letters to Fowell Buxton and others refer to the possibility of making another appeal to the British Government direct. But this time his reception in Cape Town was favourable, and his facts made such an impression on Sir George Napier that they were forwarded at once in detail to the Secretary of State by the Governor himself. His suggestions, first made in conversation, were apparently by request of the Governor embodied in a letter (25 August) supplementing that of 12 July to Colonel Hare which dealt more especially with the position of Moshesh ; it was reinforced also by appeals from Kok himself, and, on behalf of Moshesh, from the French missionary Casalis.[1] Dr. Philip's letter betrays considerable alarm. Moshesh is in danger of ' annihilation ', the Griquas of Philippolis of even more imminent attack from ' an enemy who are united in their hatred against them, and in their determination to embrace the first favourable opportunity to exterminate them and to possess themselves of their country ' —unless the Government intervene to prevent ' the bloody tragedy '. Government mediation is favoured, moreover, by ' the better part of the Boers themselves . . . who are too few in number to have any influence over the dispositions, councils or proceedings of their brethren '. The protection of Philippolis is especially urgent:

---

[1] The date of Kok's letter, 5 June, was so nearly that of Dr. Philip's departure from Colesberg (where it was written) that it was no doubt drafted even under Philip's supervision.

'since if country on the colonial borders passes into the hands of a hostile Boer republic, the free trade with friends in the colony will keep the hostile Boers so well provided with arms and ammunition that it may render all attempts nugatory, which may afterwards be taken, to save Moshesh and Waterboer and the numerous tribes of the Natives in the interior '.

This fear on the part of the missionaries is the counterpart of the charge sometimes made by the Boers that missionaries put them in danger by supplying natives with firearms. It explains why, in later letters, Dr. Philip hoped to put something like a ' ring fence ' of protected tribes between the Colony and the Trekkers. It was not in order to set the tribes against the farmers, but to protect them, by controlling and restricting the supply of weapons of war. His first remedy, however, so far as the Griquas were concerned, was to take the Griqua country within the Colony, as he had proposed to Sir Lowry Cole years before in 1833 ; so long ago as 1819, he says, he hoped for this consummation ; only on seeing the progress they had made under Mr. Wright between 1825 and 1832 did he begin to think it possible ; now, he concludes, it is the ' only possible expedient of safety '. But should the Government hesitate to adopt this plan ' till it shall have received more mature consideration '— ' as a *substitute* for the first plan, in the *meantime*, I beg leave to recommend to Your Excellency that Treaties should be entered into with Moshesh and Adam Kok '.

Dr. Philip goes on to elaborate. In spite of his fears of Boer designs, he recognized Boer rights in Philippolis, suggesting that disputes with the Griquas about leases ' may in my opinion be easily adjusted ' by the Government acting as a mediator. The Boers themselves, by submitting their leases to the Government, had made an ' acknowledgement of its right to interfere in this case '. But the Treaties ought to be strictly limited in number—an important qualification that is often forgotten : [1]

' *Were Treaties with the Government to become a common thing . . . they would lose all their value and cease to answer any good purpose,* and for that reason I would recommend that none should be made at present except with Moshesh and Adam Kok. . . . As there are few points in which these *two* chiefs can come into collision with

[1] E.g. referring to conversation with the Governor about the advisability of recognizing one Lepui, of Bethulie, Dr. Philip now points out that Lepui is there ' on sufferance only ', and his case should ' remain in abeyance '.

each other, the soundest policy the Government can pursue will be to strengthen (their) hands ; but should the Government enter into treaties with other chiefs beyond them . . . they will find nothing but rivals in those in whom in other circumstances they may find allies who may be useful to themselves, to their people and to the Colony.'

As if to justify Dr. Philip's worst fears, things began to happen in Griqualand very shortly after his return to Cape Town. Early in September the Governor took the preliminary caution of issuing a Proclamation warning His Majesty's subjects against any attempt to molest or injure the native tribes, or to take unlawful possession of land belonging to them—mentioning in particular the Basuto, the Barolong of Moroko, the Batlapi of Lepui, together with the half-breeds and Griquas. Meantime the Republican leader, Jan Mocke, had returned from Natal and begun to make his presence felt on the Orange River ; so much so that ' the better part of the Boers themselves ' took alarm, and through their spokesman, Oberholster, wrote to the Civil Commissioner of Colesberg early in October, warning him of Mocke's intention to proclaim as a republic the whole of the country beyond the Orange River.   A few days later Mr. Justice Menzies, being in Colesberg on a Circuit tour, arrived independently at Dr. Philip's solution of the difficulty, and on very similar grounds :

' I believed that every person, black or white, who would not take the oath of allegiance (i.e. to the threatened Republic) would be compelled to leave the country, that they intended no longer to recognize the right of any native tribe or chief, within their assumed territory, to the land in their possession, and to reduce them to a state of servitude.' [1]

Menzies, therefore, deeming the situation critical, took it upon himself to make a proclamation annexing, in the Queen's name, all territory east of 22 degrees and south of 25 degrees, ' not being Portuguese dominion or in lawful possession or occupation of any native chief or ruler, *more particularly and especially such portions of the said territory as are now in possession or occupation of any subjects of the British Crown* '.

Meantime, the Governor had reported to the Secretary of State on 15 September, enclosing Dr. Philip's letter of 25 August. In his own dispatch he somewhat emphasized, what Philip also recognized, that the Griqualand Boers were colonists only,

---

[1] Letter to Governor enclosed in dispatch of 11 November 1842.

with no desire to throw off their allegiance, who were being driven by numbers and land-hunger to cast greedy eyes upon Moshesh's country. At the same time, knowing how Downing Street feared and disliked extending British dominion, he inverted the order of Dr. Philip's recommendations :

' The two modes of overcoming the difficulty are either by extending the protection of the Government by means of treaties with the Native chiefs, and the promise of armed support in giving effect to those treaties, or by spreading our influence over the whole of that country by subjecting both the natives and the Europeans to British law and authority.'

On similar grounds Judge Menzies' proclamation, evidently deemed too precipitate to have any hope of gaining the approval of Downing Street, was at once disallowed, though the Governor's private opinion hardly admits of doubt : on 11 November he wrote, immediately after hearing of Menzies' action :

' I again take the opportunity of expressing my firm conviction that there is only one mode by which effectual check can be given to this system of slavery which, under the name of *apprenticeship*, prevails over a great part of the country where the emigrant farmers have located themselves, and that is the colonization of those territories.'

Even more specifically, on 13 December :

' Your Lordship is aware that I am favourable, as a question of expediency, to the extension of British supremacy as the only means of averting calamitous consequences to the native tribes.'

This December opinion was called forth by a continuance of acute unrest on the Philippolis front. The numbers involved were small and insignificant enough, but the Governor could not remain indifferent to the news that reached him. In the course of November he must have heard through Dr. Philip how the French missionaries, Pelissier and Rolland,[1] were complaining that Boers were ejecting natives from their fountains. At the same time Mr. Atkinson of Colesberg wrote expressing a fear that ' the Griquas will not tamely submit ' to the Boers, and may start a war to the extermination of one side or the other. Casalis also, from Thaba Bosigo, reported a rumour that ' they would be compelled either to acknowledge the authority of the Natal Volksraad or to leave the country '. Moshesh, indeed,

----

[1] Rolland adds : ' I am no advocate for war, but I fear the Boers must feel the weight of the British arm before they will come to their senses. . . . Proclamations are of no use. They are so much waste paper.'

had no official message from the Boers and there was no rupture, but while regretting the necessity for dragging Moshesh out of ' an obscurity so favourable to the reception of Divine Grace ', Casalis added that action is necessary, since ' Boers still creep in silently and settle (in the west) where they are aware he has least control '.   Then, on 5 December, the Lieutenant-Governor, Colonel Hare, reported that ' rebellion ' threatened in Colesberg, the trend of official opinion being further reflected in a letter from Theophilus Shepstone (to Dr. Philip, 2 December) : ' There appears no human possibility of the natives of any mission station being preserved except by the prompt and vigorous interference of the Government '.   In the course of December, therefore, Colonel Hare was sent up to Colesberg with a force of 300 infantry and 100 mounted men, whereupon the hostile Boers at once dispersed, and the military danger, such as it was, passed. In March, after another warning Proclamation by Colonel Hare, Atkinson reported first a ' temporary lull ', both sides awaiting some Government decision in the matter, then, on the 31st, that the Griquas had collected at Philippolis, ' expecting ' the Boers.   At last, about 21 and 26 April, Napier received dispatches from Lord Stanley.   These instructions, while sanctioning the annexation of Natal, now laid down that ' you will be careful not to engage in operations at a distance from the settled parts of the Colony '.   In the north, therefore, measures for the protection of the natives were to be permitted only ' under treaties entered into for the purpose with the chiefs '.

CHAPTER XIV

THE BRITISH ATTEMPT TO TAKE CONTROL—THE 'TREATY' POLICY IN THE NORTH 1843-6

IN the middle 'forties it was still just possible that the disastrous effects of unrestricted ' trekking ' might have been mitigated. Since 1836 the so-called Stockenstrom treaties had been the basis of an attempt to establish order on the old Kafir frontier. The year 1843 saw the beginnings of British administration in Natal. For about three years after Lord Stanley's dispatch of 1843, Sir George Napier and his successor Sir Peregrine Maitland persevered in the attempt to secure stability north of the Orange River by the formal recognition of the *status quo* at least in Griqualand and in Basutoland.

On the face of it, Humanitarianism was on the way to winning the battle with Economy, to become the guiding motive of British policy. In Cape Town Dr. Philip was personally consulted on almost every issue that arose, enjoying the confidence of the Government under Napier and Maitland, and the new Secretary Mr. John Montagu,[1] as, except for a few short months under D'Urban in the middle of 1834, he had never done since very early days. At this period his letters even to Fowell Buxton are few and hurried, which shows that he was ready enough to work with the local authorities when they would allow him, without making dramatic appeals to British Parliament and people.[2] This co-operation between Government and mis-

---

[1] Just possibly Dr. Philip's advocacy helped to secure for the Colony its first civilian Secretary : ' Lord John Russell ought to see the need for sending a civilian and enlightened Secretary with a military governor like Napier, not a soldier and a Tory and a nervous-minded man like our (present) who I am sorry to say does as he pleases ' (to Buxton on the dismissal of Stockenstrom, 22 November 1839).

[2] ' Having brought the Colonial Government to a sense of impending danger, I have succeeded (in getting action taken) to place the Boers

sionaries was to be expected now that Governors were no longer prejudiced by the anti-Philip mania of the Frontier Boers and of Grahamstown. The question at issue was the fate of the coloured people beyond the Orange River, and Dr. Philip had been the first to demonstrate the urgency of their case. There being no Government officials to report direct, the missionaries on the spot were the obvious source of information, and their evidence came, as a matter of course, through Dr. Philip, the Cape Town Superintendent of the London missions and the Agent also of the French missionaries in Basutoland.

But Philip's immediate responsibility for the policy of the Government has been misconceived. The ' treaty ' policy was forced alike on Napier and Maitland, against their better judgement, by the determined refusal of Downing Street to countenance any more drastic assumption of responsibility.[1] Under such circumstances, friendly co-operation with the Colonial Government had little effect on the ultimate decision, which lay with the Government in London. Philip himself soon recognized that the treaties were all he could hope for [2] and did his utmost to make them a success. Far from holding the Colonial Government on leading strings, Philip in this instance deferred too much to the exigencies of the position. He may have been ill-

at bay till the Governor shall receive more ample means and powers from Home to enable him entirely to defeat their designs. As the documents I had drawn up at his request were sent to Downing Street *with his recommendation*, we are not without hope as to the result ' (to J. Thomas, Esq., 4 April 1843).

A year later : ' Formerly the Government was opposed to me, but things are so far changed that I have now the Government with me ' (to Dr. Thos. Hodgkin, Aborigines Protection Society, May 1844). ' At present the Colonial Government does nothing as to relations with the independent native tribes without consulting me ' (to Sir T. Fowell Buxton, 1844, undated).

[1] For Napier's opinion above, pp. 205–6. Maitland, reporting the revised treaty negotiations of 1845, noted that, for well-known reasons, he was barred from any extension of the area of the Colony.

[2] Philip's opinion was notorious all along. In May 1845, when Maitland was setting out to attempt a fresh settlement in Griqualand, one Merrington suggested to Attorney-General Porter that Dr. Philip should be consulted. According to Mrs. Philip (16 May 1845) Porter replied : ' O ! we know what Dr. Philip thinks. He wants us to take in the whole of the country under the Colony, but that we cannot afford to do. There would be no end of that.' Dr. Philip himself the same week wrote independently from Port Elizabeth : ' The simplest and the only method is to take the Griquas into the Colony, and to get Moshesh to agree to have a fort in his territory to keep the way to Natal open.'

advised to neglect his friends in London and thus lose any available means of stiffening the Government attitude. For in the absence of sustained pressure, Downing Street, rather hardening in its old aloof attitude and in its hostility to Colonial expansion, countenanced the Treaty policy just so long as there was no serious explosion. A very few years later, following its natural bent, it all but washed its hands of the whole business. The treaties, in a word, were only a timid concession made by Downing Street to humanitarian concern for the welfare of the coloured people, and a half-hearted recognition that the situation in the north demanded serious attention.

Had the Government still had to deal only with the old peaceful penetration of colonists, and with Boer moderates like Oberholster, a settlement should have been relatively easy. But when at last Napier's instructions authorized him to take measures for the protection of the Griquas, the position was more complicated. The acute excitement which brought the troops at least as far as Colesberg in the end of 1842 was caused by the more aggressive tendencies of the Die-hards under Jan Mocke. The Great Trek, that is to say, was beginning to show itself in its true colours. Rather than submit to the authority of what was after all their own Government, the Trekkers in Natal had forcibly defied the Queen's commission, showing that their exodus was of the nature of a rebellion. Its character was disguised so long as the vastness of South Africa had made it possible for the malcontents to withdraw unhindered from the control they resented, and all the time no doubt the majority of the Trekkers wanted nothing so much as a quiet life, and having acquired farms, to work them in peace. Even their overbearing attitude to the natives may have sprung from a wholly intelligible nervousness and fear. But when land came to be obtainable only at native expense, there was conflict ; and with conflict on the Borders, the certainty of renewed Government concern about the doings of its Trekker subjects.

Part of the alarm in Griqua territory was probably quite fortuitous. In this lonely country of vast distances game abounded and lions were still common. Not even missionaries travelled unarmed. Boers as a matter of course carried guns with them wherever they went, if only to keep themselves supplied with food, so that the frequent semi-political meetings of these un-settled times tended to be assemblages of armed men. In times of excitement, indeed, these armed meetings became so much an ingrained habit that, long years afterwards, apologies were made for the rebellion of 1914 as originating in nothing more serious than an ' armed protest ' that could never have been so grossly misunderstood in the old days of the Republics. In the 'forties it happened that the Griquas, unlike the Bantu tribes, also had guns, and, like the Boers, were given to holding meetings. When Boer and Griqua meetings happened near the same time and place the guns were too apt to go off—with little or no premeditation on the part of their owners.

It may be, therefore, that Oberholster, rather than Mocke, was the more typical Boer, in being governed more by considerations of safety than by ambition or politics. In the opinion of Mr. W. Y. Thomson, a young and competent missionary who took charge after Mr. Wright's death in April 1843, Oberholster was ' weak ', and ' liable to be turned by too strong an opposition ', but also ' a humane man, sincerely desirous of preventing bloodshed '. The same witness wrote in July 1844 :

' The firm adherents either of Oberholster or of Mocke are extremely few. With the great mass of the emigrants it is a matter of indifference whether they belong to Government or to the " Modder River Republic " and they will assuredly adhere to the strongest party. A strong demonstration of Government on behalf of the chiefs or Oberholster would, therefore, leave the heads of rebellion destitute of adherents. . . . (Already) some who were formerly the avowed adherents of Mocke have declared themselves neuter, and some have given in their allegiance to Oberholster. And further, the Boers know that to engage in war with disciplined troops in this country, where there is neither bush nor woody ravine to afford protection to their flocks and herds, or cover to their persons in their peculiar mode of fighting, would be utter madness. The Boers know their own tactics, and the local advantages requisite to their success, and it was this consideration that caused their formidable force to vanish, as at the wand of an enchanter, when the Lieut.-Governor with the troops appeared at Colesberg (in Dec. 1842).'

However this may be, with the advent of Mocke on the Griqua border British intervention was much more likely to provoke opposition. At the same time, anything like weakness on the part of the British authorities might, as Mr. Thomson feared, have the effect of throwing the moderates into the arms of the more extreme faction. Mocke's party, moreover, as the Griqua attitude shows, was more utterly regardless of native rights and interests and, by mere addition of numbers, intensified the land-shortage. It has been argued that at the time of the Treaties there were in Griqualand ' actually more white people than

Griquas '. [1] Why then, it is asked in effect, such extreme tenderness for the rights of a handful of Griquas ? Oberholster himself, it appears from Mr. Thomson's letters, pressed merely for ' equal rights '. But the relatively large and increasing number of Boers was precisely the difficulty. Even in those days experience had shown that ' equal rights ' must very soon make an end of native or Griqua land-holding.

The increased pressure, in fact, made the situation almost menacing. Weak and divided though the Griquas may have been, they were the descendants of men who had fled from the Colony rather than submit to the very conditions that threatened again to engulf them. In their independence—as hunters or traders in ivory, as landholders, or it may be by leasing their land to Boers—they had acquired horses and guns, with some practice and skill in using them, and were by no means certainly disposed to submit quietly to complete dispossession. Several times in the latter part of 1842, when no doubt they had been better employed looking after their own farms, they collected excitedly in Philippolis to prepare to meet the Boers with united resistance. After December the unaccustomed appearance of troops in the north served to provide them with a little ready money, some of which was spent on house-building, and some, no doubt, on arms and ammunition. [2] The missionary Wright, complaining that even Boer leaseholders had taken up arms in order to expel their Griqua lessors, still feared a disastrous clash in the early months of 1843, and Dr. Philip, while continuing to keep the Governor informed of the rather alarming news that reached him, had to act at the same time as a moderating influence —urging patience both on Mr. Wright and on the Griquas :

' The Griquas must not expect too much. . . . The mad proceedings of the Boers in this instance have damaged their cause with the Government, but that is what they will soon get over, as on former similar occasions, and the Griquas will be sacrificed as a peace-offering to the Boers. Government has never withstood the tide of colonial feeling. . . . On the subject of the leases, therefore, the people must

---

[1] Theal, ii, 419.
[2] In March 1843 Mr. Wright reported great activity. The Griquas having received £578 from the Government for the use of their waggons, they had ' 25 houses in course of erection '—' but not a glass of brandy '. Nor were they without resources. In May Mrs. Wright reported that with a view to evacuation, the Government had made a fresh requisition for 50 waggons—a surprisingly large number for such a despised community.

be fair and reasonable. Anything unreasonable will transfer the sympathies of Colonel Hare to the side of the Boers. . . . Supposing the farmers are obliged to leave their farms at the expiration of their leases, what is to be done ? The land cannot lie empty, and the natives are not in a position to fill the farms with stock.'

To Mr. Wright, who remarked that the Griquas were ' not in a state to be played with ', Philip rejoined that he hoped they were ' not adopting any rash counsels '.

However futile Griqua resistance must have proved, the Government had yet to reckon with such rashness as an imminent possibility. Had the Government merely stood aside, the Griquas who had tasted freedom might not have been content to be reduced to the condition of the ' free ' Hottentots of the years before 1828. Missionary letters show that they by no means welcomed the prospect of a return to rule by Boer field-cornets. The section among the Griquas long known as *Bergenaars*, virtually bandits, had been on active commando against Moshesh's neighbours so lately as 1841 (above, p. 194) ; with their numbers increased by the pressure of Boer occupation, they might easily start more widespread ' depredations ', reproducing in the north the same effects as the old ' extermination ' on the Kafir frontier. In the end an exterminatory feud between the Boers and the Griquas was in all probability prevented only by the restraining influence of the missionaries, and even the possibility of a feud was not to be contemplated so lightly by the Government of the day, nor indeed by the Trekkers themselves, as it has been by some historians. The Government had good reason to know also that Griqualand would not long satisfy Boer land-hunger. The turn of Basutoland must come next, which, as the history of the Free State was soon to prove, would inevitably mean war, and with war in that quarter, dangerous reactions elsewhere.

Influenced by considerations like these, Governor Napier in the course of 1843 showed himself disposed to meet appeals from the Griqua leaders, and also from Moshesh, by giving them such limited protection as Downing Street was at all likely to sanction. For a moment negotiations were interrupted by the death of Mr. Wright in April ; left without a spokesman, even the Griquas, it appears, were nervous of treaties.[1] In a letter

---

[1] ' With no one to assist us,' writes one Hendrik Hendrikse, who had *Bergenaar* leanings, ' in a written agreement between two nations, one of which is highly civilized, and the other not so civilized or enlightened, it never goes well.'

dated 25 August, however, Adam Kok himself formulated his appeal, raising questions that demanded some answer. The Griqua settlement, he claimed, was sanctioned by General Bourke in 1826 and recognized at various times by later Governors. Now its integrity was threatened by Colonial Boers, British subjects ; and whereas the Griquas had ' ever been faithful in their adherence to the British Government', these Boers had, in 1842, ' assembled with an armed force ' to ' throw off their allegiance ', and ' employed both threats and promises to induce us to join them . . . but though in great danger we unhesitatingly refused and waited in patience till Colonel Hare freed us from our difficulties '. In particular :

' The insults and injuries inflicted on the Griquas by the Colonial Boers have convinced me that should I attempt to execute the laws of my country [1] respecting the lands of Philippolis, at present held by the Boers, when the leases shall have expired, nothing but the interference of the Colonial Government can prevent a war which must end in the destruction of one or both of the contending parties.'

Kok's letter was, no doubt, the result of earlier consultations, and even before it can have reached Cape Town the Government Secretary was in communication with Dr. Philip and the missionaries about the terms of the contemplated treaty.[2] In the middle of October drafts were sent for signature, both to Kok and to Moshesh, and formalities were completed—at Philippolis on

[1] An earlier appeal from Kok, sent in with Dr. Philip's letter of 25 August 1842, makes more of the vain provision of Griqua ' laws ' which expressly prohibited ' burghers ' from leasing their landholdings to colonists.—No doubt much of this Griqua correspondence was inspired and guided by missionaries. (After all, more important people than Kok have letters and speeches prepared for them.) But several letters exist that appear to have been *written* (in Dutch) as well as signed by Adam Kok himself.

[2] For example, on 29 August, Dr. Philip, who referred also to recent conversations, urged on Mr. Montagu that Kok should have at least the same salary as Waterboer, suggesting also that the Kafir treaties would have been more successful had the chiefs been conciliated by such payments.

Dr. Philip had great difficulty at this time with his London office. It was months before Mr. W. Y. Thomson was definitely established at that ' most highly important station ', Philippolis, and Moffat's influence in securing his ' District Committee ' to limit the Superintendent's powers in the north led Philip to formal resignation. The stout adherence of the abler young missionaries like Edward Solomon, W. Y. Thomson and Atkinson of the L.M.S., and of Casalis and Dyke of Basutoland, together with the friendly relations with the Govern-

29 November, and at Thaba Bosigo on 13 December. The chiefs now became allies, pledged to friendship, required to preserve order in their own territories and to co-operate with the Colonial Government in maintaining peace and order on the frontiers. To this end they were allowed small supplies of arms and ammunition, while to bind them to their alliance, and to give them standing with their own people, and with the Boers, they were put on salaries of £100 and £75 per annum respectively (sums by no means trifling for the time and place).

This treaty-making was in truth but a feeble instrument to achieve any effective settlement of the troubles that kept the North in a ferment. The creation of the Griqua and Basuto 'states' had some of the weaknesses of the old plan of making 'paramounts' of Gaika and Hintza. Though the land question was clearly fundamental, the treaties set up no machinery to deal with disputes in Griqualand, where Boers had already acquired a footing. But they failed also to effect even a strict delimitation of the boundaries of the new states. This flaw, though perhaps inevitable, was fatal; for, primitive peoples being necessarily vague in their ideas of territorial limits, even Moshesh's power and authority were weak on the outskirts of his domains, precisely where European encroachments were most considerable. Mr. Casalis, indeed, on behalf of Moshesh, lost no time in asserting the chief's full claims. On 13 December, the very day the treaty was signed, he wrote pointing out that the boundary assigned in the draft treaty excluded several miles of country which, although at present occupied with his permission by the Barolongs under Moroko, 'are undoubtedly within the territory of Moshesh'. Moshesh, therefore, signed only with reservations—in the full expectation that the matter would be adjusted. Equally promptly, however, the Rev. W. Shaw, Superintendent of the Wesleyan Missions in the disputed area,

ment, especially Mr. Montagu, kept him at his post until the domestic storm had blown over.

In November 1843, however, he wrote to his friend, Miss Wills : ' It is a curious fact, now that I have the Home and the Colonial Government both at my feet, that my last and the severest of my conflicts should take place with the Directors of the L.M.S. At this moment when the Governor is consulting me and taking my advice on the most important affairs of South Africa, the silliest creatures connected with our missions in this country, men whom it would be charity to the missions to allow them to spend their salaries in England, have more weight in the Mission House in Blomfield Street than I have.'

wrote protesting that his protégés were independent of Moshesh. The result was that early in January the Governor was consulting Dr. Philip about requests for separate treaties, not only with Moroko, a respectable chief with some 10,000 followers, but with lesser fry like Sikonyela, as well as with completely insignificant mixed breeds called Carolus Baaitje, Pieter Davids and Gert Taaibosch, who had only two or three hundred followers each.[1]

Such multiplying of treaties was to destroy any effectiveness they might otherwise have had. The French missionaries, co-operating with Dr. Philip and the L.M.S., were undoubtedly right in principle in holding that Moshesh was the only chief in those parts capable of maintaining his position ; Sikonyela and the mixed breeds would be helpless to make a fair bargain with Boers wishing to settle among them, and quite incapable of fulfilling the treaty obligation of ' co-operation ' with the Colonial Government for the preservation of peace and order. Their only hope was to stand together, and their wisdom would have been to consolidate the pacific authority of the great Basuto. On the other hand, the effective power of Moshesh did not really extend so far as his supporters claimed. Population, indeed, was already so great that many of Moshesh's vassals had begun to encroach upon the lands of their neighbours—so that Sikonyela, for example, was perpetually at feud with Moshesh. The champions of the Basuto potentate failed to make sufficient allowance for the fears of the weaker chiefs, or to convince and carry with them their Wesleyan colleagues, whose first concern was, naturally perhaps, to safeguard any special interests of their own little communities. At the same time, in pressing as they did for separate treaties, the Wesleyans showed a total lack of statesmanship and reduced the treaty policy to absurdity. The upshot was that no progress had been made with the definition of the Basutoland boundaries before the whole arrangement was thrown into the melting pot once more by Sir Harry Smith's policy of annexation in 1848.

If treaty-making was thus hampered by divisions among the natives themselves, the difficulties were still greater in the Griqua country where the Europeans were already strongly established. Here, in effect, the treaty threw upon the shoulders of an improvised ' government ' of semi-civilized Griquas a task like that which, on a larger scale, has strained the resources of organized Western civilization itself from that day to this. From

[1] Report by Field-Cornet Joubert in 1845 (quoted Cory, iv, 319).

the beginning of the Treaty negotiations the Griquas showed themselves just sufficiently informed—by knowledge of Dutch and by contact with the Colony—to be fearful and suspicious. In September 1843, Mr. W. Y. Thomson, like Wright before him, reported that only the hope of a treaty and the prospect of Government assistance restrained them from attacking the Boers —who refused to vacate the fountains—before reinforcements of Trekkers should come in from Natal. At the same time they were nervous of Government measures :

' What little news I can scrape together from Natal seems to say that a peace has been made in which the interests of the tribes in this quarter have been utterly overlooked and that we are consequently left to the tender mercies of the Boers. The consequence is that the very worst characters are leaving Natal and are trying to get a footing here and frightening the people with the story that Government will take Philippolis within the boundary and guarantee to the Boers the lands and fountains on which they now reside.'

Incorporation in the Colony, he now fears, may make many Griquas ' turn *Bergenaar* '. ' The leases and written agreements on which the Griquas would ground their claims would be mere waste paper in a court of justice. . . . The Veld Cornets, &c., would be appointed among the Boers . . . and the coloured people are not sufficiently civilized to cope with the Boers in cultivating the land, so that they would soon become mere labourers.'

Two months later the treaties arrived and were ' well received '. But Mr. Atkinson, writing from Colesberg on 17 November, at once touched a weak spot :

' There seems to be a lull, but I cannot think it will be permanent peace till something more shall have been done with the Boers (and their land claims). The great fault and the chief difficulty is with the Philippolis government and people themselves. *They* let the Boers in, and gave them the footing they have, and now they cannot get them out if they would ; and I do not believe many of them are sincere in wishing to get rid of them so long as they can get a little temporary advantage by letting their farms to them. I am afraid for them, they are so very weak and unstable.'

About the same day Edward Solomon wrote from Griquatown regretting the spirit and attitude of the Griquas ; they resent any advice or interference in their temporal affairs by the missionaries ; if they were ripe to manage their own affairs all might be well, but they ' obviously are not '. These unfortunate people were now left to the mercy of a treaty, to straighten out the tangle in their own district.

Just at first Mr. Thomson's letters indicate that even this show of British protection had eased the situation. Oberholster and the ' moderates ' were anxious to vindicate their rights to land, but had no desire for conflict either with the British Government or with the Griquas themselves. They resisted, therefore, the more extreme counsels of the republicans in their midst, and, as late as 7 March 1844, Mr. Thomson professed to fear nothing—the Boers being sharply divided among themselves. The first serious trouble arose not, as might have been expected, about land claims, but about the effect of the treaty in subjecting Europeans to the now legally recognized authority of the Griqua chief and Council—an issue on which, as it happened, Oberholster and Republicans were in large measure agreed. In January 1844, two Europeans having quarrelled, one, Mills, was killed, the other, van Staden, was arrested by Kok, and, strictly in accordance with the treaty, and with the terms of the little used Cape Punishment Act of 1836, sent to Colesberg for trial. Thereupon the Winburg Boers in uproar threatened Kok with vengeance, raising a storm that blew over only after van Staden's release.

Other cases, less well known, served to reduce Kok's legal powers to a farce, and on 28 March the Chief made an almost pitiable appeal to Cape Town. The immediate occasion was a complaint that certain Boers, in defiance of a newly enacted ' law ', were not only introducing ' large quantities of ardent spirit ' (a notorious temptation to the Griquas), but ' threatening to fire on any subject of Adam Kok who shall attempt to carry into execution the order of his chief mentioned above '. Shots, in fact, had already been exchanged between one Hans Rabie and certain Griquas, and Kok is ' grieved to inform His Excellency that he expects similar conduct from many others of the farmers from the threats and insulting language they employ '. Under these circumstances the Chief asks :

' Does His Excellency consider Kok justified in regarding all colonists resident in his District amenable to his laws ? What assistance will His Excellency be prepared to render to Kok should the violence of farmers render dangerous the maintenance of order and execution of laws in his District ? What advice can His Excellency give with regard to such colonists in his district as refuse obedience to his laws ? '

As the Governor could hold out no promise of help, but only

advise great caution, the first effect of the treaty was, in truth, to define and make patent the state of anarchy that had long existed. It subjected the Boers in this area to a government quite as power-less to enforce its behests, as they were determined to repudiate its authority. The Boers in this case had some cause for com-plaint. In the Boer Republics, for a long time to come, natives were subjected to their masters without any court of appeal. Here the Boers found themselves under the jurisdiction of Griquas who had no real courts at all.[1]

Even in face of the general refusal to submit to such Griqua jurisdiction, divisions among the Boers continued so acute as to delay a crisis. When the treaty was first signed, Oberholster and his friends—258 ' heads of families ' [2] had petitioned to be taken under direct British jurisdiction on the terms then being applied by Advocate Cloete in Natal. To this view of the matter they adhered, proposing to Adam Kok, at a meeting in June 1844, to refuse to allow in Griqualand any who repudiated British allegiance, but also protesting to the authorities that they could not hold out indefinitely against the Republicans unless prompt measures were taken to support them in their old loyalty.

Out of the chaos that prevailed there came one ray of light. Dr. Philip himself had always considered the long-vexed land question a matter for Government arbitration. Mr. Thomson elaborated the suggestion.[3] In October 1844, or early in Novem-ber, Thomson and two colleagues discussed a plan of separate Boer and Griqua areas with the Lieutenant-Governor, the latter apparently agreeing in principle, stipulating only that the Griquas must be prepared to accept the Government's decision and probably to ' forfeit the northern part of their land already occupied (hired ?) by Boers '. The missionary Hughes in reporting this conversation commented that a ' population basis '

---

[1] It appears there may be yet another side to this question. In October 1843, before the days of the Treaty, one Jan Vries was sum-moned before the Circuit Court for debt, on the application of a Boer. ' As the Attorney-General denies the right of the Griquas to indict a Boer because the jurisdiction of the Court does not extend beyond the boundary, this is giving the Griquas the severity of the English law without according them its protection ' (Thomson to Philip, 24 October 1843).

[2] Theal, ii, 422. Apparently also in August 1842, when some of them claimed to have been there as early as the Griquas themselves (Cory, iv, 283).

[3] Thomson to Philip, 17 October 1844. Also Hughes to Philip, 7 November 1844.

would secure substantial justice for the Griquas and 'compel the Boers to condense', the Griquas to be left to 'manage their own concerns upon the principles of our municipalities in England'. In December somewhat similar proposals were made to Kok by the Republicans. In substance, this was the nucleus of the plan adopted by Sir Peregrine Maitland seven months later.

The Government, however—though in February the Council proposed a Commission, which was actually appointed in April —could not be persuaded to make a real move till its hand was forced by yet another, and this time a more serious, 'armed protest'. The occasion was Kok's rather tumultuous attempt, with a 'commando' of about 100 armed men, to arrest a Boer named Krynauw, on a charge of ill-using a native servant. There seems to be no question but that Krynauw had administered a brutal flogging. On the other hand, finding their bird flown, the commando seems to have made free with some of his property, and early in 1845, with marching and counter-marching, protesting Boers came together in camp at a place called Touwfontein, some thirty miles from Philippolis. By April 1845, the Griquas having assembled in opposition, the country was virtually in a state of war.[1] The Government had delayed to intervene in a country crying out for decent administration ; only when the flame, which had smouldered while it tarried, at last burst forth, it decided to take action. In May British troops were rushed up to the Orange River, and after one sharp skirmish at Zwartkopjes, the Republican Boers withdrew to the north, leaving the way apparently clear for Sir Peregrine Maitland, who arrived at Touwfontein in person in the middle of June, to make some attempt at settlement. The restraining influence of Downing Street, however, severely hampered his freedom of action. The Governor's own report on his doings in the north [2] is evidence of the paralysing effect of this restraint :

'My object was no less than to secure their land and freedom to the numerous native tribes, inhabiting the country hundreds of miles beyond the Colony to the north-east, against the encroachments and aggressions of self-expatriated British subjects, superior in combination and arms, and too often ready as well as able to dispute successfully

---

[1] Rather significantly, the Boers did not have it as much their own way as with most Bantu tribes. In petty skirmishes, the casualties seem to have been one Griqua killed and six taken prisoner, and ten Boers killed and wounded (Cory, iv, 307).

[2] To Secretary of State, 1 August 1845.

with the rightful owners of the soil for the simple necessaries of a half-civilized life. (Of the Emigrants he notes, moreover) their independent and migratory habits, their disaffection towards the British Government, their readiness to plunge into the interior to escape the least pressure of an external power upon them, and their contempt for the natives, their indifference to native rights and native life. . . .

' I cannot keep too prominently in Your Lordship's view the extreme scantiness of the means at my disposal, for I felt bound to lay aside as utterly impracticable any plan which involved any considerable expense *either for a Civil or a Military* establishment.'

After meeting the chiefs at Touwfontein on 26 June, the Governor reminded his superiors that the state of things that had come to a head in the Griqua country was ' of much wider extent—stretching over the greater part of the country inhabited by Bechuana and Coranna tribes up to the Magaliesberg and French Mountains north of Delagoa Bay ',[1] urging also that a settlement in Griqualand ' should be framed on principles applicable to the intermixture of British subjects and Natives (up to 25 degrees S. lat.) '. In Griqua country, he adds, there was ' scarcely one Boer ' who had not obtained his farm, ' generally on lease, from an individual Griqua or their *Raad* (Council) by the payment of a valuable consideration as stipulated by a contract '. Elsewhere, however, ' the Boers generally paid nothing for the lands on which they located themselves, and in many instances held them not only without the Chief's permission, but by force, in defiance of his power to remove them '. A temporary pacification would serve no useful purpose. It became necessary ' to do something with these numerous and scattered farmers, to prevent fresh quarrels and collisions with the Native tribes, and to put a stop to the gradual process of shoving the latter out of their lands and either exterminating them or reducing them to slavery '. The Boers could not be brought back to the Colony, and to expel those settled in Griqualand would only

---

[1] Thus Dr. Philip's 1842 report on the ' Transvaal ' problem was not entirely forgotten. The Government must certainly have seen also a further report from the missionary Edwards, in October 1844, after a long journey to the north-east, to the effect that ' all the Bechuanas east of the Marico are in subjection to the Boers '. One ' Pilane ', for example (probably about the ' Pilandsberg '), had said to him : ' I can do and say nothing (relative to the placing of a missionary). I live in the country of the Boers for fear of Moselekatze. I am their servant.' The Boers had then ' all gone to seek powder, and even ordered me (Pilane) to send my warriors ', and according to Edwards, ' They are evidently preparing for a struggle with the English and could easily turn us all out of the Bechuana country.'

drive them on to adjoining tribes. ' The continued location of them, therefore, among the tribes, *under some restraining regulation*, seemed the only plan open for any consideration.' ' Extension of British sovereignty ' being equally out of the question, he concluded that since there was 'land enough for both ', they should, in effect, be ' segregated '—by measures ' confining the farmers within certain defined limits, and reserving for the natives an ample tract within which no foreigner should be allowed to acquire land '.

The faltering step taken in 1843 had not been quite in vain. The conflict between Boers and Griquas, so far from being caused by the first Griqua Treaty, had brought that Treaty into being. The Treaty obligations now forced a reluctant Government to face the solution of a problem on which depended the last hope of preserving South Africa as a political unit. It was none too soon. The basis of the settlement now proposed was the suggestion made earlier by Mr. Thomson. The native territories were to be divided into two portions, one inalienable, the other open for European settlement on terms to be agreed upon with the Colonial Government. The inalienable reserve was to be ' amply sufficient for the present and future wants ' of the tribe ; the leasable portion was to be defined by treaty, and selected, as far as could be, so as to move as few of the existing occupants as possible ; an Agent, backed by the force of the Government, was to be on the spot to deal with disputes as they arose, his authority, however, being not an extension of British sovereignty, but a delegation of that of the Chief. The tribes, in fact, were left in enjoyment of their own law and custom, with ' clusters of British subjects in their own locations ' under ' self-government '. The European settlers, finally, were to pay an annual quit rent, half the revenue to go to the chiefs, the other half to defray the expenses of the Agent, the land as a whole remaining the property of the natives under the ' sovereignty ' of the Chief. On these terms a new treaty with Adam Kok was signed in February 1846. Moshesh, however, who had agreed in principle to the new plan sketched by the Governor at the Touwfontein meeting in June 1845, had not composed his territorial disputes with his neighbours in time to come in, before events on the old Kafir frontier, which had at first distracted and hindered the northern settlement, ended by upsetting it altogether.

In spite of the sequel, this revised treaty policy was an advance on anything that had gone before, holding out some hope of a real permanent settlement. For almost the first time, it recognized that black and white must inevitably share the land between them, that their different standards make it desirable to keep the races apart as far as possible, that in unrestricted competition the backward race is at a hopeless disadvantage, and therefore, that the highly desirable separation can be maintained only by the demarcation of a minimum of native land as inalienable ' Reserve '. In the 'forties only the British Government was strong enough to carry out such a comprehensive policy. In the twentieth century South African opinion is at last more and more inclined to accept these principles as sound—slowly coming to recognize that land-hunger and congestion of population underlie a good deal of the economic and even physical ill-health of the natives—much more slowly and reluctantly, that the characteristic *malaise* of White South Africa is due to over-expansion and to the superficial taking up of land that had far better have been left as Native Reserve—as it might have been if only these principles had been applied in the 'forties.

For a short time the omens for a happy issue were not unfavourable. The missionaries, in the first place, who spoke for the native population—having evolved the essential principle of reserved areas—were striving for a reasonable settlement. As the idea of reserves shows, they by no means ignored the legitimate claims and the interests of the Boers. Edward Solomon, for example, trained by Dr. Philip, and married to Mrs. Philip's niece, rejoiced that the protection of neighbouring tribes would no longer rest on the none too strong shoulders of Waterboer. ' Additional treaties ',[1] he writes to Dr. Philip from Griquatown on the eve of the Touwfontein meeting, 26 June 1845, ' will rouse our people to see that their superiority must be maintained, not by a mere treaty with the Government, but by a steady progress in civilization and religion '.[2] ' Now,' he concludes :

[1] Dr. Philip's latest opinion was written to the L.M.S. (24 March 1846) : ' The tribes are for the present preserved from the destruction that threatened them. . . . The treaties will, I hope, afford them protection *till they shall become colonial subjects, the only thing that will place them beyond the reach of danger.*'

[2] Mr. Solomon, who was pushing on with an irrigation furrow from the Vaal River, comments on the hard struggle for existence. ' If the means of civilization were at hand I believe our people would make rapid strides.' A large body of irrigation workers from other parts, he believes, ' would settle here if they could only find means of supporting themselves '.

' Now is the time for the interference of our Government on wide and comprehensive principles. Now or never. I think that Sir P. Maitland may now by some bold and decided step settle the affairs of the Boers which have given so much trouble to his predecessors. . . . The Boers must be brought under British rule and must be separated from the Griquas. This is the only foundation on which peace can be established in this country. You will, no doubt, be using your influence with Government to direct them aright, and I thank God that you are still in the country [1] at this critical period.'

It was a great misfortune that precisely at this crisis Dr. Philip was no longer fully available to advise upon the difficult adjustments involved in the signing of new and more elaborate treaties. Early in July 1845 the old man of seventy—full as ever of affairs—had travelled as far as the Kat River on his way north, when he was summoned back to Hankey by a tragic event, the drowning of his eldest son, William, and his eleven-year-old grandson (Johnny Fairbairn.) Letters from W. Y. Thomson and others indicate that even after this blow Dr. Philip was instrumental in securing (unspecified) ' material alterations ' in Adam Kok's treaty ; but though he continued as Superintendent of the L.M.S.—' waiting for a successor '—till October 1850, he seems perforce to have stuck more to routine and was never the same man again. In January 1846 he was presented, on behalf of the Basutos, with a lamp—for his services in ' bringing them light '. But his expected second visit to Thaba Bosigo never took place, nor did he see things for himself, as in 1842. He took no part, therefore, in trying to settle Moshesh's boundary disputes, nor in talking over with the Governor in Cape Town [2] the letters that still reached him about the administrative difficulties of the Government Agent in the new capital Bloemfontein. The new crisis in Kafirland in 1846 almost passed him by, and without Dr. Philip to advocate an effective policy of ' holism ' in South African affairs, the renewed impact of black and white, Colony and Republics, finally drove the British Government into headlong flight.

[1] In 1843 Dr. Philip had resigned and for some time planned to retire to England.

[2] Mrs. Philip's letters during her husband's absence in 1845 throw incidental light on happenings not recorded when he was on the spot. On 2 May, for example, she sent Thomson's letters ' first to the Governor ', before forwarding them. A week later ' the Governor sent to ask if we knew anything of the happenings at Griquatown ' (where the Boers were supposed to be creating a native diversion to keep Waterboer from coming to help Philippolis).

Meantime in the north, the relative strength of the emigrant Boers, if not their actual numbers, made Boer co-operation and consent the first essential of any permanent settlement. The usual view is that even the revised treaty policy was unduly considerate of Griqua and native interests, and correspondingly provocative of Boer resentment.[1] At Touwfontein no doubt, Sir Peregrine Maitland, like any good Army officer, was severe towards those subjects of the Queen who claimed to treat with him as spokesmen of an independent Republic. But the Die-hards, as their quarrels with Oberholster proved, were only a section of the European settlers in Griqualand, and mattered a good deal less at that time than the later history of the Republics would suggest. The important thing just then was to keep the good will of the ' Moderates ', and the fact is that, so far as their first objective, land, was concerned, *bona fide* settlers got very good terms indeed.

In Griqualand proper the area open to lease was fully larger than the inalienable ' reserve '. At the very beginning, missionaries and Griquas protested [2] at the ear-marking of half the quit-rent accruing from leases—hitherto all their own—for the maintenance of an Agent, as it seemed to them, ' for the protection of the Boers '. The Agent was, indeed, too weak, had he wished it, to put any serious pressure on the stronger party in the territory —the Boer farmers. Mr. Thomson continued to complain not only of the feebleness of attempts to use the Punishment Act to protect natives against ill-usage, but of the failure, sometimes even of the absence of any desire, to clear the ' Reserve ' for native occupation. By a later decision of Sir Harry Smith [3], farmers might be required to vacate lands in the Reserve, but only on receiving ' compensation for improvements '; and as the Griquas were either too poor or too improvident to offer such payment, Maitland's hope that ' in forty years the Reserves will be free ' proved too optimistic. Government by a mere Agent was a further fundamental weakness of this settlement, and could not be a permanent *modus regendi*. An Agent could never have the legal and moral authority of a regular magistrate,

[1] Cf. Cory, iv, 314.
[2] (Thomson to Philip, 1 July 1845.) In November Thomson said the Griquas were rather against annexation, on the ground of the Attorney-General's ' special pleading ', i.e. tenderness for Boer interests. He wrote similarly in February 1847.
[3] Dr. C. W. de Kiewiet MSS., *The British Government and the S.A. Republics.*

B.B.B.

Q

or the police or military power behind him. But it is hard to see that the Boers were the chief sufferers from this deficiency.

As things first turned out, the shoulder-shrugging acquiescence of Downing Street in Sir Harry Smith's policy of annexation, in 1848, seemed to show that Her Majesty's Government was beginning to see that annexation was the logical sequel to the first halting steps taken by the treaties of 1843 and 1846. A period of peace and quiet must in themselves have paved the way for a more effective civil government. By 1848, moreover, Downing Street was committed to a policy of colonial devolution. Preparations for the establishment of representative institutions in the Cape Colony were well advanced. In the middle of 1851 a draft constitution for the Orange River Sovereignty actually reached Cape Town,[1] and, had all gone well, the extension of parliamentary government to the people of the Orange River Territory, whose interests were identical with those of the parent Cape Colony, must have followed as a matter of course. In that event, since their right to the land had been acknowledged, there was neither reason nor inducement for the really solid, peace-loving majority of the Orange River Boers to join the irreconcilable Republicans. The influence of Mocke and Co., apart from the later Orange Free State, and frowned upon by the official Dutch Church,[2] must have been weak and negligible in face of a liberal Cape Colony reaching to the Vaal. The Diehards might then have been left to come to their senses at their leisure, and to the ' common South Africanism ' of a later day.

It was not to be. In the late 'forties South Africa was nearer to recovering and retaining its unity than it ever was again till 1910. This hope was blasted, not so much by the imperfections of the attempted settlement in the north, as by the feelings of despair occasioned in Her Majesty's advisers by another prolonged upheaval among the Kafirs in the east, where, after years of comparative peace, a storm broke within a month of the signing of the second treaty with Adam Kok. On 1 April 1846 Sir Peregrine Maitland left Cape Town to take charge in the east, and for over two years he and his successors had so

---

[1] The draft constitution was held back by Sir Harry Smith, and apparently its existence was overlooked by his successor, Sir George Cathcart (de Kiewiet MSS.).

[2] Letters from Rev. A. Faure to Dr. Philip (e.g. on 1 January 1844) afford fresh evidence of the well-known dislike of the Dutch Church for the Trek movement, or it is sometimes said, of a ' lack of sympathy ' between ministry and people.

much to occupy them there that they left the newly appointed
Government Agent in the north very much to his own devices.
The Agent's authority was so very slender that in the best of
circumstances he could hope to make good only if he was sure
of backing from the Cape Colony. The war, however, absorbed
not only the Governor but all available troops. It also encouraged the more refractory of the Boers to persist in a restless
agitation, to the further embarrassment of the hapless Agent,
who made little enough progress with the Griqua settlement, and
none whatever farther afield on the much disputed boundaries
of Moshesh's country. In 1850, two years after Sir Harry
Smith's plunge into the policy of outright annexation which Downing Street at first half-heartedly accepted, and before this new
move had time to prove itself, there was yet another upheaval
in Kafirland. This time, without further parley, the economists
in Great Britain had it all their own way. The emigrant Boers
were left to manage their own affairs, and the natives to their
own resources.

CHAPTER XV

THE TREATY SYSTEM ON THE KAFIR FRONT 1838-42—MALADMINISTRATION AND DROUGHT

THE ' Seventh ' Kafir War was not begun, like that of 1834, and like the momentous war that followed in 1850, by the Kafirs. The immediate occasion in 1846 was a Kafir attack on the escort which was taking a prisoner from Fort Beaufort to Grahamstown for the theft of the ' axe ' which gave the war its popular name ; but this episode was in itself a mere police affair, important only because, coming when it did, it served to convince the Governor of the need for a definite departure from the treaty policy of 1836. The Governor thereupon decided to strike first. According to the Manifesto which he issued on leaving Cape Town for the front, this was only the culmination of a long chain of ' causes which rendered it impossible to refrain any longer from punishing the systematic violation of justice and good faith on the part of the Kafirs '.

On the face of it, the ' Kafir ' Treaties had a simpler function than those concluded in the north in 1843 and 1846. The Kafirs, though with divisions of their own,[1] were a compact, homogeneous community, with fairly definite boundaries. The problem was apparently only to keep peace on the border where black and white met, whereas in the Griqua country Europeans and coloured people were not only under the perennial danger of a physical clash, but had to find a *modus vivendi* side by side in the same country.

In origin the Kafir Treaties, like those of the 'forties, were a compromise between Humanitarians fighting for protection of the native tribes and economists concerned for the interests of the British taxpayer ; in practice economical motives had the

---

[1] Treaties were signed separately in 1836 with the Gaikas, Ndhlambis and Gunukwebe—later with the Tambookies (or Tembus).

effect of starving efficient administration, making the treaties—
in all their history—a poor substitute for the full responsibility
and control which were urged on Downing Street in vain. The
treaties, moreover, had a bad start in the excitement of 1836.
Land-hungry colonists, blind to the need of the Kafirs for land,
and with an eye ever upon Kafir love for cattle not their own,
were gravely disappointed. Their own hopes of new farms in
Kafirland were frustrated, and they feared that the retention of
the borderlands by the Kafirs would mean a continuance of
cattle-stealing. Yet had the boundary been extended to the Kei,
apparently they were prepared to have taken that risk. From
the beginning they were almost derisively hostile to the ' Glenelg
policy ', seeing in it only the cloven hoof of Humanitarian distrust,
and unwilling ever to give it a fair trial as a possible remedy for
frontier disorders.

Now the treaties themselves undoubtedly showed the influence
of Humanitarian and other critics of the deplorably militarist
(and futile) policy that had led to the war of 1834. Native
land-hunger being recognized as a real thing, even the long-
disputed ' Ceded ' Territory was given back to the Kafirs, not
indeed in full ownership, but on ' loan '—during good behaviour.
Military posts on the Border, like Fort Beaufort, were to remain,
but for the rest the control of the frontier was thrown on the
chiefs, colonial interests being represented by Agents resident
near the principal chiefs, but armed only with ' diplomatic '
authority. On paper, at least, there was a reversion to the
policy of non-intercourse, British subjects to enter Kafirland
only with permits, at their own risk, and to remain there subject to
Kafir law ; Kafirs, on the other hand, to enter the Colony only
with ' passes ' from the Agent.[1]

The cattle-stealing provisions were at least elaborate. Any
Kafir caught red-handed in the Colony was to be shot at if necessary, and further dealt with under colonial laws. But with old
practices in mind, the treaty-makers now laid it down emphatically that ' on no occasion whatever shall any Patrol, or armed
party of any description, be allowed to cross ' the boundary
either for the capture of alleged criminals or for the recovery
of stolen animals. On the Kafir side of the line the law of
the chiefs must prevail, with colonial interests watched or

---

[1] In practice, the colonial need for labour, and distress among
the Kafirs, led to a considerable influx of Kafirs on passes issued apparently under the 49th Ordinance of 1828. (See pp. 66 ff and 266.)

sponsored only by and through the Agents. Thus, if colonial
pursuers traced thieves or cattle to the boundary, two courses
were open to them. Either they might cross, unarmed, enlist
the aid of the nearest *pakati* (councillor or headman), and having
with his help traced the spoor, report on oath to the Agent, carry
off their own property (and no more), leaving the exaction and
payment of compensation to the chief. Or else they might appeal
to the nearest military post for an escort, and, having traced the
spoor as far as they could or dared, lodge a complaint, on oath,
with the Agent, and throw the whole responsibility on to the
chief direct. Thus the conditions to be fulfilled by the victims
of thefts, before they could lawfully recover their stock, were
onerous, or even clumsy. The hand of Stockenstrom (and of
Dr. Philip) appears in the provisions which require for example
a formal declaration, on oath, of the precise number of animals
missing, that they were properly guarded by day,[1] or adequately
secured in kraals or stables at night. It was also laid down that,
if the theft was at night, pursuit must be commenced, at latest,
early next morning—this last, no doubt, to make sure that the
animals' traces were reasonably fresh, and to check the notorious
ingenuity of ' spoor-finders '.

The stipulations were not in themselves unreasonable, but the
humanitarianism of the treaty-makers made little allowance for
the natural difficulties of the farmers scattered over an unfenced
and primitive frontier. At the same time, in such an unsettled
community, the scheme threw such a burden of responsibility
on the Kafir chiefs as could only be borne by them if the civilized
government did its share in trying to prevent cattle-stealing.
But a starved administration left the frontier line open, virtually
without police protection.[2] Thieving continuing, changes in the
treaties were constantly demanded, and always in the direction
of heaping more and more responsibility on to the chiefs, without
offering them anything in return. Prolonged wars and unsettlement must in any case have impoverished the natives. It is
forgotten how short a time had elapsed since the clearing of the

---

[1] ' The frontier farmers should remember that they got *good* land
cheap, and should not complain of having to protect their flocks as they
know they would have to do ' (Stockenstrom to Philip, 25 August 1842).

[2] Captain Stretch, e.g. on 28 September 1839, complained to the
Governor's Secretary that a body of 60 native police were not properly
remunerated. In 1836 they had been paid with cattle taken from
delinquents, but this ' fund ' ceased when ' Queen Adelaide ' was
abandoned.

Zuurveld in 1811. Men of thirty who were then driven from their homes, and old enough to feel resentment, were only sixty-five in 1846, in their full strength and vigour at least as leaders and councillors.[1] Yet in effect the Government, which had for years allowed its subjects to encroach on what the Bantu had some excuse for regarding as their own land, now expected law and order from the long harassed tribes—in short, that they should police colonial farms on its behalf.

On his first trip to the frontier in 1838 Sir George Napier seemed to accept unreservedly a colonial view, absolving the farmers from all blame—holding that the Kafirs had ' no excuse for their continued and daring depredations ', and that the chiefs did not do their part in checking them. His report to Lord Glenelg on 12 July 1838 [2] suggests that he still conceived the problem so much as a task for soldiers—' to defend the Colony from any sudden rush of Kafirs '—that he could not see how to make the troops ' at the same time a police force to check the constant stealing of cattle which must, if not speedily put a stop to, force farmers who reside on the immediate frontier to emigrate or be reduced to absolute want '. For the present he contented himself with warning the chiefs and trying to strengthen the patrol system, returning to Cape Town in October evidently under the firm impression that the treaties were a hopeless failure.[3] There, in January 1839, he decided on one step of very doubtful wisdom. In his desire to test the efficacy of the treaties in preventing thefts, he instituted a ' Not Reclaimable List ', of animals stolen (or alleged to be), but ' irreclaimable ' because their owners had failed to comply with the undoubtedly rigorous stipulations of the treaties. In practice, this list grew inordinately because farmers were able to submit records of losses ' by theft ' without the need for proof. The result was to keep excitement alive on

[1] E.g. ' His right to the Kat River is a theme Maqomo delights to dwell on ', and Maqomo being ' of a warlike and ungovernable disposition ', he and others, ' if Sandile's countenance be obtained, would scarcely reflect on the fearful and ruinous consequences to them of attempting to recover the lands Gaika lost in 1819, and which, I reiterate, I believe to be the source of existing irregularities on both sides of the Border ' (Stretch to Lieutenant-Governor, 6 March 1845).

[2] Quoted Cory, iv, 329.

[3] To Secretary of State, September 1840. ' Never were treaties more strictly and pertinaciously adhered to,' he writes, yet ' it has been impossible to prevent depredations. . . . But God forbid that I should ever be an advocate of the unjust or inhuman policy which calls for seizure of the land '.

both sides. Colonial discontents were doubled by such ' official ' evidence of their sufferings, and the much advertised ' D'Urban System ' came to be idealized by contrast. On the other hand the Kafirs were alarmed by this (unsifted) testimony against them, and protested, like Maqomo on one occasion : ' Our people steal oxen and cows but the Government steals with the pen.' [1]

Two years later, in October 1840, the Governor set out once more for the frontier, armed this time with a carefully annotated Memorandum by Judge Menzies, and hoping to secure modifications in the Treaties.[2] As a result, a Proclamation of 28 January 1841 (sanctioned by Lord John Russell in a dispatch of 17 April 1841) announced that, by agreement with the chiefs, armed herdsmen would no longer be required, that *bona fide* pursuers of stolen cattle might cross the boundary, in small parties and unarmed, without the formality of procuring passes, and that ' on recovering cattle they should be allowed to take something more than the exact quantity lost, by way of compensation for time and trouble '.[3] In thus tightening up against the Kafirs, these changes had the defect of rather lessening the need for the Colonial Government to improve its own defective police system ; but they seem to have been of some use in facilitating the recovery of stolen cattle.

The evidence is, however, that Napier's views were considerably modified by what he learned on his second frontier visit.[4] Henceforth—while trying to keep the peace by winking at the payment of compensation for ' irreclaimable ' losses—he took the alarms of Grahamstown more calmly. Not all the

[1] As early as September 1839 Stretch begins to complain of ' unofficial ' returns in the Press gaining credence, while the Agents were ignored. In support he forwarded ' statements ' from Maqomo, Botman, and Tyali, complaining of ' claims' for cattle and horses that had not been adequately traced. Such claims, he concludes, were ' the cause of the last war '.

[2] Memo. in Gubbins' Collection.   [3] Cory, iv, 353.

[4] Napier may possibly have met Stockenstrom, who returned from England to his farm near Bedford just about the time of the Governor's visit, and on 29 October wrote to Fairbairn claiming that, thanks to the treaties, the frontier was unusually peaceful, and that the Boers of the Colony rejoiced in their immunity from service on commandos. The ' Eastern ' party, however, were pressing for changes, and must be carefully watched lest their importunity make the Governor depart from the *principles* of the treaties and make a big war inevitable (Letter in Gubbins' Collection). To Dr. Philip on 26 February 1841 he ' refrained from comment ' on the revised treaties—' the amendments, appendages or whatever you call them '.

murders reported were the work of ' foreigners '; besides ' strays ', many of the thefts complained of were the work of Hottentots, Fingos, and ex-slaves, or of Xosa whom the farmers ' harboured ' for their own convenience, in defiance alike of pass laws and of the wishes of the chiefs.[1] Stretch afterwards reported that, according to Napier himself, the Governor had come to Kafirland disposed to proclaim martial law and get Stretch hanged.[2] A new note was heard in Napier's dispatch of 7 January 1841, remarking on ' the excitement kept up in Kaffraria by the movements of the emigrant farmers ', and the likelihood that ' especially the Gonaquabi ' will soon ' make a formal application ' to be brought under ' the authority and control of H.M. Government '. In the following December : ' No important merchant in Grahamstown has not within the last few years invested in sheep farms along the border '—one, Cypherfontein, sold by the Government for £1,975, resold lately for £3,500 ; another, on the Fish River, bought for £300, had sold for £1,100. ' Thefts ', he adds, are largely ' for food '. In October 1843 he wrote :

' It is the object of a party on the Frontier at present to exhibit the Kafir character in the most unfavourable light in order to prove that the effect of the treaties has been to degrade rather than elevate them in the scale of civilization ' (and he promised statistics to prove the contrary).

Finally, almost on the eve of his departure, 4 December 1843, Napier definitely opposed Colonel Hare's belief in ' coercion, prudently, justly, and judiciously conducted ', urging that this was a mere reversion to the ' Commando System ', and that ' every armed patrol would be to postpone the great object of the treaties, namely, to raise the Kafirs by an appeal to their sense of justice '. As an alternative he urged Dr. Philip's remedy,[3] the payment of the chiefs, together with the punishment of proved robbers, not by the chiefs but by colonial tribunals.

[1] For references, see Walker, p. 233.
[2] Memo. on Treaties. Gubbins' Collection.
[3] The Philip MSS. include important letters not only from Read and Calderwood but also from Stockenstrom and Stretch, and many others. But their evidence is scattered, and Dr. Philip himself seldom made any official comment. One incidental suggestion made to Secretary Montagu in a Griqua letter of August 1843 was approved by Napier (December 1843) and adopted later by Maitland : ' I consider that, the want of what is here recommended (a salary for Kok), to be the grand defect of the Caffre treaties. Had a few of the powerful chiefs been subsidized by having small salaries allowed to them we might by this time have had the affairs of Caffreland in our own hands.'

The truth is that the treaties were by no means the unqualified failure that tradition would suggest. Granting all that can be said of their futility as a permanent solution, they marked an undoubted advance on the *bellum in pace* of the years between 1811 and 1834. The reprisals and commandos of all those years contributed their share to the insecurity and unrest out of which the Trek developed. Now the burghers who remained had a rest at least from military service. In 1839 there was a fresh development of Kafir mission work, even by the L.M.S. which in 1830 had expressly diverted the French missionaries to a less unsettled area.[1] Above all, the early 'forties were a time of boom and of rising prices in the much complaining Eastern Province itself. The rise in land values, remarked upon by the Governor, as well as by Stockenstrom [2] and his friends, was due in the first place to the introduction of sheep-farming ; and though some frontiersmen abandoned their farms, whether to go on trek or to seek a safer zone within the Colony, the development of the wool industry could not have come about without a considerable measure of practical security. Before long the very success of the treaties in keeping relative peace opened wider issues. With a new demand for native labour came new difficulties about ' passes ' and about ' squatters ', thence, since according even to Napier [3] squatters sometimes stole in order to live, a new chain of ' thievings ', and a renewed attack upon the treaties themselves.

The original sin which finally led to the breakdown of the treaties was European as well as native, and the causes of failure a good deal more complex than the derisive colonial hostility by which they have always been summarily condemned would allow. The first blow to the treaty policy was the (hardly blameworthy) failure and the fall of Andries Stockenstrom. The treaties, it may be true, were conceived by their humanitarian supporters as a means of protecting the natives from the encroachments of greedy colonists. But in spite of Downing Street, Stockenstrom, who framed if he did not originally suggest them, undoubtedly thought of them as a mere preliminary ; they were to prepare the minds of the Xosa tribes for willing acceptance,

---

[1] New stations were planted by Messrs. Calderwood and Birt. (See also above, p. 75).

[2] *Cape Col. Qn.*, pp. 79, 80.

Below, pp. 245, *note* and 301.

presently, of the advantages of civilized government [1] within the Colony. In normal conditions he might have been trusted to keep the balance even—watchful, as himself a frontier farmer, of the success of his policy in protecting the frontier, and not unmindful, as an administrator, of its effects on native interests and feelings. But conditions were far from normal, and in the two years of his Lieutenant-Governorship he was so persecuted by his Grahamstown critics that, though indefatigable in organizing his department, he was left with little leisure for anything but his immediate concerns. Citing similar colonial persecution of Maynier, Philip and Fairbairn, ' May the D——l pity me ! ' (he writes to Fairbairn, October 1837). ' I am quite done up ' (28 February 1838), ' I can go on no longer '. Also—' I know my own temper.' His enemies are getting the officials ' in their fangs ' ; their evidence against him is taken ' in holes and corners '. In March 1838 Grahamstown was celebrating, with illuminations, the failure of a libel action he brought against the Civil Commisioner Campbell, on which he writes : ' I never humbled myself before any man. . . . There lives a God who will settle all this in defiance of the whole fraternity.' By July he had

---

[1] Stockenstrom wrote a long apologia to Philip on 25 August 1842 : ' This abominable Natal affair frightens me. . . . I see our political and normal advancement retarded half a century.' He pours scorn on Lord Normanby for his desire to treat the colonists with ' Conciliation ' ; ' fancying he could establish a firm government on a mere ephemeral " popularity "(!) (which Stockenstrom lacked), he unhinged the confidence of all friends of order ' . . . and ' shook the foundations of good Government and left us with almost *none at all* '. . . . ' I speak and feel strongly. Is not this my native country ? Have not the Boers always been dear to me ? Are not the English my fellow subjects and adopted countrymen ? Are not all the victims of rapacity and savage cruelty, of whatever colour and class, my fellow-creatures ? Might we not all improve and prosper together ? ' . . . After a long defence of the Boers as potentially ' the best disposed and easiest managed people in H.M. dominions ', he urges the systematic ' colonization of all depopulated territories '. As for the tribes, ' I confess that (with Sir B. D'Urban) I should be glad to see the whole of Africa one immense British Colony with our laws in full vigour through every nook of it. But . . . it is folly to talk ever of reversing the order of nature . . .'
Hence : ' Where you have depopulated territories, over which there may be scattered remnants of tribes who have lost all order or law, or never had any, and are altogether powerless against your own subjects, whom you cannot keep away from them, and who show their superiority merely by oppression and plunder and slaughter, then you must either leave those enormities to take their course, until the

decided to take leave of absence, not without the satisfaction of finding the Governor comparatively sympathetic :

' The malicious and stupid faction will be disappointed in their hopes of setting the Governor and myself by the ears. As I despise *them* and their meanness and see them with pity and contempt flourish in their disappointed fury, so much I reverence and venerate the true gentleman and man of honour.'

This being Stockenstrom's state of mind as revealed in his confidential letters to John Fairbairn,[1] his cue was naturally to seize on every fragment of evidence that went to justify the treaty experiment. From the Chumie in October 1837, he noted the surprise of Sir John Wylde, the Chief Justice, at finding that at a conference with the Kafir chiefs he and Captain Stretch went all *unarmed*, quite safe among those ' irreclaimable monsters '. Like Stretch, he insisted that a ' " Cabal " and " War Party " *want* a blow up—that they may share in the scramble '—more than once, that ' the price of land continues to rise '. The frontier is almost always ' quiet '—' only six head of cattle this week ' (January 1828). Again (27 April)—' the fellow who pretends to believe that the Hottentots and Caffres are preparing to *eat us up* gives £200 for a sheep farm *bordering on the Fish River Bush* '. In July, on the eve of departure : ' The Government sees more and more through the trick of frontier dangers ', one Major Charters having returned ' delighted ' from the front where ' *unarmed* Boers have gone into Kafirland, got a commando from the chiefs ', and ' returned successful ', with the cattle. Finally on 10 August, he encloses Reports, ' to enable you to

original population of the soil shall be completely rooted up, or enslaved, and the moral degradation shall have come to such a depth as to act injuriously upon the parent state which sent forth the venom ; or you must interfere by applying the only antidote at your command ;—you must " *swamp* " the bad by an ample supply of the good, and adapt the orphan race to a full participation in the benefits of the laws and improvements which this superior population will bring along with them, thus forming a nucleus to which thousands of the oppressed will gradually draw for protection, and planting the seed from which British law and British institutions may in process of time spread far and wide, as their virtues become known and felt and the soil becomes prepared for their culture. . . . For example, the Griquas are already thoroughly convinced of the superiority of British rule, but to force Moshesh and his tribe to become British subjects forthwith might be disastrous.'

[1] In Mr. J. G. Gubbins' Collection.

judge whether I have any cause to blush at the fruit of my labours '. [1]

Now the ' tranquillity ' of which Stockenstrom boasted was alleged also by his one whole-hearted supporter, Captain Stretch, who, as Agent among the Gaikas, the most ' turbulent ' of the clans, was in a position to know the facts.[2]   At the same time, though the farmers' complaints undoubtedly ascribed to the Kafirs all losses whatever—animals straying in an unfenced and broken country and coming to grief in holes and dongas, together with the ' sins of jackals, wolves and tigers ' now being laid to the charge of the Kafirs, as in other days to that of ' vagrant ' Hottentots—peace in Kafirland was not incompatible with thefts and ' depredations ' in the Colony itself.   On this ground it was easy enough to charge Stockenstrom with saying ' Peace, Peace ', where there was no peace.   Moreover, one effect of the persistence of his critics was that Stockenstrom himself came to judge the treaty policy by their standards—his own emphasis supporting and confirming the impression that cattle-stealing by the Kafirs was the beginning and end of the difficulty. Napier (for a time at least), and Maitland after him, absorbed to the full the still almost universal delusion that cattle-stealing was the fundamental rather than an incidental cause of the whole long tragedy of the Kafir Wars.

The cattle-stealing was of course a symptom rather than a prime cause of frontier unrest.   As the Gaika chief, Sandile, protested to Sir George Grey in 1835 : ' The patrimony of a chief is not cattle.   It is land and men.'   History and experience have since proved the Bantu to be singularly amenable to just government, even in face of the crushing pressure of European colonization itself.   As Stockenstrom at least recognized, success depended on carrying the Kafirs with them—persuading them gradually of the incalculable advantages of civilized government, of which hitherto they had had no direct experience.   What little they had seen, heard and felt, was not encouraging.   The emancipation of the Hottentots was too recent, and still too insecure, to give Kafirs convincing proof of the benefits to be expected ;   their own experience was only of ' clearing ' their

[1] He rejoices also that not only did Maqomo and Eno come to say ' Farewell ', but Governor and staff, with Colonels Peddie and Hare, were present at a farewell dinner ' given me ' by the 72nd Highlanders.
[2] ' With the exception of the slanderer's tongue, everything is quiet on the frontier ' (Stretch to Philip, 22 July 1838).

country by commandos and military ' reprisals ', and their judgment of Hottentot history is significantly preserved by Captain Stretch who, in July 1845, warned the authorities that even Tembu and Ndhlambi chiefs agreed that they must ' stand by the House of Gaika, *lest we be broke up as the Hottentots were* '.

But if even Stockenstrom set such store by evidence that ' depredations were on the decrease ', their continuance was the all-absorbing fact with his successors. On the fall of Lord Glenelg, in 1839, in spite of the best efforts of the Humanitarians in England [1] to save the one official who could be trusted to give their policy a fair trial, Lord Normanby decided that his extreme unpopularity made Stockenstrom's return inadvisable, and he was superseded by a very ordinary soldier, under whom the independence and prestige of the Lieutenant-Governorship steadily declined. The new Lieutenant-Governor, Colonel Hare, had no special qualifications for his highly difficult administrative task. Never original nor creative, he was a faithful soldier, soon convinced of the necessity for coercion, but without any appreciation of the wider aims that were an essential part of the treaty policy as it was conceived by Stockenstrom. If he was not hampered like his predecessor by personal unpopularity, neither was he so independent ; indeed the claims and clamours of his neighbours in Grahamstown so filled his communications to the Governors as to shut out from their minds the need to consider also the effect of policy upon the interests of the Kafirs.

The treaties were conceived in a moment of unusual Humanitarian ascendancy ; but from the fall of Stockenstrom the pendulum began to swing in the opposite direction. Both the Governors of the time, Napier and Maitland, were honest and painstaking, but apart from official reports, especially those from Captain Stretch, received little independent evidence of the effects of frontier policy. The missionaries, unfortunately,

---

[1] The dismissal of Stockenstrom is a commentary on the evergreen South African tradition that British ministers trembled at the nod of ' Exeter Hall '. ' We have done all we could to sustain Stockenstrom by urging the Governor to sustain him,' writes Freeman of the L.M.S. to Philip (14 August 1838)—' we ' being the newly reorganized Aborigines Protection Society. A year later, 5 September 1839, Fowell Buxton, no longer an M.P., reported to Dr. Philip his despairing effort to change Lord Normanby's decision against the most trusted of humanitarian officials : ' By Stockenstrom's desire I made an effort to do him service with the higher powers, but as usual with my applications, no good came of it.'

were unusually silent. Scots and Wesleyans who between them had many important stations in Kafirland, had no obvious spokesman ; the L.M.S. were represented chiefly by the Reads, father and son, on the Kat River, and by Mr. Henry Calderwood,[1] at Blinkwater, near Fort Beaufort, but these two were in such sharp antagonism that their reports were largely about their own quarrels, and what time and energy his Northern preoccupations left to Dr. Philip were devoted to keeping them at peace. Dr. Philip's former close watch on the workings of frontier policy was sadly missing. Calderwood, moreover, seems to have been dictatorial and, resisting the blandishments to which so many others fell, failed to make a friend of his important parishoner, Maqomo, actually alienating him by the changes he advocated in the treaties.[2]

The constant demand for such changes was in itself unsettling, suggesting how the treaties were judged more and more exclusively as police measures for the protection of the farmers' cattle—what time, as Captain Stretch complained,[3] the Government refused to find the money for the police force needed to make a success of them even in this limited respect. In these circumstances the chiefs, who were still sore at their earlier losses [4] rather than elated by the respite of 1836, were left for the most part to sulk in silence, without any spokesman with the Government. Insensibly, therefore, the treaties which began

[1] Mr. Calderwood, who joined the L.M.S. about 1838, seems to have had abilities above the average, and considerable ambition. In his early days on the frontier he unburdened himself to Dr. Philip (from Grahamstown, May 1839) : ' I see it is *impossible* for a missionary with a conscience and a heart to live in Caffreland and refrain from doing what will be *called political*. And if it be political to stand between oppressor and oppressed I am determined by the Grace of God to be *political*.'
During Dr. Philip's absence on tour in 1841–2 Calderwood ' supplied ' for a time at ' Union Chapel ' in Cape Town. On his return to Kafirland he disliked and disapproved of Read's conduct of the Kat River, and his ' familiarity ' with the coloured people, whose confidence, however, he himself did not entirely capture. The friction with Read drove him to take a rather ' official ' view and in 1846 he found a new ' field ' as a Kaffrarian magistrate.
[2] Philip to L.M.S., 11 March 1845.
[3] Notably in *Memo.* on the failure of treaties. In Gubbins' Collection.
[4] Maqomo's heart was always ' sore about the land ', especially the Kat River Valley (Cory, iii, 52, 276—fully confirmed by Stretch and others in letters on eve of the war of 1846).

with some idea of the need for controlling all the mutual relations
of colonists and Kafirs—even including the safeguarding of the
Kafirs against colonial encroachments—came to be regarded by
the chiefs with suspicion, scorn and overt hostility, as measures
subtly designed against them for their still more complete
undoing.

As the Kafirs' first experience of anything but naked military
force, the experiment of the Stockenstrom treaties was inaugurated
under peculiarly adverse conditions. In the first place, the retrocession of the territory conquered in 1835 must have been in
itself perplexing. Contact with Europeans since 1778, especially
under the more intensive régime of the years between 1811 and
1834, had given the Kafirs little reason to appreciate the benefits
of just and efficient civil government, and the purely repressive
policy of all these years now brought Nemesis in its train. The
new policy had first to live down the not unnatural feelings of
suspicion and distrust engendered in the Kafir mind by all that
had gone before. But that the change was interpreted by them
as a confession of weakness is a deduction, not unnatural, perhaps,
to European minds that clung to their faith in the efficacy of
' Powder and Ball ',[1] but resting on no further evidence than
the reiterated assertion of nervous frontiersmen. Nerves were
on edge the whole ten years,[2] and the colonists, constantly looking
for ' trouble ' from the Kafirs, magnified what there was. The
constant agitation in Grahamstown reacted on the Kafirs, persuading them that this was only a temporary and suspicious lull
in European aggression.

For it is a mistake to suppose the Kafirs unobservant of events
on the colonial side of the frontier, and beyond. Their expressed
fear of sharing the fate of the Hottentots is proof to the contrary,
and they soon had reason to believe that the change of attitude
in 1836 was too good to be true. Before the treaties were two
years old Grahamstown had succeeded in making things too
hot for Stockenstrom, whom the Kafirs knew to be their friend ;
a year later it was known he was gone for good, and Stretch,
another obvious friend, was threatening to resign.[3] As Dr.

---

[1] Phrase used by Duncan Campbell, later Civil Commissioner
of Albany (*Cape Col. Qn.*, p. 121).   [2] Cory, iv, *passim*.
[3] To the dismay of Dr. Philip and the missionaries (Philip to Buxton,
22 November 1839 ; Birt to Philip, 13 September 1839 ; Calderwood
to Philip, 11 November 1839).

Philip at once prognosticated,[1] there soon began the process of tightening up the treaties by changes that invariably threw more responsibility on the chiefs, making these instruments, perhaps always imperfectly understood, more and more bewildering. On top of their old war losses, almost incessant ' nagging ' shook the prestige of the chiefs and their already weak hold over their own people,[2] at the same time disposing them to try to impress their followers by some show of bravado—or even by cattle-raids that brought new demands, and more outcry from Grahamstown about the futility of the treaties. The doings of the emigrants beyond the Colony were indirectly even more disturbing. The Trek itself was no doubt in defiance of the Government ; but it was not lost on the Kafirs that the first result was the overthrow of Moselekatze and Dingaan, the second, the occupation of vast tracts of land both in Natal and in the north. The prolonged war and unrest behind them in Natal, and latterly in Griqualand, with the land-grabbing of the Trekkers, could not but make the Xosa feel uneasy for their own security.

In Kafirland itself the times were such as to test severely the resource even of the strongest government. For a full generation now the Kafirs had been torn by internal dissension as well as, occasionally, by external war. The arrival of Europeans on the Fish River had put a definite term to an expansion that had gone on unhindered for generations, demanding a considerable modification of their mode of life and putting a heavy strain on their primitive agriculture. In addition, since at least 1811 they had had to provide as best they could for those of their number definitely thrown back out of the Zuurveld. One immediate result was the feud between Gaika and Ndhlambi (chap. iii) that left the Xosa very seriously weakened and divided. But now, having met more than their match in the Europeans, they not only got fighting among themselves but began to find

---

[1] ' Captain Stretch is likely to resign,' and if so, ' the last link that binds the Colony and Kafirs on amicable principles will be dissolved ' (Philip to Buxton, November 1839).

[2] As early as October 1838 Rev. J. Brownlee reported inter-tribal fighting which he ascribed to the loss of authority by chiefs, as a result of earlier happenings. Gaika, a weak Paramount, was dead, and Maqomo only a Regent. Among many later references, Stretch, in December 1844, reported Gaika's heir Sandile as saying : ' I am not as your Governor. If he speaks he is obeyed. My people are disobedient and will not hear.'

that they were between two fires. Behind them, to the north-east, the pressure that had sent their fathers so far afield continued. At this very moment it was redoubled by the rise of Chaka, and from 1820 onwards the advance guard of the Bantu migration in what is now the eastern Cape had to deal with a succession of organized ' hordes ', or ' broken fugitives ', killing or stealing or seeking new homes, or all these things together. Besides the weak and scattered Fingos, and the Mantatees more to the north, there were the comparatively well-organized Bacas, and the Tambookies or Tembus, from whom the Xosa suffered many raids, and for some of whom they had to make room in their already straitened country. The Tambookies presently settled down, to the north of the Xosa and behind them. The Fingos were beginning to do so when, so far from bringing peace, the D'Urban settlement opened the long feud between the Fingos and their former masters, or protectors, the Xosa. It left a rankling sore, that though the Xosa undoubtedly had a grievance (above, pp. 112–3), the last clauses of the Stockenstrom Treaties expressly required them to ' abstain from molesting ' not only the Fingos remaining on Gaika land ' near the Gaga ', but those more firmly planted among the hitherto almost unoffending Ndhlambis at Peddie. This humane provision, unfortunately at the expense of the Xosa both in land and in cattle, served presently to drive even the loyal Pato into hostility to the Government and into the arms of the Gaikas, and all the time to keep alive the unsettlement for which the Xosa had so much excuse. While the Xosa stole colonial cattle, vast numbers were also taken from them, or destroyed. It had taken a heavy toll indeed of colonial cattle to make up the losses and the tribal disorganization of so many years of virtual anarchy. Obviously it was no time for the easy accumulation of wealth on either side of the border.[1]

Finally pure mischance contributed not a little to the tragic denouement. Any hope there was of peace and recuperation was dashed by the cruel hand of nature. There is evidence that, throughout the story, occasional dry years were years also

[1] Statistics of cattle taken by one side or the other are equally worthless. The estimate by the Rev. W. B. Boyce (quoted Cory, iii, 129) deserves notoriety. Having proved to his own satisfaction that the 60,000 head said to have been captured by troops early in 1835 could not have been more than 30,000, he adds laconically the *precise* number stolen from the Colony, 111,418.

of unusual unrest and of Kafir cattle-stealing.[1] Now, on this unlucky frontier, the early and middle 'forties seem to have been a time of prolonged drought which, had there been nothing else of note, might have made the period memorable for an acute famine. In the winters of 1841 and 1842 the Civil Commissioner of Albany so far relaxed restrictions as to allow two friendly chiefs, Kama and Zibi, to reside temporarily and graze their cattle in Bathurst, at the source of the Koonap, and even in Albany itself.[2] Early in 1842 Dr. Philip, on tour beyond the Stormberg, described devastating swarms of locusts. In the end of 1844 drought distress was still acute, and, according to Stretch's Diary, crops failed both in 1845 and 1846, while in July or August 1845 snow and cold rain played havoc with the starved animals. After four such years the provisioning and the movements of the troops in the campaign of 1846 [3] were gravely impeded by the impoverished condition of the transport cattle, this rather suggesting that the drought was particularly felt on the more densely populated Kafir side of the frontier. It was as in the days of the prophet Joel :

> That which the palmerworm hath left,
> Hath the locust eaten,
> And that which the locust hath left,
> Hath the cankerworm eaten ; . . .

The fire hath devoured the pastures of the wilderness
And the flame hath burned all the trees of the field.
For the water brooks are dried up,
And the fire hath devoured the pastures of the wilderness.

The drought was the crowning disaster to make the Kafirs acutely conscious of the pressure of population, and their fear turned to dismay at renewed threats that they might, after all, be expelled from the ' Ceded ' Territory.[4] All this conspired with their other perplexities to bring home to them their elemental need of Land.

[1] Statistics both of cattle theft and of rainfall are too unreliable to detail. But there is no doubt about the droughts of the critical years 1834, 1845 and 1846.
[2] The vagaries of South African climate make it quite possible that, for example, Albany had benefited from local showers that missed Kafirland.
[3] Cf. Cory, iv, 463.
[4] See below, p. 252, and Cory, iv, 377, for the ' Springbok ' speech by Mr. J. M. Bowker, who declared that to ' see the Kafir *sink* before the European, as the herds of springbok had already vanished, could occasion me no feeling but pleasure '.

CHAPTER XVI

THE DRIFT TO WAR AND CONQUEST, 1842-8

THE lull and comparative calm that followed Governor Napier's amendment of the treaties in the end of 1840 were not very long-lived. It is true that 'no shot was fired' during Napier's term of office, but by the middle of 1842 a culmination of causes gave the Colony one of its periodical war scares.[1] In May 1842, charges of witch-craft implicating the Queen-Mother Sutu in the death of the important chief, Tyali, with the beer-drinking and fighting which accompany such great occasions among the Bantu,[2] gave Colonel Hare some cause for anxiety. A year earlier Gaika's heir, Sandile, had come of age, and while he does not seem to have had very striking gifts or presence, (he had a deformed foot,) these changes had a two-fold effect. Maqomo, shaken in his regency, became restive ;[3] at the same time probably the younger bloods were roused to greater bellicosity. None the less, towards the end of the year troops could be moved from this frontier to deal with the Griqua and Boer disturbances about Colesberg and Philippolis, though in May 1843 they were somewhat hurriedly recalled. A few months later Colonel Hare had reached his conviction of the necessity for 'just and prudent coercion.' The Governor, on the other hand (above, p. 232), was more disposed to agree with Stockenstrom and Stretch, reinforced about this time by the Wesleyan missionary W. B. Boyce, that the rumours of unrest were spread chiefly by a War Party among Europeans on the

[1] Alarmist rumours reached as far as W. Philip at Hankey, May 1842.

[2] The months May, June, July are the time of harvest, and the new season's beer, brewed from the Kafir corn or millet, is often responsible, even yet, for local disturbances and faction fights at harvest time.

[3] Calderwood repeatedly suggests the restlessness of Maqomo, and on 29 May and 19 July 1842 even the Reads (both to Philip).

frontier : ' A war and nothing but a war ' will satisfy these people.[1]

While domestic happenings were disturbing, the dominant fact continued to be the distress due to the drought. In the Colony the rainless weather and the sickness of hope deferred were in themselves a severe nervous strain, and enforced idleness or stagnant trade gave both farmers and traders too much time to think about their grievances.[2] Drought also made it difficult for the Colony to absorb the Bantu labourers forced across the border by starvation, though this influx, so far as it meant cheap labour, was not altogether unwelcome to farmers. For years Mr. Justice Menzies had been trying to tighten up the administration of the old 49th Ordinance, pointing out to the Governor how farmers liked to encourage a ' reserve ' of labour. In a fashion that still survives native families were given land, grazing, and hut-room as ' squatters ', in return for the unpaid services—if need be of the whole family ; and in times of dearth these people, being cut off from the communal life of any tribe, were almost driven to steal in order to live.[3] In the early months of 1842 the magistrate of Fort Beaufort roused himself to put pressure on Mr. Read to secure the removal of Fingo and ' foreigner ' squatters from the Kat River Settlement. Mr. Read's protests [4] raised some pertinent questions. Why, he asked, should the ' Hottentot burghers ', and not the Boers, lose the valuable services of ' squatters ' [5] for herding and harvest ? To remove them at that moment would deprive them of their *pay*—their own harvests. The Fingos themselves protested that, if forced out, they would leave the Colony altogether, presumably to ' live by their wits '. Such practical considerations, together with the land shortage that already existed in Kafirland, seem to have prevented any serious attempt to check squatting on colonial farms.

---

[1] Stockenstrom quoting Boyce to Philip, 9 August 1843.

[2] It has sometimes been suggested that, for example, the South African rebellion of 1914 could hardly have happened had the drought-breaking rain, that made the campaign a double misery, come a month earlier and set the farmers in the affected area ploughing.

[3] Menzies to Napier, 12 October 1840, and January 1843, the latter quoting a ' Report ' of October 1838. Also Napier to Secretary of State, July 1841.

[4] To Borcherds, 14 January, and to Philip in January and February.

[5] Read makes early use in this connexion of a now familiar Dutch word—*bijwoners*.

By 1844 the authorities were increasingly perplexed. On 10 June 1844 Mr. Moore Craig in an official Memo. ascribed most of the alleged thieving, like Menzies before him, to ' wandering natives encouraged to squat by farmers, in defiance of repeated orders of Government and of Ordinance 49 ', the law of passes being in utter confusion (above, p. 67). The Tembu Agent, Mr. Fynn, presently showed how and why.[1] In terms of the treaties, passes were to be issued by the Agents ; in practice, they were obtained, ostensibly in terms of Ordinance 49, from any magistrate, field-cornet or J.P., on a printed form which, however, ignored the stipulation of the Ordinance that passes to natives going ' in search of work ' should be valid for only fourteen days. Thefts, he concluded, were often due to

' natives who, having served in the Colony and acquired a knowledge of Dutch, ingratiate themselves into the favour of the Dutch colonists by whom they are too frequently permitted to rove the Colony without passes '.

But two considerations outweighed all protests against this use of the legally defunct Ordinance : ' No description of servants ', wrote Mr. Fynn, '—or such an abundant supply—could be so well suited to the wants of the frontier farmers. The colonists are materially benefited and many a native in times of need is saved from famishing.' And so, throughout 1844 and 1845, in spite of redoubled outcry against ' thieving ', reports, and the diaries of Agents like Fynn and Stretch[2], continue to record streams of Kafirs passing through to ' seek employment in the Colony '—and presumably to find it.[3] In the end of 1845 the Rev. R. Birt, making his annual report to the L.M.S. from his Kafirland station, gave the Kafir side of the picture : ' The great difficulty of finding some means of employment for the natives becomes more pressing every year.'

The truth is that drought and war together had thus early given South African officials their first experience of the modern Native Problem in some of its complex essentials. The prolonged unrest in Kafirland, and the influx of broken tribes and clans from beyond, had severely shaken the stability of the original Xosa tribes. In the ferocious drought that followed to put a

[1] Memo. on Ordinance 49, 20 September 1844.
[2] Stretch especially, in a very full Diary in Cape Town Archives.
[3] According to Stretch, 11 November 1844, the ' normal ' pay for twelve months' service was ' one cow and calf, with keep '.

further strain on their sorely tried social system, it was difficult even for brethren to dwell together in unity—far more to welcome the stranger within their gates (new-comers like the Fingos forced upon them). Since those days, experience and dire necessity have taught the Bantu to accustom themselves to far more straitened conditions than were imposed upon them in the 'forties, till Europeans have come to accept their endurance as a matter of course. But for those who have ears to hear, the intense resentment roused in the long-suffering Bantu by the restrictions of the Land Act of 1913 must have been but an echo of their protest in those more spacious days when first they were called upon to adapt themselves to relatively crowded conditions. Even then there was one possible way of escape. There were plenty of needy men or adventurers (Xosa and Fingo) ready to try the experiment of seeking an outlet among the farmers of the Colony—and some, no doubt, merely looking for peace and quiet. The position of the squatters of those days was economically perhaps better than now—land and grazing rights at least being more generous. In such conditions, when firm control was specially necessary, the administration was thoroughly ineffective. Magistrates were few and feebly supported where they were sorely needed not so much to make the white man's law feared as to teach the natives—what happily their children have long since learned—to know and honour its impartial justice. Severely shaken as they had been, there was yet a limit to Kafir endurance. And so in his Diary for 11 February 1846, Captain Stretch recorded that the farmers' servants had 'suddenly deserted'.

But large considerations of Native Policy found a secondary place in the minds of Governors and officials who, after the fall of Stockenstrom, tended to concentrate more and more on the absorbing and troublesome accident of cattle-reiving. Though Sir George Napier's more alarmist views were modified after 1840, the last months of his governorship were marked by a well-intentioned step which, in the long run, probably did more to rouse Kafir anxieties about their land than to give increased security to the Colony. Frontier disturbances so alarmed Colonel Hare that, having failed to persuade the Government to sanction the removal of the Gaikas altogether from the Fish-Keiskama country, in October 1843 he induced the chiefs to agree to the establishment of a fort, Post Victoria, in the heart of the ' Ceded ' Territory, for the better control of a chief described by Sir

George Cory as 'the horse thief Tola'. From this point, Security definitely dominated Policy.

In March 1844 Sir Peregrine Maitland took charge, at a time when, as the Agents' reports show, distressed natives were steadily seeking work in the Colony and 'depredations' were loudly complained of. The frontier trade in guns,[1] it also seems possible, helped to make the younger Kafirs more daring. In July a farmer named de Lange, in pursuit of his stolen horse, died of wounds received in an exchange of shots with Kafirs near the Fish River. As shooting made this a more serious affair 'the Lieutenant-Governor moved with alacrity '.[2] ' He decided, at length, upon the military occupation of the Ceded Territory '—and this time there was no Napier to say him ' Nay '. Instead, Maitland proceeded himself to the frontier, with some haste, arriving at Port Elizabeth on 10 September. Barely a week later he reached Fort Peddie, and, on the 19th, summarily abrogated the old, and dictated new treaties to the chiefs of the Amagqunukwebi (Pato and Co.) there assembled. From Peddie he went on to Fort Beaufort, and, having made similar new treaties with the Tambookie chiefs who met him there,[3] only then turned to deal with the Gaikas, who, as much the most important of the frontier tribes, took occasion afterwards to feel aggrieved at this slight on their dignity. On every ground the Governor would have been well advised to move more slowly.

The Colony's joy at the abrogation of the Stockenstrom Treaties, and at new 'shackles' for the Kafir[4], did not at all help matters, serving still further to rouse Kafir suspicions at ' changes ' not very material in themselves, merely because they were changes. The innovations were, perhaps, sufficient to give some warrant for their uneasiness, and to justify Captain Stretch afterwards in holding that the Governor's visit was ' disastrous ', and the final doom of all hopes of making a success

---

[1] Cory, iv, 336 ff.

[2] de Lange undoubtedly suffered violence. But the occasion was reminiscent of old Scottish Border forays. In the pursuit of his horse he came upon Kafirs driving ' a large number of cattle, *presumably stolen* ' (Cory, iv, 375), thereupon ' hurriedly returned and collected a number of farmers ', and gave chase—and in the inevitable mêlée that followed, was shot. Such was Cape Border law and practice.

[3] A few weeks later, to complete the ' chain ' of ' Treaty States ', Mr. Shepstone concluded treaties with Kreli for the Gcalekas and with Faku for the Pondos.

[4] Cory, iv, 380.

of any treaty policy.[1] The Kafirs were left, as before, in possession of the Ceded Territory ; but Post Victoria was regularized
by a clause which gave the Government permission to plant
forts there. The cattle clauses were similarly stiffened up ;
animals identified in Kafirland might now be reclaimed, with
compensation, even if not followed up at the time they were
lost, while the Chief was made responsible for cattle that were
definitely traced to his territory, whether actually discovered
there or not. Alleged thieves and criminals, moreover, even
belonging to Kafirland, were to be tried *in the Colony*, and a
Court of Appeal was to be established, independent of the
Agents. This clause caused considerable difficulty, since as
the Kafirs protested, the Agents they at least ' knew '.[2]

The onus of carrying out the treaties again lay too much with
the Chiefs. The weakness of the new order, like that of the
old, was due as much to the deficiencies of administration on
the colonial side of the border as to the sins of the Kafirs. Relying
on its new treaty rights, the Government did as little as ever
of its own share of ' prevention '. Captain Stretch again gives
the clue, in a frankly worded private letter :

' The Dutch farmers are dissatisfied with the treaties because they
would like to be their own magistrates in deciding cases of theft. On
the other hand the English . . . are in favour of rubbing in the military
side of civilization. . . . The troops are likely to have plenty to do
—for they have been allowed to slumber for the last five years and
not a thief was caught in the Colony by either the civil or military authorities, all being demanded from the unfortunate Caffre chiefs. £200,000
has thus been enriching the Grahamstown shopkeepers while they
were calling out at this outlay on account of the Treaties.'

Stretch wrote in November 1844. His ' not a thief ' may be
understatement. The substance of his criticism stands. In the

---

[1] Stretch, Memo. on Treaties.

[2] The Gaikas also objected strenuously to an attack on their authority
by a clause specially safeguarding the rights of their Christian subjects.
The clause as drafted made a rather sweeping and old-fashioned attack
on native custom (for example on the payment of *lobola*, long criticized
as ' the sin of buying wives '). Rightly or wrongly the Native Administration Act of 1927 shows the modern trend, and has newly recognized
such Native Custom for the whole Union.

This clause was of importance for its effect in putting missionaries
out of favour, especially Calderwood : ' The Gaika chiefs have no
advisers, no intercourse with the missionaries, and no confidence in
them, because at the time of the Governor's visit they in a body recommended changes in the treaties in a way that the chiefs disliked ' (Philip
to L.M.S., 11 March 1845).

year that followed there was no substantial improvement in the efficiency of Government preventive measures. By unanimous testimony 'depredations' were worse. During, or because of, Boer and Griqua excitements, in the hard winter months of 1845, Stretch,[1] Fynn, and Shepstone alike reported numerous thefts ; and by the end of the year, or the beginning of 1846, thefts gave place to deeds of violence which were some warrant for fearing a general attack on the Colony.

If the 'first duty of History is to understand ', it should be possible to see, in some measure, from the Kafir side of the frontier, how these poor people were driven to the folly and violence that were their own undoing. While already they had some, doubtless not uncoloured, knowledge of what was passing in the Colony, about this time the true inwardness, as it seemed to them, of colonial designs was forcibly brought home to the Kafir 'man in the kraal'. In October 1843, Colonel Hare, as above, obtained leave to plant 'Post Victoria' among the Kafirs in the Ceded Territory. But it was only during the Governor's treaty-changing visit that the modest fort was erected and troops sent to garrison it ; and the fort, coming together with the new treaties in this way, was ominous. Notoriously, leading colonists, and their newspapers, had long assumed that the only real remedy for their grievances was the expulsion of the Gaikas from the Fish River Bush [2] and the Fish-Keiskama country (which included what remained to the Kafirs after 1829 of the delectable modern districts Bedford, Adelaide, Fort Beaufort, Stockenstrom (the Kat River) and Victoria East). Here then was another step [3] in the execution of this well-known programme. In March 1845 Captain Stretch emphasized to the Lieutenant-Governor how difficult it was for the young

[1] Stretch takes occasion to note also (July 2) that animals alleged to be *stolen* but found *strayed*, are not reported found. One de Lange, he says, having told Colonel Somerset of fifty horses stolen, afterwards reduced the number to twenty in Somerset's presence in Stretch's office.

[2] Cory, iii and iv, *passim*. An extreme, but common, view is recorded in a conversation of 1843. A farmer pressing for ' the D'Urban System ' was asked : ' If we did return to it, and the lands of the Caffres were secured to them—what then ? ' ' Oh,' he observed, ' what better would we be then ? we want the country.' (Enclosures, Stockenstrom to Philip, 3 August 1843.)

[3] In 1819 and after the Kafirs had already lost Bedford, Adelaide, the Kat River and Fort Beaufort, whence their grievance.

Paramount, Sandile, had he wished, to control the 'National Party' of Maqomo and the late Tyali, who chafed at Gaika losses—'more particularly' (he underlined the words) 'as (depredations) *have been principally confined to the country they always speak of*' (i.e. Bedford, Adelaide, etc.).

In the middle of the year, when unrest was considerable, the Land Question came more and more to the front. 'I feel convinced', wrote Fairbairn to Dr. Philip, who was then on his way to the frontier, 'there is a design for handing over the best part of the country between the Colony and Natal to the colonists '—to the 'final destruction of the natives from sea to sea '.[1] On 6 July some such rumour had reached not only Stretch, but the Rev. J. Brownlee at King Williams Town. This good Scot found the frontier position 'aquard' (awkward !) ; a message, he says, has threatened chiefs who protect thieves with 'forcible ejection from the Ceded Territory'. The same day Stretch tells Dr. Philip, as he had already told the Governor, how the Kafirs all fear to be 'broke up as the Hottentots were ' by expulsion from their lands : 'You must eat your corn ', they are saying to Botman, 'and make yourselves strong ; prepare *veld schoenen* (shoes) also that may stand fast '. On the 13th to the Governor : 'Allow me to solicit ' no patrols in the Ceded Territory ' till the excitement has subsided '.[2] Next day Maqomo thanked the Government for ' reassurances '—' we hear now it is only against thieves '. On the 31st Stretch, in an interview with the chiefs, 'refuted ' the current statement that the 'Gaikas had been threatened with expulsion ', but added in his official letter :

'It is obvious that considerable efforts have been made at Fort Beaufort to involve the Kafir chiefs in war, which, it cannot be concealed, is more desired by the colonists than by the Gaika chiefs.'

The charge that colonists wanted war is too facile. There were a good many who believed that force was the only remedy ; on the other hand, as Maitland complained, the fears of the farmers may even have 'given the Kafirs self-confidence '. What is at least certain is that in their own anxiety colonists saw nothing of the effect on the other side of the frontier of their ideas of policy. In August and September farmers' meetings 'broke out ' once more,[3] with petitions from the Eastern

[1] Fairbairn, missing the help of Fowell Buxton, whose health was gone, now suggested an appeal to Lord J. Russell.

[2] On the same day he adds that ' the Rev. J. Laing alleges ' that Boers were ' inciting ' Maqomo.   [3] Cory, iv, 400 ff.

Province, one of which, from Albany and Lower Somerset, wanted ' the immediate removal of the Kafirs from the Ceded Territory ', another holding that ' savage hordes are quite incapable of appreciating treaties '—a half-truth that forgot the failure of the civilized government to do its share of the police work. In reply, both the Government Secretary (Mr. John Montagu) and Attorney-General Porter held the farmers' complaints to be ' exaggerated ', the latter taking a philanthropic view ' without being a philanthropist '. But the complaints made their mark, and the Governor, forwarding petitions to London on 17 November, agreed that, though exaggerated, the charges were partly true, ' depredations ' being ' inevitable so long as an uncivilized race greedy of cattle . . . lies along such a frontier '.

The Governor's first thoughts at this time, like those of Dr. Philip, were still for the danger in the north, whither troops had had to be moved—if he ' would not suffer our allies the Griquas to be exterminated by the emigrant British subjects ' :

' Should affairs North (he continued) again demand an armed force, an entrance into the Colony by Kafirs in force might not be unlikely.' Treaties are no good unless to work on the fear or interest of the chiefs, and a line of posts is useless ' on such a frontier '. ' I do not mean I think an inroad probable, at least while the present force is maintained. But it is difficult to calculate on the movements of an uncivilized race —to a considerable extent irritated by our endeavours to control their plundering habits.'

This dispatch shows Sir Peregrine Maitland fair-minded and just in intention, but as far as ever from understanding the essential problem. Like his predecessors—soldiers all of them—he conceived the tribes as first of all a serious military danger. Since 1838 at least such exaggerated fears of a systematically planned invasion had in effect immobilized the troops. Since they must be kept together, at considerable expense, as a garrison, they were not available for their far more important function of acting as a police force, nor were there funds for additional enrolments, for magistrates, or even for prisons. The Governor had, moreover, thoroughly absorbed the less excusable fallacy that his sole task on the frontier was to check cattle-stealing.

Meantime, the forces that found an outlet in cattle-lifting had Kafirland in a growing ferment, worse for the continued failing of the summer rains and the threat of famine. In October 1845 Sandile raised objections to Post Victoria : ' The country is now quiet ', he urged. ' I therefore wish the soldiers to go home . . . where they were useful against thieves.' [1] In November a German missionary, a Mr. Scholtz, was murdered in the country of the once friendly chief Pato. That his assailants mistook their victim for the Government Agent, Shepstone, made the deed no less ominous. In the end of December two hundred natives were wounded in a collision with troops near the unwanted Post Victoria. On 13 January Sandile himself made a ' raid ' and helped himself to goods from a store near Captain Stretch's house, Stretch reporting two days later that the Kafirs said of ' stealing '—' We are only taking what belongs to the Kafirs and Hottentots '. Next day, ' missionaries report kraals of observation, building '. On the 25th ' traders are preparing to leave '. On the 27th Fynn reported that his Tambookies were excited, the Gaikas and Ndhlambis having promised Pato help in refusing to surrender the murderers of the missionary Scholtz. On top of all this excitement the Government took a disastrously false step. So far from agreeing to abandon Post Victoria they proposed to move it to a more convenient site near ' Block Drift '. About 20 January engineers arrived, and, apparently by the mistake of a subordinate, began a survey *on the Kafirland side of the river*.[2] Had it been intended to provoke a native attack no surer way could have been taken, and yet on 7 February Stretch reported that Sandile was ' sleeping in the bush for fear ', while on the 14th, Colonel Hare himself reported one Captain Smith as advising against ' provoking a collision ' by the establishment of a new post ; on the 24th traders and even missionaries arrived at Fort Peddie, ' feeling insecure under the present excited state of the country '.

At this crisis Henry Calderwood wrote Dr. Philip a letter, for which much may be forgiven him,[3] showing real insight and profound understanding :

BLOCK DRIFT,
18 *January* 1846

Several of the Brethren have wished me very much to visit Cape Town with a view to converse *privately* and *fully* with those who may have influence in the Government, but the way does not seem quite open. . . . In the meantime I wish on my own responsibility to

---

[1] Stretch's Diary, 2 October 1845.

[2] The site was that of ' Fort Hare ', now happily transformed into a University College for Natives.

[3] Most of the missionaries, and some officials, were severely critical of any attempt to combine the missionary with the official.

state a few things to *you* in the hope that you may be of some use . . . if you have the ear of the Government. There is, however, a serious difficulty in the way . . . I cannot *at present* see my way clear to *write* nearly all I know, and therefore *much* caution is necessary in saying anything to Government. But it is the unanimous opinion of the Missionaries that unless the Government determine to *understand* the Caffre Question better than they *now* appear to do, it is almost certain that the Caffres will be destroyed, and our missions too, but not before a terrible blow shall have been inflicted on the Colony.

We have most certain evidence that the great bulk of the Caffre people were bent on war a few weeks ago. . . . The feeling is deep and bitter in the extreme. The approaching famine—and the somewhat formidable preparations on the part of the Government and the farmers—appear to have overawed them in the meantime. I have seen Macomo very often just now and he sent most of his chief men to me to speak on the present state of things. He very urgently declares that he will not fight and that *most* of his *people* will sit still with him. Perhaps he himself would really sit still—but he certainly could not restrain the great body of his people in the event of war—unless it should happen that the Caffres were *instantly* repulsed, and this they could not well be.

The feelings of the *Nation* seems now to be against all *white* men, and in the event of war mission property would all be destroyed, and even the lives of missionaries would be placed in extreme peril. I fear that the *political* circumstances of the people are now such that until a decided change is effected the success of our mission will be of a very limited description. It is deeply to be regretted the Government should so easily have fallen into a false position with the Caffres in the affair of Sandile's violation of the treaty the other day. The Government with much simplicity allowed the vexatious land question to be mingled up in the dispute. The Government had no *just* power to send engineers to survey ground for a Post (*Block Drift*) in Caffreland, and this leads me to notice two or three other points, which deserve serious consideration, without attempt to illustrate them.

(1) Amongst all the vexatious questions between the Colonial Government and the Caffres, the most vexatious is what may be styled the *land question*. The Caffres are evidently so sensitive on this point that they *cannot* and *will* not consider *any* question calmly when *that* is mixed up with it.

(2) The Caffres are, either from ignorance or design, exceedingly disposed to mix up the *land question* with every other between them and the Government. Thus the movements of Government are rendered much more intricate and liable to misconstruction than they otherwise would be.

(3) The agitation of the *land question* is a powerful engine by which the war party can work upon the feelings of the more peaceably inclined and thus effectually endanger the peace of the country.

(4) It is equally clear that the Government in all their interviews with the Caffres have by their language fostered this feeling in the Caffre mind by *always threatening* the *expulsion* of the Caffres from their country, if the demands of Government were not complied with. The difference between the neutral territory and any other territory

is only one of words, and at this moment the *mind of the nation* is in a perfect fever on the land question. There never can be a really sound understanding between the Caffres and the Colony until this is set at rest and that for ever.

The Government ought instantly to use any possible means to cause the mind of the Caffre people to comprehend and believe this fact—that the colonial boundary cannot on any consideration whatever be extended so as to deprive the Caffres of *one inch* of ground. There must be no more *threatening*. The Caffres *never threaten* when they *really intend* to do anything. Expulsion must never be thought of —far less threatened. . . .

Let the Government place the land question on its only proper footing and take their stand simply on cases of theft and oppression of Europeans received by themselves into the Caffre country—and punish *vigorously* and *promptly* all such cases as are *well authenticated, even at the risk* of war. Let this be fully understood, and the evil-disposed in Caffreland will stand more alone than they do now.

The Caffres can understand what it is to be punished for *stealing* and *murder*—but no argument will ever convince them that it is either *just* or *reasonable* to take their *land* from them. It will be a hard task to teach a barbarous people that there is very great harm in taking the cattle of the Colony so long as it is threatened to take their *land* from them—seeing, as they say, *so much has been taken from them already*. If the Caffres require to be punished—as I think a very large body of them do—in the name of *mercy* and *justice* let them be punished *where they are*. Let the policy of the Home Government have a fair trial on its own merits. But it *cannot* have that if the Caffres *can* be every now and then threatened with *expulsion* from their *lands*. . . . [Second sheet of letter missing.]

This letter of Calderwood's almost certainly reached the Governor and made its impression. On 21 March he wrote to Lord Stanley, clearly recognizing now the importance of the land question :

' The hint that they hold the Ceded Territory only on good behaviour has them ready to *unite* to oppose our endeavours to put down depredations, on the ground that the land is the object aimed at. Expulsion is likely to keep up an irritation about the land, which is better avoided.'

But it was too late to save the situation. Almost before it can have reached Cape Town, the episode of the Axe had happened (above, p. 228). On 21 March Colonel Hare decided to take action, and by 1 April the Governor had sanctioned a declaration of war. There was no question this time of the war bursting on an unsuspecting Colony. The Kafirs had been so refractory that even missionaries had fled betimes, and Maitland was satisfied that the tribes, if left to themselves, ' would probably have assumed the offensive in the spring or summer '. He knew also that it would not be possible to fight the Gaikas alone, that even beyond the Kei, Kreli was alarmed, and that he ' must be prepared to grapple with the whole Caffre nation '.[1]

Nor was there any excuse for the dominant party among the colonists to complain of the ' machinations ' of an Anti-Colonial Party. The restrained though negative and unimaginative treatment of the Kafirs in the last ten years seemed to have put them in the wrong, united all parties against them, and in the end left them without any effective advocate in their hour of overwhelming defeat. Captain Stretch was sad at their sullen recklessness, and almost silent. Sir Andries Stockenstrom presently led the burghers against them. The Reads also were definitely alienated [2] by attacks that did not spare the Hottentots of the Kat River, and were driven for many months to the shelter of the fort at Elands Post (now Seymour). Fairbairn and the *Commercial Advertiser* supported Maitland's policy.[3] Dr. Philip (much troubled by a ' shake ') was generally of Fairbairn's way of thinking, but when it came to a settlement, too frail to do more than ' collect information ' for Dr. Hodgkin and the Aborigines Protection Society,[4] which made no obvious use of it. Yet in one essential, the restraint of all these Philanthropists was not inconsistent, except with the popular conception of their policy in 1835. As Dr. Philip himself wrote to the L.M.S. (13 May) :

' You will remember that, while I was opposed to the last war as a war of extermination, I was also decidedly of opinion that the Kafirs having

---

[1] Hare to Maitland, 4 April, and Maitland to Gladstone, 15 May 1846.

[2] Joseph Read, a mission teacher, shocked even his father by serving as a combatant. But the old man wrote in July of the ' national antipathy ' of the Hottentots against the Kafirs on account of ' aggressions by their ancestors '.

[3] For the paper's differentiation between this war and the policy it had fought in 1835, see, e.g., *Commercial Advertiser*, 14 October and 2 December 1846. On 10 October Fairbairn's sister-in-law, Mary Christie, wrote to her mother, Mrs. Philip, remarking on the attitude of Fairbairn and the Reads. ' It seems so very strange ! '

[4] So he tells Miss Gurney, 24 July 1847. His ' collection ' includes most illuminating letters, e.g. from Stockenstrom, Stretch, the Reads, Calderwood, Fairbairn, the Rev. J. Niven, and for the North, W. Y. Thomson, Solomon, Casalis, Dyke, Rolland. Had there been anyone to marshal these often trenchant criticisms of the policy of the Settlement after 1847, as Philip would once have done, South African history must have been profoundly influenced.

given in their adhesion and taken the oath of allegiance to the British Government, ought to have been retained as British subjects, and that the expense of such a measure was the only objection urged against it. *Every one here is now of my opinion,* but the result might have been no better had it been acted upon. . . .'

There was thus an unusual consensus of opinion in the Colony. But in spite of this, and of ample warning, the attempt to take the offensive was marked by more than traditional ' British muddle ' and incompetence. A whole series of ' unfortunate incidents ' [1] in April and May, with the loss of two large baggage trains, gave the Kafirs confidence so that they even took the initiative. Following on wholesale, partly defensive, destruction of the property of traders and missionaries in Kafirland,[2] they exacted toll once more in the Colony, burning houses, raiding cattle, and forcing refugees to take shelter in towns and villages, thus forcing the troops on to the defensive. The 28th of May was ordained a ' day of humiliation and prayer ', which moved Dr. Philip, in his old age, to show a gleam of grim humour : ' The question is not what to do with the Kafirs, but what will the Kafirs do with us ? ' On 11 June, Maitland commented : ' We or they must abandon the country.'

The Kafirs had soon shot their bolt. In the end of May they plucked up courage for a futile attack on Fort Peddie. In June unusual carelessness or over-confidence on their part exposed an ' army ' to severe punishment by a surprise cavalry charge ' on the Gwanga '—this episode, which was the nearest approach to a set ' battle ' [3] in the whole campaign, being followed

---

[1] Cory, iv, 428 ff. Some responsibility attached to Colonel Somerset, who first appeared on this frontier in the time of his father, Lord Charles Somerset. One of his earliest semi-independent exploits (1825) was known as ' *Somerset's blundering Commando* ' (Cory, ii, 239). For his share in precipitating the war of 1834 see above, ch. viii ; for his doings in this war, see Cory, iv, 434 *note*, and below, p. 263). It may be significant of the power of ' uncles at the Horse Guards ' (Stockenstrom's gibe) that Somerset, now a Major-General, was still active, in a subordinate capacity, in the war of 1850-2.

[2] ' The ruin effected by Caffres upon mission property erected for their salvation is most striking and lamentable. I dare say most of the mission property has been destroyed that the invading force might have no shelter. Except near Peddie and Block Drift, all stations of London, Scottish, Wesleyan and German Societies this side the Kei have been destroyed. It is a sad blow to us all ' (Calderwood to L.M.S., 13 August 1846).

[3] The attack on Grahamstown in 1819, the ambush of a column in the Boomah Pass, 1850, are almost the only ' Battles ' (?) in the whole series of Xosa wars.

B.B.B.   S

by a long series of ' Smithfield Market cattle-driving ' expeditions that scoured Kafirland, with little further active opposition. The Xosa, indeed, whatever the Zulus may have been, were never an organized offensive military power. But their deeds in the early days of 1846 served to give a new and fatal confirmation of the fixed idea that the only way of safety for the Colony was to appropriate more of Kafirland.

The British campaign continued to be very badly conducted. With drought and transport difficulties as some excuse, burghers and regulars quarrelled among themselves.[1] The burghers were, perhaps, half-hearted, knowing in advance that Governor Maitland held out no prospect of farms for Europeans ;[2] but the Governor also justly deplored the weakening effects of the Boer emigration which had removed so many of the stoutest fighting men. Even so the Kafirs were helpless, except against scattered farmers who, to protect themselves or their cattle, had been fain to invoke the organized power of the Government to take still more native land and to break up and disperse the tribes. The Bantu could only retaliate in their own way. Now, against organized military attack, the Xosa fell back on non-resistance, the attacking columns of troops being met and surrounded by crowds of women and children ' begging for food ', sometimes in return for bundles of fuel or thatching. Many chiefs protested, as Maqomo had done even in 1835, that they were not fighting, would not fight, and asked only for peace.

But the tragedy had to be played out—the ' power ' of the tribes broken. Even the short-lived half triumph of ' Philanthropy ' in 1836 had made the worst of both worlds, offending the colonists, without giving the natives any feeling that their human interests and feelings were really safeguarded. With this one interlude, for more than seventy years this essentially police problem was given the dignity of exclusively military treatment. The one thing never tried was honest civil government, which, recognizing the Xosa as subjects with secure rights to a share in their own land, would have punished wrongdoers, in Mr. Calderwood's phrase, *where they were.* The policy of such a course, tried and abundantly justified since with many only very partially conquered tribes throughout Africa, was learned—if it has been fully learned even yet—only after the sacrifice of the alert and cheerful Amaxosa.

[1] Cory, iv, cc. 9 and 10.
[2] Maitland to Stanley, 21 March 1846 and 20 January 1847.

In August or September 1846 Sir Peregrine Maitland was seriously thinking of the ' ultimate settlement ' for which the situation had not been ripe when he reported on 11 June. By September Maqomo and others had surrendered ; the discontented burgher forces were disbanded (or seized an excuse for going home), and even when, after this month, rain made fresh movements of troops possible, Kafirs still in the field made no resistance. It now fell to this mild and humane Governor to make a decision which was so generally approved at the time that, even yet, its consequences have never been appreciated. All agreed, even Downing Street,[1] that British control must once more be extended to the Kei. But for some time the Governor's mind had been running on the plan of ' clearing ' another slice of country and ' filling up ' instead with Fingos, friendly or mission Kafirs, and Hottentots. The country to be cleared, moreover, included the whole of the ' Ceded ' Territory, and in addition ' the Amatola fastnesses '—the most beautiful country in all that area and the cherished home of the Gaikas. Since, in Sandile's words, ' the patrimony of a chief is land and men ', the chiefs felt that they might as well resist where they were as accept another and more drastic uprooting ; the new ' locations ', to be assigned by the Governor at his own pleasure subject to the good behaviour of their already unruly tribesmen, meant an end to their dignity and independence. Moreover—' How in the world ', wrote Jas. Read[2] to Dr. Philip on 6 October, ' could Sir Peregrine think of trying to come to such terms of peace just after all the Boers and many of the coloured people [i.e. all the colonial forces] had left the frontier and he and Colonel Hare retreated to the Colony ? ' The Governor's resolve left nothing for it but war à outrance.

It was not for this that Sir Andries Stockenstrom had come out in April ' to serve his country '. As commandant of the burgher force he was allowed some discretion, and the task that had fallen to him was to organize and conduct a march through the heart of the drought-stricken country to deal with Hintza's successor, Kreli, the great chief beyond the Kei. While he agreed that the tribes needed punishment, and a forcible reminder

---

[1] Grey to Pottinger, 2 November 1846. See p. 261, *note*.

[2] Read, to his credit, soon got over his anti-Kafir phase. From this point, letters which reached Dr. Philip from Read, Stretch, Stockenstrom, and others, show that Maitland and his two successors had begun to have their critics.

of the power and efficiency of the white man even in face of drought, he had never contemplated a war of conquest and extermination. His hope was to get Kreli's sanction for the annexation of the Cis-Kei, and to bind him by a treaty which would give the Government a warrant, such as they now lacked, for compelling him to do his share in keeping the Cis-Keian tribes in order. Having fulfilled this mission, he returned in the end of August to find that the Governor, leaning to a more drastic policy, bluntly repudiated the treaty he had made with Kreli. To add to Stockenstrom's easily roused chagrin, one of his companions, Colonel Johnstone, contradicted his version of the interview with Kreli. He found, moreover, that posts he had planted for the protection of the roads into the Colony had been moved in his absence, and an expedition sent off to the north to chastise the Tembu chief, Mapassa. This diversion he resented as an encroachment on his sphere of campaign, and at the same time as liable to prejudice the success of his own mission. With a parochial zest for petty personal details, the South African account of Stockenstrom's second withdrawal has fastened on the ' acrimonious ' letters which Stockenstrom presently inflicted even on the Governor.

But Stockenstrom was extremely touchy. He ' knew his own temper '. The ' difference ' with the Governor, which soon brought about his resignation, went deeper than ' personal pique '.[1] Its root was in the Governor's growing determination to carry the war to extremes, in what Stockenstrom knew by experience must be a prolonged and costly effort to hold the tribes in peace, not by reason and good government, but by crushing them into helpless subjection. Calderwood at this time (to the L.M.S., 26 September) claimed to have made the Governor see the justice of retaining the Kafirs on the land, and on 7 October wrote to Dr. Philip that the Governor had put his name to a message, declaring ' *he will not give the land to white people* '.[2] Next day Calderwood had accepted office as a magistrate to do his best for the location of the Gaikas, and in doing so he bound himself also to take his official orders. But on the 14th Maitland had hardened again and wrote to the Secretary of State that the Gaikas must go. Further, their passive resis-

---

[1] ' You need not fear that I shall resign from personal pique,' he wrote, explaining his views to Read on 12 and 17 September.

[2] Maitland (to Secretary of State, 18 September) is against white farms, but favours towns and artisans.

tance made it necessary to continue ' systematic devastations ' till the Die-hards should cross the Kei, where, he airily assumed, there was ' plenty ' of land for them. A month later he had hopes that ' famine ' would compel surrender, and in the same week accepted Stockenstrom's resignation.

Thus with Stockenstrom's second departure from the frontier, the flame of philanthropy which he had tried to keep alight, after a last flicker, finally died. As in 1835, the authorities soon found that the extreme measure of driving the tribes across the Kei was impracticable ; but deprivation of lands now came to be the recognized penalty for native ' rebellion ', till the old Kafirland had degenerated into the congested ' Cis-Kei '. The Kafirs, after another year of ' war ', were compelled for the time being to submit. But they could not ' feel that it was *intended* for their benefit '. They were left with so little to lose that the train was well laid for the ' terrible war some years hence ' —no later than 1850—which Calderwood again had prophesied, in his pre-official days (13 August to L.M.S.), would be the inevitable consequence of uprooting the Kafirs, or even holding over their heads the threat to drive them from their chosen land.

Sir Peregrine Maitland had but a few months left, Earl Grey deciding that a younger man, armed with fuller discretion as ' High Commissioner for South Africa ', was needed to complete a settlement.[1] In October Maitland was busy about a scheme of redistributing the lands of the still protesting Kafirs among Fingos, Hottentots and friendly Kafirs, ' in some measure organized for defence, under British superintendence and supported by the military posts ', with the ' desirable addition ' of a missionary.[2] On 14 October the *Commercial Advertiser*, satisfied that the object was ' not the acquisition of territory, but self-defence ', agreed that ' a different class of settlers must be interposed between these two races ' ; it also understood ' Fingos,

[1] The High Commissionership was a recognition also of the necessity of annexing Kaffraria, since ' the welfare of our uncivilized neighbours, and not least the welfare of the colonists, require that the Kafir tribes should no longer be left in possession of the independence they have so long enjoyed and abused ' (Grey to Pottinger, 2 November 1846).

[2] This was in accordance with a ' Memo.' by Mr. W. Shaw, communicated to Dr. Philip by Brownlow Maitland, the Governor's son and Private Secretary, on 19 October. Dr. Philip gave qualified approval to a ' swarming off ' of Hottentots from the Kat River and remarked to the L.M.S. on the 23rd : ' You will see that I shall find some work to do on the frontier of Caffreland.'

Hottentots and others, hostile to the Caffres as any could desire, to be ready in thousands to accept frontier locations '.[1]

But Maitland's energies were soon again fully absorbed in continuing the war, and Sir Henry Pottinger, who took over in January 1847, was a good deal less favourably disposed to the Hottentots or ' Coloured People ', whom he presently described as ' pampered and spoiled '. In February and March, by insisting on their serving in ' levies ' instead of as ' free burghers ', he began to sow the seeds of discontent that ripened into the ' Hottentot Rebellion ' of 1851. Even Genadendal (the Moravian settlement) was a ' Hottentot Elysium ', where Hottentots got ' three or four times what they would receive as soldiers '. The Kat River settlement, which had suffered very severe losses by deaths on service, by drought, devastations, and interrupted industry, was soon (12 March) ' memorializing ' against the new policy and the threat to stop war rations—(had they but known it, the very next day the Governor was listening, with not unwilling ears, to new demands for laws against *vagrancy*,[2] for which ' the laws in force do not impose such restraints as are desirable '.) The Governor, therefore, was disposed to accept the verdict of Mr. Biddulph, a Settler magistrate, who in October sounded the knell of fresh ' Kat Rivers ' by an adverse report on that settlement. Sir Andries Stockenstrom thereupon wrote in its defence, even to Earl Grey (20 November), and Dr. Philip momentarily roused himself to write in protest to the Governor. But by this time even the Hottentots had grown suspicious : ' The new plan turned out to be a system of *Martial Law*,' wrote Dr. Philip (to L.M.S., 18 January 1848), ' but it received no countenance from the coloured people. They would have been between two fires, between the white man and the Caffre.' In this way Maitland's plans for the Hottentots miscarried, and nothing was left for it but to ' fill up ' as his successors soon began to do with European farmers.

Still less did Maitland make progress with the resettlement or ' location ' of the hostile Kafirs. In the closing months of 1847 he began a system of registering those who gave up their

[1] Fairbairn had some difference with his friend Stretch on this issue, and noted, on 26 December, Stretch's retirement and the disappointment of ' his expectation of a *peaceable* union of Caffreland with the Colony '.
[2] Pottinger to Secretary of State, 13 March, 14 April 1847 (*Cape Col. Qn.*, 276, 279 ff.),

arms and made submission as British subjects, planning to ignore
the authority of the chiefs and to place them under the direct
rule of magistrates. Some 3,000 Gaikas submitted and got
crops planted ; but it was estimated that 7,000 Gaikas remained,
besides Pato and others nearer the coast, who never even asked
for terms, and on 6 January a message from Downing Street
recalling him found Maitland himself still superintending cattle-
driving expeditions [1] on the far side of the Kei at Butterworth.

Now, if Maitland definitely came down on the side of stringent
military enforcement of tranquillity on the Kafir frontier, he
did so almost in amiable despair. It remained for his peppery
successor, Sir Henry Pottinger, to apply the remedy with a
ruthlessness that remains almost without parallel, and for Sir
Harry Smith, after him, to carry on by submitting the territory
he conquered not to the civil government it so badly needed,
but to the rigours of a continuance of martial law. When
Sir Henry Pottinger took over early in 1847, the Colony itself
was war-weary, disappointed of its hopes of farms [2] and sore at
quarrels with the regulars. The pressure he applied to the
Hottentots was, perhaps, more relentless for the poor response [3]
made to his frequent appeals for burgher help in bringing the
Kafirs to complete submission. His first concern was Pato,
whom Colonel Somerset attempted in April to clear from the
country towards the mouth of the Kei—what time Captain
Stretch snorted at the prolongation of the ' campaign ',[4] with
gibes at Colonel Somerset, for whom, said he, Pato was ' as good
as a walking annuity '.[5]

But besides the last-ditcher, Pato, poor Sandile was not done
with. Once more in June, the time for beer, some of his people,
having reaped the crops grown by those who had submitted
to Maitland, seem to have stolen ' fourteen goats ' from the
Kat River settlement. Under Pottinger, the chief who had been
ignored if not deposed by Maitland was now held responsible
for restitution of the goats and the surrender of the thief, and

---

[1] Cf. Theal (iii, 35) for numbers of cattle taken, and how few Kafirs.
[2] Cf. Maitland to Grey, 20 January 1847.
[3] Cf. Theal, iii, 40, 45. Read to Philip, 13 October.
[4] ' Whoever writes on the Caffre tragedy to be acted yet will have
to record British Justice to her Colonies ' (to Philip, 14 April 1847).
Also ' You did not record the 100th part of the sufferings of the Hottentots in your Researches '. He thought Stockenstrom's return ' the
ony hope ' (26 June).
[5] For Somerset, see above, p. 257, *note*.

only partially [1] complied with the demands made upon him.
Thereupon the Governor ordered his arrest. When a patrol
sought him out, Sandile, mindful, according both to James
Read and to later frontier tradition, of the fate of Hintza, had
fled to the bush. But the patrol was fired on, and though Sandile
now sent a ' peace-offering ' of twenty-one head of cattle, ' the
season was favourable for military operations ' (says Dr. Theal) and
the Governor resolved on drastic measures for his total expulsion.

On 27 August Sandile was proclaimed a rebel or outlaw, and,
for the encouragement of volunteers, it was announced that
cattle were to be kept by their captors as *booty* ; on 7 September
General Berkeley was given confidential instructions that, while
the Governor thought the ' booty ' Proclamation would suffice,
any cattle that could not be driven off were to be *killed*—hostilities
to cease only when all arms were surrendered in token of complete
submission. On the 24th the Governor further demanded
complete renunciation by Sandile of his claims West of the Kei,
till even the General (Berkeley) protested that, unless Sandile
was given some location, his ' predatory hordes ' would impose
an impossible strain on the military machine. Operating with
an elaborate system of cattle-receiving depots as bases, ' all that
the forces could accomplish in the Amatolas was to destroy the
huts and prevent the Kafirs from settling anywhere ',[2] but in
less than a month Sandile surrendered at discretion.

Finally, in October, the troops moved on to the Kei to carry
out a ' similar plan ' against Pato. Stockenstrom was now moved
to protest (20 November to Earl Grey) that the *loot* policy was
' worse than commandos ', which at least professed to recover
stolen property ; this, on the contrary, allowed thefts and murder,
' by men who never lost nor possessed a cow or a shilling '.
Scouting ' the surrender of a miserable starving chief ', and
scoffing at ' newspaper victories ', he warned Earl Grey that
the result would be to leave ' four or five times fifty thousand
robbers ' on their hands, with the chiefs on Robben Island and
their cattle in the Colony, and endless expense to ' keep the
Kafirs conquered '.[3]

The ' similar plan ' against Pato was the end for the time

---

[1] Read, writing to Philip from Kat River on 29 June, says categorically that the goats *and cattle* sent by Sandile as fines ' miscarried ',
but ' have since been delivered '.　　　　[2] Theal, iii, 48.
　[3] To Dr. Philip, on 11 December, he wrote in similar strain, adding :
' The Gospel may follow the guns and do good in the end, but the
Gospel might have got in without the guns.'

being, and for Sir Harry Smith, who took office on 17 December
1847, it remained only to make a definite Proclamation (on the
23rd) of the annexation of ' British Kaffraria ', and to dictate
terms of peace. Kafirland and its tribal system were now in
parlous plight. The effects had long been visible. Off and on,
throughout 1847, the Agents or the new magistrates made reports
that showed some of the social consequences of drought and war
following a prolonged period of unrest and instability. In
March and April, Henry Calderwood, now Commissioner with
the Gaikas, noted that among these tribes (the ' strongest ' in
Kafirland, and occupying the ' best ' of the country), there was a
breakdown of tribalism, many natives taking up residence on
one chief's land while still professing allegiance to another. If
a census that was taken is at all reliable, two years later the Gaikas,
who in 1836 were estimated at 55,000, had shrunk to 30,000,
many being absent owing to ' the scarcity of food '.[1] At the
later date, 1849, natives of Kaffraria were allowed to choose only
between assigned ' locations ' and ' service '.[2] But even in
1847 the characteristic modern ' search for work ' caused by
landlessness and hunger had fairly begun. In April the Government approved of Calderwood engaging even the lately independent Xosa for service with masters who were prepared to
' take charge of and provide for them on their own premises '.
In spite of passes, and ' thieving ', other Commissioners [3] found
at the same time that farmers ' gladly welcomed ' war refugees,
being ' in great distress for servants '. The Government itself
met the farmers' wants, and its own embarrassments on the
frontier, by encouraging recruiting through the Commissioners,[4]
and the evidence is, moreover, that wages were not rising—
the ' cow and calf ' per annum referred to earlier by Captain

---

[1] In an 1849 Report Calderwood estimated that another 20,000
Gaikas were dispersed with chiefs beyond the Kei as well as in the
Colony. The Ndhlambis had rather surprisingly grown from 10,000
to 34,000. At the later date Calderwood and others remark on land-
hunger even among the Tambookies north of the mountains where there
was an influx of Europeans.

[2] Smith to Grey, 26 October 1849.

[3] Fynn to Government Secretary, 17 May 1847.

[4] Cf. Reply to one van den Berg of Riversdale (*Private Letters*,
1847, Cape Town Archives) who was recommended to take *not* children,
but *families*. On 18 November Calderwood despatched 170 natives
and expected many more applications ; he also recommended that
families be sent, and ' as far into the Colony as possible ', though another
Commissioner, McKinnon, reported that natives were against going

Stretch were by one account ' one cow ' only.[1] Incidentally, in attempting to control the comings and goings of these working Kafirs, the authorities at last discovered that the 49th Ordinance was no law at all (above, p. 66). Further convincing evidence of the acute distress of Kafirland comes from far-off Griquatown, where, in August 1847, Edward Solomon reported the arrival of a ' party of Caffres who had come 250 miles ',[2] locating themselves under Waterboer ' near the Great River ' and ' asking for instruction '.

Dr. Philip recounts a shrewd remark made some years earlier by an old native : ' The Boers are like buffaloes ; they have hard heads, but we see them before they attack us. But the English are like the tiger ; they have too much here ' (pointing to his head), ' they spring upon us before we see them '. The ' peaceful penetration ' of Hottentot and native land by the earlier Boers was indeed as nothing to the systematic havoc wrought among the Amaxosa ; neither had the Republics the military resources to shatter the tribal system of the Bantu so utterly, except on the open High Veld where they found it already in ruins.[3] The British ' tiger-spring ', when it came, was far more thorough.[4] Once the conquest was complete the disastrous

to the west. After the war a Proclamation of 27 January 1848 referred to ' the present attempt by a system of " apprenticing " young natives, to add to scanty supply of labour ', and at the same time ' reclaiming a number of the youth of British Kaffraria '. This also was to ' contribute to the peace of this important province '. Applications presently came from as far afield as ' Piketberg ' and Colesberg. Beaufort also ' could use four times as many '.

[1] In 1848 B. Moodie of Swellendam has a note on wages : for the first year, one cow ; for the second and third years of *contract*, two cows ; for girls, six she-goats ; *or*, for men, £1 per annum.

[2] To Philip, 15 August, ' We are at a loss how to meet their wants.'

[3] Hence, in all probability, the republican (and Natal) practice of ' indirect ' rule, leaving much responsibility to the chiefs. In the Cape, largely even in the Transkei, British Government came in only when the chiefs had in fact been broken, and found it convenient to rely more on the European magistrate.

[4] Rev. T. D. Philip, in a draft ' Life of Dr. Philip ' written about 1900 but never published, suggested the efficacy of British policy for wringing from the Bantu the two things they possessed—land and labour ; having taken up a position on the outskirts of Bantu country, the British became involved in war for the suppression of cattle-stealing ; in the war they destroyed Bantu wealth in cattle, at the same time seizing land as a penalty for theft—thus at one blow reducing the native people to economic dependence and forcing them to supply labour, or starve.

effects of this policy of Thorough were in the end mitigated
by strong and fair administration and by the boon of complete
political freedom.

When Sir Harry Smith took charge at the close of this devastating war, there was no political freedom even for the Cape
Colony, and no Kafirs capable of exercising political rights. Sir
Harry's system, born of the war and unrest which made it hard
for officials, and still harder for colonists, to think except of
the need for ' security ', was Martial Law. The still exaggerated
fear of the Xosa as a military power, blind to their lawful aspirations as human beings, came near to driving them to desperation,
as it certainly made them fair prey to their own false prophets.[1]
With a stroke of the pen (and a spectacular show of Sir Harry's
fireworks) the treaties were finally swept aside, and the land
annexed to the Crown : ' I make no treaty. I say this land is
mine ' [2]—the chiefs being given to understand that their ' locations ' would be where they were sent.[3] At the same time the
chiefs solemnly bound themselves (under *force majeure*) to
repudiate ' witchcraft ' and ' the sin of buying wives ', and to
other conditions ' subversive of the whole framework of Bantu
society '.[4] A few months later, though, as a magistrate reported,
the natives were ' slow to believe ', the Ceded Territory—the
fair Chumie Valley above the modern Lovedale—was being
planted with villages of soldier settlers—the Auckland, Woburn,
and the rest, of the Christmas Day massacre of 1850. In January
also the north-eastern district of Albert, for some time contested
by farmers and Tambookies,[5] was annexed to the Colony : in
March the Governor told Earl Grey of his plan—a ' financial
expedient '—to sell farms to war-enriched frontiersmen.[6]

Measures like these, with the alternatives of new and less

---

[1] ' Umlangeni ' had appeared in 1850–1, and was the precursor
of their cattle-killing in 1857.

[2] Smith to Grey, 7 January 1848.

[3] *Sandile* : ' Your children require land as they are crowded.'

Governor : ' All up to the Kei ' (i.e. not the old ' Ceded ' Territory)
' is Sandile's.'

Sandile : ' I do not know that country.'

Whereupon, Smith threatened total expulsion from Kaffraria (*ibid.*)

[4] Theal, iii, 57. E.g. on behalf of their people the chiefs were called
upon to acknowledge no chief but the Queen of England.

[5] Read to Philip and to the Lieutenant-Governor throughout 1843.

[6] ' Frontier settlers having, generally speaking, acquired large fortunes by the war expenditure, they are prepared to pay large prices for
these lands ' (Smith to Grey, 23 March 1848).

spacious locations, or service,[1] were the beginning of the process
that has reduced the ' Cis-Kei ' to its modern conditions.[2] In
the more settled parts, officials tried to bind native settlers to
their holdings by an annual quit-rent, virtually a land tax, of
£1 per holding. James Read protested that this meant £200
from 200 Fingos in his neighbourhood for 2,000 morgen for
which a European would pay £4, and Mr. Calderwood in 1849
urged at least a temporary reduction to 10s. per holding. But
the natives generally were in no mood to attend to Sir Harry
Smith's well-meant efforts to help them. In his concern for
their ' first step to civilization ' he was presently consulting
Dr. Philip and others about how best to teach them to plough
and to follow habits of industry, to see ' the necessity of wearing
clothes ', and the use of money, and how also ' to establish
schools on such a footing as would ensure hereafter teachers
from among themselves ' ; ' too much pains ' cannot be taken
to wean them from the use of blankets, and ' of all things His
Excellency requests ' the use of English in the schools, ' to the
total exclusion of the Kafir dialect '.[3]

In the early days of the peace the Rev. R. Niven returned
to his station near the Chumie, to find only Burnshill reoccupied.
' War ', he wrote to Dr. Philip on 18 January 1848, ' has changed
the missions sadly for the worse '. He was, he felt, ' walking
among tombs and haranguing the dead '. Writing of the settlement and of the prospects for the future, he deplored the ' evil
of depriving them of so much land and giving Europeans a
position in the little that is left, which will, I fear, end in the
Caffres becoming a nation of degraded servants on their own soil ' :

' Our Governor is attempting too much, denouncing social evils which
his system cannot punish, and which in that case had better be left
to the progress of light among this unhappy people, who have suffered
equally from themselves and others. Time is needed and must be
allowed for maturing an incipient scheme in the hands of such an
ex tempore character as Sir Harry Smith.'

But within six weeks of his assumption of office this ' ex tempore
character ', having launched ' British Kaffraria ', dashed off
through the Orange Territory and found new worlds to conquer.
On 3 February he was writing of his doings from the banks of
the Tugela in Natal, having left behind him a ' peace ' founded
on poverty and prostration.

[1] Smith to Grey, 26 October 1848.
[2] Facts in pamphlet Land, Natives and Unemployment (1924, now
out of print).
[3] Circular by Richard Southey, Secretary, 17 April 1848.

CHAPTER XVII

THE ANNEXATION AND ABANDONMENT OF THE NORTH, 1848-54

WAR on the old Cape Frontier interrupted for a time the handling of the complex issues raised in the rest of the country by the Great Trek. Sir Harry Pottinger's short term of office was so fully taken up by his exertions in Kafirland that almost his only contribution to northern un-settlement was to snub the Transvaal leader, Andries Pretorius, who journeyed some hundreds of miles to seek an interview that was refused him. With Kafirland settled for the time being, Sir Harry Smith, being not only Governor of the Cape Colony but High Commissioner for South Africa, at once set about using his authority ' for the settling and adjustment of the affairs of the territories . . . adjacent or contiguous . . . to the frontier '.

There were indications, perhaps, that Downing Street was now more disposed to shoulder its South African responsibilities —provided always this could be done with a minimum of expenditure, and in such a way as to lighten the financial load for the future.[1] The institution of the High Commissionership was in itself an advance, and in private talk before he left England the new Governor must have discovered that in Earl Grey he had to deal with a Secretary of State who had definite and constructive notions of colonial policy. But the speed and decision with which Sir Harry acted, even before hearing that Downing Street was prepared to accept the inevitable and sanction the annexation of Kaffraria, were peculiarly his own ; and when, soon enough, the storms began to blow again on all fronts, it quickly appeared that even Earl Grey was in no position to carry through a ' forward ' policy.

The attitude of the British Parliament was very different from what it had been in the 'thirties, when Humanitarians

---

[1] The 1846-7 war had already cost a round £1,000,000.

almost alone took any active interest in South African affairs. The ' Clapham Sect ' was no more—the fervour of anti-slavery Humanitarianism, and of the Evangelical Revival itself, almost utterly spent ; Dr. Philip's breakdown in health, his final retirement in 1850 and death a year later, left the champions of native interests in South Africa leaderless and without efficient spokesman—even the L.M.S. fearing to be ' branded as political '. [1] The direct and continuous influence of these forces, even in their zenith, has been much exaggerated ; now there was no one at all, no Fowell Buxton, still less a Wilberforce, to champion the sentiments loosely attributed to ' Exeter Hall '. On the other hand, the Colonial Office had almost more persistent and watchful critics, with a wider popular appeal as the champions of the interests of the British taxpayer. The Free-Traders led by Richard Cobden were at one with colonial reformers like Sir William Molesworth in wishing to save expense by devolving responsibility upon colonial legislatures, [2] and even Tories like Peel and Graham, as well as Disraeli, were so far from the Imperialism of a later day as to ' betray ' a leaning to the heresy ' that we have no interest in preserving our colonies and ought, therefore, to make no sacrifice for that purpose '. [3]

With these opinions so much in the ascendant, every one that mattered was prepared to take responsibilities to South African natives very lightly. A faintly uneasy conscience was satisfied if all that ' Exeter Hall ' had stood for was paid the homage of a clause, like that in the Sand River Convention of 1852, by which the Transvaalers agreed neither to permit nor to practise *slavery*, at the same time that Her Majesty's Government expressly repudiated ' alliances with the coloured nations '. These it now abandoned to the unfettered control of its own quondam subjects, many of whom had sought to repudiate their British allegiance precisely because their view of native rights (and of their own obligations to natives) was so radically opposed to that hitherto maintained by Her Majesty's representatives. The continued failure of attempts to establish peace in South

[1] R. Niven to Stretch, from London (1852), when he failed to get any hearing for representations made on behalf of the Kafirs.

[2] In March 1848 Earl Grey himself had accordingly drafted a minute, instructing Smith to warn the Colony that it would in future be held responsible for its own expenditure—this actually before he had heard of the annexation of British Kaffraria.

[3] Howick Papers. Grey to Elgin, 18 May 1849. Quoted by J. L. Morison, *British Supremacy and Canadian Self Government*, pp. 266–7.

Africa strengthened the prevailing belief in *laisser-faire*, and opinion in Great Britain itself was presently responsible for the most decisive and far-reaching climb-down in the whole history of British rule in Southern Africa.

Sir Harry Smith's most pressing concern in 1848 was in the north. In January he made a characteristic dash through the country. With no Dr. Philip to check him, and Mr. Thomson removed to Grahamstown, the Governor swept aside Kok and his two treaties (1843 modified in 1846—above, chap. xiv) as of little importance, depriving him of control beyond the ' inalienable ' reserve. He also acted the part of a confiscatory land-reformer, giving Kok permission to eject time-expired Boer lessees but only on payment of compensation for improvements [1] —' as if ', remarked Sir Andries Stockenstrom, ' by *lending* a room in your house, you forfeit the whole '. To Moshesh, a ' great chief ', Smith was more polite, gaining his ' magnanimous ' concurrence in the view that ' some great and paramount authority'. was necessary, for ' peace, harmony and tranquillity ', for the purpose also of ' maintaining inviolate the hereditary rights of the chiefs, and of effectually restraining the Boers within limits and upon the locations they now possess '. [2] Being satisfied further that at least the considerable Oberholster party of Boers was well disposed, and having apparently ' sounded ' even the Transvaalers, through Pretorius,[3] he tarried no longer, but on 3 February issued a Proclamation from the Tugela, extending the Queen's ' sovereignty ' over the whole of the country of Moshesh, Moroko, Kok and others, from the Orange to the Vaal and the Drakensberg—this

' with no desire or inclination whatever on the part of Her Majesty to extend or increase her dominions . . . but on the contrary with the sole view of establishing relationships with those chiefs and protecting them from any future aggression . . . '

British subjects, it was laid down,

' were to be subject to the laws of the colony of the Cape of Good Hope, and guaranteed the *full possession of the rights of citizens of the said*

---

[1] Stockenstrom was moved to indignation : ' What statesmanship we are at the mercy of ! ' ' Hiring ', he had written to Earl Grey, ' was preferable to trespass.' (Quoted by Read to Philip 11 June 1848.) This was ' contrary to all law ', comments E. Solomon (December 1848).

[2] *Agreement* with Moshesh, 27 January 1848. Eybers, p. 269.

[3] Walker, p. 240.

colony, subject to the payment of an annual quit-rent for the lands they now occupied ; the proceeds of this revenue were to go first *to the fair and honest remuneration and indemnification of the native chiefs*, secondly, to defray the expenses of (British) government ; any surplus, with the proceeds of traders' licenses (at £50 each, as in Kaffraria), was ear-marked for churches and schools, "*for the exclusive benefit of the population north of the Orange River* "—loans being also promised to supplement any sums locally subscribed for church building.'[1]

With surprisingly little demur, Earl Grey, who in March had feared an extension of ' risks ' by the annexation of the north-eastern district of Albert, on 28 June approved of Smith's action, rejoicing in the ' success of the measures for bringing the emigrant Boers once more within the control of regular government '. And so, had fates proved kinder, the hesitations of ten years or more might have ended by the effective re-union of far the greater part of this divided South Africa.

Throughout, Sir Harry Smith was full of consideration for the welfare of ' his children ', the Boers. Even the high-handed treatment meted out to Kok and the Griquas was in Boer interests. Edward Solomon, the judicial father of two well-known South African judges, concerned for native welfare, considered Smith's policy, as a whole rather than in particular, ' too dogmatic and bullying '. James Read, the younger, wrote with less restraint :

'Many sensible men on the Frontier begin to think that he will inflict a more severe blow on the rights of the natives of this country than any former Governor.'[2]

In spite of this, the irreconcilable Northern Boers were the first obstacle to South African re-union. In the winter Sir Harry was forced to dash post-haste all the way from Cape Town to the rescue of Major Warden, the British Resident Agent, who was ejected from his capital Bloemfontein by Andries Pretorius and a force from beyond the Vaal. In August Smith defeated the malcontents near the Orange River at Boomplaats, put a price on the head of Pretorius, whom a little earlier he had tried to bait with the offer of a commissionership in the new province, and drove them out of the Sovereignty to nurse their grievance and to continue their own quarrels with their friends beyond

[1] Eybers, pp. 270 ff.
[2] ' What ', Read adds, ' does he mean in one of his familiar epistles to the Boers, I think to Potgieter, by saying that he would locate some of the natives among them ? Some years ago such hints would not have escaped the eagle-eyed Philanthropists here and in England.'

the Vaal.[1] On this episode Edward Solomon commented again from Griquatown (to Dr. Philip on 9 September) :

' I think it is fortunate for the natives that from the first this outbreak has assumed the character of decided opposition to the Colonial Government. Sir Harry Smith appears to me to have formed too favourable an opinion of the Boers, looking upon them rather as unfortunate than as criminal, and inclined to side with them when their interests and those of the natives clashed. He appears anxious to clear them from the imputation of being rebels, but now in spite of his conciliatory manners and the really kind measures adopted for their benefit, they have put themselves in a posture of opposition and insulted the British Government by expelling its agents. . . . I rejoice that this has not originated in any dispute between Boers and Griquas (but in) open hostility which necessitates a real settlement and the removal of the ringleaders from this country.'

Still, the Governor was long-suffering, refusing to eject even rebel lessees of Griqua land, and in the end Mr. Solomon advised Dr. Philip (March 1849) that it would be wiser to ' encourage the Griquas to make what use they can of the lands that are left to them than to go on quarrelling about what they have so unjustly lost '. ' This ', he concludes, ' is advice the Griquas little relish and is, therefore, the more important.' And there the long political battle fought by the L.M.S. on behalf of the Griquas virtually ended.[2]

In 1849 and for part of 1850, Sir Harry Smith's attention was sufficiently engrossed in Cape Town by the hectic agitation of all parties in the Colony against Earl Grey's plan of making the Cape a convict settlement.[3] During these fateful months difficulties that demanded the care of a wiser and a stronger man than the Resident Agent, Major Warden, came near destroying all hope of a satisfactory permanent settlement in the newly annexed Orange River Sovereignty. The Griquas, as the Governor had quickly divined, were weak and submissive, and their discontent made little difference ; but the delay caused by the Kafir War in carrying out the revised Treaty policy of 1845 had by this time made the fixing of Moshesh's boundaries a more intractable question than ever. Even Moshesh who, for a Bantu chief, had done wonders in binding broken fragments of tribes into a Basuto nation, enjoyed no precise territorial sover-

---

[1] See, e.g., Walker, p. 257.
[2] In the 'sixties and later, the Rev. W. Dower shepherded the trek of the Philippolis Griquas to their new home in Griqualand East (Kokstad).
[3] *Cape Col. Qn.*, p. 260.

eignty. On the undefined borders, where his authority was necessarily weak, European colonists had now considerably enlarged their claims by bargains with lesser potentates, whom such insidious, and by no means disinterested, flattery had elevated into rivals who appeared of greater importance than they actually were.

As in Kafirland, the real dispute was not merely about land, but about access to the very best land in all those parts. The broad valleys of the Caledon and its tributaries are much the best watered and most fertile in this part of the country, and constitute one of the only two or three considerable wheat-growing districts in the whole Union. Originally, the rise of the Basuto power, following hard on the Chaka wars, was possible only because of the security afforded by the mountain fastnesses of the Maluti Mountains and the Drakensberg. But the people of Moshesh, as times became more settled, and their confidence in the Chief's protection more assured, had by this time spread once more over the agriculturally much more tempting, but less easily defended, open country lying to the north and west. In this area, however, the lesser people like Moroko and Sikonyela, and other ill-organized refugees, had a footing ; and here also, through the very weakness of these chiefs, Boer farmers had staked their claims, characteristically wide, out of all proportion to their numbers. For straightening out this tangle Major Warden's authority was pitifully inadequate. He was, moreover, largely dependent on the goodwill of burghers, on whom, for want of a garrison, the defence of the territory rested. For in spite of Sir Harry Smith's optimistic appropriation of the revenue due from quit-rents, funds were very short ; and in the last resort both Smith and Warden knew very well that Earl Grey was prepared to tolerate the experiment of the Sovereignty only so long as it was self-supporting.

Warden's first step was to appoint a Land Commission composed exclusively of officials and burghers. In spite of the ' native danger ', farmers and natives were inextricably mixed up together, and any line that sought merely to recognize the *status quo* must have made an impossible frontier. Very careful handling was needed to secure a workable compromise, but, in the event, in the absence of any even unofficial sponsor,[1] native

---

[1] The French missionaries were the constant advisers of Moshesh, but, as foreigners, needed such backing as Dr. Philip had given them. In 1848, moreover, Revolution in France left them very short of financial support. There was a danger of their giving up altogether.

interests received short shrift in the delimitation of the boundary that became famous as ' the Warden Line '. The consequences were very soon apparent, especially as acute land-hunger was the prolific cause of rivalry among the natives themselves. ' For three years ', wrote the Rev. Mr. Dyke of Morija to Dr. Philip, on the Christmas Day of 1848, ' the Government had promised arbitration ' to settle a dispute about an area claimed by the Basutos, though occupied in part by Mantatees under Sikonyela ; ' but the delay and recent acts of the Government in reference to other parts of the country were but little calculated to inspire confidence '. The result was that, as ' unfortunately Sikonyela has never been long without giving provocation ', an ' act of hostility ' on his part, following the Boomplaats rebellion in September,[1] led to a Basuto counter-attack, with the killing of about twenty Mantatees and the capture of two or three thousand head of cattle. In this and other instances Moshesh made reparation to his troublesome neighbours ; but Mr. Dyke continues :

' We have just heard of a plan for a boundary proposed to His Excellency by Mr. Southey and one of the magistrates in these parts. . . . To facilitate the Government of British subjects who have emigrated into Moshesh's country, these gentlemen kindly propose to take in all the part of Moshesh's country in which emigrants have set themselves down, and who in very many cases are living side by side with villages of natives (Bassoutos). The plan says that emigrants living in (areas) not embraced by the new British line will have to remove. . . . Naturally the natives taken in by the line must retreat over it so as to leave room for new emigrants—a cunning plan certainly, and very fair, seeing that for five or six families of Boers to be displaced, thousands of natives must remove. . . . This scheme is the more unjust as Moshesh never took a farthing from any emigrants who have settled in his country. His limits were settled by treaty in 1843, after which he was requested by Sir Peregrine Maitland to grant a portion of land which would be exclusively for emigrants. This he did and now he is told by Mr. Southey that he proposed to the Governor to set aside all former limits and establish another which cuts off half of Moshesh's country, or rather the Bassouto country—that is, of the habitable part of it. . . . The Governor may perhaps see the enormity of the plan proposed and try by his answer to Moshesh to allay the angry feeling which is already excited. . . . I only trust the Bassoutos will be patient and see what can be done without war. War

---

[1] E. Casalis had written from Thaba Bosigo on 1 September 1848 : ' Moshesh having ever been faithful to his treaty has naturally been an object of great suspicion to the rebels who have kept him closely watched, endeavouring at the same time, by every means, to stir up the Mantatees and other tribes to attack the Bassoutos.'

must ruin them but who would wonder if they resort to it, seeing that they know not where to look for redress.'

This proposal of Mr. Southey's concerned the extreme south-west, the area round the mission station of Beersheba. Two months later Mr. Casalis, Moshesh's most intimate adviser at Thaba Bosigo, wrote with rising indignation of the delimitation of a boundary that involved the removal of ' at least forty villages (*Basuto*, not Mantatee or Barolong) ', and threatened to leave the great Morija mission station, chosen as it had been for its *central* position, on the very border outskirts of Basutoland (where it now remains). Indeed, the crowding of the modern Basuto population into the narrow strip of habitable country along the Union border points again to the real significance of the long feud of the Basutos with the Free State—the mountainous interior has begun to fill up only in our own over-crowded day—and Mr. Casalis' letter deserves to rank with that of Mr. Calderwood (above p. 253) for its clear recognition that in Basutoland, as in Kafirland, the objective of colonists and of Bantu alike was land :

The Rev. Dr. Philip
DEAR SIR,
That Sir Harry Smith should feel vexed at the manifestation of dissatisfaction among the natives is by no means surprising. But His Excellency is very much mistaken as to the personal dispositions of the French missionaries, and the amount of influence they possess on the minds of the natives in such matters, if he supposes that this dissatisfaction originates in any interference on our part.

Up to the conclusion of the late wars with the Boers the natives have given the most satisfactory proof of their confidence in Government. The rebels used every exertion to induce them to join in the revolt. On the other hand, had the natives not felt assured that Sir Harry would regulate the affairs relative to their territory with upright-ness and equity, they had it in their power to burn the houses and destroy the gardens of the emigrants interspersed among them—most of the farms having been abandoned and left entirely unprotected by their owners. It appears then that there must have been something in the working of the present system which has created suspicion with regard to the real intentions of Government.

All men who believe that generosity and a disinterested interference may yet find their place among political principles understood that the Sovereignty proclaimed beyond the Great River, being neither the result of conquest nor the infliction of a deserved chastisement, was the extension of a wholly paternal impartial authority over parties who might well be taken in the light of children in a state of minority. Could it have been suspected to be anything else every honest heart would have repudiated it as the most refined piece of imposition ever contemplated. The possession of the places they already occupied was secured to the Boers, and this the native chiefs (the Basuto chiefs) consented to, because they were assured both in private conferences and through public proclamations that no further encroachments should be suffered, and that their rights and authority over their people should be respected.

One of the first acts of the magistrate of Smithfield has been to seize the person of a subaltern chief belonging to the family of Moshesh, because he refused to allow a veld-cornet to take an account of the number of the people and of their property. The chieftain was afraid that this might be a preliminary to making soldiers of his men, and insisted on the contemplated measure being first communicated to Moshesh. The chieftain was seized and dragged to Smithfield and only released when one of his people offered to stand bail for him. The incident created great excitement among the natives.

At the same critical moment the disaffected Boers were using every means in their power to work upon the feelings of the natives, telling them that the sovereignty of the Queen had bereft them of all rights to their own country, that they would be placed under British Law, be obliged to pay taxes, to serve in the Cape Corps, &c. On another hand the boasting and haughty behaviour of the farmers, who were willing to abide by the new regulations of Government, their utter disregard for the feelings of the natives among whom they lived and whose rights they had till then outwardly respected, seemed to confirm the interpretation which the disaffected gave of the new system of policy. At the same moment rumours were rife that it was intended to draw a limit between the Boers and the natives. The latter were under the impression that the object of Sir Harry Smith in changing the former treaties and proclaiming the sovereignty had precisely been to preclude the necessity of a boundary. They understood that *intermixed* as the Boers were with them, it had been found impracticable to operate a perfect separation, whence flowed the necessity of bringing black and white under the general protection and supervision of Her Majesty.

Moshesh had, himself, expressly asked His Excellency what would be done in the case of the Boers living near native villages, to which it had been *explicitly answered* that each party were to remain as they were. Thus the natives were led to think there would be between them and the farmers nothing more than a moral limit—that Government would accurately ascertain the number of Boers already settled in their country, define the extent of their farms, restrain them from further extension, govern them where they were, and leave to the natives the free occupation of all those portions of their territory which remained yet in their possession. They felt conscious that if a boundary was established, some one must be removed, and they thought from indications which they had already observed, that they had much reason to fear that necessity should be laid on them.

Hence I suppose the reluctance of Moshesh to meet personally the land commission to make a limit. But had he no reason to demur before becoming a party to any such arrangements ? I received information of the boundary proposed by the Commission and found to my utter amazement that it is such as will require (if carried out) the removal of at least 40 villages of Bassoutos including the personal

residence of a brother of Moshesh. That boundary would pass within
25 miles of Morija, one of the most central stations. It detaches entirely
from the remainder of the tribe the stations of Beersheba and that of
Hebron. It deprives the inhabitants of Beersheba of 23 cattle posts,
actually occupied by them, and from which their flocks must be driven.
It places at the disposal of Government a large portion of territory in
which only a few families of Boers reside at the extremities, whilst the
central parts are occupied by the natives. Happily the Commission
have left to Moshesh the liberty of expressing his opinion to Sir Harry,
before the proposed limit be confirmed, and I hope he will have availed
himself of that his right.

My conscience has not allowed me to remain silent, and I have
taken the liberty of respectfully stating my opinion to the High Commissioner by a letter. No one laments more than I do the estrange-
ment of the confidence and the affections of the Bassoutos from the
British, which even the mere proposal of such measures must unavoid-
ably occasion. It will eventually prove the ruin of the natives, and
if improved by the disaffected farmers may very soon involve the
Colony in great difficulties. I apprehend it will also materially impair
the credit of the missionaries in the tribe, as we have always endeavoured
to persuade the Bassoutos that the British Government was animated
with the most generous and upright intentions towards them.

I have long been convinced that the natives, brought as they have
been in close contact with a white population, are unable to govern
themselves, and I believe they had a sufficient perception of this to have
yielded to the authority of Government, had they not been threatened
of being dispossessed of the very fields they cultivate. I fear much
confusion arises from the very limited and erroneous ideas generally
entertained respecting the statistics of the Bassouto country. The
population is under-rated, the actual and future wants of the tribe are
not taken in consideration. It is no childish debate about useless wastes
that takes place at this moment. The present lamentable war of the
Bassoutos and the Mantatees which originates in nothing else than a
land question, shows sufficiently how keen and deep are the feelings
of the natives on that subject.

Excuse this long letter, and believe that in thus frankly expressing
myself, I only yield to the desire of acknowledging the proof of interest
you have given us by writing.

I remain, Reverd. and dear Sir,
Yours most respectfully,
E. CASALIS

GRAHAMSTOWN,
22nd February, 1849

Two months later still (25 April 1849) Mr. Rolland of Beersheba, a less regular correspondent of Dr. Philip's, put the
truth about the land in a nutshell, making the important point
that this was ' not even a question of boundary between Colonial
territory and native land, but of *taking a certain part*, hitherto
in their undisputed possession, *from the natives* '. ' The new line ',

he continues, 'takes in nearly all the white inhabitants', and decrees 'the removal of *some hundreds* of native villages, inter-mixed with their farms, including our mission station of Hebron with the whole of its population'.

Nor are these outbursts the mere fulminations of missionary Philanthropists. Major Warden, having no sufficient power behind him to interfere with European farmers, or to enforce their removal, was guided exclusively by their interests and advice. Without, it would seem, in a single case disturbing farmers in actual occupation,[1] Warden's Commission issued certificates of possession, giving the Sovereignty a definite boundary, and the farmers a legal title, to which they clung even after the abandonment of the Sovereignty a few years later. At the same time, while, as missionaries protested and officials affirmed,[2] the Government paid little regard to the rights of native occupants, it was yet powerless to carry out the evictions it proposed. The 'settlement' was unduly tender to the claims of the petty tribes, giving them more than they really required —perhaps from fear or jealousy of Mosesh, and usually at the expense of the Basuto.[3] As the farmers' legal title to the land remained, masses of Basuto and others became squatters without rights, and a rare legacy of native discontent was bequeathed to the later Free State.

Such, in short, was the fulfilment of the bargains with Sir Harry Smith, by which Moshesh agreed to the establishment of British Sovereignty 'for the purpose of effectually restraining the Boers within limits and upon the locations they now possess'. As Dr. Philip had pointed out in the beginning, and as the Governor at first realized, Moshesh was the one chief whose friendship and co-operation were worth keeping. Even now, over and over again, in spite of all provocation, he showed himelf not only sincerely anxious to keep the peace and to maintain good relations with the Government, but willing to keep a

[1] Clerk to Newcastle, 10 November 1853, and de Kiewiet, *British Government and Boer Republics*, MSS., ch. v.
[2] De Kiewiet, *op. cit.*, Basutoland Records, ii, pp. 29-30.
[3] One Molitsani, who in the end adhered to Moshesh, having been crowded out by the 'Warden Line', was given a 'slice' of Basuto country, 'that a recognized chief should not be without a country' (de Kiewiet, *ibid.*). On the other hand, Warden was unable to make room for some 12,000 Barolong except at Basuto expense, because he was unable to remove 'two or three Boer farmers', who between them claimed 'some 100 sq. miles' (Warden to Smith, 23 December 1848).

bargain, and able to enforce it on his own people. For years Boers and Basuto had in fact been living side by side with a minimum of disturbance. In 1848, isolated Boers were left unmolested during the excitement of the Boomplaats campaign, and Sikonyela was reimbursed for not unmerited losses at the hands of the Basuto ; in 1849, Moshesh agreed, under protest it is true, to the new boundary line, even when Major Warden absurdly recognized the petty chiefs (who more readily consented to white occupation) as independent rulers, and presently as ' allies ' against the Basuto.[1] Only a very strong hand could have enforced such a settlement. The restraint and control maintained by Moshesh were remarkable, but in the end his followers, threatened with dispossession by tribes they probably despised, inevitably came to blows with their old enemies, now the special protégés of ' Government '.

Towards the middle of 1851 Major Warden, who continued to accept the view that the unrest was due, not to his own dispositions, but to the greed and ambition of the Basuto, demanded compensation for attacks, again not unprovoked, on Sikonyela and Moroko. Even now, with the available Government forces heavily drawn upon for another Kafir War, Moshesh kept faith and paid up 2,500 head of cattle. At last, as inter-tribal fighting continued (always in the disputed cornlands), Warden decided to take ' strong action ', called up the burghers and his native allies, and prepared to march against the Basuto chief. But now, to the burghers, Basutoland farms were one thing, the suppression of the unrest to which their occupation gave rise, quite another.[2] This was an inter-tribal quarrel and no concern of theirs. The burghers, therefore, obeyed the summons in very small numbers, and in June 1851 the punitive expedition was badly defeated at Viervoet on the very borders of Basutoland, Warden being forced to fall back on Bloemfontein, and to remain there on the defensive till the High Commissioner should find men and leisure for the vindication of British authority and prestige.

The situation was nearly desperate. From Bloemfontein Major Warden seems to have fulminated against those burghers

---

[1] For other instances and references, see Walker, pp. 254-5, 259, 267.

[2] Many of the farmers would undoubtedly have welcomed a British garrison to protect them in the enjoyment of their new lands, but Downing Street tolerated the Sovereignty only so long as it was self-supporting and self-protecting.

who had left him in the lurch. The burghers for their part, with the frontiers in confusion, and the Basuto once more in effective occupation of the lands assigned to the native ' allies ', had their own grievances ; even if the tumult and unrest were not all of native origin, the tribes were fighting each other and farms were unsafe.[1] Some of the Boers, still hankering after independence of British rule and of its inconvenient obligations, appealed for help and protection to the outlawed Transvaaler, Pretorius, who, with a forbearance that brought him a quick reward, refused to intervene. Others objected, not to British rule in itself, but to the autocracy of Major Warden. It was impracticable under the circumstances to think of allaying discontent by promulgation of the Letters Patent of a liberal constitution, which seems to have lain in Cape Town till its very existence was forgotten.[2] But the decisive fact for the authorities who had to deal with this situation was the event which precipitated the crisis ; the action at Viervoet made it appear that the ill-used Moshesh stood as an enemy to peace and settlement— most unjustly, even as a new ' native menace '.

Even now, had this been all, Sir Harry Smith's experiment might have been saved from complete break-down. The parliamentary constitution for the Sovereignty had already been authorized, and Moshesh was still for peace though he could hardly have been the victim of more tactless blundering than that perpetrated by Major Warden. Events, however, quite unconnected with the affairs of the Sovereignty, sealed the fate of Sir Harry Smith's plans for a general settlement. As in 1846, Kafirland was the Achilles' heel. In that long harassed province the Governor's hasty and rather blustering settlement endured for less than two years. The summer of 1849–50 seems to have been another period of drought,[3] and, therefore, probably of

---

[1] Some who had marched with the expedition were harried by the ' disaffected ', Warden being powerless to protect them (Warden to Smith, 24 August 1851). Other evidence indicates that Zulu levies did some ' thieving ' and that even European adventurers ' fished in troubled waters ' (de Kiewiet, *op. cit.*).

[2] Dr. de Kiewiet makes the point that in 1853 the Law Officers were in some doubt as to the legality of abandoning the Sovereignty except under an Act of Parliament, till it was pointed out that the Representative Assembly under this draft had never been formally constituted (*British Government and Boer Republics*, ch. vi).

[3] And in this crisis, two veterans were out of action. Old James Read wrote to Hankey in September 1850 that he would fain see Dr.

stock-theft, if only by Kafirs drifting into the Colony in search of work. This drift put a heavy strain on the workings of the pass-system, and Ordinance 49 being found at long last to have lapsed,[1] ' Vagrant Laws ' were threatened, to the further alarm of the Kat River Hottentots. An attempt was also made to root out their ' squatters '.[2] Hard times, moreover, were little favourable for the collection of the new quit-rent (above, p. 268) which caused some discontent even among loyalists. The Kafirs, meantime, had to choose between service with farmers, and their newly defined ' locations '.[3] The younger Read was apprehensive ; in August 1849 he wrote :

> ' I fear (this) stringency will bring another collision with the Kafirs. A conquered people should be ruled with leniency. . . . I saw Macomo the other day. He said : " I did not fight in the last war. I fear not death, as I would rather die than have Smith's foot on my neck— but I fear God." There is a certain point at which nations become reckless of death and would rather commit *felo de se* than be exposed to indignity.'

This notwithstanding, the Governor was able to report (both in April and June 1850) peace and great progress. Then, in October 1850, the Governor called a general meeting of chiefs at King William's Town ; but Sandile, the Paramount Chief, mindful once more of the fate of Hintza, failed to appear and was summarily deposed. In November came ' reassuring notices ' by frontier officials. In December Sandile was to be ' fetched '. On Christmas Eve the fetching expedition was ambushed, with heavy loss, in the bush of the Boomah Pass ; on Christmas Day the soldier settlers of the villages in the Chumie Valley were horribly butchered ; and not long afterwards raiding parties got to work in the Colony itself.

Nor was this the end. In January came the unprecedented

Philip ' once more in this world '. But he could not ride, and the oxen were unfit to travel ' owing to the severe drought '. Some time earlier, in 1847, Dr. Philip wrote probably his last letter to the Buxtons : ' My own health is very precarious, but if the Lord has any more use for me He can yet give me a few more days : if not He can carry out His work without me.'

[1] Enclosures from Smith to Grey, 7 and 28 August 1849 : on 27 September McKinnon urged Proclamation in restraint of passes, where-upon (3 October) Attorney-General gave opinion, quoted above, p. 67.

[2] Read's letters to Philip, especially March, April 1849, with personal reassurances in private letter from Smith to Philip, 2 April 1849.

[3] Smith to Grey, 26 October 1849.

news that numbers (much exaggerated [1]) of the Hottentots of
the Kat River and Theopolis had joined the rebel Kafirs. And
in spite of the apparent danger to the Colony, the European
farmers were slow and unwilling to turn out once more on commando in adequate numbers.[2] Left with such troops as he could
muster to bring the Kafirs, rebels as they now were, to sufficiently
abject submission, the Governor's campaign made little or no
progress, and in May 1851 he reported cheerlessly that the
attempt to ' civilize the Gaikas ' (all in two years) had proved an
' awful failure '. Not many months later (January 1852) when
he stigmatized the natives as ' perfidious, treacherous and
bloodthirsty ' he reflected only too faithfully the now dominant
opinion that the real source of all the trouble was Bantu original
sin. The news from Basutoland in June was the last straw.
Earl Grey in Downing Street was now at the mercy of his critics
in the British Parliament, and their impatience determined the
issue, and closed this decisive chapter in South African history.

From the point of view of these critics, every possible plan
had been tried save one. After war and reprisals, a ' neutral
belt ' ; then reprisals and war once more ; thereupon ' recognition ' and ' equal treaties '. That the treaties had failed to
give the natives the one thing needful—absolute security on
their land, with just and effective civil government, was entirely
overlooked ; humanitarianism, so it seemed to Sir William
Molesworth, had made the Kafirs better fighters but worse
savages,[3] and, treaties having failed, annexation with strict
military control had ended again in war on two fronts. British
money had been squandered in vain, and to stop this ceaseless
drain all that remained was to leave South Africa altogether to
its own resources.

When news of the Kafir War reached England the storm
broke. While Sir William Molesworth denounced the attempt to
civilize such ' barbarous and sanguinary wretches ', Mr. Gladstone joined in the attack on a policy which ' for no benefit to

[1] *Cape Col. Qn.*, pp. 279 ff.
[2] (Smith to Grey, 21 January 1851.) The reluctance of the burghers
to serve was partly due to the lapse of the old Commando Law, whose
amendment was disallowed in 1834, above p. 84, and partly perhaps
to the withdrawal of so many on trek. But a cry of the ' country in
danger ' could not have evoked so poor a response had it not been clear
that the Kafirs were already a broken people.
[3] *Materials of a Speech*, p. 10.

South Africa . . . ensures the recurrence of wars with a regularity which is perfectly astounding '.[1] Sir Charles Adderley, with some local knowledge of South African conditions, pressed for a Commission to investigate the relations of Europeans and natives on the spot. The Cabinet, temporizing, met this demand by appointing a Select Committee, but privately, Earl Grey, doubtful of his own policy, and with shaken confidence in Sir Harry Smith, decided before the end of May to send two Commissioners, Messrs. Owen and Hogge, to report, and to help the Governor to restore order and to settle the country on some more permanent basis.[2] Earl Grey, in truth, was himself leaning to the abandonment at least of the Orange Sovereignty, and in September warned the Governor that unless the colonists were prepared to assume a full share of responsibility for the defence of the country, no British interest would be served by continuing the British connexion. Grey himself, however, like Sir Charles Adderley—who was left, in the end, a voice crying in the wilderness [3]—was still uneasy ; remembering that Britain had a responsibility to the native population, he still feared ' the destruction of the less civilized races ', with much suffering to the Boers themselves in the process. Sir Harry Smith had different reasons for opposing a withdrawal, and again voiced the feeling that the natives were less a responsibility than a danger. Catching the trend of Earl Grey's thoughts and anxious to save the Sovereignty, his own creation, he replied on 12 November :

' If H.M.'s Sovereignty over this territory were rescinded, the step would be regarded by every man of colour in South Africa as an unprecedented and unlooked for victory to his race, and be the signal for revolt and continued resistance to British authority.'

The rest of the story is to be gleaned from the ' minutes ' endorsed on the documents that were handled by the Colonial Office. Before ever the Governor had penned this letter, or the Commissioner had time to report, a minute, apparently in the handwriting of Lord John Russell himself, noted on 21 October : ' The ultimate abandonment of the Orange Sovereignty should be a settled point in British policy.'[4] On 12 January 1852, Earl Grey, who meantime had resolved on Smith's recall,

---

[1] Quoted by C. W. de Kiewiet in *loc. cit.*
[2] Grey to Hogge and Owen, 31 May 1851.
[3] Cf. speech on Abandonment, which he deplored as a short-sighted plan for shaking off ' present difficulties ' (Hansard, vol. xxxiii, pp. 52 ff.).
[4] Draft of a reply to Smith's dispatch of 20 August.

minuted, a little less finally, for the instruction of the new Governor, Sir George Cathcart :

' It is a question for serious consideration whether the attempt (to civilize the natives) which has thus failed can be renewed, or whether the exercise of British authority in South Africa must not be restricted within much narrower limits than heretofore. . . . Apart from the very limited extent of territory required for the security of the Cape of Good Hope as a naval station, the British Crown and nation have no interest whatever in maintaining any territorial dominion.'

In February the Russell Ministry was defeated, and Earl Grey, the greatest and most active Colonial Secretary of the period, escapes responsibility for what followed. In the end of the month Sir John Pakington took over, under Lord Derby, who, as Mr. Stanley, had made the first notable concession to humanitarian concern for the Bantu by his instructions to Sir Benjamin D'Urban in the end of 1833. The Bantu were now ' the enemy '. In the urgency of the crisis ministers showed no consciousness of the land pressure and the blundering which had helped to make them dangerous.

As it chanced, some of the first letters to be dealt with by the new Colonial Secretary reported the appeal of the still outlawed Transvaaler, Pretorius, to be allowed to enter into regular peaceful relations with the British Government. Though Major Warden thought he was not to be trusted, Pretorius had shown good faith and refrained from taking the opportunity of stirring up more trouble in the Sovereignty. He might yet make difficulties by working on the feelings of the ' disaffected ' ; on the other hand, the natives were dangerous, and Pretorius might be an invaluable ally against them. It went for nothing that the Transvaalers were those who had gone farthest into the wilderness to escape restraint, and in its first week the new administration gave decisive evidence of its conversion from humanitarianism in native affairs back to a policy of uncompromising military repression. A minute of 4 March welcomed the prospect of agreement with Pretorius expressly on the ground that :

' If we could obtain the co-operation of men trained in and accustomed to Bush warfare, *the Caffres would no longer appear such dangerous enemies.* No time should be lost to *repair the errors* that have made these men our enemies instead of friends and invaluable allies.'

This was really the end. Faced by the dangers that beset the Sovereignty, and interpreting with accuracy the wishes of their superiors in England, Earl Grey's Commissioners, Messrs.

Hogge and Owen, though without precise instructions, had already, on 16 January 1852, signed the Sand River Convention, by which the Transvaal Boers received their independence, with a pledge of ' non-interference ' that was to be mutually binding on British and on Boers. ' As we should object ', wrote Governor Cathcart in approval and support,

' to the Boers beyond the Vaal forming alliance with Moshesh . . . so it appears to be just that we should disclaim alliance with those North of the Vaal River, amongst whom the Boers can only live by exercising a requisite supremacy for their control. . . .'

Not long before this, Dr. Livingstone had complained of the loss of his household goods at hands of the Boers ' exercising requisite control ' ; within a few days of submitting the Convention for approval, Sir George Cathcart was pleased to retort that the injury he had sustained was but ' incidental to a state of war or to life in remote regions '. Livingstone was not yet a famous popular hero and his protest could be disregarded. The Convention was received in Downing Street with ' great satisfaction ' and the Transvaal was free.[1]

Now the guiding motive of Hogge and Owen, and still more of Sir Harry Smith in lifting his ban on Pretorius, was, if possible, to save the Orange Sovereignty. As an enemy, Pretorius might rally the malcontents of Winburg and threaten not merely Bloemfontein but Natal. His benevolent neutrality must be bought. But since the whole object of the Sovereignty had been, in Earl Grey's words, to bring these emigrant British subjects ' once more within the control of regular government ', and to save the natives from oppression or ' extermination ', there was no obvious reason why, if these principles were renounced for the Boers beyond the Vaal, they should be maintained, possibly at heavy cost, in the Orange Territory. The overwhelming desire of the Molesworths was ' that a limit be put to the extent of the British dominions in South Africa ', and the Orange River was a more effective limit than the Vaal. The abandonment of the Orange Sovereignty followed as a matter of course and was now a mere matter of arrangement.

Towards the end of 1852 Sir George Cathcart had sufficiently beaten the Kafirs to be able to turn some of his attention northwards, and on 12 October he plunged for withdrawal, without qualification :

[1] Cathcart to Grey, 12 April (for Livingstone), 20 April (enclosing the Treaty), and to Pakington, 28 July 1852.

' An acknowledged foreign state will be far more easily . . . and economically controlled by respect for the power of H.M.'s armed forces within the Colony, and will form a more secure barrier against barbarians from without than can ever be accomplished by British political interference and attempted Government, without an expensive military establishment for its support.'

This dispatch arrived on the eve of the fall of the Derby Ministry, but Sir John Pakington left his successor a minute approving of Cathcart's recommendation. Very shortly afterwards, on 14 March 1853, further alarmed, perhaps, by news of an ill-starred attempt by the Governor in December to vindicate British authority with Moshesh, the Duke of Newcastle pronounced for abandonment. The principle he ' considered as settled ', appointing yet another Commissioner, Sir George Clerk, to see the thing through.

The preliminary matters to be ' adjusted ' were to induce the settlers as a whole to undertake the responsibilities of self-government, and to persuade those who disliked the enforced loss of their rights as British subjects to fall in with whatever plans could be made. At various meetings of delegates, ' loyalists ' were fully more vocal than the republicans, and to the end the Boers showed no marked enthusiasm for the greatness of ' independence ' that was thrust upon them. Even in the Volksraad of the later Republic the old ' loyalists ' continued to have a fair share of the representation, showing happily that the schism was free from British-Dutch racial feeling. The defence of the country was the crux, and the Boers were as hesitant to assume this dangerous responsibility as the British authorities seemed determined to escape it. There was still, various delegates reminded Sir George Clerk, an only partially settled land dispute with the Griquas, and there was always Moshesh ; and both received such curt treatment as redounds little to the credit of the British authorities responsible for a precipitate renunciation of moral obligations.

When he reached Bloemfontein in October 1852, Sir George Cathcart, had he examined the evidence even then available,[1] must have seen how hardly and unjustly the land claims of Moshesh were dealt with by Major Warden, and how, in spite of this, his bearing was conciliatory. The Governor, however, while somewhat cutting down the colonial claims against him,

---

[1] Theal's *Basutoland Records*, 3 vols., published, with three more volumes, *Miscellaneous Basutoland Records*, in Cape Town Archives.

had in the end of 1852, without parley, given Moshesh three days in which to collect 1,000 horses and 10,000 head of cattle from his scattered dependent chiefs. Within the time limit Moshesh duly paid 3,500 head of cattle, and asked for time : whereupon, giving effect to his ultimatum, the Governor marched against Thaba Bosigo. As in Kafirland, war meant cattle-driving ; and cattle in this instance, for all his previous experience, were at once the undoing of the Governor, and in the long run the saving of the situation. In December the invading force became ' entangled ' with its captured cattle, and was severely checked by the Basuto at Berea ; Moshesh, however, protesting his honest desire for peace, persuaded the embarrassed Governor that his captures met the bill, and the Governor agreed that it was peace, and that Moshesh was still the Queen's ally. In the following year Moshesh once more kept his own people in control, incidentally chastising Sikonyela and other disturbers of the peace.[1] At last Sir George Clerk, recognizing the injustice of the Warden Line, but unable to reach a new agreement with the burgher delegates, and only anxious to be gone, left the matter as he found it.[2] Moshesh, for all the ' wily astuteness ' with which he is credited, remained under the impression that his old 1843 Treaty, with its wider boundary, stood. The burghers, however, strong in their possession of land certificates, felt that they were quite free to deal with the Basuto as occasion demanded or offered. The Free State wars with the Basuto were not long delayed.

The treatment of Kok and his Griquas was similar, but more immediately final in its results. Even under the Sovereignty, the unstable Griquas not only failed to pay the ' compensation for improvements ' demanded of them by the time-expired lessees of their land, but continued to make new leases and sales even in the inalienable Reserve. Having failed to secure Kok's assent even with the bribe of a pension of £300, the Commissioner signed the Convention recognizing the independence of the Orange Free State in February 1854, and left Kok to his own resources ; on the flimsy pretext that leases and sales were the

[1] Walker, p. 266, and references.
[2] Sir George Clerk, in dispatch of 3 December 1853, having his doubts, comforted himself and his superiors as follows : ' So long as Moshesh and Sikonyela maintain the degree of control they now exercise . . . their wars either among themselves or with Europeans will not deserve to be characterized as exterminating or atrocious.'

practice, not only did the Convention promise ' measures affording every facility ' for such land transactions, but privately Clerk left it to be understood, not by Kok, that land sold by the Griquas would henceforth form part of the Free State. Within ten years, as Dr. Philip had prophesied, the Griquas had trekked *en masse* to the new Kokstad.

Such was the Native Policy of the early 'fifties ; and the ' abandonment ' was in effect the cementing of a defensive alliance of British and Boers against the natives. British recognition of the Republics came thus as an act of friendship, marking a season of harmonious co-operation between the two white peoples. But this act held all the seeds of the disputes that were yet to tear South Africa to fragments. Britain had, indeed, agreed with her adversary quickly whiles she was in the way with him, but the apparently friendly recognition of the Republics was far from being based on any mutual understanding.

Great Britain had no more contemplated accepting the Boer view of the place and rights of the coloured population than the Boers thought of modifying their old attitude. Nor had Great Britain wittingly relinquished her right as, almost necessarily, the suzerain of the new Republics, to assert her own views if and when occasion demanded. The Boers of the Sovereignty had come near accepting British rule and its implications, and might almost certainly have been made part of the Colony. But recognition had the effect of hardening the Boers in general in aloofness and in their old way of thinking. It was not as if the Republics had become any less a part of the essential South African whole. They were hardly even strong enough to stand alone, continuing under British influence ; and their dealings with natives, as later with Uitlanders, could not fail to have reactions on British South Africa. But the disputes and differences that now arose were not those between a Government and its own subjects, but between a strong Government and weak Governments strongly and nervously assertive of their rights, not least that of managing natives as their own responsibility in their own way. In recognizing the Republics as she did, Great Britain for the moment turned her blind eye on the fundamental cause of the disputes which had rent the country for two generations. Thus established, the Republics, while learning more and more to cherish their own ' independence ', came little nearer recognizing the sovereign virtue of broad human freedom.

B.B.B.   U

CHAPTER XVIII

CONCLUSION: THE SHORTEST WAY WITH THE BANTU—THE NATIVE PROBLEM 'MADE'—CONDITIONS IN THE UNION

THE British authorities had little need of their Boer allies for the work of conquest that still lay to their hands in Kafirland. Economy being now the rule, it seemed to Governors and officials that the shortest way with the Bantu was to make an expensive recurrence of war in the British zone as nearly as could be impossible. Under Sir George Cathcart, the last as it happened of the long line of soldier governors, the military view which began to recover its former unchallenged ascendancy under Sir Peregrine Maitland in 1846, had it all its own way. Cathcart's guiding principle (above, p. 287) being, avowedly, ' an effective barrier against Barbarians . . . without an expensive military establishment ', his policy was to reduce the tribes to impotence by systematic invasion and confiscation of their lands.

It was as a voice crying in the wilderness that the Scottish missionary, Niven, urged: ' Let the Government show that it does not conquer in order to dispossess.' Even while the Northern Bantu were in process of being handed over to the Republics who were to exercise the ' supremacy requisite for their control '—requisite also ' to preserve proper relations between master and servant '—the tragedy of the Amaxosa was played out with a devastating thoroughness which the slender resources of the Boers never quite equalled. In the fullness of time the economic consequences of this peace by conquest have come to be called the Native Problem.

The facts of the story stand out from the very baldness and obvious lack of imagination that mark Dr. Theal's pages.[1] Sir Harry Smith in his last year, 1851, achieved little, and troops and burghers being short, Kafir raids on the Colony continued

[1] Theal, iii, pp. 98 and 111 ff.

for some months. But when, on the arrival of reinforcements,
' active operations ' commenced, the ' forests and jungles were
scoured '—and scoured again—if only for cattle, ' most of which
had been driven across the Kei ', to the Gcaleka Paramount
Kreli. In December 1851, accordingly, ' two columns were
directed to that quarter, with the double object of punishing
Kreli, and depriving the rebels of their sources of supply '.
Thus true to type, this Kafir war, like each of its predecessors,
had its storm centre just a little farther east than the one before
it ; first the conflict was near the Gamtoos, then, in succession,
in the Zuurveld, the Fish River Bush, on the Keiskama, twice
in the Amatolas, now beyond the Kei, finally, in the rebellion
of 1878, which ranks as the ' last ' war, on the Bashee and
beyond. So now Kreli's country was ' scoured . . . with great
damage to the crops and kraals '—and some to the Gcalekas
themselves ; till in January, General Somerset, old hand that
he was, ' returned to King William's Town with 30,000 head of
cattle, a few horses and 14,000 goats ' ; the second column
' brought out 7,000 Fingos, with 15,000 head of cattle, which
these people had seized from the Gcalekas and were allowed to
retain for themselves '.

Still, says Dr. Theal, only a small number of burghers re-
sponded to the Governor's appeal in February 1852, the month
of the epic disaster to the troopship *Birkenhead*. For the hearten-
ing of the Kafirs, moreover, and of their ' prophet ', Umlanjeni,
the summer was a good one, and the crops cut down by the
troops early in the season sprang up again, giving them new
courage to prolong the agony. In the winter the campaign
began again in earnest with the burning of Kreli's principal
kraal, and the capture of 10,000 head of cattle. Now also,
improving on the 1847 device of cattle depots, and anticipating
the blockhouses with which Lord Kitchener helped to end the
Anglo-Boer War of 1899–1902, the Governor hit on the plan
of throwing up numerous ' small defensible turrets in commanding
positions on the line of march '. These ' proved themselves
most admirably adapted for South African warfare ', and made
the next ' scouring ' of the Amatolas and other Kafir ' fastnesses '
so effective that in October surrenders began. In November
only ' a few wretched fugitives' remained to be dealt with, and
the Governor felt he could safely withdraw 2,500 of the troops
for the work in Basutoland.

In February 1853 the Governor returned to dictate peace,

and, now that the tribes were broken, provided the frontier with what Captain Stretch had so much needed, a thoroughly efficient police force, the famous Cape Mounted Rifles. The best of the Ceded Territory and the Amatolas were now indeed ' forfeited for ever ', and ' the Gaikas ', says Dr. Theal, ' having lost most of their cattle as well as the rich valleys of the Amatola, were poor and weak '. But wiser at least than the D'Urban of May 1835, Sir George Cathcart refrained from attempting total expulsion, and promised them *locations* ' in the large tract of open land ' to the eastward, nearer the Kei. The Fingos, on the other hand, were now well provided with ' some of the choicest lands in the country . . . the best portions of the Tyumie and upper Keiskama valleys, as well as extensive locations farther north '. Nor were ' the operations and speculations of Europeans ' forgotten. What remained of Victoria East (the Tyumie district), with lands forfeited by Kat River rebels, and strips of farms round the forts in Kaffraria proper, were allotted on military tenure—the first deliberate exploitation of the plan of making South Africa a chessboard of black and white. A large part of the Tembu country, round what was named Queenstown, was similarly dealt with, the object being to place a buffer between Kaffraria and the Colony : ' the portion of the forfeited territory allotted to Europeans ', says Dr. Theal of this area, ' contained about 400 farms, and there were at least three times as many applicants '.

Under Sir George Grey, a humane and enlightened civil Governor, whose character and disinterestedness have brought him high praise, the Cape took its first serious steps towards civilizing the natives. Henceforth they were to be ' inhabitants of one country ' along with their European conquerors. To be not only a notable pioneer of native education, but the originator and founder, before the days of medical missions, of the first great hospital for natives, were distinction enough in themselves ; but in addition, or along with measures of this kind, Sir George Grey did much to set Cape administration on the lines it has followed ever since—the natives themselves associating his name with the introduction of their Parliamentary franchise. Before this, the peace of 1853 had contemplated ' indirect ' rule through the chiefs themselves. Grey, however, saw it desirable to ' assist ' the chief by associating with him

' a talented and honourable European gentleman who will hourly interest himself in the advance and improvement of the entire tribe, and must in time gain an influence over the native races which will produce beneficial results.'

The chief, therefore, was put on a salary, and gradually weaned from the exercise of criminal jurisdiction, though left for a time with sufficient authority, so it is claimed, to keep alive the communal spirit of the tribe.[1]

But Sir George Grey's innovations were really put to the test only under totally changed conditions. The truth is that in the Cape Colony the effective supersession of the chiefs by European officials, or as it is now called, ' direct ' rule, was made easy, if not inevitable, by the utter destruction of the chiefs themselves a very few years later. At once, indeed, even the loyal Fingos gave the Colony cause for anxiety, being disturbed at the prospect of subjection to European laws and customs which they mistrusted; and before the experiment could be tried out, the Xosa were driven to desperation by the rigorous land policy in which Sir George Grey all too faithfully adhered to and developed the plans laid down by his predecessor—with disastrous consequences. Not content with a ' buffer ' of Europeans on the borders, he began almost at once to press forward a favourite scheme for planting 1,000 men of the German legion (newly freed from service in the Crimea) in the very heart of Kaffraria itself. Meantime, the transplanting of whole tribes of Amaxosa to new and uncongenial homes could hardly be done in a day, nor a year ; as Dr. Theal narrates, ' the chiefs were clamorous for more land, and if they were permitted to occupy any tract temporarily, were loud in their complaints if they were afterwards required to abandon it '. The authorities, however, like so many others before and after them, treated these complaints as mere ingrained native habit, and turned deaf ears and a blind eye to the disturbing effects of discontent that was not unwarranted by the real congestion of the population. On Dr. Theal's showing the principal clan was forced to live at 60 to the square mile ; 10 or 12 to the square mile would have been enough for their untutored methods before the days of supplementary wage-earning on the mines.[2]

[1] Cf. Brookes, pp. 91 ff. Though the object was avowedly to allow European law ' by imperceptible degrees to take the place of their own barbarous customs ', magistrates continued, on their own responsibility, to settle disputes in accordance with native custom.

[2] Theal, iii, p. 181, *map*. Sandile, Maqomo and Bothma between them had 500 square miles. As Sandile alone had over 30,000 followers, this meant a population of over 60 to the square mile. By way of

The Bantu people, in times of unsettlement, have often shown themselves ready to be led, and even led astray, by ' prophets '. After the expulsion from the Zuurveld in 1812 it was Makana. Lately it had been one Umlanjeni, who ' sank into contempt ', and died, ' an object of derision ',[1] in 1853. In the circumstances of 1856, with little more to lose, the Xosa and the Tembu were fruitful soil for sowing by false prophets. The mantle of Umlanjeni now descended upon a young girl called Nonquase, and her uncle Umhlakaza, who began to dream dreams and to see visions of revenge. In the course of this year, inspired by these two national enthusiasts, the leading tribes ' went into training ', killing their cattle freely, and squandering their stores of grain, to eat and make themselves strong against a day in February 1857—a Great Day of the Lord—when grain was to sprout, cattle were to spring out of the ground, and warriors to come back from the dead ; then, with the help of a ' great hurricane ', they were to sweep the white man into the sea. The Day came and the sun went down as usual ; but ' when the chiefs called upon their warriors, they were answered by the wail of a starving people '.[2]

This was nearly the end. The Amaxosa were now a humbled and decimated people. ' Immense numbers ',[3] it is said, died of

contrast, the long-contested Fish-Keiskama districts had in 1921 only from 7·5 in Bedford to 10·5 in Fort Beaufort, and even Stockenstrom (the old Kat River) only 31·9 (*Union Year Book*, No. 6, p. 145).

[1] Theal, iii, 117. [2] Professor Walker's phrase, p. 298.

[3] Dr. Theal, iii, 198, estimates the number of dead at not fewer than 25,000, and ' possibly double that number '. The likelihood is, as usual, that contemporary estimates would be exaggerated.

The significance of any figures would depend on the total of the native population, and this, for reasons suggested above (p. 173), tends to be underestimated, just as the modern increase is probably exaggerated. Polygamy is one of the reasons often suggested as making for an inevitably rapid increase in time of peace. Its effect is no doubt to reduce the number of unmarried women, but the effective increase depends not on the crude birth-rate, but on survival, i.e. on the excess of births over deaths ; and all the evidence shows that under existing adverse conditions of health and over-crowding the native death-rate is quite abnormally high. In a passage that throws light on South African mentality in native matters, Dr. Theal (v, 255) cites as evidence of ' the enormous *rate* of increase ' of the Bantu (once they were ' prevented from killing each other in war and on charges of witchcraft '), the bare fact that ' in 1904 the population of the Transkei *was* 817,867 '. —The *apparent* modern increase of the native population can only be accepted with proof that the population in earlier days has not been grossly underestimated.

starvation, and whole districts were, for the time being, depopulated. A census of Kaffraria indicated a drop in population from 105,000 in January 1857 to 37,000 in July ; in the course of the same year of famine, Sandile's clan had decreased by death and flight from 31,000 to 3,700 ; Pato, Maqomo and one Stokwe, between them, could muster fewer than 10,000 in all ; Umhala's people were reduced from 23,000 to 6,500.[1] Clearly this was dispersal, not disappearance. ' Thousands ', as Dr. Theal himself says, ' poured into the Colony ', begging for food—' nor did they ask in vain ' ; many more scattered beyond the Kei—anywhere out of the old war zone, which, poor to begin with, was the scene of the most thorough cattle-killing and destruction. Now, if ever, was the time for a mild and generous settlement, to rebind the broken fragments of a scattered and a chastened people, and to guide their feet into the way of peace. Helpless as the Xosa were, it was not to be. Deliberate policy completed the scattering they themselves had so effectually begun.

Full of the idea of the Kafirs as a military danger, short-sighted officials saw only that the cattle-killing was part of a plan for a general rising, took the will for the deed, and prepared to punish them as rebels. Frontier colonists, in spite of the native ' menace ', knew that much long-coveted land was now within their grasp ; and the Governor himself, full of ideas of civilizing by example, carried on the work with a will, confiscating the larger part of such land as remained to the ' rebellious ' chiefs, and planting it systematically with Europeans. King William's Town now lay open, not merely for the thousand men of the German Legion, planned for in 1856, with their Irish wives, but for another 4,000 peasants obtained direct from Germany.

Not content with this, Sir George Grey was for keeping the Basuto in check by planting Europeans and Griquas in the sub-mountainous district of Nomansland.[2] He was disposed also to carry on the work of civilization by promoting European land-settlement in the Transkei itself—an area which, Dr. Theal

[1] Theal, iii, 197.
[2] The modern districts Barkly East, Elliot, Maclear, Mount Fletcher, Matatiele and Griqualand East, the last taking its name from Adam Kok's people who were planted there in 1863. This area, good in parts for agriculture, and admirable for sheep, was gradually alienated in large part to Europeans. Its relatively scanty population is in striking contrast to the crowding of the very similar country, to the north of the mountains, which is Basutoland.

adds in an inadvertently illuminating aside, ' it is surprising that the Cape police had been able to keep open as long as they did '. In the end only the doubts of Downing Street, and the sound sense of Grey's more humdrum and unpopular successor, Sir Philip Wodehouse, put a term to this madness. To the grievous disappointment of ' hopes that were raised throughout South Africa, particularly in Kaffraria, that vacant land beyond the Kei would at last be allotted to European settlers and the influence and power of the civilized race thus increased ', [1] Wodehouse in 1864 decided against further squeezing of the tribes. Europeans got a firm footing in the country about Queenstown. But Umtata, the capital of the Transkei, became the centre of a new Tembuland, and the Transkei itself happily survived to become the proudest boast of native administration in the Union.

The mischief in the ' Cis-Kei ' had already been done. Confiscation of sufficiently tenuous locations [2] confirmed the effects of the dispersal of 1857, finally preventing the reunion of the fragments, or the possibility of preserving even a decent nucleus of the Amaxosa as a people, like the Basuto. The Cis-Kei could not now become even a compact unit of administration like the Transkei. Again the stark facts stand out from Dr. Theal's narrative.[3] Kreli, first, too far away to be himself a . cattle-stealer, must be punished, like Hintza, for aiding and abetting his kinsmen in the west ; it must be put out of his power to do more harm, so a strong force was sent over the Kei ' to expel him ', with the remnant of his people, ' from the territory that had been the principal abode of his tribe for many generations '. The police ' kept possession of the country between the Kei and the Bashee ' till 1865, when Kreli was allowed to ' occupy a portion ' of his old land, while his old dependants, the Fingos, converted the bulk of it into ' Fingoland ' (which it still is). In 1877 the Xosa not unnaturally came to blows with their dispossessors, the Fingos, and in consequence also, with the Government ; and so Kreli, ' tall, erect and splendidly formed . . . deeply versed in traditionary lore and ever ready to impart his knowledge ' (to Dr. Theal among others), was driven once more to live on a ' small tract of land ' given him by a lesser chief in ' Bomvanaland ' (Elliotdale) beyond the Bashee, where he lived on till 1893. His son, Sigcawu, succeeded him

[1] Theal, v, 44 ; Walker, 312–13.   [2] See *note*, p. 293, above.
[3] Theal, iii, 200 ff.

in the chieftainship, ' but the dignity of the position was gone for ever '.

The fate of some other well-known figures in this frontier story was more tragic. Maqomo, ' the most intelligent of all the Rarabe chiefs, brave in the field and exceedingly capable as a guerrilla leader, though addicted to drunkenness . . . wandered into the Colony and was arrested ' in August 1857 [1]—like so many humbler natives since—' *for being without a pass* '. For this dire offence ' he was sentenced to imprisonment for a *year* '. But such a doughty prisoner could hardly escape even so lightly, and ' he was afterwards convicted of having been accessory to the murder of a petty chief who refused to destroy his cattle . . . and was sentenced to transportation for twenty-one years '. It is good to read that on Robben Island the old charm, which had impressed people so different as Colonel Somerset, Harry Smith and Captain Stretch, and many missionaries, seems to have re-asserted itself, and that he was there treated ' more as a prisoner of state than as a convict ', being allowed ' the company of his favourite wife ', and ' other indulgences '.   In 1870, ' under promise of good behaviour ', the veteran was allowed to return ' to the country of his birth ' ; but he ' began immediately to foment disturbances ', and was removed once more to Robben Island, where he died, ' at an advanced age ', in 1873.   His son, it seems, then prospered sufficiently to *buy* a farm, again in the old family home near the Kat River, where even now the clan gathered ' increasing strength ', which was its final undoing. Like so many others, Maqomo's son and people joined Kreli against the Government in the war of 1877–8.   This time their leader was taken in war and banished to Cape Town ' as a convict ' ; thereupon the members were ' dispersed ', and the ' history of the clan came to an end '.

The Gunukwebe chief, Pato, much lauded for his loyalty in the war of 1835, but a ' last ditcher ' ten years later, was, Dr. Theal adds, ' utterly ruined ', his people either joining his more consistently pacific brother Kama, or being ' dispersed ' in the Colony.   For ' an offence ', he also visited Robben Island, returning only to find himself ' almost forgotten ' ; ' his allowance from Government ', however, ' supported him till he passed away almost unnoticed '.

Finally Sandile, the crippled heir of Gaika—British ally in 1819, and Western Paramount—was graciously allowed to retain

[1] Theal, iii, 202.

a ' portion ' of his former share of some 500 square miles, about the modern Stutterheim. His clan, very naturally, began to come together again as soon as the crisis of 1857 was past— Dr. Theal's version being that it ' grew rapidly under British rule '. Sandile, however, with a great many more, including one considerable chief Umhala, son of Gaika's old rival Ndhlambi, and lesser people like ' Anta and Botumane ', became involved on the side of Kreli in the conflict of 1877. In this war, which began as a fight with their supplanters the Fingos,[1] Sandile ' was killed in an engagement with the colonial forces '. Thereupon, these tribes, being now British subjects, suffered what for many years was the normal penalty for rebellion. One after another, what remained of their locations—after Sir George Grey in 1857 had been ' enabled to give complete protection to the long harassed farmers of Albany ' by filling ' vacant ' land with more farmers—were confiscated, divided into farms, and ' sold to *Europeans* ', the people, like their predecessors in 1812, being ' removed ', or ' dispersed '.

It is only in our own day that the full consequences of this dispersal have begun to be felt. The clans were not wiped out, as the precise reckoning of 1857 would indicate ; as Dr. Theal himself says, ' the greater number of the young men and women ' remained in service in the Colony ;[2] it was all they could do. Nor is the comforting assurance that there they ' lost their (old) antipathy to Europeans ' and ' gained some knowledge of civilized ways . . . and acquired habits of industry ' much more to the point. There were, and are, in the Colony almost more than in any other part of the Union, far more homeless natives than farmers can fully or efficiently employ in ' service '. The excessive supply of labourers has made wage levels in the Cis-Kei too miserably low to support as much progress in ' civilized ways ' as might have been hoped and desired ' :[3]

---

[1] Local tradition suggests unmistakably that this Government patronage of the Fingos helped materially to provoke one last rising of the tribe of Pondomisi in Tsolo, east of Umtata, in 1880.

[2] Theal, iii, 200.

[3] Two years ago wage rates ran as low, in some districts, as 6s. a month, with ' keep ' ; even at 10s., the evidence was that servants rarely saw cash, their wages going to pay the employer for additional food. Ploughing or grazing rights may or may not go with the wage, but ' development ', especially the growth of sheep farming, has definitely restricted such privileges both for native and for European squatters.

the Cis-Keian farmers complain as constantly of ' stock-theft '
as their predecessors did of ' cattle-thieving ', for even natives
must live, and, as judges and police alike assert,[1] steal to supplement inadequate wages. Since women and children must have
a home, the men are not free to take their labour to a better
market ; if they leave the farmer they expose their families to
the risk of eviction. The very number of these under-employed
natives has, in addition, called into being one peculiar Cape
institution, the so-called ' private locations ', where some of the
' surplus ' natives (to use the word beloved of the Trekkers
in the north) swell the revenues of European land-owners in
districts like Komgha, by paying rent for the right to live their
own life as semi-independent peasants, some of them no doubt
on ancestral land from which they were never ' cleared '. But
the final result is that the steadily increasing poverty of the
natives is a heavy drag on the well-being of the whole Eastern
Province.[2]

In the Cape generally the process of confiscation, sometimes
for quite trivial offences, begun in 1853 and intensified in 1857,
continued unchecked long afterwards. The disintegration was
carried still further by the systematic transplanting of fragments
of ' unruly ' tribes,[3] a good many of them, in early days, to take
their chance ' beyond the Kei '. In the Cape, it is true, natives
were not prevented from relieving congestion by purchase, but
they were quite unfitted to face the free and open competition
of Victorian *laisser-faire*, so that with individual tenure and
free trade in land [4] as the last straw, the natives of the Cape,
first of all, were reduced to the landless and dependent condition
more slowly and gradually reached by those of all the other
Provinces in turn.

The Bantu, that is to say, are no longer, even remotely, the
military danger which drove distracted Cape Governors to subor-

[1] *Cape Col. Qn.*, pp. 30 *note*, 239.
[2] *Ibid.*, pp. 177-8, and pamphlets there cited.
[3] Like the Pondomisi in 1880 (above, p. 298 *note*). One late example
was the confiscation of a large block of comparatively good farms in
the Langeberg, west of Kuruman, for a trivial ' rebellion ' occasioned
by tactless handling of *rinderpest* (cattle-plague) regulations in 1896.
[4] In Kaffraria I have seen the title deeds of land now owned by
Europeans though the ' title ' is expressly described as ' Native '. In
barren Gordonia, land granted ' in perpetuity ' to men of colour for
services in Bechuanaland in 1885, has been largely absorbed by Europeans in the same way (Article in *Rand Daily Mail*, May 1922). See
also *Cape Col. Qn.*, pp. 284-6.

dinate the policeman to the soldier, and to trust to martial law rather than to civil government. ' Cattle-raiding ' has given place to ' stock-theft '. Masses of the natives are homeless, living, by virtually forced service, under highly uneconomic conditions—a largely rural proletariat in a self-consciously European state. The problem is one of adjustment to this complex, but European-made, position.

What time the Kafirs of the Cape were being reduced by systematic conquest, the other Provinces of the present-day Union were set on their different ways. Though the Cape, by the very thoroughness of its conquest of the Amaxosa, has, in old Kafirland, as thorny and difficult an economic problem as any part of the Union, it has also, in the relatively unmixed Bantu area known as the Transkei, evolved what is by general consent the model Native Reserve. Moreover, in spite of the bad beginning in the 'fifties, and the time of adversity which followed, the natives of the Cape entered the Union in 1910 a loyal, peaceful, law-abiding, and even a contented, people—their salvation being that, once conquered, they came into the heritage of legal and political freedom won for the Hottentots in the struggles of the 'twenties and 'thirties. Not that their contentment has survived these eighteen years ; lapse of time, with the cumulative effect of repeated droughts on a people already starved for land, and the general unsettlement of the Great War, with high prices and almost stationary wages, have brought discontent enough. Even so, the Cape by itself might have weathered the storm. But a demand for change in the Cape political system has now come from the Northern Provinces, and, the ostensible objective being the establishment of a uniform policy for the Union, the Native Problem is to be ' tackled ' by bringing the Cape natives down to the political level of the rest, rather than by extending the long-established privileges of the Cape to the whole country. South Africa generally, that is to say, has hardened in the ways it took when the Provinces parted company with the Mother Colony in the 'fifties.

In Natal, first, the major difficulties facing the British authorities when they occupied the country in 1843 were a relic of the spacious days of the early Republic, when Natal had been supposed to be ' empty ' of natives. On this assumption, the Volksraad had promised burghers two farms each, together with an *erf*, or town building-plot for a ' Sunday house ', to be used on visits to market and *Nachtmaal*, *i.e.* Holy Communion, and Commissioner Cloete at once found their leaders claiming not merely two, but ten (in one instance forty) farms each,[1] the standard Boer farm being 6,000 acres. Cloete's task was to limit and apportion these extravagant claims.[2] It became imperative also to provide for the ' surplus ' natives, and a Land Commission appointed in 1846 to mark off native reserves inevitably included in the native areas farms claimed by Boers, besides leaving others of them uncomfortably close to such unwelcome neighbours. This tenderness for native rights so irritated the Boers that probably a majority of the Trekkers withdrew rather than abate their full claims; but Sir Harry Smith's efforts [3] sufficed to retain, especially in the inland districts of Natal, a small permanent colony of Dutch-speaking farmers.

From the earliest days of Mr. Cloete's administration American missionaries had been watchful of native interests, and in October 1843, Mr. Secretary Montagu assured them, through Dr. Philip, ' that the determination to respect the claims of the natives to the lands in that territory was distinctly and emphatically announced ' in Mr. Cloete's original instructions (enclosed). To reinforce this assurance, Mr. Montagu enclosed a copy of supplementary instructions, dated 11 October : [4]

[1] Cloete to Napier, Private and Confidential, 20 June 1843 (Bird's *Annals*, ii, 191). Pretorius claimed ten farms, Commandant Rudolf forty.

[2] Cloete at once offered to register claims to 6,000-acre farms for all who could prove occupation for twelve months previous to his arrival, limiting other grants to only 2,000 acres. The confusion of these twelve months, however, made it difficult to prove effective occupation, and the offer was accompanied or followed by demands for an annual quit-rent of £4, and the payment of survey fees, together with mention of an ' upset ' price of 4s. an acre for Crown Lands—innovations that in the old Colony had helped to provoke the Trek itself (Walker, p. 204, and references).

[3] These included the offer of farms on the larger 6,000-acre scale to those who would take occupation within six months and undertake not to sell or mortgage them within seven years.

[4] Letter of Montagu to Philip, in reply to representations of the Rev. Alden Grout. Mr. Grout pointed out to the Governor, 11 February 1844, that ' were the question of right to be decided by previous occupation, a great proportion of the present inhabitants would be claimants ' by right of birth or previous residence, but that the testing of such claims would be utterly impracticable, while any attempt to enforce the expulsion of the ' surplus ' from Natal would either expose them to the ' remorseless vengeance of Umpandi ' (the Zulu chief), drive them ' upon the assagays of Faku ' (the Pondo), or ' precipitate

' I am to request you will make it known to the Emigrant Farmers
and native tribes that you were directed in May last to cause the
claims of the natives to lands which they either held or occupied to be
scrupulously respected. You will also make it known that . . . the
natives are not to be restricted in locating themselves to any particular
spots or districts, nor are they to be excluded from occupying any
land whatever which remains at the disposal of the Crown. The
Government will neither disturb them, nor permit them to be disturbed in their occupations or selections.'

In spite of this the Commissioner seems to have leaned to
the Boer Volksraad plan of complete ' segregation ', disposed—
by one missionary account—to make ' any sacrifices, concessions
or compromises that he consistently can for the sake of peace '.
. . . ' Many say he gives the Boers reason to believe that
things may be arranged far more to their advantage than there
can be any reason to believe (possible) '. The Boer plan was
for a time favoured apparently even by Theophilus Shepstone,[1]
but later, through him, with help from Lieutenant-Governor
West, the real problem of Natal was set on a fair way to solution.
In the end, Mr. Shepstone handled the natives with great tact,
shepherding a large proportion of them after 1846 into what
were for a long time fairly adequate reserves. Instead of subjecting them to European Common Law, he recognized native
law and custom, reconstituting their broken tribal system, with
the Lieutenant-Governor of Natal (1850) as ' Supreme Chief '.

them upon ', and ' leave them to the mercy of the (Northern) farmers '.
In the same letter Mr. Grout argued strongly against the proposal to
' place the natives under the authority of chiefs ', holding that ' few
things could be more unfavourable to their improvement. For my
own part I see no difficulty in placing them at once under British Law
and in that case there would be no objection against placing the most
intelligent and best characters among them as local magistrates, remov-
able at pleasure. . . . The sooner we can weaken (old prejudices)
by withdrawing from their minds what has a tendency to strengthen
them, and familiarize their minds with British forms, principles and
ideas, the better.'
In an earlier letter to Dr. Philip, September 1843, Mr. Grout
remarks : ' Mr. Lindley says if the natives are located in small bodies
as proposed, it will be simply that they may become servants to the
Whites, and root them ultimately out of the land as was done to the
Hottentots, and he consequently says that if the Government so locates
them he would not on any account work among them as he thinks they
can never become *Men* under those circumstances.' Mr. Lindley
soon after this gave up his mission work and devoted himself entirely
to the service of the pastorless Trekkers.

[1] Brookes, pp. 28 ff.

The reserves, however, are even now little more than one-eighth part of Natal Proper, with much good land, but also more than a fair proportion of what certain of their own prophets have described as ' country for baboons '.[1] They were a device in fact for leaving perhaps rather more than a fair share of the acreage of Natal open for the ' occupation and speculations ' of Europeans. Even to-day Europeans number barely one-tenth of the total population.

Though the demarcation of Reserves made little provision for the natural expansion of the native population, this growth at first found outlet. Crown lands were expressly left open to the natives in accordance with the instructions to Mr. Cloete in 1843, being only slowly and gradually swallowed up by new white settlers. European farmers, moreover, or absentee land-lords, welcomed labourers or share-paying squatters as tenants on their own broad domains. By reason, therefore, of the very smallness of the European population, for a long time all was well. But it was almost in spite of the Reserves. While Shep-stone's administration, with the naturally peaceable disposition of the Bantu themselves, deserves full credit, the abundance of land actually available for native occupation contributed materially to keep the almost unbroken peace which marked the first half-century of the Colony's existence, even during the tumult of the Zulu War of 1879.

The sequel is less reassuring. In the twentieth century Natal has come into its own as a farming country ; its coast lands are thickly planted with sugar-cane and sub-tropical fruit and vegetables ; its ' High Veld ', with a relatively good rainfall, fills up with active and progressive ' mixed ' farmers. The old easy days of unlimited native squatting are gone, leaving a new and crabbed problem to be dealt with by Europeans, in a spirit narrowed by the smallness and isolation of the country's past. In spite of the peaceful disposition of the natives of Natal itself, the tiny European population has grown up in mortal fear of their overwhelming numbers—a fear accentuated by the near proximity of the traditionally formidable Zulus. In 1856 the isolation of Natal was emphasized, when it was cut off from the liberalizing influence of the Mother Colony at the Cape. In 1893 Natal became a self-governing Colony on such terms as to leave the vast native majority in the unfettered political control of the exiguous white population. In 1897 Zululand

---

[1] R. Russell's *Natal*, p. 203. (See above, p. 177, also p. 294, *note*.)

also was incorporated in Natal, and after ten years of self-government, only three natives [1] had succeeded in getting over the ring fence that barred them from qualifying to share in the political privileges of the great minority. In 1906, almost the first native ' rebellion ' was suppressed with the ruthlessness of nervousness. In 1910 Natal joined the Union, reinforcing, and to be reinforced by, the anti-native tradition of the old Republic. In 1913 the Union Natives Land Act proclaimed anew the policy of ' segregation ', pronouncing also against the age-long practice of native ' squatting '.

Economic pressure on the Natal natives has now begun to be felt in full force. According to an authoritative estimate of 1915, even then barely half the natives of Natal proper were located in the sufficiently crowded reserves.[2] To-day the evictions due to the progress of European farming have enormously increased the pressure on the available land, and the artificial tribal system, which there is reason to believe (as Mr. Grout feared in 1844) has been rather an obstacle to the civilization of the natives,[3] threatens to break down altogether.[4] The natives in Natal, in short, present a sufficiently complex problem, a broken and conquered people, little advanced by eighty years of contact with civilization, relatively rather better off for Reserves only by contrast with the land famine in some other parts, while, by the hardly avoidable accidents of history, the dominant

[1] Native Affairs Commission, 1903–5.

[2] The estimate of the Beaumont Commission (U.G. 19, 1916, vide Appendix 'iv) was that 12,742 natives were still on Crown lands, 80,070 on unoccupied European-owned land, 346,641 on occupied European-owned farms and 37,199 in urban or mining areas ; thus accounting for 476,652 out of a total native population of 823,720. Since 1915 the pressure on Reserves has unquestionably increased owing to the development of European farming in Natal. In 1915, native areas ' scheduled ' under the Land Act of 1913 amounted to 2,414,203 acres, out of a total of 15,864,660 in Natal Proper, besides 3,887,100 out of a total of 6,651,105 in supposedly ' native ' Zululand. This brings the total Reserve for Natal and Zululand combined to between one-third and one-fourth of the whole area.

[3] Even in free tribal Basutoland, progressive individuals have been known to seek Government protection against the jealous exactions and persecutions of backward chiefs, and in Natal itself, and Zululand, the ' progressives ' seem to prefer mission-controlled Reserves, or privately owned farms. (See also Brookes, pp. 30, 47.)

[4] In 1927 I found one sugar-belt magistrate tearing his hair to make provision for a ' good little tribe ' whose huts had been reduced, by eviction from European farms, from more than 100 to barely 10.

Europeans of the Province (save for experiments in their own Education Department) are very far from liberal in their approach to the problems that now perplex them.

The Orange Free State was always a smaller affair, and less important in native policy. Whereas in Natal there are nearly nine natives to each European, in the Free State there are barely three to one. The provision for its natives is so small as to be ridiculous, ' Reserves ' amounting to less than one 250th part of the area of the Province; and after 1854 almost the first action of the newly established Republic was, almost as a matter of course, to bar any coloured person from holding land or acquiring rights as a free *burgher*. Here, however, Dr. Philip's work was not wholly in vain, and served presently to save the Free State from the consequences of this dearth of land and lack of rights for the native population. The recognition of the Griquas persisted even after the treaty experiment of the 'forties and the short-lived annexation of the Orange Sovereignty. Waterboer's state came to life again as Griqualand West in the Diamonds Fields dispute of 1871, and when, almost inevitably, Kok's people were being crowded out of the independent Free State in the early 'sixties, the Cape Governor, sensible of old treaty obligations, gave them one more chance of establishing themselves across the Drakensberg. Thereupon, in ' Griqualand East ', though again their economic weakness lost them their independent land-holding, the Griquas retained their political freedom, and have since become merged in the free ' Coloured ' community of the Cape Colony.

The fate of the Basuto treaty was different. After the abandonment of the Sovereignty, Moshesh, more favourably placed geographically, stronger in man-power and in sagacity than Adam Kok, carried on a not unequal war with the Free Staters ; and when at last, in 1868, he was hard pressed, his old status as an ' ally ' aroused a sense of responsibility in the British Government, and induced them to take him and his state under the Queen's protection. This action was hotly resented by the Free State, but in the light of later developments it has been more than justified. The Free State had already shown its conception of ' Native Policy ' by parcelling out as Boer farms the whole of the ' Conquered Territory ', a valuable strip of the Caledon corn-lands taken from the Basuto in 1866. The British Protectorate of 1868 saved what was left of Basuto-

land from a similar fate, and by so doing ' solved ' the Free State
Native problem—at once guaranteeing a highly necessary Native
Reserve, and relieving the Republic of the onerous task of governing a huge dependent native population. The establishment
of the Basuto Protectorate, therefore, gave ' the tight little Free
State ' that comparatively homogeneous character which was
long its pride, its strength, and its safety.

In the Transvaal Trekker ideas of native policy had it all
their own way. For the area beyond the Vaal the old theory
of depopulation will not hold. From the beginning, the Reports
and Resolutions of all the numerous republican *Volksraads*—
and the ascendancy everywhere of the *Krijgsraad*, the military
arm of the governing authority—show conclusively that the early
settlers in the Transvaal were at once ' faced by the same problem '
(of surplus natives) ' that was at that moment confronting the
Republic of Natal '.[1] Before ever Boer settlement had begun
to have serious effect upon the tribes directly under the influence
of the L.M.S., Dr. Philip, after his great tour in 1842, had
expressly warned the Government of the danger of a clash in
the north (above, pp. 199 and 221). Just about this time, Moselekatze having been expelled by the Boers, the Bechuana had
begun to ' creep back ' to their old homes, only to find the whole
territory claimed, whether occupied or not, by the conquering
Boers. By the late 'forties the clash Dr. Philip had foreseen
had come about, and, even the weak and divided Bechuana
making some show of resistance to Boer encroachment, constant
bickerings and commandos kept the country beyond the Vaal
in a ferment. Robert Moffat was equally severe in his judgment
of the Boers, and apprehensive,[2] but he was in no mood for co-
operation with Dr. Philip—the only missionary in close touch

---

[1] Agar Hamilton, pp. 53, 75 *et passim*.

[2] Moffat writes to the L.M.S. in an undated letter about 1847 :
' No real friend of the Aborigines could give the Boers credit for good
intentions, but the very reverse. Their perpetual aim and object
is the entire subjugation of the interior tribes, having already appropriated the most fruitful part of the country, while its rightful possessors
are driven to the waste places. How Sechele can receive missionaries
from the Boers is a puzzle to me . . . for certain it is, they care nothing
about the eternal interests of either Sechele or his people, but would
dance a jig to hear them all, great and small, cry " Baas " (a most servile
epithet demanded by the Boers of all coloured persons).' He continues
that of course he cannot hinder the Moravian newcomers, or interfere
in any way.

with governors, and with the situation as a whole.¹ In the crisis
of the early 'fifties, when Philip was no more, Moffat and even
Livingstone, while no more successful in conciliating the Boers,
failed even to keep the Government well informed of what was
happening under their own eyes.² In itself the remoteness
of the area covered by the conquering Boers would have hindered
a less unwilling and more fully informed Government from following up and trying to control the actions of its self-expatriated
subjects ; and in 1852, embarrassed by events in the Orange
Sovereignty and in Kafirland, it agreed to recognize the inde-

¹ E.g. on 19 March 1849, Edward Solomon wrote from Philippolis
to Dr. Philip, who was still ' Superintendent ', to tell him that ' Hughes
told him ' that he ' had heard from Moffat ' that ' Mr. Potgieter, who
called himself Commandant ' had written demanding the withdrawal
of missionaries, ' especially Livingstone ', from the interior, on the
ground that they were supplying natives with guns and ammunition.
This aloofness ruined the old-time effectiveness of the L.M.S. The
quiet and ignominious expulsion of the Society itself (in the persons
of Inglis and Edwards) from the Transvaal in 1852 would have been
almost unthinkable in the days of Dr. Philip.

² Of DR. JOHN PHILIP's *personal share in all these doings*, it may now
be said that all the evidence finally contradicts the tradition that Dr.
Philip had a meddlesome itch for ' intrigue ' and interference. At
a great many points his intervention was important and effective. But
in every instance he delayed, usually till the scandal was too great
to permit him to keep silent, always till he had first-hand knowledge
on which to base his representations. The first example of his delay
was in taking up the battle for Hottentot rights (see *Cape Col. Qn.*,
p. 138). A second concerned the Eastern Frontier—his first serious
tour was in 1830, his first official letter was written only in March 1834,
when a crisis was imminent (above, ch. viii).

About the Trek itself he kept almost complete silence till after
his tour of investigation in 1842. Even then he dealt with what he
knew best, unfortunately keeping silence on what was to develop into
the Transvaal problem ; on this, though he had seen more than any
official, his evidence was less complete.

Finally, till the breakdown of his health in 1845, when he was seventy
years old, he continued to confine himself to the questions of the moment
which concerned the Griquas and Basuto, most unfortunately giving
little or no attention to the administration of the other treaties on the
Kafir frontier.

It need not now be stressed that his vision of what was required
went far beyond ' Dr. Philip's Treaty States ', for which he has been
so much censured. He tried to make the best of the ' Treaty States ',
but they were none of his originating. On the whole he did more
and saw further than any contemporary, and a little more ' interference ' on these last two questions (the Transvaal and Kafirland) might
have been of inestimable service.

pendence of the Transvaal. The Boers, therefore, had their own way of it.

As far as they safely could, the Transvaalers ignored their native population, satisfied if only, in the words of their own *Grondwet* (Constitution), they could ' keep the Kafir chiefs to the performance of their duty ', and ' suppress vagrancy and vagabondage '. Effective government was, indeed, hardly to be looked for from this scattered handful of farmers, living from hand to mouth in the wilds of a savage country. The attitude of the written *Grondwet* (1858)[1] of the South African Republic tells its own tale, even in the often quoted exordium ' that the Republic (*het volk*) admits no equality between coloured and white inhabitants, either in Church or State '. ' No coloured persons nor half-castes ', it continues, are admitted to meetings of Volksraad, nor to any civic privileges.[2] On the other hand, the ' *Krijgsmagt* ', or army, comprises ' if necessary '—as they might be, to keep each other in order—' all the coloured people in this country whose chiefs are subject to it ' (par. 96). Native administration, most vital and absorbing of governmental duties, comes very significantly under the heading ' *over de Krijgsmagt en den Krijgsraad* ' (pars. 104 & 105) : ' To the Assistant Field-Cornets, and Field-Cornets, is entrusted the *preservation of order* ; to the Commandants, the commandos, in case of internal insurrection of the coloured population '—disaffection on the part of Europeans being reserved for the higher dignity of the Commandant-General. ' By *preservation of order* ', the next section reads, ' is understood seeing to the observance of the laws, the execution of sentences . . . the observance of measures of general and local concern, *besides the supervision of the coloured population and the suppression of vagrancy and vagabonds in the field-cornetcies.*' Finally, some definitions, as e.g. (par. 104) ' by *commandos* in case of internal insurrections of the coloured population is understood, *keeping the Kafir chiefs to the performance of their duty* '. The problem of the native consists, in fact, in keeping him in order, and forcing him to do his ' duty ', that is to say, to come out to labour as and when required. This obligation

---

[1] Eybers' *Documents*, p. 363 (translation sometimes modified in text).

[2] Clause 8, in which the sovereign people make profession of the obligations of their own religious faith and duty, concludes as follows : ' The people *permit* the spread of the Gospel among the heathen, subject to definite safeguards against fault and deception.'

carried with it no corresponding right even to security of land-tenure, and the ' Kafir ' Question ended, so far as any chief or tribe was concerned, when the tribe's power was broken and the chief ' finally crushed '.

An arbitrary claim in the earliest 'forties to the disposal of all the undefined conquests of Moselekatze is typical of the Republicans' general attitude. Land was their first objective ; the second a plentiful labour supply, with ' proper ' relations between master and servant. The possibility that the primitive natives amongst whom they found themselves could ever attain to civilized status, or become a political problem, never entered into their calculations. Where the natives were powerless, as in the Sechuana-speaking area, some few chiefs were given lands and ' burgher ' status,[1] with the right to continue approximately where they had always been. The great majority paid a ' labour tax ', which, like that of the *villein* of old, was variable and indefinite in amount. A few weak tribes voluntarily ' surrendered ' their independence ' for the privilege of settling within the domains and under the protection of the Republic ',[2] for the most part as rightless ' squatters '. Now in taking over the ' depopulated ' conquests of Moselekatze, the Boers took also the responsibilities of a governing race. Without these their title was no better than his. Boer government, however, meant control by a close oligarchy of farmers, and masters, nervous for and jealous of their own exclusive interests, highly sensitive to farmer opinion, but quite unchecked by a strong independent Bench.

It can, perhaps, be said for the old Transvaal ' policy ' that it put down inter-tribal wars. In view of the scanty return the tribes received for their surrender of ' independence ', and the long record of ' commandos ' and ' wars ' which marked its history, too much has been made of the ' security ' given by the Republican Government. Significantly enough, while the Cape had its distinctive ' Kafir ' wars, and the Free State repeated wars with the Basuto, the history of the Transvaal is a record of what were for some time almost annual ' commandos ' against malcontent but isolated native chiefs—Montsioa, Makapan, Sekukuni, Mapoch, Malaboch ; on the very eve of the war of 1899 General Joubert led an almost bloodless expedition to the north and

---

[1] i.e. exemption from the cruder labour exactions, but never ' political ' rights.
[2] See Agar Hamilton, p. 76, and for ' Labour Tax,' ch. x.

drove the Bavenda chief, Mpefu, into temporary exile across the Limpopo.

The Transvaal, that is to say, most completely illustrates the way in which the Great Trek 'turned the flank' of the Bantu, laying the tribes open, one by one, to forfeiture of their lands, and to subjugation—military, economic and political. The real aim of the Trekkers was perhaps a foggily conceived plan of segregation. But, as in Natal at the very beginning, segregation was little more than a warrant for shutting their eyes to the inconvenient presence of a 'surplus' population which destroyed the unity and harmony of their peasant republic. They sought to apply it only after their labour needs were plentifully secured, and after they had appropriated for themselves more than all the land they could possibly use, regardless of what was necessary for the locating of the native population. It is true that the Transvaal Republic, finding its resources unequal to the complete subjugation of the Low Veld tribes, commonly practised the now much favoured method of 'indirect' rule—to the extent that it left them, without any help or guidance, to their own devices. Where tribal resistance, with malaria, proved formidable (as in the Zoutpansberg, where, by 1870, the Boers had actually lost ground they once held), the natives remained, legally unrecognized, but with tribal institutions undisturbed.

Conquest, it may be, brought the Transvaal Bantu into touch with civilization, so that individuals among them reached out, earlier than they might otherwise have done, after all that Europeans could teach them. At the same time, labour conditions were what masters chose to make them, with some supervision of actual physical ill-treatment by field-cornets and *landdrosts*. Such service, uncertain and variable in quantity, with no effective appeal against the lord and master, was of the very essence of the *unfree* tenures of the Middle Ages. Native rights, even in land, were so insecure that in the whole of the central High Veld, from Bloemhof in the west to Ermelo in the east, a stretch of country some 300 miles long, barely 35 square miles remained so definitely native as to come to be 'scheduled' as Native Reserve by the Land Act of 1913.[1] Since, in addition, native labour could not be fully used, the Transvaal has become the province *par excellence* of the rightless native squatter, so that in

[1] 17·8 square miles in Potchefstrom, 16 square miles in Wakkerstroom.

1915, apart from squatters on farms, nearly one-quarter of its rural native population were resident on land *owned* but unoccupied by Europeans.[1]

Thus, on the whole, Transvaal conditions epitomize the main features of the Native Problem, and since the trend to-day is against extending the privileges of the Cape natives to the rest of the country, the Transvaal attitude tends to give the lead to South African opinion. The natives to-day [2] fall into two main classes—those with a home base in ' Reserves ' and those without. Throughout the Union, such land as is definitely native is usually overcrowded, and the total area utterly inadequate to maintain the population, unless it were to be worked with more than Chinese industry and efficiency. In fact, of course, native agriculture is still primitive ; (Lecky recalls that as late as the eighteenth century there were West Highland peasants ploughing with a wooden share, and using a harrow, without harness, tied to the horse's tail !) Europeans have hardly given a thought to the native as an independent wealth producer. In early days he was a dangerous enemy, latterly a source of cheap labour—the less land he had the more useful as a labourer. These considerations having so long governed policy, the Bantu have had to adapt themselves almost in one generation to an economic revolution that for Western Europeans developed only in the course of eighteen centuries. For if Europeans brought with them great new opportunities for the Bantu, they have also imposed on them the necessity of learning to live on a mere fraction of the land which they once roamed without restriction. It has brought them as yet the very minimum of capital expenditure on such first essentials of closer cultivation as roads, railways and fencing, and very little even in the way of direct instruction in the better use of the land. The result is that the Reserves themselves have everywhere come to be all but completely

[1] Report of Beaumont Commission, U.G. 19, '16. Total native population 1,382,285 : Witwatersrand (largely mine natives, imported) 272,938 : on unoccupied European-owned land 232,082 : on farms, i.e. including labourers and ' labour-tenants ', 390,332.

[2] For facts in fuller support of statements made in this chapter, I have drawn on pamphlets and papers, e.g. The S.A. Agrarian Problem (1919), The Land, Natives and Unemployment (1924), Articles, *Cape Times*, 12–24, April 1926, and an unpublished Economic Survey of the district Herschel which I made, in 1926, for the Government Department of Statistics.

dependent on wages earned outside ; nor can they easily be
made more adequate merely by belated works of development
or by suddenly teaching the natives ' improved methods '. Even
in 1915 barely half the natives of the Union appeared to have
homes except on land owned, though not necessarily used, by
Europeans,[1] and since that date the development of European
farming, especially in Natal and the Northern Transvaal, has
had the effect of multiplying evictions of hitherto unmolested
' squatters ' to make room for new farming enterprises.'

Inadequate as they are, however, the Reserves are a considerable mitigation of a problem that would hardly exist if
the natives possessed more land. Without the existing Reserves,
the problem would, indeed, be overwhelming. It is true that
the dependence of the native areas on wage-earning is a serious
complication. For the older people their patches of land serve
as an Old Age Pension, affording the State an enormous relief
from the burdens of a Poor Rate. But the Reserves operate
also as a subsidy in aid of wages. The fact of having some
homes of their own saves masses of the natives from such exploitation as was suffered by the old Cape Hottentots (and still is by
many farm natives) ; but it also enables labourers from the
Reserves to accept a rate of wages that disastrously lowers the
standard for those others, a growing class, who have no such
home base. Even so, the purely native areas, being compact,
are comparatively easily administered ; their people are, on the
whole, contented (as in the Transkei), and constitute no serious
political problem.

On the other hand, the dispersed natives—the direct result
of conquest in the Cis-Kei, and of more gradual extrusion elsewhere—are the crux of the whole problem. The often mentioned
' squatters ' are the typical remnant of the dispossessed native
population, left, often where they were, without legal security,
but practically undisturbed in the use of what is in many instances
their ancestral land. Squatting, in fact, in undeveloped districts,

---

[1] It is significant of the unscientific approach to the ' tackling '
of the problem that the estimate of the Land Commission (1915) is
the latest available. About 1925 district returns were collected from
magistrates to guide the preparation of an amended Native Land Act,
but these have not been made available. There is, therefore, no direct
evidence of what proportion of natives employed in European areas
really have homes of sorts in Reserves. The probability is that it is
still considerable. But even in the Transkei no native, however progressive, can *legally* acquire more than one holding, 6 or 8 acres.

with a kind (or even a lazy) landlord, may often yield a fair measure of comfort. The tragedy is that this insecure and unsatisfactory tenure still offers better life prospects than the only alternatives, whole-time labour, or the so-called 'labour tenancy' (90 days' service, not necessarily continuous, in return for house, ploughing and/or grazing rights). The more typical squatter has to give his own services, often unpaid, and usually those of his whole family as well, for the mere right to live where he is, and perhaps, to 'plough' a small patch of land, or 'graze' a limited number of cattle. But he dare not move for fear of having his family evicted ; he cannot readily take his labour to the best market, or even where it is most needed—one result of the extreme immobility of the landless natives being an almost chronic shortage of labour throughout the country, even in the more developed farming districts, especially perhaps on the mines and in industry.

The almost wantonly increased pressure of the Natives' Land Act of 1913 has brought about something like a crisis. The sponsors of this Act made a dead set against the essentially unsound practice of squatting without putting anything even as good in its place—missing the essential truth that squatting with an easy master is the best living the ordinary landless native can hope for. Farming on 'shares', and the hiring or leasing of European land, are expressly forbidden to natives who (though in practice the law is set aside or evaded) cannot now legally make their homes on the farms except by rendering labour service. At the same time native right to purchase land except with the express sanction of the Government is heavily restricted —to areas that have not yet been defined. The result has been an immeasurable unsettlement of 'farm' (i.e. landless) natives ; many have been evicted ; others, rather than tolerate their straitened conditions have broken away, and, further upset by 'War' prices, which at the same time made the cramped conditions more acutely felt even on the Reserves, natives of all sorts have betaken themselves to the towns and dorps in almost unmanageable numbers—there to nurse their grievances, of which almost the bitterest is the restrictive Land Act. But in the towns they have met a new rival. Land-hunger, *fons et origo mali*, has meant also that the more land Europeans superficially absorbed from natives, the less they were themselves compelled to learn real agriculture. Now the wheel has come full circle, and the essence of the 'Native' Problem of to-day is that an exodus of starving unskilled Poor Whites from imperfectly developed European farms is brought into violent competition for unskilled labour with the still cheaper overflow of natives from farms and from congested ' Reserves '. The foundations of economic life could hardly be more thoroughly unsound than in modern South Africa.

Such has been the unlooked-for result of the ' extermination ' of so many native tribes. It came, not without warning which went unheeded in days when South African society might possibly have been set on a more stable basis. The hard case of the Poor White has aroused increasingly serious attention only within the last twenty years, and the first result has been to drive South African politicians to short-cuts—anything to meet the panic of an overwhelmingly European electorate at the danger threatening their ' white ' civilization. But civilization is not ' white ' or ' dual ', and the talk of segregation to-day, with its stress on a ' dual ' policy of ' separate development ', too often merely runs away from the essential problem—the established contact of advanced and backward peoples as parts of one South African community. Increase the ' Reserves ', by all means, and so mitigate the rigours of this economic clash ; but for the rest, policy is to be judged as it operates to lessen the fatal difference between European and native standards, and to raise the mass of landless natives from that state of backwardness which is precisely what makes them a ' problem '.

That the Bantu are capable of civilization outstanding individuals among them sufficiently show. However different the outlook of the races, physiological testimony to the innate superiority of the European race remains in the region of pure speculation, and estimates of the varying capacity of Bantu tribes are so contradictory as to leave an impression that differences are accidental, and that the race as a whole has a certain quality. There is strong testimony, for example, backed by the high authority of Dr. Theal, to the superior qualities of the (militarist) Zulus, who, however, seem to have produced fewer educated leaders than some less famous tribes. On the other hand, experienced officials have often remarked on the greater capacity of some of the mixed tribes like the Fingos and Basuto, pointing out how the despised Fingos tend to become Headmen, or even small capitalists, among the backward Pondos, as also do Basuto even among the Zulus of Natal.[1] For the backwardness of the masses their history amply accounts, and some further allowance must be made for our own failure either to learn their language or to be at pains to teach them ours. (The best of us might appear stupid enough to masters shouting instructions at us in an unknown language.) When all has been said, there is little doubt that the relatively advanced natives of to-day are those who, like the Fingos, have been better placed to reap the first-fruits of European education, and the Cape alone has in any adequate degree fulfilled the functions of the state as a civilizing agency.

The distressingly unwholesome economic conditions, especially their insecurity on farms, the only homes so many of the natives know, are sufficient to account for a great deal of ' raw ' backwardness that unhappily survives even in that Province. But a great many individuals, both Xosa and Fingo, have risen above their surroundings, some few as independent farmers, a good many more as teachers and clergymen, a handful in journalism or even in the professions ; so that in these days when adverse conditions are obliterating old tribal dissensions and giving the Bantu the beginnings of national self-consciousness, an overwhelming majority of their leaders and spokesmen are Capeborn or at least Cape-educated. When, not many years ago, the Union recognized the rise of the Bantu, and Bantu aspirations, by the establishment of a University College for Natives, its inevitable site was in the Cis-Kei, at Fort Hare, next door to the greatest of the older native training institutions, the Scottish foundation, Lovedale.

The natives of the old Cape had one great stimulus. For the small and only very slowly growing number who attained the fairly exacting standards required,[2] the privilege of the Parliamentary vote lay open. This effectively ensured that though native interests might be, even grossly, neglected by the old Cape Parliament, they could never be too blatantly countered ; a sufficient number of its members were under the necessity of remembering that a section of the South African community

---

[1] Cf. evidence of the late Mr. John X. Merriman on the Natal natives, chiefly Zulus : ' You have not elevated the natives in Natal ; you have not educated them ; they are barbarous and you have designedly left them in a state of barbarism.' Quoted by Dr. Brookes, p. 47.

[2] Johannesburg Joint Council of Natives and Europeans. *Memo.* No. 4, *In Defence of the Cape Franchise.*

is native. The Cape natives were, for example, strikingly free from the unconscionably irritating pin-pricks of an old-fashioned repressive system of Pass Laws, and by contrast with other Provinces, the Cape Government was almost generous in its provision for native education. The success of the Transkei itself has been not merely that its people have felt their local administration to be their own, and entirely devoted to their interest, but that in the last resort their voice could be heard in the national councils at Cape Town. And everywhere, for the few who attained, the vote was a treasured right, which gave them a status in national affairs ; for the rest a hope and an aspiration. The trial of freedom has been abundantly justified under conditions which the havoc wrought by the Kafir wars made the most intractable in the whole country.

None of the other Provinces has made any comparable contribution to the ' solution ' of the Native Problem. Everywhere the rapid development of European farming is steadily increasing the economic pressure on the natives, and the numbers of landless to be provided for. Except in the Cape, the Land Act restricts even those who would and could relieve the pressure by the purchase of land. The Cape natives themselves become a ' problem ' as soon as ever, through the stress of their own adverse economic conditions, they drift in search of work, for example to the wealthier and more highly developed Transvaal. There they find themselves subject to old-fashioned Masters and Servants Acts (which, for example, make a strike an illegal desertion of duty), ' barred ' (by their colour) from a rise to the better paid posts in industry, excluded from the political privileges of their fellows in the Cape, and left, often enough, ' a prey to agitators '. The all but entirely European controlled Union Parliament leans, in fact, more and more heavily away from the Cape policy and tradition. Acutely ' political ' Governments are of necessity guided by their voters, and the Cape native vote being even now a very small influence, native interests yet get more attention in that [Province than elsewhere. The Cape natives, therefore, cling to what they have, and native leaders in general feel that to substitute for the Cape vote a restricted ' communal ' franchise, even for the whole country, could only mean that all but an insignificant handful of members of Parliament would be entirely free from any obligation to consider native interests. Even educated natives could then, at most, look for what their rulers would think to be for their good. This, with the experience of eighteen years of Union, appears to them a forlorn hope enough.

The past is still too much with us. The new policy which South Africa threatens to evolve is, in fact, inspired by ideas which have too long passed current as historical truth. Filial devotion, rendered a little blind by the accidents of British-Dutch quarrels, still inclines a strong section of South African opinion to make the heroes of the Great Trek their pattern in all things —even in native policy, to which they are the poorest guides. The pioneer work, the hardihood, and the independent spirit of the Voortrekkers evoke nothing but admiration ; but modern South Africans must recognize also that many of the peculiar difficulties of the modern question, and even more the mental attitude with which they are approached, are a legacy from early days. Granted that there is room for both black and white within the borders of South Africa, and that, without the Europeans, there would be no progress for the Bantu ; that the Trekkers carried civilization over a wide area and laid the foundations of the modern Union; yet they also set and confirmed the disastrous fashion of ignoring the very existence of a native population, and of looking at South African problems with eyes exclusively for European interests. Placed as they were Settlers and Trekkers alike thought and acted as they did, not from considered policy, but largely as economic necessity and physical safety suggested. This people also stoned their prophets —the critics who rightly strove all they could to prevent wholesale ' extermination ' of the native population, and to temper the process by which, all over north and central South Africa, ' civilization ' and ' barbarism ' were brought into such close and inextricable contact. Inasmuch as he, at least, more nearly than either Government or Trekkers, saw the problem as a whole, John Philip was yet the best South African of them all.

If the full recognition of the rights of the original possessors of the land, which Stockenstrom would seem to describe as the accepted policy of the late 'thirties, was impracticable, the application of the modified Griqua settlement of 1845, with its alienable farm land, and definitely inalienable reserves, might have gone far to secure adequate native reserves, compelled the pioneers to concentrate and to learn more intensive agriculture, mitigated the problem of ' Poor Whites ', and saved us a ' Native Land ' problem. It might even have made ' segregation ' possible, with the European areas more homogeneous, and the great bulk of the Bantu concentrated in compact, relatively easily managed areas, like Basutoland and the Transkei. The wholesale appropriation of native lands, on the contrary—since there is no obvious disposition to undo this work by enlarging the Reserves—has left fully half the Bantu people directly dependent on European landowners, and, therefore, an inseparable part of the South African whole. Perhaps, indeed, the strongly voiced desire for a new policy suggests that the old complacency is being shaken. Native landlessness may yet in some degree be remedied by enlarging the Reserves which even now provide in some sort for nearly half the native population. Much needless anxiety and fear arise from the habit of looking at the natives as abstract and overwhelming millions. A very few thousands are in any way self-conscious, a mere handful to be reckoned with in the body politic. The danger would be were these few, who are still eager and willing to be led—content with a humble place in the One South African Society—to be driven into increasingly bitter racial opposition. In face of the facts, there is no ' solution ' in any policy which, under whatever disguise, denies to this little group of progressive and dispossessed Bantu, when and as they attain to civilization, full rights of citizenship in the Union which is their only home. Given such rights they may easily be led and won.

INDEX